A PRESS FREE AND RESPONSIBLE

Other books by the author

Gladstone and the Bulgarian Agitation, 1876
The Crisis of Imperialism, 1865–1915 (Paladin History of England)
The Age of Disraeli, 1868–1881: the Rise of Tory Democracy
The Age of Salisbury, 1881–1902: Unionism and Empire
Gladstone, I: Peel's Inheritor, 1809–1865
Gladstone II: Heroic Minister, 1865–1898

A PRESS
FREE AND RESPONSIBLE

Self-regulation and the
Press Complaints Commission,
1991–2001

'To my murmured question, "How can a press free to
behave responsibly, be prevented from behaving irresponsibly in a free society without censorship?" I
received no persuasive answer.'

Lord McGregor of Durris,
Rights, Royals and Regulation: the British Experience

RICHARD SHANNON

JOHN MURRAY
Albemarle Street, London

First published in 2001
by John Murray (Publishers) Ltd,
50 Albemarle Street, London W1S 4BD

The moral right of the author has been asserted.

A catalogue record for this book is available from the British Library.

ISBN 0-7195-6321 6

Typeset in Monotype Garamond by
Servis Filmsetting Ltd, Manchester

Printed and bound in Great Britain by
St Edmundsbury Press Ltd,
Bury St Edmunds, Suffolk

CONTENTS

PREFACE AND ACKNOWLEDGEMENTS

This book originated in a feeling among people at the Press Complaints Commission in Salisbury Square, Fleet Street, that they would like a historical record of the Commission's management of the system of press self-regulation in the UK to mark its tenth anniversary, in January 2001. Guy Black, director of the Commission, suggested the project to me, a retired and *désoeuvré* professor of Modern History and a fellow member of Peterhouse, Cambridge. I was very willing to undertake the book, provided that I could have unrestricted access to whatever archival holdings the Commission possessed and that in no respect were my findings to be subject to any vetting or approval by the Commission beyond the usual precautions relating to the laws of libel and copyright. The officers of the Commission were perfectly ready to meet my requirements and stipulations. Lord Wakeham, the chairman, declared his cordial endorsement of the project and offered all assistance in his power. The result is what you see before you.

It seemed to me that the PCC's story is well worth the telling. A free press is one of the great and exemplary British traditions. A self-regulated free press as administered from 1953 by the Press Council and from 1991 by its successor the Press Complaints Commission lends that tradition an extra and unique lustre of fascination. I hope I have succeeded in conveying at least some of that fascination to the reader. Which is not to say that the reader will find in this record an unalloyed celebration of the PCC as a brilliant story of success. The record is mixed. Therein lies indeed the fascination. The PCC is trying to do an impossible thing. It is regulating in the highest ethics of journalism at the behest of a free press as free to be irresponsible as responsible. It is a creature of the body it regulates. The press industry grudgingly created it as an evil less than threatened state regulation. It has no sanctions against its creator. Any judgment on the record of the PCC must allow for the impossibility of, let alone the other disadvantages attaching to, its remit.

I must record my gratitude to the people who have helped me by their willingness to be interviewed and by assisting me otherwise to access sources or by giving permission to quote copyright material. My first acknowledgement is to Nellie, Lady McGregor of Durris, widow of the Commission's first chairman, for her kind encouragement and generosity in making available valuable material from the late Lord McGregor of Durris's private archive. Guy Black has been indefatigable in his help and goodwill without in any way cramping my authorial independence. The same is true of invaluable information and assistance from Professor Robert Pinker, the only member of the original Commission in 1991 still in post. I am grateful to many other people who have allowed me the benefit of their experiences as participants in the story of press self-regulation: Sir Louis Blom-Cooper QC, Mr Mark Bolland, Lady Elizabeth Cavendish CVO, Mr David Chipp, Mr Cyril Glasser, Mr Roy Greenslade, Mr Mike Jempson, Mr Simon Jenkins, Mr Michael Leapman, Lord Lester of Herne Hill QC, Mr Brian MacArthur, Mr Kenneth Morgan OBE, Mr David Newell, Mr Dugal Nisbet-Smith CBE, Sir Edward Pickering, Mr Peter Preston, Sir Harry Roche, Sir Frank Rogers, Mr Alan Rusbridger, Mr Robert Satchwell, Mr Raymond Snoddy, Mr Grahame Thomson, the Right Hon. Lord Wakeham of Maldon, Mr Charles Wilson and the World Press Freedom of Reston, Virginia, USA. I must add that of course responsibility for any attributed quotations remains entirely with me.

I am grateful also to members of the staff at the Commission for invaluable assistance in guiding me to sources housed at Salisbury Square: Mrs Kim Baxter, Mr Michael Birtwistle, Mr Damian Fürer, Mrs Caroline Jaroudy, Mr Tom Roberts and Mr Tim Toulmin. Mr Philip Candice has been very helpful in assisting research. I am much indebted as well to the expertise of Ms Christine Bertram, Mr Patrick Higgins, and Professor Julian Jackson.

The expertise and efficiency of Mr Ian Shackleton and the Chatham Archive and Document Storage Company have likewise been invaluable. The British Library's microfilm facilities at King's Cross and especially its newspaper collection at Colindale have naturally provided me with the most part of my materials. My method has been to use the *UK Press Gazette*, the newspaper and magazine industry's weekly trade paper, as the primary lead, supported by mutual monitoring of *The Times* and the *Guardian*. Other papers have been consulted as occasions seemed appropriate.

Richard Shannon

PROLOGUE

The idea of a self-regulated press in Britain

How shall I speak thee, or thy power address,
Thou god of our idolatry, the Press?
By thee religion, liberty and laws
Exert their influence and advance their cause;
By thee worse plagues than Pharaoh's land befell
Diffused make earth the vestibule of hell.
Those fountains at which drink the good and wise,
Those ever-bubbling springs of endless lies,
Like Eden's dread probationary tree,
Knowledge of good and evil is from thee.

William Cowper, *The Progress of Error*, 1782

Formal self-regulation by the newspaper and periodical industry in the United Kingdom* began on 21 July 1953 in the board room of the Press Association and Reuters, Fleet Street, City of London, with the inaugural meeting of the General Council of the Press. This, as the Council observed in its first annual report the following year, 'marked a new departure in the democratic institutions of this country. For the first time in our history, the free press of Britain was to be given a ballast by a self-elected body which would both safeguard its liberties and rebuke its excesses.' Exalted a little, perhaps, by the historic éclat of that moment, the Council indulged itself in edifying supposition.

When the founder-members assembled they were perhaps slightly oppressed by a sense of the occasion and of the responsibility awaiting them. Possibly they

---

* 'Britain' and 'British' are used in this book for the usual reasons of convenience as synonymous with 'United Kingdom of Great Britain and Northern Ireland'. It is to be understood that the press in Northern Ireland has always been eligible to participate in the self-regulatory systems administered by the Press Council, 1953–90, and the Press Complaints Commission, 1991 to date.

felt a little apprehensive about what they might encounter in the uncharted territory which lay before them. They had to feel their way, make their own rules, define their own scope and authority and create their own precedents. But they 'found themselves' with surprising speed and by the second meeting the sense that they represented different interests in the profession had largely disappeared and had been replaced by the feeling of corporate existence.[1]

For nearly forty years to come that corporate body of twenty-five or so representatives of the newspaper industry, metropolitan and regional – proprietors, editors, journalists and, later, begrudged lay recruits from the 'great and good' – the Press Council (as it was renamed) in its quarters at No. 1 Salisbury Square, off Fleet Street, felt its way through uncharted territory, made its own rules, defined its own scope and authority and created its own precedents. By the late 1980s it had reached a state of terminal discredit. As from 1 January 1991, the industry which had created it summarily abolished it and replaced it with a smaller, less ambitious body – the Press Complaints Commission.

The perception at the time of the Press Council's death throes was that its twin vocations of defending the liberties of the press and rebuking its excesses, instead of being complementary and integrally interdependent, had become contradictory. Such was the disgrace into which popular mass journalism had sunk, dragging the industry as a whole down with it, that press self-regulation would henceforth confine itself, in effect, to rebuking excesses. 'Henceforth', moreover, was defined as a probationary eighteen months only. After June 1992 the question would be whether self-regulation itself would best, in the public interest, be abolished and replaced by legislation setting up some statutory regulation of the press with a view to compelling it to be accurate, unintrusive, decent, fair-minded and generally alive to its obligations and responsibilities to foster social and political advancement.

Some such form of statutory regulation of the press in Britain would indeed be even more 'historic' than 1953's 'new departure' of self-regulation in the form of the Press Council. It would be a matter of 'some constitutional significance', as one Conservative minister put it when confronted starkly with the option.[2] After all, print, including public newspaper print, has not been directly regulated by government in the countries which make up the United Kingdom since the seventeenth century. Defeat of royal prerogative government in State and Church in the Civil War, ratified by the Glorious Revolution, unsettled all previous assumptions about the right and duty of public authorities to censor or suppress matter deemed to be injurious to the commonwealth. Parliament attempted to fill the vacuum thus created by setting up in 1643 an elaborate system for vetting books and other prints. This proved ineffectual. Its one memorable consequence was to incite *Areopagitica: a Speech of Mr John Milton for the Liberty of Unlicensed Printing to the Parliament of England*, published in 1644. Cromwell set out in 1655 to make a proper job of it. His system of 'prior restraint' was finally abandoned in 1695.

From then until 1953 newspaper print in Britain was indirectly regulated in a free market of selling and buying. A seller of newsprint is free, like any other subject of the Crown, in the absence of any law positively and specifically inhibiting his freedom. There are laws of libel and defamation, sedition, obscenity, blasphemy and contempt. Sedition laws were aimed drastically against the dissident popular press in the era of the repressive 'Six Acts' in the restive days after Waterloo. There have been restrictions on the reporting of Parliament. Punitive duties have been slapped on advertisements. There have been customs and excise duties designed to make paper expensive. Restrictions on parliamentary reporting were tacitly abandoned after spectacular failures of repressive prosecutions. Stamp taxes were abolished in 1855 (by a government eager to damage and punish *The Times*). The other 'taxes on knowledge', the paper duties, were abolished by Gladstone in 1861 after a struggle against Lord Palmerston and the House of Lords.

Against such alleviations politicians and lawyers have made Britain's libel law among the toughest in the world; and since 1889 an all-pervasive governmental culture of secrecy has been legalized in a series of Official Secrets Acts. Freedom of information legislation, often promised, seems unlikely on present indications to make much of a dent in that secretive culture. Added to this is the current process of incorporation into British law from October 2000 of the European Convention of Human Rights. This presents the newspaper press with the conundrum of reconciling its interest in a guaranteed right of freedom of expression with everyone else's interest in a guaranteed right of privacy.[3]

That the British press remains not merely unregulated but self-regulated is by no means unconnected with historical circumstances stemming from the seventeenth century. The press became 'free' because government efforts at regulation failed. That failure became the central feature in a constitutional tradition whereby the liberty of the press took its honoured place in the pantheon of British liberties celebrated defiantly throughout the eighteenth century and consecrated in the vast expansion of newspapers and newspaper readership which marked the Victorian epoch, when the 'educated' press dominated the field and gave to newspapers a prestige never enjoyed before – or since.

For all the claims for a free press to be, in Lord Bathurst's words, the 'greatest liberty of the subject', press freedom as such in the United Kingdom has never been (at least until the absorption of the Human Rights Convention) specifically asserted, let alone guaranteed, by law. Bathurst's supplementary proviso, that therefore all inconveniences arising out of press freedom 'are to be submitted to', has never been part of the official British frame of mind. In this respect the British case – along with historically affiliated offshoots in the Irish Republic* and Australia – remains very much the exception to the general rule of societies in the Western democratic tradition. The seventeenth century, even in the relatively advanced England of Milton and Locke, was not a time for proclaiming the rights of man. It would take a generation or two of enlightened thinking before such a thing became possible after the rebellion of the American colonies against the British Crown led to the creation of the United States. Even there, the Constitution had to be amended in 1791 to provide that Congress shall make no law abridging freedom of speech, or of the press. That famous First Amendment in effect became the historical precedent, one way or another, later or sooner, for every other Western democratic culture apart from Britain and her affiliates. The essence of the matter is that constitutional or legislative guarantee from government is reciprocated by some degree of acceptance on the part of the press of a corresponding obligation of acknowledgement.

There is not, nor ever has been, any such reciprocity, any such corresponding obligation of acknowledgement, in the culture of Britain's press. The historical peculiarities of the emergence in Britain of a newspaper press which government has tried and failed to regulate go far in helping to explain the peculiarities of the British press – especially the popular or 'tabloid' press – in the twentieth century. Those peculiarities are mainly to do with what have been identified as the uniquely depraved habits of the 'rough old trade'.

Lord Bathurst's supplementary proviso has ever been the watchword:

---

*Ostensibly the Republic, under the 1937 constitution, has a guarantee of press freedom modelled on the United States, but so hedged as to be in practice little different from the UK's, with an even more stringent law of libel.

freedom is indivisible; a free press is a press as free to be disreputable as reputable. The price of a free press, as a hallowed cliché of British journalism has it, is some bad newspapers. But *so* bad? Concomitantly, journalism in Britain has never been much noted for inculcating a professional ethos. In fact, strictly, as Geoffrey Robertson QC has pointed out, there is no such thing as professional journalism in Britain. 'Journalism is not a profession. It is the exercise by occupation of the right to free expression available to every citizen. That right, being available to all, cannot in principle be withdrawn from a few by any system of licensing or professional registration.'[4]

Anyone can start up a newspaper. Anyone can write for a newspaper. Considerations which compel official regulation of the electronic media – the fact that airwaves and television channels are scarce public resources – do not apply to print. Nor have considerations about the imperative of testable competence and public responsibility in relation to the professional activities of physicians, surgeons, dentists, barristers, solicitors, engineers, architects, accountants, academics, parsons and so on, ever been anything like as imperatively applied in the case of journalists. Yet exemption from formal qualification does not make the temper of the trade any sweeter. 'There is a professional hardness of attitude', admitted David Lipsey, when associate editor of *The Times*, '– journalists being outraged by complaints.'[5] Raymond Snoddy, a notable student of his trade, offers some pertinent comment:

> Three characteristics seem to mark the behaviour of British newspapers: an almost pathological reluctance to admit errors and say sorry, a deep sensitivity to criticism and a marked distaste for thinking about what they do. . . . The degree of complacency and defensiveness involved is a small symptom of a much greater malaise – the lack of self criticism in the newspaper industry, a characteristic noted by the first Royal Commission on the press as long ago as 1947.
>
> The newspaper industry is almost unique in its low level of research into the quality of its product and into the effects of the lack of sustained quality control, even though this concerns the most important factor affecting the reputation and credibility of a newspaper – its accuracy.[6]

Added to this must be noted the consideration that the roughness of the rough old trade in the special case of Britain's press is in good part attributable to the simple geographical fact of Britain's being a smallish but very densely populated island. England's political culture, especially, is highly centralized, with an unusually dominant metropolis. Nowhere else in the world are there published so many newspapers with national coverage. Nowhere else do popular tabloid newspapers have such huge circulations, easily the largest market-oriented in the world. The total circulation of daily newspapers in Paris in 1999 was less than half that of the *Sun*. And nowhere else, unsurprisingly, do such newspapers compete more fiercely, and occasionally unscrupulously, in the circulation market.

How did it come about that after two and a half centuries of non-regulation of the press, the newspaper industry set up and funded in 1953 a system of self-regulation? The verses by William Cowper quoted above attest to an early yet profound sense of ambivalence in the public mind arising out of the gap between high press pretensions and low press performance. Those verses were quoted in 1914 by J.D. Symon, a former *Illustrated London News* man, as an appropriately ambivalent epigraph for his somewhat disenchanted *The Press and its Story*. They were quoted also, as a suitable epigraph, by Professor Oliver McGregor, chairman of the third Royal Commission on the Press of 1974–7, in his *Final Report*. In the intervening sixty-three years the newspaper industry had certainly not diminished as a perceived social problem. For Symon it was a matter of looking back over twenty or thirty years to the high Victorian epoch and observing glumly that the press was no longer as well regarded as it had been then. In 1894, when J.B. Mackie published his celebratory *Modern Journalism: a Handbook of Instruction and Counsel for the Young Journalist*, quoting Cowper would have been incongruous. Without a hint of irony, Mackie could extol editors as 'professors of the "People's University"'. The men who exercised the 'higher functions of journalism', he counselled young journalists from his editorial chair at the *North-Eastern Daily Gazette*, 'not only directly instruct the public mind and purify the public conscience, but they directly and powerfully help, correct, and to no small extent control the most gifted intellects and the most dominant enthusiasms of the day'.[7]

It is highly likely that those young entrants to the trade could already discern a credibility gap between Mackie's generation and their own. It would be only two years on, in 1896, when the defining moment came – Alfred Harmsworth's launching of the *Daily Mail*, flagship of the populist 'New Journalism'. Harmsworth's genius was to cater for a new suburban readership which had neither time nor taste to read the established educated sectarian press, the pride of Victorian journalism. The *Daily Mail* proved a portentously brilliant success. Symon could read the signs of the time.

There were members of a younger generation who shared his regrets. A dismayed G.M. Trevelyan grieved in 1901 that 'the Philistines have captured the Ark of the Covenant (sc. the printing press) and have learned to work their own miracles through its power'. A second defining moment came in 1908 when Harmsworth, by now ennobled as Lord Northcliffe, bought *The Times*, famed but bankrupt 'Thunderer' of the Victorian age. It can be surmised that L.T. Hobhouse had this ominous event in mind when in 1909 he deplored the way the press was becoming 'more and more the monopoly of a few rich men', and thus 'from being the organ of democracy' was on the way to degradation as the 'sounding-board for whatever ideas commend themselves to the great material interests'. To Hobhouse and his fellow casualties in the 'strange death of moral England', it was now evident that tension had grown dangerously between an ideology which claimed 'the Fourth Estate' as its own, 'and the forces of production which by then had made the press into an industry, subject to the logic of an expanding market'.[8]

Hobhouse thus defined the central dilemma of the modern newspaper press: the profoundly uneasy relationship within an industry which on the one hand is an industry like any other, making (or failing to make) a living in a market that is not only expanding but also intensely competitive, and on the other a form of production crucially necessary to the democratic health of the body politic. The example of the 'yellow press' in the United States, embodied most menacingly by William Randolph Hearst, offered salutary warning. As the press barons who succeeded Northcliffe after the Great War waxed in power and influence as proprietors of populist newspapers with huge circulations, that uneasy relationship steadily forced its way towards the head of the public agenda of national problems. The defining moment that passed into industry folklore of those times was Stanley Baldwin's denunciation in 1931 of Lords Rothermere and Beaverbrook, as proprietors aiming at power 'and power without responsibility – the prerogative of the harlot throughout the ages'.[9]

It was also in 1931 that a 'liberal-socialist think-tank', Political and Economic Planning, was formed to map out the shape of a collectivist future. Its survey of the press was published in 1938. Here, seemingly for the first time, was the germ of the idea of 'some sort of body' which would both protect the public against the press and also guard the press against illegitimate government encroachment. To George Murray, *Daily Telegraph* veteran and sometime chairman of the Press Council, this was a 'remarkably percipient peering into the future'.[10] PEP noted 'disturbing tendencies' observable with the rise of mass-circulation papers which made press shortcomings more conspicuous: triviality, intrusion, inaccuracy, over-emphasis on sex, all exacerbated by frenzied circulation competition. The National Union of Journalists had much the same aim of inculcating ethical standards when it formulated its Code of Conduct in 1936. PEP proposed a 'Press Tribunal' to be set up by the industry under a lay chairman with judicial experience, assisted by two assessors chosen from panels of proprietors' and journalists' organizations. The tribunal would have no legal authority and no power to inflict fines or other punitive measures. It was to be assumed that shaming publicity would prove a 'very powerful sanction'. Thus would a series of case decisions be built up which would form a working code of legitimate practice. PEP proposed also an academic Press Institute under the auspices of London University to lend the newspaper industry a dressing of intellectual respectability and to temper the crudity of the market.

War in 1939 pushed all such matters to the margins. Rationing of paper inhibited circulation competition. From time to time the press irritated Churchill's government. Powers of censorship were invoked. But much more serious was a Labour government with a landslide majority in 1945. The new socialist political climate would be reflected in a sterner attitude to the egregiously capitalist press industry. The idea of a collectivist post-war order would include taking up once more the kind of proposals left floating by the PEP.

The Attlee government took a very cautious view of direct legislative intervention to ensure a socially responsible press industry. Ready enough to transfer other industries such as railways and coal to public ownership, it drew back from any measure that might bear the character of national-izing the press. What were held to be the constitutional implications for 'the freedom of the subject' were formidable and daunting. Pressure from the National Union of Journalists, however, made it certain that something had to be seen to be done. What was arranged was that two MPs who were NUJ members moved in the House of Commons on 29 October 1946 that

having regard to the increasing public concern at the growth of monopolistic tendencies in the control of the press and with the object of furthering the free expression of opinion through the press and the greatest practicable accuracy in the presentation of the news, this House considers that a Royal Commission should be appointed to inquire into the finance, control, management and ownership of the press.

The motion was carried in a free vote by 270 to 157. For the first time in its embattled history, the 'rough old trade' would be subjected to having its entrails exposed to searching official examination. A Commission, appropriately briefed, was accordingly set up in 1947 under the chairman-ship of Sir David Ross, former provost of Oriel College, Oxford. It included two journalists: Sir George Waters, editor of *The Scotsman*, and R.C.K. Ensor, then with the *Sunday Times*. The Commission delivered its report in June 1949.

Its findings cleared the newspaper industry of monopolistic tendencies. But in several other respects it found serious shortcomings. The Com-mission noted particularly that 'the marked rise between 1937 and 1947 in the circulation of the *Daily Express* and the *Daily Mirror* is evidence of the large and expanding public for sensational newspapers'. Overall, the Commission concluded that the press had failed to keep pace with the requirements of society. That failure, the Commission found, was attribut-able largely 'to the plain fact that an industry that lives by the sale of its products must give the public what the public will buy'. A newspaper could not therefore 'raise its standard far above that of its public and may antici-pate profit from lowering its standard in order to gain an advantage over a competitor'.

How was a higher quality press keeping pace with the requirements of society to be promoted? Not, the Commission was clear, by changes in ownership and control. 'Free enterprise is a prerequisite of a free Press, and free enterprise in the case of newspapers of any considerable circulation will generally mean commercially profitable enterprise.' The Commission preferred 'to seek the means of maintaining the free expression of opinion and the greatest practicable accuracy in the presentation of the news, and, generally, a proper relationship between the Press and society, primarily in the Press itself'. The Commission, moreover, impressed by the industry's conception of its own function as shown in evidence before it, and the high standards of public responsibility that it acknowledged, felt encouraged to expect that the press 'will recognize and accept the part which it can thus play in developments which are vital to the future of democracy'. The industry needed 'to consider where it is going and consciously to foster those tendencies which make for integrity and for a sense of responsibility to the public'.

The Commission therefore went on to recommend that the industry itself should create and fund a central organ calculated to achieve these ends. It would be called the General Council of the Press, and consist of at least twenty-five members representing proprietors, editors and other journalists, together with five or so lay members representing the public interest, including the chairman. The lay members were to be nominated jointly by the Lord Chief Justice of England and the Lord President of the Scottish Court of Session, who would consult the chairman about the nomination of his fellow lay members. The Commission envisaged that a heavy burden of work would fall on the chairman, and recommended accordingly that he be paid. 'The objects of the General Council should be to safeguard the freedom of the Press; to encourage the growth of the sense of public responsibility and public service amongst all those engaged in the profession of journalism – that is, in the editorial production of newspapers – whether as directors, editors, or other journalists; and to further the efficiency of the profession and the well-being of those who practise it.' For the furtherance of these objects the Commission rec-ommended that the General Council should take such action as it thought fit under ten headings. These included a general review of any develop-ments likely to restrict the supply of information of public interest and importance, measures to improve methods of recruitment, education and training, issues relating to pension schemes, technical training and research, links with international press organizations, production of periodic reports, and so forth. It was item four on this list which, as things turned out, calls for particular notice.

(4) By censuring undesirable types of journalistic conduct, and by all other possible means, to build up a code in accordance with the highest professional standards. In this connection it should have the right to consider any complaints which it may receive about the conduct of the Press, to deal with these complaints in whatever manner may seem to it practicable and appropriate, and to include in its annual report any action taken under this heading.[11]

Raymond Snoddy was to comment forty-three years later on this Commission's report: 'Today, many of its preoccupations seem to belong to the age of post-war austerity. Yet in its 361 pages reside all the issues now being tackled by the Press Complaints Commission which began operating in 1991.'[12]

INTRODUCTION

The long road to the Last Chance Saloon, 1953–1989

'I do believe the popular press is drinking in the last chance saloon.'

David Mellor MP, Channel 4 *Hard News*, 21 December 1989

That the press industry would have to swallow at least the major elements of this invitation to set up its own self-regulatory apparatus was not in doubt. The alternative of some regulatory system imposed on it from outside was certain to be even more distasteful. The option of simple defiance, though no doubt tempting, would have been impolitic. The temper of the Labour party was best not provoked. The obvious initial recourse was dilatoriness and procrastination. Industry bodies began a leisurely process of wrangling and intrigue.

The Newspaper Proprietors' Association (NPA), founded in 1906, spoke for the English metropolitan or national press. (It prudently changed itself into the less provocative-sounding Newspaper Publishers Association in 1968.) The Newspaper Society (NS), founded in 1836 and the senior publishers' association in the world, spoke for the English, Welsh and Northern Irish regional and local press. These were the two big players. There were Scottish counterparts. The Periodical Publishers Association dated from 1913. There were also the press agencies: the international Reuters had its origins in the 1850s; the national Press Association in 1868. The Guild of British Newspaper Editors was a recent foundation, in 1946. The Institute of British Journalists, a polite trade union in the guise of a professional body, stemmed from the 1880s; the more abrasive National Union of Journalists (NUJ) from 1907.

Churchill's Conservative government came in in 1951, but it became clear that this would not spare the press from swallowing its self-regulatory pill. The House of Commons began to betray signs of impatience. A debate in November 1952, inspired by a private member's Bill which would have required the industry to set up a general council, aired more radical notions of quasi-statutory disciplines for newspapers. The proprietors reluctantly conceded that the non-regulatory game was up.

Thus it was, eventually, in February 1953, that the industry swallowed its medicine – not without choking. It choked particularly on the issue of lay representation. It was received wisdom and trade folklore that only journalists understood the 'old black art'. The two journalist commissioners, Sir George Waters and R. C. K. Ensor, had recorded their reservations on this point. 'As an old member of the journalistic profession', Ensor could not put his name to the proposal that the Council should have members appointed from outside. 'It is not usual in analagous bodies, and I am aware of no peculiar disability among Pressmen calling for such an innovation.' So it was that the new General Council of the Press would include neither lay members nor an independent lay chairman. Its first chairman would be no lesser figure than the head of the profession, so to speak: Colonel the Hon. J. J. Astor, proprietor of *The Times*. There were to be fifteen editorial and ten managerial nominees, with elaborate provision to encompass national and regional groups, journalists' unions, and Scottish interests. Pretty well all the subsidiary proposals recommended for inclusion in the Council's brief by the Ross Commission were dropped. The tasks of the Council were to be simply 'to safeguard the Freedom of the Press – and combat abuses of that freedom'; very much in that order. The Council had the conventional abuses in mind: intrusion into privacy, 'callous methods of enquiry' in the reporting of crime, and sexual titillation.

Nor was the industry too cowed to make clear that there would be strict limits set to the scope of such combat. No procedure for receiving and dealing with complaints specifically or regularly was envisaged. Meetings would be private. The Council regarded 'building up a code of conduct' with much the same distaste as it regarded lay membership. That was the sort of thing the Swedes and the National Union of Journalists had. The ethos and tone of the Council would be in-house, empirical, informal, part-time, and cosy. The industry, after all, was financing it, and would tolerate no powers of punitive sanction. The Council's authority would be purely moral. Rebarbative notes also were sounded. Intrusive journalism was defensible on public-interest grounds. The industry's lawyers insisted that complainants must waive resort to legal redress as the price for having their complaint attended to. Areas of 'difficult and disputable ground' were pointed to: questions of taste, offences against a 'general sense of decency'. In its 1954 report on its first year of activity the Council declared itself confident. That it wielded no sanctions seemed not to be a disability: its 'less spectacular methods will probably be most effective, and our appeal to conscience and fair play has rarely been in vain'. It was encouraged to hope 'that by its influence the Council may do much to encourage and justify the confidence and good will of the public towards the Press'.[1]

Of the Press Council it must be said that its disastrous end in 1990 was in its flawed beginning in 1953. It was flawed because it was grudged. Behind the scenes and façades of the 'important experiment' in press self-regulation was an industry that did not want it and did not like it. In 1949 *The Times* had doubts as to whether the Commission's recommendation was necessary or workable; 'the paper saw in the proposal a potential threat to press freedom'.[2] Those doubts were discreetly veiled in 1953 and after, but they lingered on not far below the surface of life at Blackfriars. Sir William Haley's prescription for the ills of the industry was to look, despairingly, to the proprietors. 'The only men who can change it are Lord Beaverbrook, Mr King, Lord Rothermere and Mr Thomson.'[3]

Within less than a decade the Council's manifest managerial and structural deficiencies were addressed by a second Royal Commission on the Press, which reported in 1962. The Shawcross Commission in effect rebuked the industry for evading the Ross Commission's recommendations for lay membership and an independent lay chairman. The industry in 1963 sulkily appointed the eminent judge Lord Devlin to the chair and a small group of lay representatives on to the Council. By this time it was evident that the Council's main work by far would be fielding complaints against press behaviour. In its early years the Council had dealt with an annual average of a mere sixty-odd complaints. By the middle and later 1960s complaints were running at four to five hundred a year. The terms of reference now focused primarily on complaints, and the budget was accordingly increased. New procedures for handling them were put in place, with a specialist complaints committee.[4] A problem here was that the Council admitted complaints from parties not directly involved: 'third-party' complaints. This increasingly put a strain on the machinery.

Thus given a second wind, the Press Council (as it was now renamed) for a while gave the impression of making its way successfully under the chairmanship of a series of prestigious lawyers: Devlin, Pearce, Shawcross, Neill. It became the object of admiring academic attention,[5] and a model for other countries to observe. It was the obvious precedent for the advertising industry to refer to – rather ironically, as things turned out – when in 1962 it began to set up its own self-regulatory mechanism, the Advertising

Standards Authority. The Council did some service to its industry, initiating investigations and defending journalists reporting the Aberfan coal-tip disaster from the menaces of the Attorney-General. George Murray, a former chairman, declared in 1972 that the Council 'in its present form has abundantly proved its value. It has become rooted in the British system and will undoubtedly endure.'[6] Also in 1972 the Younger Committee on Privacy commented that all press representatives had testified to the effectiveness of the Press Council, alleging that it was 'respected, feared and obeyed' by journalists and that it commanded the confidence of the public.[7]

Press representatives had no interest in testifying otherwise; but in any case pious pronouncements availed little as the tide of journalistic events began to engulf the Press Council. The era in which Northcliffe's *Daily Mail* was the exemplary specimen of the rogue newspaper was succeeded by the era of Beaverbrook's *Daily Express*, which was succeeded by that of the *Daily Mirror* under Hugh Cudlipp. The Sunday *News of the World* had always occupied its own special niche in this rogues' gallery. In 1969 the paper was acquired by the Australian Rupert Murdoch, whose father had learned his journalism under Northcliffe. Later in 1969 Murdoch bought the *Sun*, which he and his editor Larry Lamb converted into a stunningly successful daily tabloid by exploring the murkiest depths of the market. Here was the most roguish of all the rogues. By the early 1980s Murdoch's *Sun* with four million or more circulation had shouldered aside Robert Maxwell's *Daily Mirror*. In the House of Lords Murdoch was denounced as having done more than anyone else 'to lower the standards of journalism in this country'. The *Sun* was pilloried as 'one of the nastiest newspapers published in any Western democracy'.[8] Never had the rough old trade been rougher.

The Press Council fulminated against Murdoch, to little avail. Murdoch dismissed it as 'a pussy-footed arm of the establishment'. He saw it, as he saw the Australian Press Council modelled on it, as 'interference by failed editors and retired schoolmasters'. His *Sunday Times* editor, Harold Evans, got the message: 'he didn't give a damn'.[9] This was important. Murdoch, 'the Digger', had cast himself as the scourge of every thing class-bound, stuffy, effete and retrograde in British life. He had a plausible cause. His and his tabloids' 'great pleasure' was to 'puncture the pompous, or, at times, to brush aside the "chattering classes"'. Like Northcliffe, Murdoch too would take over the moribund *Times*. But unlike Northcliffe, Murdoch disdained any ambition to become a press baron in the House of Lords. As a new type of populist proprietor, Murdoch's not giving a damn about the House

of Lords could be taken there as a kind of compliment; but his not giving
a damn about the Press Council proved to be the most infectious wound it
could suffer.

There were to be many painful collisions between Murdoch's papers and
the Press Council through the 1970s and 1980s. As the last chairman of the
Council, Louis Blom-Cooper, was later to testify, the 'element of journalistic and editorial irresponsibility became more pronounced by the changing
characteristics of press ownership and fiercer competition in the 1970s'.[10]
The Labour party in July 1974 published *The People and the Media*, with a view
to altering the political balance of the press in the interests, as the party saw
it, of effective public choice. Industry turmoil and the start of Harold
Wilson's second Labour government led to yet another Royal Commission
in 1974, the chairmanship of which was taken over in 1975, on the death
of Sir Morris Finer, by Oliver McGregor, Professor of Social Institutions
at the University of London. Reviewing the 'responsibilities, constitution
and functioning of the Press Council' was part of its brief. The McGregor
Commission's *Final Report* in July 1977 found that there were still 'flagrant
breaches of acceptable standards' among newspapers, and there was 'a
pressing call to enhance the standing of the Press Council in the eyes of
the public and potential complainants'. The Council needed more generous
funding from the industry to advertise itself and speed up its procedures.
It needed a lay majority to demonstrate its independence from the industry.
It needed to draw up a coherent code of practice out of its adjudications,
and not make do with occasional 'declarations of principle' – as on chequebook journalism in the aftermath of the Moors Murders case, or on privacy
as related to certain egregious gossip columns in 1975 and 1976.

2

The Commission was divided on the question of complainants waiving
legal redress (a waiver which had been endorsed by the Younger Committee on Privacy). The Commission accepted the Council's case against
its being empowered to fine or suspend contumacious papers. There
were implications for censorship. There were implications for legal representation and all that would follow therefrom. There would be 'severe
practical problems' about levels of fines in relation to resources. And
whom, precisely, to fine? All these questions and answers were to be
rehearsed over many years in the debates on press regulation. For the time
being, the McGregor Commission fell back on faintly trusting the larger

hope. 'We prefer to rely on the sanction of censure by an independent and forceful Press Council.'

A code of practice would, in itself, the Commission urged, conduce towards forcefulness because it would emphasize clarity and consistency. This in turn would assist the Council to toughen up its stand on accuracy and bias; a toughening-up much needed, in the Commission's opinion. The Council, further, should persuade the industry to give critical adjudications prominent publicity. The Council should do more to instigate its own investigations into press behaviour. And it should express its condemnations more forthrightly. In sum, the Commission concluded that the Press Council should be, and be seen to be, an independent self-regulatory body pressing upon its industry 'the emphasis which we believe' the Council must give 'to protecting the public interest'.[11]

So, what it all amounted to was that the Press Council – to use a phrase which had earlier resonated amid the industry – had failed to keep pace with the requirements of society. In response the newspaper industry, in its accustomed grudging manner, conceded the recommendation of the Commission for a lay majority on the Council. This was a painful concession indeed, bespeaking loss of nerve. It did provide more money. In its turn the now distended Council did some of the things bidden it. It undertook more initiatives. It expressed its condemnations more forthrightly. A notorious case in both points was that of the *Daily Mail*'s breach of the Council's declaration of principle on chequebook journalism in relation to the Peter Sutcliffe (Yorkshire Ripper) affair in 1981. It was evident that several editors and executives had lied about their conduct of financial negotiations. Sir Patrick Neill's excoriating report *Press Conduct in the Sutcliffe Case* was immensely impressive and was duly applauded in Parliament. But, perversely, what came out of it was not public awareness of a new, tougher Press Council, but public awareness that the Press Council had yet again been flouted. What was remembered in the end was not Neill's report but its insolent dismissal by David English, editor of the *Daily Mail*, as 'short-term, short-sighted and smug', 'proving yet again that the Press Council still does not truly understand the concept of a Free Press'.[12]

The press industry, moreover, still refused to countenance a code of conduct or practice for journalists, particularly now when journalists would be judged by a lay majority. To that majority the industry did not reconcile itself. It became, in fact, the main reason why the Council failed to restore its standing with journalists.

The McGregor Commission, instead of bolstering the Press Council in the manner of the Shawcross Commission in the 1960s, had the effect of undermining it. McGregor's brief was wider than those of his predecessors. His *Final Report* was undoubtedly the most comprehensive and brilliant analysis of the British press.* It was at its most revealing in its exposure of scandalous trade-union malpractices. Its otherwise implicitly Leftish agenda hinted at the Labour party's *The People and the Media*. It stimulated socialist critiques of the press industry in general and the Press Council in particular: the one as being (in Raymond Williams's words) 'the Press We Don't Deserve'; the other as being a fraudulent imposture to gull the public into thinking that self-regulation was making newspapers wholesome and publicly accountable.[13] There were revived notions of state intervention. Renewed attention was directed to public subsidies in Sweden, Finland, Norway and, less approvingly, France.[14] In 1980 the National Union of Journalists withdrew its four nominees from the Council on the ground that it was 'wholly ineffective' and 'incapable of reform'. At the height of its Fleet Street power, the NUJ had established its own Ethics Council to police its Code of Conduct, with punitive sanctions. Then in 1983 came the severe critique instigated by the Campaign for Press Freedom, with Geoffrey Robertson QC in the lead. Among its proposals for a 'new settlement between public and press' was a reformed Press Council, with a published code of conduct, duties of monitoring and auditing and reporting to the Monopolies Commission, and responsibility for compulsory professional conduct courses in training schemes for journalists.[15]

All this contributed to what Louis Blom-Cooper later described as the 'drip-drop of discredit' which eroded the Council's credibility. Robertson mocked its inability to publish up-to-date reports. Of more moment was that Robertson arrived early at the conclusion at which the Calcutt Committee of 1990 arrived later: that the objective of protecting press freedom had proved incompatible with the Council's now primary function of fielding complaints. But, in a curious and paradoxical way, the Robertson critique of press self-regulation as administered by the Press Council was also a critique of the 'ham-fisted ideas' of those who wanted to replace press self-regulation with statutory regulation. If Robertson and his friends helped to undermine the Press Council, they also provided the best arguments for keeping media law at bay and giving self-regulation 'one final chance' in 1990 to survive and prove itself. 'If the existence of the Press

---

*McGregor made much of his being the first trained academic historian to chair a Royal Commission on the press.

Council justifies the argument against such expedients', Robertson observed of statutory bodies, 'then for this relief it deserves much thanks.'[16]

It was essentially on the strength of that kind of argument that voluntary press self-regulation – without powers to fine or suspend or expel, unhindered by any privacy law, and free from fees or costs to complainants – survived the crisis of 1990 ('Calcutt Phase 1'), then survived the crisis of 1993 ('Calcutt Phase 2'), survived the sacking of its discredited chairman in 1994, survived all manner of scandals and panics arising from the grievances and wiles and fate of Diana, Princess of Wales, and survives to this day. If the publication of *The People against the Press* justified the case against statutory regulation, it deserved well of the press industry.

But the Press Council, for all the thanks it deserved, did not survive. It was killed off by the circumstance that the 1980s were identified as the pits of British popular journalism. They are also identifiable as a decade of unprecedented change and instability in the industry. Proprietorial stresses intensified technological strains. Indeed, there were veteran newsmen, echoing William Haley in 1962, who by 1984 could see only one slim chance for the industry. 'Ultimately we must hope for some benign intervention from the proprietors, who are still the strongest influence on the national press.'[17] But the greatest proprietor of the time had other priorities in mind. It was Rupert Murdoch, aided by Eddie Shah in Warrington, who rode the whirlwind and directed the storm as the old Fleet Street was abolished and Wapping in the East End became the eye of a newspaper revolution.

The Press Council simply could not cut a figure to any credible degree commensurate with the scale of events, whether of tabloid degradation or of industry tumult. When in 1988 Sir Zelman Cowen QC, the Council's fifth independent chairman, presented his last report, *Difficulty, Damage, Danger – but Hope*, he referred to warnings given by ministers that if the Council could not secure compliance from newspapers to its rules and adjudications, the government might feel obliged to intervene with stern measures. Timothy Renton, minister at the Home Office, declared that if press self-regulation was seen manifestly to fail, 'it could not be imagined that nothing would be put in its place'.[18] Cowen pointed out that Kenneth Morgan, the director of the Council,[19] had warned the industry, citing particular cases, where trouble and danger lay.

The immediate trouble and danger lay in the 'avalanche of criticism' of the Council's failure to impose its authority over the *Sun* in the McCabe case, where an adjudication upholding the complaint of a lorry driver who had refused to cross a picket line at Wapping was treated by the paper with deliberate and repeated contempt. As Cowen commented, the 'conduct of the editor, which was surprising, and in my view entirely wrong, was declared to be in some way evidence of failure and weakness on the part of the Press Council'. Cowen added that those 'who would give teeth to the Press Council – and sharp and long teeth at that in terms of heavy money penalties – should consider the implications. . . . it would in practical terms turn the Council into a court, with formal and full hearings, supported by counsel and with rights of appeal'.[20] This argument – that bringing in statutory press regulation with sanctions meant bringing in lawyers which would mean time and expense to complainants – was subsidiary to and supportive of the larger arguments about state intervention and censorship put forward against 'media law' by *The People against the Press*; and it was to prove a vital component of the defence of press self-regulation then and since.

3

Yet no amount of such components could inject vitality into the Press Council by 1988. 'The Council appeared publicly to be retreating in hugger-mugger', as Blom-Cooper put it, 'oblivious to the impending threat to its continued existence.'[21] An attempt by a former director, Noel Paul, to provide a substitute code in *Principles for the Press* (1985) was dismissed by Lord McGregor as a 'jumble of potted digests' and an 'essay in incoherence'.[22]

In many ways the natural successor to Sir Zelman Cowen in 1988 would have been Professor Lord McGregor of Durris. The acclaimed chairman of the 1974–7 Royal Commission, he had been duly rewarded with a peerage in 1978. He was generally agreed to have made a good fist of chairing from 1980 the equivalent self-regulatory body for the advertising industry, the Advertising Standards Authority. Having taken early retirement from London University, McGregor was groomed for the ASA by a former chairman who went on to be chairman of the Independent Broadcasting Authority, Lord Thomson of Monifieth.[23] McGregor had good connections: he had been a trustee of Reuters since 1984 and chairman of Reuters Founders' Share Company since 1987. He had published and lectured widely on press matters and on general questions of industry regulation. He was the author in 1983 of *Press Freedom: the Role of*

UNESCO, in which he demolished with academic precision the pretensions of the promoters of the New World Information and Communication Order. He was *persona grata* with influential figures in the main industry bodies. The Newspaper Society director, Dugal Nisbet-Smith, who was anxious to see the back of Cowen, encouraged McGregor to make himself available as Cowen's replacement.

But of course when McGregor appeared before the Council as candidate, he appeared as the author of the report which had damned the Council as having 'failed to persuade the knowledgeable public that it deals satisfactorily with complaints against newspapers, notwithstanding that this has come to be seen as its main purpose'. And he appeared as the author of eighteen recommendations for improving the Council's performance, very few of which had been adopted. McGregor later recounted of his interview how he held back nothing in telling the Council 'everything that was wrong with it. I got the impression that my contribution was not well received', adding that he would not in any event have taken the job had it been offered.[24] Kenneth Morgan, the Council's director, recalled of McGregor on that occasion: 'He did not endear himself.'[25]

Certain alternative candidates – one was said to be a former Conservative Chancellor of the Exchequer – were thought inappropriate. Cowen, desperate to unload the job, sounded a fellow QC, Louis Blom-Cooper, a prominent barrister of libertarian reputation. For Blom-Cooper, Cowen's sounding came out of the blue. He had not thought of himself as a welcome or even plausible candidate. He was not particularly well regarded by the principal industry bodies. The Newspaper Publishers Association and the Newspaper Society (who between them paid more than 80 per cent of the Council's costs) resented his being behind newspaper articles advocating reforms, especially the ending of the waiver of legal redress. They were nervous of his intention to set up a review of the Council's constitution and procedures.

But from the Council's point of view, the one thing to be said for Blom-Cooper was that he was not McGregor. In the end that was enough. Blom-Cooper's contract was for three years at £50,000 a year. Nisbet-Smith recalled being 'staggered' when he heard of the appointment. He was not aware that Blom-Cooper was in the running.[26]

Once installed in the chair at the beginning of 1989, Blom-Cooper energetically set about rescuing the Press Council. He conferred with the Home Secretary, Douglas Hurd. He activated his review committee. He initiated five investigations, including one into allegations of scandalous press behaviour in the Hillsborough football stadium tragedy in April 1989. He floated the notion that privacy legislation need not be incompatible with press self-regulation. He followed up in 1990 with further inquiries, including one into irresponsible and sensational reporting of the Strangeways Prison riot.

On his appointment Blom-Cooper had been sent a message from Geoffrey Robertson: 'To Louis – good luck – you will need it!'[27] The new chairman got little of it. There was recalcitrance among industry nominees on the Council. On the review committee James Evans from the NS and Bernard Shrimsley from the NPA were stiffly resistant on the legal waiver and code-of-practice issues. Meanwhile, with the Hillsborough scandal, a gross and repeated libel of singer Elton John, and heartless intrusion into the last days of the television personality Russell Harty, the tabloids were at their atrocious worst.

Two private members' Bills, one on the right of reply and the other on the protection of privacy, were making their way through the Commons. For the Home Office, Timothy Renton spoke of the press being on probation, and needing to put its house in order within a couple of years. In the Lords, McGregor opened the debate on the Press Council's thirty-fifth annual report. He observed: 'Public and parliamentary censure of the press has never been so severe.' He observed also that for many years 'the Press Council's response to criticism of its constitution, procedures and effectiveness was arrogant, self-righteous and petulant'. Yet the point of McGregor's argument was that statutory tribunals armed with punitive powers would cause far more troubles than they cured.[28] He was seconded by the industry's principal spokesman in the Lords, Lord Stevens of Ludgate. But although the Bills ran out of time, the tide of public and parliamentary censure was running too high to be ignored.

Blom-Cooper and his busy review committee soon found themselves out-flanked on both the government and the industry sides. Ministers, uneasy at implications for the 'constitutional' principle of press freedom, and perhaps even more uneasy at the prospect of offending their powerful political allies in the press, were anxious not to have their hands forced. Another Royal Commission would be absurd. But something would have to be seen to be done. Hurd and Blom-Cooper had agreed that some official review of press self-regulation was urgently needed. Blom-Cooper trusted that Hurd would hand the task to the Press Council's own committee. However, Hurd announced in July 1989 that a Home Office committee under David Calcutt QC, Master of Magdalene College, Cambridge, would be set up:

in the light of recent public concern about intrusions into the private lives of individuals by certain sections of the press to consider what measures (whether legislative or otherwise) are needed to give further protection to individual privacy from the activities of the press and improve recourse against the press for the individual citizen, taking account of existing remedies, including the law on defamation and breach of confidence.[29]

Calcutt was asked to work speedily and produce his report in the summer of 1990.

On the industry side there was uneasiness at the heightened threat of statutory regulation to traditional press freedom. Broadsheet journalists were incensed that tabloid antics would drag the whole industry under the stern arm of a press tribunal. Some were ready to break ranks. Hugo Young of the *Guardian* declared that it was time 'to end the professional blackmail by which it is pretended that the interests of the *Sun* have anything in common with the interests of the *Guardian*'.[30] Some editors were moving towards the idea of a privacy law to save the press from worse. In the Newspaper Society there was talk of breaking away and setting up their own self-regulatory system. A *British Journalism Review* was launched by Geoffrey Goodman, industrial correspondent of the *Daily Mirror*, to provide the press with an analytic organ of debate about promoting newspaper standards, and to repair its lack of self-criticism. There were schemes to import American practice and appoint internal ombudsmen at newspapers. But the industry thought that something more resonant was required.

In July 1989 the Newspaper Publishers Association set up a committee of five editors, with Andreas Whittam Smith of the *Independent* in the chair, to plan a manifesto from the editors of national newspapers to defend press freedom. Expanded by November 1989 to include all national editors, the committee accepted that in the current atmosphere it would be politic to concede the code-of-practice point. Blom-Cooper could thus see his own plans being upstaged by national editors as well as the Calcutt Committee on Privacy and Related Matters.

By November 1989 Sir Frank Rogers, chairman of the NPA, was in conference with Lord McGregor, chairman of the ASA, about 'proposed self-regulatory machinery'. This would include a code of practice and would 'consist of a lower tier of readers' representatives spread through-out national newspapers or groups, and a higher tier of the council of the NPA which will have supervisory powers throughout the system'. It can be surmised that Rogers had McGregor in mind as the possible head of some possible replacement of the Press Council, or at least of some body dealing with the national press. Evidently that contingency was already on the NPA's agenda. McGregor was particularly concerned to give the scheme 'a better chance of being accepted if it were to be given a degree of independence in appearance and fact by setting up a body, or committee, or council between the NPA and the national newspapers'. He thought 'some such form of organization with lay representation is the minimum requirement to secure public confidence and hence to give a reasonable chance of defeating the threat of legislation'.[31] Possibly these discussions involving the national papers ran in tandem with the regional press debate about setting up their own arrangements.

However that may have been, amid the turmoil of those hectic months, as public and parliamentary disgust with the errant tabloids fuelled the pressure for disciplinary legislation, a topical move by the independent television Channel 4 was to launch a press coverage review called *Hard News*. It was to this programme that David Mellor, who had succeeded Timothy Renton as minister of state at the Home Office, was invited on 21 December to be interviewed by the journalist Raymond Snoddy. Mellor, oppressed by the tabloid press's dismal record for 'intrusion into people's private lives and its morbid coverage of national tragedies' – he had the Hillsborough case particularly in mind – declared himself 'almost ashamed and embarrassed to live in the same society as journalists who wrote such stories'. He was disgusted and disturbed at seeing the consequences of 'sensationalism driven by the circulation war'. The government was reluctant to intervene but it was painfully aware of 'widespread detestation' of the press in Parliament. It remained to be seen, of course, what the Calcutt Committee would recommend to the Home Secretary. 'I do believe', Mellor concluded, 'the popular press is drinking in the last chance saloon.'[32]

CHAPTER ONE

'An industry in a panic': from Press Council to Press Complaints Commission, 1990

'What matters in the Calcutt debate is that the case for self-regulation was considered and won the day.'

Simon Jenkins, *UK Press Gazette*, 2 July 1990

'The minority view, that editors should have nothing to do with Calcutt and defy the Government to legislate, has considerable bravado appeal but it has lost the day and it is time that everyone made the best of what we all accept is a bad job.'

UK Press Gazette, 2 October 1990

At the beginning of 1990 the British newspaper industry was disquieted and apprehensive. Calcutt and his Committee on Privacy and Related Matters had been taking evidence for several months. The Committee consisted of one Social Democrat MP, one former member of the Press Council, three lawyers and two journalists, one of whom was Simon Jenkins, then editor of *The Times*. It was known that they were seeking information from France, Germany, Canada and the United States. Would they opt for something drastic in the way of privacy legislation? Or, even worse, a regulatory tribunal with powers to discipline the press? There were MPs demanding that newspapers deemed guilty of repeating 'untrue' allegations be subject to punitive suspension. The Labour party policy review envisaging statutory press supervision was in preparation. Mellor's quip about drinking in the last chance saloon took on a life and notoriety of its own, much bandied about in newsrooms and pubs in the spirit of black comedy and *absit omen*.

It was not beyond conjecture that the government might use Calcutt's forthcoming report to clear away the Press Council and absorb press regulation into an inclusive statutory media complaints body. Observers of David Mellor's handling of the new Broadcasting Bill felt they had reason to suspect that the statutory Broadcasting Complaints Commission (BCC), established in 1980, was being promoted as a model for the press; that indeed Mellor seemed to have in mind the advantages of co-ordinating media regulation in both press and radio and television. This, Mellor seemed to be saying, was preferable to a privacy law. And if the Calcutt Committee was minded to take the statutory option either by proposing a transformed Press Council or an entirely new body, they would find the Home Office in support.

To the newspaper industry the BCC model was a dangerous one. The BCC dealt with programme-makers who were already guidelined and regulated by strict codes. The print medium was an entirely different breed. Rather than start down this slippery slope, press interests urged, it would surely be better to give the Press Council a chance and let the ombudsmen being appointed by newspapers have time to prove themselves. The Press Council, after all, had just published its tough Code of Practice. 'A statutory complaints commission sounds like a modest step', *The Times* pointed out, 'but it is more like crossing the Rubicon.'[1]

To many in the industry the Council's Code was itself quite enough of a crossed Rubicon to be going on with. Blom-Cooper proposed that the Council commence operations on the basis of its Code as from 1 March. In *The Press and the People: the 36th Annual Report of the Press Council, 1989*, Blom-Cooper argued his case with an accomplished barrister's skills. On the one hand he stuck to his guns on the theme of the Council's unique vocation to integrate defence of press freedom with rebuke of press excesses. None of the three Royal Commissions, he pointed out, had given the 'slightest hint' that there was any incompatibility. This was the burden, of course, of Blom-Cooper's evidence on behalf of the Council to Calcutt. And he now had his Code to display as an earnest of good faith. His main failure in the Council review was not to get the waiver of legal redress past James Evans and Bernard Shrimsley.

On the other hand, as a result of that Council review, Blom-Cooper now was armed with 'several radical proposals which have concerned newspaper editors and proprietors'.[2] The sixteen-point Code of Practice was not in itself at the head of this industry agenda of concern about Blom-Cooper's doings. The NPA editors' group under Whittam Smith were gearing up to formulate their own version. What an unmollified industry was looking at was a series of disciplinary procedures with which the Council proposed to arm itself and which was designed to put editors invidiously on the spot. The Council now expected its censure to 'discredit

editors and journalists at whom it is aimed and to be weighed by their
employers'. One proposal in particular was eventually, after various
permutations, to have interesting repercussions. 'That in appropriate,
serious cases where the Council itself rather than a complaints committee
adjudicates against the conduct of an editor, it should invite the proprietor
or publisher to recall the commitment he has given to uphold the Council's
principles, and ask what he intends to do about the conduct of his paper in
the future.' Blom-Cooper's strategy was to woo Calcutt with this strong
medicine for the industry while trusting that Calcutt would not follow the
Geoffrey Robertson line that a press freedom body could no longer be a
convincing press rebuke body. In the end, by trying to have it both ways,
Blom-Cooper failed to have it either way.

Meanwhile, having not endeared himself to the industry by prescribing
nasty medicine, Blom-Cooper then endeared himself even less to his pay-
masters by asking for more staff and a budget of a round £1 million for
1991. The Council was facing charges of £850,000 with an income of
£574,000. The industry was reluctant to pay up. Edward Pickering recalled
how he and his fellow Times Newspapers executive Denis Hamilton used
to make the rounds of press offices on Friday nights with a begging bowl
to cadge money for the Council.[3] Industry people, it appeared, responded
to the new financial demands with 'barely concealed fury'. The Newspaper
Society stumped up to save self-regulation, not to save Blom-Cooper. The
chairman, indeed, was thought 'now likely to have to listen even more carefully to criticism' of his Council's review. That the NUJ chose this moment
to return to the Council they had flounced out of in 1980 probably did little
to boost Blom-Cooper's sagging credit. It looked too much like a case of
the hacks rejoining the sinking ship.

Then, as Calcutt loomed, the industry scored a spectacular own goal. A
popular television actor, Gorden Kaye, badly injured in a freak accident, lay
desperately ill in Charing Cross Hospital. A reporter and a photographer
from the *Sunday Sport* contrived access and subjected the stricken man to
their attentions. The *Sunday Sport* editor thought this exploit a 'great
old-fashioned scoop'. Even for what was disdained as an entertainment
sleaze-sheet rather than a newspaper, this was held to be a scandal too far.
The Committee on Privacy and Related Matters naturally took note of
what instantly became a landmark in atrocious intrusiveness.

Defence of the press was now pushed on to the back foot. The Press
Council's solemnly proclaimed principles evidently were floutable with
impunity.[4] At the Guild of British Newspaper Editors' conference at

Nottingham the theme was 'Has the Press gone far enough in its attempts at self-regulation?' Brian MacArthur at *The Times* extolled the *Washington Post*'s Code of Practice as a model which would 'hinder not one jot our ability to report and investigate but would raise us significantly in the eyes of the public. . . . I can vouch from my own experience that even editors most guilty of previous excesses now read the writing on the wall.' Editors must make the Press Council work. The 'stark truth' was that for journalists who believe in extending the freedom of the press, 'the Editors' Code and the Press Council are our last options if we are not to get government regulation of the Press'.[5]

In truth the writing was already on the wall. The Press Council's status as any kind of option was fading fast. Its embroilment in the case of a tabloid referring to homosexuals as 'poofters' exposed it to mockery and ridicule as a body of 'pompous laymen and self-important journalists' straying 'too far into the jungles of taste and discretion'. The *Sun* insulted the Council as a 'bunch of loonies'. It was true that the industry often found Blom-Cooper's pronouncements baffling and wayward, reflecting growing sentiment that his appointment in 1988 had been a mistake. The *Press Gazette*, the weekly trade paper, complained of 'hectoring encyclicals'. Peter Preston, editor of the *Guardian*, dismayed at 'dotty' and 'infantile' squabbles in the shadow of Calcutt, issued a call to order and advised Blom-Cooper that his 'new Council will not succeed because it is nurse (in place of something worse) but because it argues its corner with ferocity and verve'.[6]

Ferocity and verve were qualities not in ready supply at the Council. Blom-Cooper had shot all the bolts he had to shoot. But among those giving evidence to Calcutt, oddly enough, were none other than Kelvin MacKenzie, fabled rogue editor of the *Sun*, and his even more fabled rogue proprietor, Rupert Murdoch. MacKenzie, who had been one of the national editors subscribing to the projected Whittam Smith code, assured Calcutt that statutory regulation was superfluous 'now the tabloids have reformed themselves'. With a certain verve he produced thirty recent copies of his paper. 'These days, he said, there was nothing in it he could not show to his maiden aunt.'[7] Whether the Committee (which had a reputation in the industry for being grim) took this stunt in good part is not clear. No doubt they took Murdoch's presence more seriously. That presence was stage-managed by Sir Edward Pickering, a veteran journalist who interpreted Murdoch to his editors, and was reputed to be the 'wisest man in Fleet Street'. Now, seconded by the New Zealander Andrew

Knight, who had recently come across from Conrad Black's Telegraph Group, Pickering interpreted Murdoch to the Calcutt Committee. Their purpose was to sustain press self-regulation. Between them Pickering and Knight smoothed 'ruffled feathers in the corridors of power'.[8]

How successful they were in smoothing Calcutt's feathers remains conjectural. One of the members of the Committee, the Liberal Democrat MP John Cartwright, told the House of Commons how evidence was given by a long succession of prominent proprietors and editors 'who came before us to repent of past sins and assure us that they had all now turned over a new leaf'. But of course every inquiry into the press for the past forty years ' has heard the same pleas and has been persuaded to grant one last chance'.

2

That was precisely, in the end, what the Committee on Privacy and Related Matters did. 'Our first main recommendation is that the press should be given one final chance to demonstrate that it can put its house in order.' Calcutt's report was in the Home Secretary's hands by 16 May. It was published on 21 June. Calcutt's own preference from the start was for a tough privacy law. He was thwarted in his hope for unanimity on that score. 'Nowhere', the Committee concluded, 'have we found a wholly satisfactory statutory definition of privacy.' A tort of infringement of privacy should not, therefore, presently be introduced. Nor should there be any extension of the law of defamation. Nor should a statutory right of reply be introduced. However, in the light of the Gorden Kaye case, three new criminal offences involving intrusion by journalists should be created, all concerning varieties of trespass on private property. There should also be further restrictions on press reporting of court proceedings.

So far, from the industry's point of view, a mixed bag, mostly good; but the proposal to criminalize acts of a specific social group was thought both offensive and undesirable in principle. 'We have no evidence of a golden age of media responsibility', the Committee further declared, 'and anecdotal evidence to the contrary is probably tinged with nostalgia.' But the past two decades had seen a new degree of tabloid competition. And it was clear that the Press Council had failed to exert a self-regulatory authority adequate to cope with the problems ensuing. There was need for a 'fundamental over-haul of the present structure and a complete review of the assumptions upon which it depends'. The Press Council's own review did not go far enough to expunge the image of ineffectiveness that it suffered from. 'In our view the two distinct functions of defending the freedom of the press and adjudicating on complaints sit uneasily together, and only an independent body can effectively carry out that second task.' Calcutt specified that the uneasiness he referred to arose out of the Council's being 'an overtly campaigning body' for press freedom. He therefore recommended that the Press Council be abolished and replaced by a Press Complaints Commission, which would apply itself to providing an effective means of redress for complainants. Revealingly, Calcutt cited the statutorily based Broadcasting Complaints Commission as a model in point, not the self-regulatory Advertising Standards Authority.[9]

Calcutt recommended that the press industry be given a year to establish the new Commission. He specifically advised that the existing Council secretariat not be transferred to staff the Commission, even on an interim, transitional basis. The evidence, then and later, suggests that Calcutt thought of the Commission as an interim transitional body, halfway to his ultimate objective of a statutory press tribunal. He stipulated that, should the industry fail to demonstrate that self-regulation could be made to work effectively, a statutory system for handling complaints should forthwith be introduced. He was careful to offer a model for that. The Calcutt report was as much concerned with the machinery of a potential Press Complaints Tribunal as with the machinery of the proposed Press Complaints Commission. There seems little doubt that Calcutt expected that 'maverick publications' would prove as impossible for the PCC to discipline as they had been for the Council. Giving the industry a period of 'probation' in which to demonstrate the efficacy of its new apparatus – this was eventually set at eighteen months – had the tactical advantage of giving the government a breathing-space timetable in which it could nerve itself to jump through the statutory hoop of flames.

The Committee proposed detailed specifications for the designated Press Complaints Commission. It should publish, monitor and implement a Code of Practice. Calcutt thought the Press Council's version 'too vague'. His own example, decidedly stiff, eschewed any 'public interest' qualifiers to which editors might appeal. The PCC should operate a 'hotline' (much as the Council had already advocated) on a 24-hour basis by which editors could be alerted before publication of potentially objectionable matter. The waiver of legal redress by complainants would be abolished. The Commission should have a chairman independent of the industry and no more than twelve members in sub-committees adjudicating on complaints under delegated powers. Members of the Commission should not be nominated by industry bodies, though a majority of them should have 'experience at the highest level of the press'. Editors, in other words, would be obliged to monitor each other. Nor did the Council's lay majority seem now a particularly persuasive precedent. Appointments to the Commission should be made by an Appointments Commission, itself independently appointed, possibly by the Lord Chancellor.

In sum: if the newspaper industry wished to maintain self-regulation it should manifest its commitment by providing the money to set up the new machinery within twelve months. 'It must now demonstrate that it can discharge its responsibility and that, through its own conduct and self-regulation, it can command the confidence of the public.' If it was not prepared to put and keep its own house in order, 'further legislation must follow'.[10]

3

The Home Secretary, David Waddington, welcomed the Calcutt report. He confirmed that this was 'positively the last chance for the industry to establish an effective non-statutory system of regulation'. Ministers at large welcomed it, as well they might. It let them off several awkward legislative hooks – privacy, defamation, right of reply – which were inconveniently popular in both Houses of Parliament. Best of all, it postponed having to attend to the most awkward hook of all, subjecting the press, most of it Tory, to statutory regulation. To Calcutt's initial grace of a year to the industry, add eighteen months of probation, and you are at the beginning of 1993; and in any case there would have to be a general election by 1992. As for the recommended legislation against journalistic intrusion, that would be 'carefully considered'. Waddington concurred in the new Commission's being modelled on the Broadcasting Complaints Commission. Ministers recognized that the press industry had made some attempt in the past year to respond to public concern about abuses, and high tribute was due to the chairman of the Press Council for his valiant efforts to modernize and make effective the existing system of self-regulation; but ministers could not offer a reprieve against Calcutt's verdict and sentence of death. For the Labour party Roy Hattersley gave the report's recommendations an 'unqualified welcome' and undertook to 'happily co-operate in their implementation'. He was particularly concerned to endorse Calcutt's stiff definition of what would constitute demonstrative failure on the industry's part: a 'single maverick paper ignoring the proposed new code of conduct' would trigger statutory regulation.[11]

For Blom-Cooper and his Council, Calcutt's verdict and sentence, and the government's refusal of reprieve, was a horrifying shock. Even more shocking, in its way, was the failure of the industry to rally to the Council's defence. The industry disliked Calcutt; but that dislike was not translated into any better liking for the Council. That the NUJ rallied to the Council's support only confirmed the inevitability of non-reprieve.

Of journalism's luminaries, Charles Wintour, ombudsman for *The Times* and the *Sunday Times*, was one of the few with a kind word to say for the doomed Council. He thought Waddington 'unnecessarily brusque'. But of course the press could not expect sympathy. Still, 'in view of his extraordinary failure so far to consult the industry he is so close to confining in a statutory strait-jacket he might yet be persuaded that reform of the Press Council along the lines recommended . . . would be far more sensible than his current plan'. Surely, Wintour urged, the Press Council, with the spur of this report behind it, could reform itself far more rapidly and effectively than a commission could be established. 'It is half-way there already. An office is manned; a chairman whose reforming zeal is fully acknowledged by Calcutt sits already in place.'[12]

It would be that zealously reforming chairman's fate to sit vainly in place. For the most part reaction from the industry shared the government's relief but not the government's satisfaction. Statutory regulation had not been summarily imposed; but the reading of Calcutt prevalent among journalists was that, in the words of Ian Beales, chairman of the parliamentary and legal committee of the Guild of British Newspaper Editors, its 'great danger' was that it appeared 'to open the way to statutory control'. The Guild announced that it looked as if the aim was 'to fit the press out with a strait-jacket and invite us to do up the straps'. The Association of British Editors, a lobby group of senior media figures, accused Calcutt of being 'another turn of the screw against the free working of the press in Britain'. There were aggrieved protests against the invidious anti-intrusion proposals and the abolition of the waiver of legal redress. Proprietors contributed their thoughts. Robert Maxwell at the Mirror Group was rather bland and non-committal, perhaps reflecting the suspicion the *Mirror* people nursed that Murdoch's espousal of self-regulation was manipulatively self-interested. Lord Rothermere, on the other hand, on behalf of his Associated Newspapers empire denounced Calcutt's line of reasoning as illogical and unjust: 'that if just one of our number – even if a sleaze sheet rather than a proper newspaper – steps out of line, then the whole lot of us will have statutory fetters clamped on us'.[13]

For the regional press, the Newspaper Society was inclined at first to resist. The fate of the Press Council, insisted the Society's director, Dugal Nisbet-Smith, was not up to outsiders. 'The Press Council is thankfully not a creature of the state. It is not for Mr Calcutt, or the Government, to determine its fate without legislation.' The Society was seeking urgent meetings with the Home Office and other newspaper industry bodies to explore the implications for press freedom.[14] Nicholas Herbert, editorial director of the Westminster Press regional group, advocated telling Calcutt to do his worst. Talk among the regionals about setting up their own regulatory arrangements uninfected by the tabloid nationals had faded in the face of the practical difficulties involved. There were too many structural links with the metropolitan press to make divorce feasible. The NS had in fact already proposed the formation of a Press Council Board of Finance, advised by George Bogle, who had set up the model, Asbof, the Advertising Standards Board of Finance, which levied its constituent bodies.[15] Here indeed was the origin of Pressbof, the Press Standards Board of Finance, established in 1990, with Nisbet-Smith as its prime begetter; but the Press Council was not to be the beneficiary of it.

From the nationals, meanwhile, responses were no less doubtful. At the *Daily Telegraph* the editor Max Hastings felt it remained to be seen 'whether the most serious betrayers of press standards take Calcutt's warnings seriously. I still believe that the difficulties of defining offences against acceptable behaviour in a form that can be codified are somewhere between very great and insuperable.'[16] Peter Preston at the *Guardian* explored the theme of 'heavy boots on a slippery slope'. Calcutt, having abolished the Press Council, 'thereupon creates the most curious quango known to political man'. The report's 123 pages were wholly lacking in evidence of an overwhelming 'public demand'. There was irony in the Press Council's having made a sweeping refurbishment just as its death warrant is signed. Calcutt creates a 'painstaking sort of half-way house' and calls it the Press Complaints Commission. 'That is the curious quango.' Its membership, Preston foresaw, was to be 'handed down from Whitehall via the corridors of London clubland. . . . One awaits, heart in boots, for the emergence of Lord Rees-Mogg as chairman designate.' Calcutt was an 'alpine vista of slippery slopes'.[17]

At *The Times*, Simon Jenkins, one of Calcutt's colleagues, decided that some calling to order would be salutary. There was no clear or conclusive evidence, he insisted, that press behaviour had worsened or that self-regulation could not work. The press was always unpopular when passing

through phases of intense competition. The Calcutt Committee, 'after prolonged debate', decided that self-regulation in the matter of privacy should
be given a last chance. Most witnesses agreed that the press was behaving
better than it had been just a year ago. 'But we had to accept that a wide
range of public and political opinion felt that the Press Council had insufficient authority.' Some new body was needed specifically to investigate complaints, independent of the industry and with more staff and money to act
swiftly. Publishers, Jenkins urged, should back the new Commission, and
ensure that editors make it work. What was the alternative? A law against
intrusive journalism would become a shambles. Either it would not protect
the weaker, or poorer, victims of press intrusion, or it would lead to the
litigation virus infecting American newspapers. There privacy laws had
become a surrogate for libel. 'The freedom to search out news is worth
keeping outside the courts or the control of the state. A framework for
such freedom is on offer. The press should seize it.'[18]

As dire prognostication about Calcutt followed upon dire prognostication, Jenkins returned to his unapologetic defence. The press was 'too
gloomy about Calcutt'. Notions that there was a threat to press freedom
were 'absurd'. 'Press freedom grows ever more fragile when the press reacts
to criticism with the same cry as do lawyers and doctors: "A great
profession at work, public keep out."' What mattered in the Calcutt debate
was that 'the case for self-regulation was considered and won the day'. Of
course the industry could sit tight on its dignity and tell the 'get tough with
the press' lobby that it was right all along. That would put the clock back a
year, a year in which the press had largely neutralized the 'get tough' lobby.
'The dogs are sleeping', Jenkins urged. 'They will never go away, but at least
we have a chance to let them lie.'[19]

At the *Sunday Telegraph* a different order of question was being asked. If
the Home Secretary 'gave every sign of being genuinely outraged' by the
excesses of the tabloid press, what of the Prime Minister herself? For not
only did Mrs Thatcher regularly invite Mr Murdoch, owner of the *Sun*
and the *News of the World*, to Chequers; she also knighted Larry Lamb,
'the creative editorial genius who launched the *Sun* on its triumphantly
successful muddy path'. A barony was conferred as well on the owner of
the *Daily Star*, David Stevens.

The reason Mrs Thatcher favours Mr Murdoch and the other offending tabloid
proprietors and editors ... is because she draws great political benefit from their
editorial support. It is said, probably rightly, that the support of *The Sun* can

make or break the fortunes of the Tory Party. On the one hand, the Prime Minister honours and encourages these invaluable political partners; and on the other, her Home Secretary threatens to prosecute them for vile intrusions of privacy. A certain hypocrisy here.

The question that really ought to be asked, thought the *Sunday Telegraph*, was 'why these offending newspapers, the nastiness of which is not equalled anywhere else in Europe and North America, are so enormously popular'. People 'love to read the muck'. That was the real problem, which Calcutt will do little to solve. All that will be done will 'amount to brushing the dirt under the carpet'; and sacrificing press freedom 'seems to be a heavy price for doing that'. Why does not the Prime Minister set an example by herself 'ostracising and publicly attacking the offending proprietors in the vastly effective manner of Stanley Baldwin, her brave predecessor, who compared them . . . to prostitutes exercising power without responsibility?'[20]

The short answer to that question was that, for all the fame of his execration of hostile proprietors, Baldwin cultivated friends in the press as assiduously as any other political leader. The larger question about the relationship of a political party to its invaluable partners in the press vis-à-vis policy on press regulation would echo, unanswered, for years to come.

4

The Press Council reacted naturally with dismay. After all the labour of its review, after all the evidence it had contributed, Calcutt's verdict seemed ungrateful as well as cruel. The Council was a going concern. Its offices at Salisbury Square were indeed manned. Its reforming chairman indeed sat ready in place. A six-hour crisis meeting on 26 June produced a defiant response: 'neither the Calcutt Committee nor the Government has the right or power to wind up the Press Council'. It vowed to resist abolition rather than submit weakly to the death sentence.[21] Defiance was applauded by the NUJ. The general secretary, Harry Conway, denounced Calcutt as a charter for the protection of the establishment against an inquiring press. The chairman of the Australian Press Council, Professor David Flint, extended fraternal solidarity. As befitted one leading a movement for a World Association of Press Councils, he advised a more cautious response to Calcutt by British government and press industry. 'Britain is still seen as a model for many countries. Throughout the centuries, the freedoms that the British people have enjoyed have made her a beacon, a land where, at times almost totally surrounded by tyranny, freedom of speech and a free Press have flourished.'[22]

But the game was up. Sir Frank Rogers, the national industry chief, took Calcutt in his stride – or rather, had already taken Calcutt in his stride. He called his Newspaper Publishers Association Council together on 26 June to give 'full support' to the setting up of the Press Complaints Commission. The NPA would 'seek consultation on the means of supporting it and wanted to ensure that its costs were controllable'.[23] Not the least extraordinary thing about this crucial NPA Council meeting was that Rogers had in his pocket a 'personal view' from Louis Blom-Cooper that, in the interests of preserving press self-regulation, it was expedient to set up the PCC as quickly as possible, and that the Press Council would best reconcile itself to extinction and not spend time in futile and possibly damaging resistance. Blom-Cooper communicated in the same terms with the Newspaper Society and the other constituent bodies of the Council. He was convinced that Calcutt was not a first step on a slippery slope leading to statutory regulation. He saw it as a genuine last chance to make self-regulation work. He was encouraged by Roy Hattersley's endorsement of Calcutt, which he interpreted as a significant shift away from the Labour party's hitherto entrenched partiality for statutory controls.

The problem for Blom-Cooper was that his Press Council by no means shared his noble instinct for self-sacrifice. Its chairman went off to the 'crisis' meeting on 26 June, having already conveyed his personal capitulation to Rogers's NPA meeting the same day. Not even Blom-Cooper's best friends would extol him as a faithful team-worker or a dutiful committee man. He arrived at Salisbury Square expecting to persuade the Council that surrender was the best policy. On apprehending the Council's defiant mood, he quickly abandoned his intention and found himself swept along in the emotional current of resistance. As he put it, he could see that his own view 'would not be helpful in the circumstances'.[24] Blom-Cooper's initial personal embarrassment soon became a collective embarrassment for the Council once the confusion came out into the open. 'He sabotaged any chance we had of keeping the Council alive', one of its members grumbled. 'Some Press Council members are critical of Mr Blom-Cooper's conduct', it was reported. 'Some members have been urged by national and provincial newspaper representatives to call for his resignation.' That drastic recourse was not pressed: it seemed better to let the Council depart with dignity.[25]

That the game was truly up was signalled publicly by Rothermere at an Institute of Journalists reception. 'Some no doubt would like us to cling on to nurse – in the unlikely form of Louis Blom-Cooper – for fear of something worse. For my part, I recognise that we will have to untie ourselves from those now somewhat frayed apron strings and strive to make the best, for the public and the profession, of the new proposed Press Complaints Commission.'[26] Rothermere, head of a press group of which the *Daily Mail* was flagship, spoke from inside knowledge both of proceedings at the NPA and of meetings of editors who formulated guardedly positive responses to Calcutt. 'While in public they may have broadly welcomed it', commented *Private Eye*, 'many strongly disagreed with aspects of the report. In one matter only were they united and cheerful: the abolition of the Press Council was a very popular recommendation if for no other reason than that it gets Louis Blom-Cooper out of the way.'[27]

Rothermere, however, was not in a position to speak so boldly as he did until the Newspaper Society, the other major player in the industry game, came into line with the NPA. There had been a time when it seemed that a 'significant gulf' was opening up within the industry over who should police the press. Rapprochement came only on 4 July, when the NS decided 'reluctantly and conditionally' to accept Calcutt. Dugal Nisbet-Smith, the Society's director, reflected the resentment among the regionals and locals at being tarred with the metropolitan tabloid brush. What was being given to the NPA as a punishment was being given to the NS as a reward. But it was conceded that going it alone with the Press Council was not a feasible option. Nisbet-Smith made it clear that the NS decision was more a recognition of the reality of the threats accompanying the government's acceptance of the Calcutt Committee's report than a full acquiescence. 'If we don't oblige the government by abandoning genuine self-determination for imposed regulation, we will get statutory regulation.' Doubtless this was the message conveyed with relish at the Home Office. 'The tone of the statement', commented the *Guardian*'s media correspondent Georgina Henry, 'was less accommodating than that of the Newspaper Publishers Association. . . . But it spells the end of the Press Council which now has neither of its two most important constituent bodies supporting it.'[28]

Blom-Cooper was now the embarrassed captive of his Council. It summoned him back from Antigua, where he was professionally engaged, to attend to its now desperate affairs. He had already declared that he would not be a candidate to head the new Commission which for him embodied the industry's ignoble abdication of its role of defending press freedom. But even at the eleventh hour the Council envisaged saving something from the wreckage. A working party was set up to 'consult constituent bodies and others' about the 'viability of continued self-regulation'. And what of the Council's 'continuing with its role of defending press freedom'?[29] Senior figures in the industry, however, were known to rate the Council's chances of even residual survival as 'none whatsoever'. 'They have been critical of Blom-Cooper and will refuse any longer to fund the Council.' The Commission would need a budget of at least £1 million a year. This was where the new era of press regulation would take shape. The NS's earlier proposal to apply Asbof arrangements as practised by the Advertising Standards Authority to the Press Council were now diverted into setting up a Press Standards Board of Finance applied to the Press Complaints Commission. 'Pressbof' would co-ordinate the industry's actions on self-regulation; and would comprise representatives of the NPA, the NS, the Periodical Publishers Association, the Scottish Daily Newspaper Society, and the Scottish NPA. Initially it was hoped that James Evans, one of the senior men in the Thomson Organization, would take the chair. It was Harry Roche of the Guardian Group who took it on.

'So farewell then, the Press Council', wrote Charles Wintour elegiacally of its last, spurned struggles to stay alive. 'There could scarcely be a more blatant demonstration of the contempt with which the council is now regarded by senior figures in the industry.'[30]

5

Wintour had other insights to offer. Calcutt's recommendation had been that the PCC should be constituted by an Appointments Commission, itself constituted by preference by the Lord Chancellor. That was Calcutt's mode of securing the Commission's independence from the industry. Wintour could see, however, that in the interests of speed and simplicity it was likely that the industry chiefs would 'leapfrog' that stage by themselves appointing a chairman 'of acknowledged stature and independence who would be agreeable to the Home Office'. In this Wintour was precisely correct. The chiefs were not going to accept supinely every jot and tittle of Calcutt. Wintour could see a heavy burden bearing on Sir Frank Rogers, chairman of the NPA. Together with Rogers were Nisbet-Smith of the NS, James Evans, and the patriarchal Sir Edward Pickering. Wintour fretted at the 'terrifying prospect' that the chiefs were setting in being a body that could far too easily be transformed into a statutory body. 'With Roy

Hattersley as Home Secretary in waiting, the publishers must be well aware of the risks.' The state, thought Wintour, 'is becoming far too enmeshed with the future regulation of the press'.[31]

The chiefs were no doubt well aware of the risks. They had no intention of taking the Broadcasting Complaints Commission as their model. They would have shared Wintour's assessment of Hattersley rather than Blom-Cooper's. Their strategy, in essence, was to create a genuine system of press self-regulation out of the somewhat ambiguous, or 'half-way house', elements of Calcutt by sheer rapidity of movement. For what was most remarkable about the response of the industry chiefs to this crisis was their astonishing turn of speed. Calcutt had allowed them a year to get things up and running. What became clear very soon after June 1990 is that they aimed to have the Press Complaints Commission in being and in operation by 1 January 1991. Pressbof was soon in formation. It would effectively be the powerhouse of the whole machine. With Roche in the chair it would include Rogers, Evans and Nisbet-Smith. George Bogle of Asbof would work out for it an efficient financial equation for levying the industry. Scotland's contribution, courtesy of the Scottish Daily Newspaper Society, was to provide managerial headquarters and staff in Glasgow, under the care of Grahame Thomson. Harry Roche and his team were in place by October.

6

At this moment the industry was in a most curious state. As the chiefs hastened purposefully to their objectives, the Indians danced their ritual dances. The NUJ had the Trades Union Conference debating Calcutt's failings and deficiencies. The *British Journalism Review* lamented the 'fateful day' when editors and publishers agreed to a code of practice.[32] The Association of British Editors organized a poll to assess reaction to Calcutt, the results to be available for a seminar in London in October run by ABE and the International Press Institute. Their necks, as they saw it, were 'in the noose'; they wondered that the 'powers that be' in the industry seemed to be so little galvanized at the 'sinister' prospect before them.[33]

The powers that be were in fact much more galvanized than ABE or the Institute knew. There was the question now of who would head the new Commission. Rogers had been cultivating Lord McGregor at the Advertising Standards Authority since at least November 1989. There appeared to be no hint of any serious alternative. Pressbof now had him in focus. McGregor's contract with the Authority would lapse in December 1990. He was perfectly placed. His credentials were impeccable. He had demolished UNESCO's pretensions. He was the author of the unsurpassed 1977 Royal Commission report. He had scholarly expertise as an economic historian. 'I've read a lot of Victorian newspapers which printed court news verbatim', he declared. 'There's no real evidence that there has been any decline in standards between then and now. The agitation we see for a proper complaints body is the product not of declining standards but an improvement. The public has come to demand more from newspapers.' That sort of thing was music to the industry's ears. As for self-regulation, McGregor's reputation as its champion was such that it was widely acknowledged that there could 'hardly be a fiercer defender of the freedom of the press to regulate its own affairs'.[34]

To all appearances an 'affable and soft-spoken man', McGregor had followed his time at Aberdeen University and the London School of Economics with a spell of farming, following his father, in Yorkshire before 'choosing the route of poverty, academia'. After a distinguished university career in Hull, Manchester, Oxford and London, McGregor took over the Royal Commission in 1975. He took his seat as a Labour peer in 1978, having been a member of the party since 1937. He moved to the Social Democrat benches and then to the cross benches in the 1980s when chairman of the ASA. His 1991 paper on *Self-regulation in Britain: the Cases of the Advertising Standards Authority and the Press Complaints Commission* offers valuable insights into his understanding of the British self-regulatory tradition, stemming from the Factory Acts of the first half of the nineteenth century.

But after his experience with the Press Council in 1988, would he take the Commission on? He was now 69, but his energy seemed unimpaired. Pressbof delegated Dugal Nisbet-Smith to seek McGregor out at his Hampstead home. Nisbet-Smith recalls McGregor's responding to his offer of a three-year contract at £60,000 a year with such enthusiasm as almost to shake his hand off.[35] Not becoming Press Council chairman in 1988 now seemed the most fortunate of all contingencies. Thus it was announced by Harry Roche on behalf of Pressbof on 10 October that the first chairman of the PCC would be Oliver, Professor Lord McGregor of Durris. And thus was Calcutt's prescription as to the procedure of appointments decisively 'leapfrogged'.

On his appointment McGregor announced himself confident that the newspaper industry could get its house in order, with the help of the

PCC, within the eighteen months allotted. 'The Advertising Standards Authority has been able to secure obedience to its adjudications and effectively handle complaints on misleading and offensive advertisements without a single legal sanction in its armoury.' Those newspaper editors who agreed in November 1989 on a declaration of principle and a code of practice in the wake of the mounting public concern over press standards, McGregor pointed out, were now showing willingness to make self-regulation work. McGregor confided that he first became convinced of the dangers of statutory regulation while Royal Commission chairman. 'A large number of people on that occasion wanted the Press Council to have power of legal sanction. I remember going home and sitting down to sketch out what such sanctions would be like. After three hours' work, I recognised that one would create a body which was a Frankenstein [monster] available to any government ill-disposed to the press, all or some of the time.'[36]

Another consequence of the speed with which the industry chiefs were driving the process was that a bold short-cut sliced through Calcutt's prohibition against bringing Council staff over to the Commission. Recruiting anew would hold things up. Kenneth Morgan, the Council's director, and his senior assistants Raymond Swingler and Bill Field, the complaints secretary, had in any case recently been given substantial salary increases by the Council to help them negotiate better redundancy terms if not taken on, or good terms if they were. Even *Private Eye* conceded that Morgan was a 'sensible' director of the Council; and his general repute was as 'one of the more amiable adornments of the journalistic profession'.[37] It was understood that Press Council staff would join the Commission 'in an interim capacity to aid the transition'. Lord McGregor would determine how long their employment would be extended.

Further details emerged of the new machinery. The Commission would have a budget of £1.5 million, and would be a 'streamlined' body of sixteen members, nine of whom would be editors, serving for mandatory six-month terms. As Andreas Whittam Smith later remarked, 'journalists don't respect the opinions of lay people'. Editors should be judged 'only by their peers and not by Mr and Mrs Great and Good'.[38]

Calcutt's purpose was to prevent editors fobbing off the Commission with substitutes, as had been the practice with the Press Council. In view of earlier developments in the Council and later developments in the Commission on this question of the industry/lay equation, Calcutt's prescription for an industry majority was one of his recommendations to which there was no demur. Nor was there demur about ending the waiver of legal recourse by complainants, though there was foreboding in the industry on the press's liability to double jeopardy. It was thought expedient also not to challenge Calcutt's prescribing a 'hotline' telephone and fax arrangement. A plan was announced to install one on a 21-hours a day, seven days a week basis; but nothing ever came of it. There was always too much resistance to it as 'prior restraint' censorship.

Another of the streamlining design decisions for the Commission pressed for by Whittam Smith was that it would not follow the Council's practice of accepting 'third-party' complaints. Thus would a heavy burden be lifted. About half the complaints dealt with by the Council were from people not directly concerned. The activities of 'people like Bob Borzello' would be avoided. This fabled scourge of the press, from Chicago, had lodged some 220 mostly successful complaints with the Council, mainly on race issues. Borzello protested: 'If the Whittam Smith rule had been in force none of these complaints would have been heard although they were obviously based on newspaper stories which violated Press Council and national newspaper guidelines.'[39] Whittam Smith was unrepentant. 'It is a waste of time and money if the Commission gets sidetracked into general complaints when it should be handling the real complaints.' Newspapers would be allowed a week to resolve the complaint internally before the Commission would be called in to take over. Most complaints, it was assumed, would be so resolved. There would be no time-consuming hearings as had sometimes been the case with the Council. All the PCC's business would be conducted swiftly on paper.

Meanwhile, at the unlikely offices of the *News of the World*, an editors' committee assembled by Pressbof continued the work of the earlier Whittam Smith NPA committee in drafting a Code of Practice to be circulated to industry bodies. Tactfully, the Calcutt code was used as a matrix. The *Mirror* editor Roy Greenslade, 'motivated by mischief', as he later confessed,[40] nominated Patricia 'Patsy' Chapman, editor of the *News of the World*, to become the first head of the Code Committee, the third constituted organ of the new self-regulatory apparatus, after Pressbof and the PCC itself. The Code Committee would be responsible for drawing up and amending the Code of Practice which the Commission would administer. The point was that it would be the industry's code, not the Commission's. That was at McGregor's insistence, and would become his most important legacy to press self-regulation. The Code Committee would be autonomous of both Pressbof and the Commission. It cost nothing and would meet as convenient either at the NPA's offices in Southwark Bridge Road or at the Newspaper Society's offices in Great Russell Street, Bloomsbury. Its chairman would be a member ex officio of the Commission, not subject to the six-month rule for editors. Patsy Chapman thus became one of the first two tabloid editors to serve on the PCC (the other being Brian Hitchen, editor of the *Daily Star*). There were initial fears that tabloid editors waging circulation wars could not be trusted fairly to adjudicate disputes involving each other's papers. And, for that matter, would the public accept the editor of the *News of the World* as a reassuring guardian of press ethics? McGregor insisted on gambling on the opportunity of training poachers to be gamekeepers.

Final touches to the code were completed by the end of October. Chapman's colleagues included Roy Greenslade of the *Daily Mirror*, Brian Vine, managing editor of the *Daily Mail*, Geoffrey Elliott of the Portsmouth *News*, Ian Beales of the *Western Daily Press*, and Jeremy Deedes, executive editor of the *Daily Telegraph*. They grappled with the difficult task of drawing up a code which would 'not be seen as too soft by the politicians, while being acceptable to the industry'. The key thing was just the right degree of flexibility to prevent constant fracture. The Code Committee's version was stiffer than the NPA editors' but more relaxed than Calcutt's. A 'public interest' defence was included in the manner of the now upstaged Press Council code. McGregor ratified it as 'a proper basis from which his commission can start to work'.[41]*

Peter Preston, editor of the *Guardian* and one of the leading editorial figures pushing movement forward, declared on BBC Television his conviction that the new self-regulatory system was sound and would be workable. 'We have made swift strides towards a clearer, better system for the reader.' Roy Greenslade at the *Mirror*, however, had doubts as to how tabloid editors could find time to devote to the Commission. Simon Jenkins of *The Times* called it 'a ghastly sentence on our time', but newspapers would have to agree to it. Whittam Smith informed a seminar of editors on 16 October that there had to be 'substantial peer-pressure' among editors, not their deputies or associates. Regional and local editors still had misgivings. Although they provided a good half of the Press Council's business, the Council was not being wound up because of their misdemeanours.[42] There were queries also as to where the proprietors were. 'It is high time', complained the industry's organ, the *UK Press Gazette*,

---

* See Appendix.

'that whatever authority they were wielding internally should have a public face.' If the new system was to succeed, it must have the unreserved support of the industry and its opponents must be brought into line.

> If editors are required to take a turn on the commission for periods of time it is vital that all editors take a turn and not just . . . quality editors. There is already a feeling growing that national tabloid editors won't want to. Proprietors must ensure they do . . . The minority view, that editors should have nothing to do with Calcutt and defy the Government to legislate, has considerable bravado appeal but it has lost the day and it is time that everyone made the best of what we all accept is a bad job.[43]

There were plenty of Indians still dancing their ritual dances of protest at the bad job. The Association of British Editors and Geneva-based International Press Institute preferred to see Calcutt as a 'position paper' rather than tablets of stone. There were calls for lobby groups to 'fight Calcutt'. The Guild of British Editors protested to the Home Secretary. The NPA came under attack as 'absolutely spineless'. There was high anxiety about Calcutt's recommending legislation against press intrusion. At the beginning of November the Press Council's swansong, *The Press and the People: the 37th Annual Report of the Press Council, 1990*, included 'Epitaph: a Critique on Calcutt, a Personal View by Louis Blom-Cooper'. This was, unsurprisingly, a sustained polemic on Calcutt's 'seriously flawed' report: 'unless great care is taken, the outcome may be a complaints system which is more readily convertible into statutory control and stands in closer relationship to newspaper and magazine publishers than the Press Council has done'.[44] Blom-Cooper drew attention to a crucial ambiguity in Calcutt: wanting a body independent of the industry, but with a majority of members drawn from the 'highest level of the press'. This ambiguity would cost the Commission dear in critical times ahead. The Council had indeed, in the words of the *Press Gazette*, 'hit back from its deathbed'.[45] The new self-regulatory system had by no means heard the last from Louis Blom-Cooper.

The *Press Gazette* wavered back to the Press Council's line: 'PCC – final solution or lame duck?' There were persistent doubts as to whether the Commission would be effective in seeing off the Calcutt threat. 'That being so, perhaps the fingers-up approach might have been better!'[46] All this provoked Simon Jenkins once more to denounce the 'hysterical outcry' in the press. Calcutt, he assured the Media Society, was 'something of a triumph for those who gave evidence' and 'argued against what, just 18 months ago, was the near certainty that there would be statutory legislation to control the Press'. The new PCC, Jenkins argued, was not a step towards statutory legislation; it was the old Press Council 'to all intents and purposes'.[47] The Pressbof heavyweights rebuked the *Press Gazette* for its faintheartedness. For his part, McGregor expressed 'pleasure and relief' that the recent Queen's Speech at the opening of the new parliamentary session made no mention of Calcutt's proposed legislation to criminalize press intrusion. He also conceded that the PCC might use its discretion to allow third-party complaints in certain exceptional cases. It was a matter he would raise with his colleagues when appointed.[48]

McGregor himself had been appointed by leapfrogging Calcutt's proposed appointments procedure. Pressbof squared the Home Office about that. An appointments commission for the PCC would in due course be formed: the fourth of the organs of the new self-regulatory apparatus. It would consist of the chairman of Pressbof, the chairman of the Commission, and one independent member. But that was not yet. For the present McGregor, in consultation with Pressbof, leapfrogged his own Commission into being. He already had the tabloid editors Chapman and Hitchen. He made up the rest of his industry contingent with Max Hastings of the *Daily Telegraph*, Michael Clayton of *Horse and Hound*, Robert Ridley of the Manchester *Metro News*, William Anderson, managing editor of the Dundee *Sunday Post*, and Andrew Hughes of the *Sunderland Echo*. Instead of fulfilling Calcutt's formula with two further editorial appointments, McGregor decided to temper the active industry presence by recruiting veterans who would reflect journalistic experience at the highest level while yet remaining at a strategic distance from the day-to-day trade. In this way he hoped to neutralize the flaw noticed by Blom-Cooper: the ambiguity between independence and an industry majority. His two neutralizers were Sir Edward Pickering, vice-chairman of Murdoch's Times Newspapers, and David Chipp, former editor-in-chief of the Press Association. The 'great and the good' were represented by Lord Colnbrook, who as Humphrey Atkins was a former Conservative Cabinet minister, Dame Mary Donaldson, former Lord Mayor of London and an eminent quangoist, Professor Lesley Rees of St Bart's Hospital, and Sir Richard Francis of the British Council.

McGregor, it might be noted, included no lawyers. He thought the Press Council had been disadvantaged in 'having as its Chairman for many years a succession of brilliant lawyers' who had discountenanced a code of practice. He thought lawyers made bad members of self-regulatory bodies because they focused attention on the language of rules and statutes, and excluded the spirit. Calcutt, he felt, had been lawyer-dominated.[49]

From the ASA McGregor brought across two highly valued colleagues: Lady Elizabeth Cavendish, with royal connections and valuable experience as a magistrate, and Robert Pinker, Professor of Social Work at the LSE. These appointments, designed to reflect 'broad views', were announced on 28 December. The Press Complaints Commission would be ready to open for business at Salisbury Square on 1 January 1991. Technically, like Pressbof, it was a public company limited by guarantee, with articles of association. In summary, these were to handle speedily and judge fairly complaints which raised prima facie a breach of the industry's Code of Practice; to give advice to editors about both the interpretation of the Code and journalistic ethics; to report to Pressbof any apparent ambiguities and shortcomings in the Code disclosed in the course of the Commission's work or by public and parliamentary comment; to secure support from the public, Parliament and the press by achieving recognition that the Commission was accessible to complainants and independent of press interests in its judgments; and to promote generally established freedoms, including freedom of expression and the public's right to know, and defence of the press against improper pressure from government or elsewhere.

The PCC was grudgingly welcomed by the press industry pretty much as the Press Council had been in 1953: making the best of a 'bad job'. There was, however, one big difference: the industry understood well in 1990 what it had not well understood in 1953. The best really had to be made of a bad job. But would the PCC, even so, enjoy any better fortune than the Press Council?

CHAPTER TWO

'The most curious quango known to political man': first phase of probation, 1991

'The underlying dilemma may be incapable of resolution. A free press must be free to offend people. Any mechanism put in place to protect those unjustly pilloried will equally be used as protection by others who have something to hide – something it would be in the public interest to expose. A purely free press would rely on a market mechanism, in that a paper offending too many readers will find its circulation dwindling. That happened to the *Daily Star* during its brief link-up with the *Sunday Sport*, yet sales of the *Sun* and the *News of the World* began to sag only when their editors signed the self-restraining declaration and were persuaded by their proprietors to abide by it. The lowest common denominator remains a powerful marketing formula.'

Michael Leapman, *Treacherous Estate: the Press after Fleet Street* (1992)

The 'self-restraining declaration' referred to above was that of the clutch of national editors gathered by Andreas Whittam Smith in 1989 who accepted the need to improve methods of self-regulation and who declared their commitment to a common code of practice to safeguard their independence from official control. The editors now had their Code of Practice. They now had their Complaints Commission to police it. But they also still had their dilemma and the tabloids still had their lowest common denominator. It would be McGregor's task to grapple with a seemingly irresolvable dilemma.

One of the formative things McGregor brought to that task was an ingrained distrust of politicians. His opinion of the security of press freedom in the hands of politicians, as he later recounted, was formed when, as chairman of the Royal Commission in 1975–7, he interviewed more than a hundred MPs of all parties. The duty of the Royal Commission, they almost invariably advised, was to recommend curbs on the irresponsibility of the press. 'To my murmured question, "How can a press free to behave responsibly, be prevented from behaving irresponsibly in a

free society without censorship?" I received no persuasive answer.'
McGregor emerged from those interviews convinced that the phrase
'responsible press' was one of the most insincere incantations in English
political speech. 'I emerged also with a deep suspicion of the honesty of
politicians who affect to uphold freedom of expression.'[1]

McGregor also brought to his task a formula framed to answer
persuasively his own murmured question. Thus he defined his resolution
of the dilemma of a free press free to offend: 'I believe that we found it in
self-regulation with the Press Complaints Commission serving as the
conscience of the industry, upholding its ethical Code of Practice and
dealing with complaints of citizens.' And how was this to be achieved? 'We
need an intermediate and tenable position between . . . unfettered freedom
for the press and the subjection of public expression of opinion to some
form of government control.'[2]

Here McGregor had moved from safe ground in the 1970s to dangerous
ground in the 1990s. To some extent this was inherent in the irresolvability
of the dilemma. As chairman of the PCC he had to define publicly some
notion of a principle of operation. The fact that he had not answered
persuasively his own question hardly mattered in practice. No one was likely
to point to logical contradictions involved in the idea of an 'intermediate
position' being calibrated on freedom. Where McGregor did expose indications of vulnerability was in his emphasis on his Commission's being the
conscience of the industry. Again as a general notion it was unexceptionable. The mode in which it was applied would be what mattered.

McGregor at one level was a conventional enough academic with a
professorial outlook on the world. At another, he was a passionate moralist
and an excitable practitioner of the politics of conscience. He was a disciple
of T. H. Green and Lord Beveridge, as mediated by Barbara Wootton. He
took on the PCC as he had taken on the Royal Commission and the
Advertising Standards Authority: as an important exercise in his academic
expertise, social institutions, and in the public welfare that good social institutions can generate. He saw social institutions as moral agents. He saw the
self-regulatory tradition inherited from the Victorian era as social morality
at its best: the voluntary politics of inner conscience, needing no imposition
from outside. McGregor had very high ideals about the immense public
welfare that a responsibly self-regulated press could generate. That is what
made it impossible for him, in the last resort, to operate consistently with
his own murmured question to the politicians. What press freedom and self-
regulation are most in need of is resourceful and successful defence of press

irresponsibility. The great irony of McGregor's career at the PCC is that, though he championed press freedom and self-regulation against the politicians, in two of the three critical junctures of his chairmanship he came down heavily on the same side as the politicians. This, unimaginable in these early days, started to happen in 1992.

The industry set about boosting McGregor. 'If anyone can make the Press Complaints Commission work it is Lord McGregor', enthused the hitherto very unenthusiastic *Press Gazette*. 'As he settles in this week, we wish him well. He, and his colleagues, undoubtedly represent the best chance the Press has of avoiding Government legislation.' His evident determination to 'run a very businesslike PCC' was highly encouraging. 'Keeping to specifics, avoiding hectoring encyclicals, shunning the open court style of adjudication and insisting on top-level representation from all shades of newspaper – all this suggests that he will avoid offering too many hostages to fortune.' Early indications in 1991, thought Raymond Snoddy, were that the PCC, and with it the last chance for self-regulation in the UK, was 'not yet a lost cause'. Lord McGregor, it appeared, was 'a man of independent mind who is determined to make the Commission work, if given half a chance'. Brian Hitchen, editor of the *Daily Star* and one of the tabloid commissioners, proclaimed his belief that the PCC would not only be a firm and necessary regulator of press behaviour, but in time would evolve into a doughty defender of the press. 'The PCC is going to work because we are all going to make it work. And that's a fact.'[3]

For his part, McGregor set about reacquainting himself with the industry. He had made an ingratiating start by indicating that he would scrap plans for a prior-restraining 'hotline'.[4] At the annual lunch of the Newspaper Press Fund he stressed the point that the PCC was 'not a body external to the Press, not something imposed on you from outside'. It was not imposing its own rules. 'You created us and you will suffer if you have made bad choices.' It was not the PCC's role to 'sit in judgment or make pronouncements but to interpret and enforce the code of practice which has been drawn up and approved by publishers and journalists'.[5] Adoption of the Code and abolition of the waiver of legal action were key features of the PCC's claim to embody a new order. 'In this way, the industry moved forward from the old Press Council to a full self-regulatory system.'[6]

Interviewed in the *Independent* by Michael Leapman, McGregor further distanced himself from the deposed Council. 'The Press Council was a rather *de haut en bas* body, operating as an outfit external to the industry.' The Commission would be 'an integral part of the industry, set up by the industry to do a job'. One of the first things decided in January was that the PCC would move to new premises, 'and these were now being sought'. (They were never found.) There must be 'regular and unceasing dialogue between the commission and the Press'. McGregor was 'adamant' that the tabloids had to be properly represented: 'I didn't want it to be editors of posh papers sitting in judgement over the tabloids.' At the end of the day, 'if we can't capture the tabloids we've failed, and we can only capture them by getting them to work on the commission with us'. They had eighteen months in which to 'carry the Home Office', McGregor pointed out. 'But we've also got to carry the Opposition, who share the Government's view on the Press.' Because editors were short of time, and their deputies unacceptable, McGregor hoped to limit formal meetings of the Commission to half a day every month. Only if any member disagreed with an adjudication drafted and circulated by the director, Kenneth Morgan, would it be debated at a meeting. Leapman concluded with some critical observations. 'Despite the rationalisation of its procedures and the high calibre of its membership, the PCC will suffer from the contradiction inherent in the very notion of self-regulation: it is hard to project a body as impartial when it is funded by the Press and dominated by its representatives.'[7] Leapman was here pointing to what was to prove the PCC's most vulnerable point. Meanwhile, there were administrative loose ends to deal with. What to do about the backlog of cases left over from the Press Council? It was decided that a fresh start was desirable; and the ghost of the Council was conjured up and left to wind up its business. The first meeting of the Commission, on 30 January, considered other matters left over from the old order. The argument was put that 'it would be a serious political mistake to outlaw third-party complaints wholly'; and it was agreed to accept them at discretion when they related directly to the Code.[8] It was also agreed on the same grounds of good public relations that the PCC might initiate inquiries at discretion. Another cautionary note was sounded: the newspaper industry had accepted the ending of the legal waiver 'without enthusiasm'; and it would be prudent to bear that in mind when any question about the good faith of complainants arose.[9] Would the PCC deign to include the sleazy and maverick *Sport* sheets in its remit? It was felt that, even if Pressbof failed to levy money from their proprietors, to dodge accepting responsibility for disreputable 'newspapers' would compromise the Commission's credibility.[10] And in the interests of promptitude it was determined that no provision for appeals would be allowed in the Commission's procedures except if procedural fault could be demonstrated.[11]

In March the PCC delivered its first adjudication, upholding a complaint about treatment by the *Daily Mail* and the Wolverhampton *Express and Star* of an IRA shooting, which might have compromised the security of a nearby chief constable. Thus so early did a kind of 'privacy' issue arise. Roy Hattersley, the Labour opposition's shadow Home Secretary, assured the Media Society that he did not believe the PCC would be able to protect the privacy of individuals. 'I hope, but I must say I doubt, it will succeed.' For its first great test was already upon it.

2

On 23 January Clare Short, Labour MP for Birmingham Ladywood, described in the House of Commons her distressing experiences with the *News of the World* and the *Sun.* 'Members will be aware that Patricia Chapman, the editor of the *News of the World*, is a member of the new com- mission – [Hon. Members: "Shame."] – established, I understand, on 1 January.' She recounted a campaign of vilification in these papers conse- quent on her Bill in 1986 to ban 'pornographic' Page Three girls. She called for remedial legislation. She called for Chapman to be sacked from the Commission. Chapman retaliated with what she described as a 'measured response' to a 'vicious attack made under cover of parliamentary privilege'. Short complained to the PCC about articles in the *News of the World* which intruded into her private life without justification in the public interest in breach of Clause 4 of the Code of Practice, and which breached Clause 1 with respect to published material which was inaccurate and misleading.

Here was a high-profile case which it was crucially important the Commission dealt with authoritatively and convincingly. It was embar- rassing that the editor complained of should be a member of the Commission; but, if things went well, that could be turned to advantage. Chapman played no part in the Commission's consideration and adjudica- tion. It was soon apparent there would be no chance of conciliation. The Commission thought it advisable in this instance to get assurances from both sides that they would await its adjudication and would not initiate or pursue any legal proceedings about the issues in dispute pending the adjudication, which was delayed because of the need to await supporting evidence on Short's behalf from witnesses to events in the 1970s. The substantive question in the privacy issue was the special status of a public figure. Short fully accepted that, as such, she was not immune from legitimate inquiry in the public interest. Her grievance was that the newspaper investigation yielded no valid story. The upshot was that Ms Short's complaints were upheld.[12]*

Debate about what the *Press Gazette* called a 'hot potato' and what Robin Hunt in the *Guardian* described as a 'ticklish case' which 'gives the PCC the opportunity to flesh out the code of conduct', especially where 'public interest' was ill-defined, centred on Chapman's assertion that 'any MP is fair game for special treatment'. 'We do believe a newspaper in a democracy is most certainly entitled to make inquiries about an elected Member of Parliament, whose wages you pay and whose character is likely to be coloured by his or her experiences in life, just as yours or ours might be.' Donald Trelford at the *Observer* disagreed with that formula, arguing that the case had come 'too soon'. The Code of Practice should have been drawn up using test cases; instead, Clare Short had *become* the first test case. Trelford held that politicians should be allowed their private lives as well as their public ones. 'Was there a genuine public interest? I'm very doubtful, given the special animus which the Murdoch papers have to Ms Short because of her stand on Page Three girls.'[13]

The Commission's great concern was whether its adjudication had yielded a valid reading of the Code of Practice. Its dilemma, as Robin Hunt pointed out, was that 'it must send early signals to the Government that it can help the newspaper world to heal itself by deciding exactly where public interest stops and invasions of privacy begin'.[14] The adjudication, published in May, was described as 'bullish' by none other than Louis Blom-Cooper. Even David Calcutt conceded that it was 'encouraging'.[15] Trelford was in no doubt that 'the Clare Short adjudication was a landmark'.[16] A partly analogous case in which Neil Kinnock, the Labour leader, complained that his privacy had been invaded by an inaccurate piece in *Today* gave the Commission an opportunity to finesse the issue. 'Leading politicians seek, experience and must expect regular exposure in the press', adjudicated the Commission. 'This article dealt largely with trivia . . . in which people might be interested. The PCC does not regard it as malicious or as an intrusion into privacy which breaks the Code of Practice.'[17] Considering that the Clare Short adjudication made the fundamentally important distinction between 'the public interest' and 'what interests the public' – a distinction applauded by Blom-Cooper – this reference to trivia 'in which people might be interested' was careless. It was duly to be pounced on by Blom-Cooper.

---

* See boxed adjudication, pp. 64–7.

3

Opinion in the industry held that the Commission had acquitted itself well in its first landmark test. Patsy Chapman exploited to the hilt her discomfiture for its benefit.

> Lord McGregor put me in the hot-seat with a place on his Press Complaints Commission. . . . A funny old choice, some said. . . . After just one meeting Clare Short MP put me in an even hotter seat. An editor is not allowed to sit in on complaints against his or her paper. I was sent out of the room like a naughty girl. . . . I was found guilty and sentenced to print an adjudication which ran to 2,300 words. A WHOLE PAGE. This was punishment indeed for a tabloid editor with so many interesting tales to squeeze in.[18]

Among those not amused by Patsy Chapman was Roy Hattersley. He had already expressed doubts about the PCC's likely efficacy. Now he told the legal and parliamentary committee of the Guild of British Newspaper Editors that he thought the Sunday papers 'broke the PCC's Code of Practice every week'. In doing so he revealed that Labour's plans for the media went beyond its Charter of Rights policy document, and would combine privacy legislation with its proposed freedom of information legislation. 'You'll get it because I shall be deputy Prime Minister and I believe in it.' A Bill would be introduced in the first session of a Labour-led Parliament, and the first breach of the Code would trigger statutory press regulation.[19]

The Guild editors protested that Hattersley was prejudging the issue, and demanded evidence of the alleged Code breaches, or of public concern. The matter was not without a larger relevance, since June 1991 was the anniversary of the publication of the Calcutt Committee report. The *Guardian* celebrated the occasion under the headline 'Cowboys cool it in the last chance saloon'. Calcutt himself was invited to assess the results of the year and look to the future. He stressed that a body which provided an effective means of redress for complaints against the press was ipso facto a body defending the freedom of the press. His report, he felt, had been widely misunderstood on that point. He thought that there were now 'signs that there may be a general acceptance by the press that an unwarranted intrusion into a person's private life is simply unacceptable'. He thought the PCC Code represented 'a considerable advance on anything that has previously come from the press'. But he was unhappy at the insertion of the 'public interest' subclauses. He still considered his own code better, because it was more specific in identifying areas of legitimate concern. He deplored the lack of action on the 'imaginative' hotline procedure. He approved the general shape of the Commission, but was unaware of any arrangements to ensure that appointees would be independent of the kind of industry bodies which used to nominate to the Press Council. 'This may yet, I fear, lead to difficulties.' Calcutt trusted, also, that something would be done, sooner rather than later, about his proposed criminalization of physical press intrusion.[20]

Other luminaries were invited to contribute. Blom-Cooper drew attention to the Calcutt recommendations which had either been ignored or not acted upon. He regretted that because the PCC was a narrow, exclusively complaints body, it was unable to do what the Press Council would undoubtedly have done: set up a general inquiry into coverage of the Gulf War and child-abuse cases. 'Who will now take on this vital role on the public's behalf?' Tony Worthington, a Labour MP and sponsor of the 1989 Right to Reply Bill, thought it 'worrying' that the vindictive editor who had been censured in the Clare Short case was the 'architect' of the PCC's Code. Roy Greenslade, now aglow in the merit of having been sacked as editor of the *Daily Mirror* by Robert Maxwell, pointed out that the PCC had no more teeth than the Press Council 'but everyone realizes this time that it is the last chance saloon'. He pointed out also that if Gladstone had been 'exposed' in a tabloid newspaper for his interest in prostitutes, it might well have prompted widespread public odium. 'However, such activities do not necessarily make William Ewart a bad prime minister. That is the view held by most politicians.' Donald Trelford at the *Observer* thought the jury was 'still out on the PCC though early signs have been more encouraging' than he expected. He had been a sceptic. He feared the industry's 'colluding' with Calcutt might turn out to be the first steps to statutory control. But he was now impressed by the 'speedy, robust, non-bureaucratic, non-legalistic way that the commission has so far gone about the business of admitting or rejecting complaints'.[21]

The Commission's immediate problem was not opinion in the industry or public but opinion in Parliament. There the Clare Short case was not celebrated as a 'landmark'. It provoked angry debate. Government exploited its notoriety, much as with the Gorden Kaye affair, to turn the screw on the industry. 'We have given the Press 18 months to get its act in order by self-regulation', announced a senior Home Office spokesman, 'but it appears many newspapers are breaking the code. It leaves us little option but to draw up plans for statutory or Government regulation.' On the other hand, it was easy to calculate that, allowing for the PCC's probationary concession, there could be no legislation this side of a general election.[22] McGregor, evidently rattled at the failure of the politicians to strike a positive note, hit back at Calcutt. McGregor dismissively declared himself 'not the slightest bit worried' by Sir David (as he had now become). It was not the Commission's duty to frame the Code but to enforce it. There were no advantages to be had from a hotline which the Commission did not already possess. He disagreed 'very sharply indeed' with Sir David's implication that the Commission's members were not independent of the industry.[23]

4

At that juncture it was neither politicians nor Calcutt that McGregor needed to worry about. In February and April 1991 stories in the *Daily Express* and the *Daily Mail* reported serious strains in the marriage of the Prince and Princess of Wales. On the first day of his chairmanship the Buckingham Palace press office invited McGregor to be briefed on how Charles and Diana were being hounded. He declined the invitation 'but it was a significant pointer to problems ahead'.[24] There had been a long record of gossipy tittle-tattle about the Waleses' marital affairs. Now American magazines were running sensational stories that the marriage was on the rocks.

Concerned at the more strident tone of these stories, David Chipp, one of the Commission members, got in touch with Charles Anson, an old acquaintance from Chipp's Press Association days, who was now press secretary at Buckingham Palace. Anson and Sir Robert Fellowes, the Queen's private secretary and Diana's brother-in-law, lunched with McGregor and Chipp at Salisbury Square. The context of this meeting was the dismissal by the Palace of the stories as 'complete rubbish'. Fellowes and Anson confirmed this. Nonetheless the stories persisted. On 9 May McGregor, Chipp, Lady Elizabeth Cavendish and Sir Edward Pickering lunched at the Palace 'where they discussed a plan for "mutual co-operation" in handling the delicate matter of reporting the royals'. Conversation centred on the problems faced in common by the Palace and the Commission. The Commission arranged a further meeting at which Palace officials met the ombudsmen attached to the national newspapers. The Commission and the Palace continued their exchange of views. McGregor and his colleagues, perhaps rather naturally, accorded great authority to the Palace's denials.

Then later in May McGregor attended a conference in Luxembourg called to concert resistance to moves in Brussels to impose dirigiste statutory press controls in the European Community. At a private dinner Vere Harmsworth, Lord Rothermere, as he later recounted, 'informed him from information at my disposal that it appeared to me that the royal couple were seeking to use newspapers to present their own cases and that this was extremely dangerous for the monarchy and for the newspapers and would present particular difficulties for the Press Complaints Commission'.[25]

McGregor returned to Salisbury Square seemingly somewhat non-plussed, stranded uneasily somewhere between Sir Robert Fellowes's assurances and Lord Rothermere's warnings. McGregor felt 'sufficiently concerned to share his information with Fellowes and Anson'. He was troubled by press treatment of the royal family's private lives and the Palace's 'relative impotence to contain it when their principals went over the heads of the official palace machine'.[26] But the evidence suggests that McGregor felt that Rothermere had rather 'overstated the case'. Perhaps that was why McGregor failed to be alerted by a front-page lead in Rothermere's *Daily Mail* on 2 July, 'Charles and Diana: cause for concern'. This was fed by friends of the Prince ('camp followers became media messengers to fuel battle royal in the press'). A riposte appeared immediately in the *Sun* the following day, written by one Andrew Morton, a tabloid reporter with good contacts in the Diana camp. 'Diana's close circle honed in on Andrew Morton.' To the casual reader – as a *Times* media team, Alan Hamilton, Tony Dawes and Brian MacArthur, later commented – 'it might have appeared as yet another royal row story. It was, in fact, the start of a campaign to manipulate the media by rival camps supporting the Prince and Princess of Wales, a campaign that inadvertently led to the biggest threat to the freedom of the press in Britain for decades.'[27]

As later events indicated, McGregor's position amid all this frenzy was a proneness to blame the messengers for the message. A devoted monarchist with an avuncular, chivalric protectiveness towards Diana, he saw the matter as essentially a press problem rather than a royal marital problem. Anthony Beaumont-Dark, a Conservative MP, wrote to *The Times* protesting that media attention to the private lives of the royal couple had 'reached the level of harassment'. 'Surely, the time has come when the media, and particularly the tabloid press, should stop their unhealthy and damaging ... daily inquest into the Prince and Princess of Wales's marriage.' Some months of self-denial, Beaumont-Dark suggested, would be the best present the media could offer on their anniversary, instead of 'raking over' their private lives.[28]

This response almost certainly reflected accurately McGregor's own attitude. He saw himself confronting a gross instance of press intrusion into privacy, with a 'public interest' pretext about the future of the monarchy manufactured out of exaggerated gossip. He preferred not to take seriously the indications that were there to be taken that, as the *Times*'s team put it, 'far from being exaggerated, press reports about the death of the royal romance were systematically planted by courtiers operating with scant regard for the health of the fourth estate'.[29]

An intervention by Andrew Morton lowered the temperature. In a piece in the *Sunday Times* on 7 July he disclosed that 'the air had cleared' and that a 'truce' had been settled: an artful way of implying there was a war without actually saying so. What Morton could see, as Diana's circle led by her brother Charles Spencer and her friend Carolyn Bartholomew pressed their information upon him, was a brilliant opportunity for the book that would make his fortune. He cancelled his American holiday and set to work. Press manipulation on both sides continued at a more subdued level throughout the summer. It was not until December 1991 that McGregor decided that he might make an initiative in view of the damage in prospect: 'knowledge was growing of an impending book by Andrew Morton that would blow the marriage apart'.[30]

5

In the meantime the Commission had plenty of business to attend to. The European Community's Commission in Luxembourg was being invited by the consultative *Assises européens de la presse* being held in Brussels to implement a European media policy. While deprecating any notion of media control, the European Commission was considering the benefits that would come from replenishing the 'national authorities ruling the press' with a number of 'specifically European norms'. Since the Luxembourg conference in May the UK newspaper industry chiefs had been preparing their lobbying riposte. 'For a country like Britain', declared *The Times*, 'where there is no "ruling" national authority and the press is subject to the same laws as other citizens and companies', these restrictive implications were worrying. 'The scope of the agenda at Luxembourg implies that this could include EC laws on the right of reply and privacy, the regulation of freelance journalism, a European press card which could amount to a licence to practise, and cross-subsidies within the press through special levies on advertising.' Draft directives had been prepared banning tobacco advertising and restricting food, drug and alcohol advertising.

> There is no common European tradition governing the relations between government and the press. Few have a truly national press. Most continental countries single the press out for special treatment, whether through subsidies or legal constraints. Many, such as Italy's, are leftovers from pre-democratic days. France has press laws dating from 1881 which prohibit bringing public authorities into disrepute, and has plans further to impose 'responsibility' on the press by bringing in an enforceable, government-drafted, code of ethics.

All such proposals, *The Times* pointed out, disregarded 'the reasonably successful British experience of self-regulation'.[31]

Lord McGregor, custodian and practitioner of that allegedly reasonably successful British experience, was naturally to the fore. The fear was that the *Assises* heralded the making of a new European 'information order' with directives on the press ushering in statutory controls in each member country. There were nightmare reminiscences of the UNESCO scheme for a 'new world information order' ostensibly to protect journalists and promote high standards of journalism, which for two decades Britain had been helping to fend off. 'Nearly all other European countries have specific legal regimes for the press', McGregor warned; 'they are all accustomed to it. But we have never had a press law and feel that direct legal intervention will be a very dangerous development.' The industry was already anxious at the prospect of possible privacy and right-of-reply legislation threatened by Conservatives and promised by Labour; and of limits also on media ownership.[32] In the industry's new weapon in this propaganda war, *Press Freedom in Britain* by Nicholas Herbert and David Flintham, published by the Newspaper Society and issued on 5 July, McGregor's message was blunt. If the scorpions of privacy law and statutory regulation were to be avoided, the press would have to submit to the whips of a strong self-regulatory organ seen to be independent of industry interests.[33]

This was the PCC self-servingly twisting the screw. The same whips-or-scorpions line of argument was evident also in McGregor's contribution to the Association of British Editors' seminar on 'media watchdogs' later in July. When the eighteen-month probation for the PCC expired next summer, who would be the judge? A Labour government or a Conservative government? McGregor's guess as to the latter was that Tory ministers would back self-regulation if the Code was demonstrably being observed. He would not attempt to predict what the view of a Labour Cabinet would be. Labour's home affairs spokesman, Robin Corbett, offered some hints. In a candid address to the seminar he derided the PCC as a watered-down version of Calcutt. He promised that Labour, in the event of the PCC's being deemed a failure, would replace it with statutory regulation. Corbett reminded the editors: 'You have eleven months left.'

It suited McGregor also to make editorial flesh creep by adding his own chilling account of how government would set about its review. It would look carefully, he envisaged, at the number of complaints upheld against individual editors. The 'critical test' would be two or three breaches of the Code. McGregor offered a specimen case in point of privacy intrusion: the *Sun*'s picture of Prince Andrew swimming naked in France. Though it had not been complained about, it was nevertheless a breach of the Code as a 'clear invasion of privacy and one that cannot be justified in the public interest'.[34]

This was the context for a complaint that Andrew did make about surreptitiously snatched photographs of his naked baby daughter Eugenie, published in the *People*. The Commission promptly returned what was intended to be a stinging verdict of 'flagrant contempt of the newspaper industry's system of self-regulation'.[35]* The particular significance of this case was that the *People*'s editor, Bill Hagerty, adopted a mockingly defiant attitude to the PCC, with the full endorsement of his proprietor, Robert Maxwell. Their case was that the picture was charming and innocent. But the sting of their defiance was to call McGregor's bluff on the whips-or-scorpions issue. They took exception, on principle, to the Commission's citing their deliberate undermining of self-regulation as an invitation to the government to bring in statutory regulation. 'It is not the role of the Commission to anticipate what Parliament might do. If Parliament wants to pass even more restrictive laws upon the press, the Commission should be opposing it, not threatening in advance what it believes Parliament might do.'[36] This was shrewd comment on what events were to disclose as McGregor's great weakness as the protagonist of self-regulation.

6

Colliding openly with one of the great tabloid proprietors rampantly defending his defiant editor was, for McGregor, much more than an affair

---

* See boxed adjudication, pp. 67–8.

merely of being subjected to 'severe discourtesy'. Was Maxwell playing a deeper game, calculating that statutory regulation might be more damaging to Murdoch's empire than to his own? Quite apart from that, however, was the bruising impact on the PCC's reputation. *The Times* asked whether self-regulation was 'proving an adequate answer to those who continue to hanker after statutory control of journalistic ethics? The answer, sadly, is "not yet".'[37] If the PCC was the press's 'Last Chance Saloon', the *Press Gazette* concluded, 'then it is getting perilously close to drinking up time'.[38]

The timing was especially unfortunate. McGregor was about to release the PCC's interim first report – 'the gospel of self-regulation' – on 11 September. This was a public relations exercise designed to give the PCC a higher profile with both the public and the industry. A long list was drawn up of persons of influence to be targeted.[39] It would feature an outline of complaints and adjudications for the first six months of the probation period, up to the end of June. Over the summer McGregor had been preparing the way by meeting editors and a variety of voluntary bodies, and planning a meeting soon with the Home Secretary, Kenneth Baker. In a preliminary interview with Melinda Whittstock, the *Times*'s media correspondent, McGregor lamented that eighteen months was a very short period in which to persuade politicians and a doubting public that the worst abuses of the tabloid press could be curbed by continued press self-regulation. The task was even more daunting if, as some suggest, 'newspaper readers are not aware of how to complain about newspaper coverage or conduct'. Yet it was this issue which would ultimately determine 'whether centuries of freedom from government control will come to an end next June'. With just ten months now left, the PCC, reported Whittstock, 'is planning a campaign to alert politicians and the public to its complaints procedure and code of conduct, and also to its performance so far'. The Commission was being criticized for its low profile, particularly compared with Lord Rees-Mogg's Broadcasting Standards Council. To Louis Blom-Cooper all this was quite understandable: 'Its low profile has prevented anyone outside from making a real assessment of the success or otherwise of the commission.'[40] Blom-Cooper had his own imminent assessment very much in mind.

A particular disappointment to McGregor was what he lamented as the 'ringing silence' in the press about individual adjudications other than in those papers with complaints against them upheld. This neglect he planned to redress with monthly complaints bulletins, providing not only details of handling and verdict, but also drawing attention to trends and issues. 'We need more analysis in the press of fundamental issues which affect newspapers fundamentally, such as what is and what is not in the public interest', McGregor insisted. 'Not one newspaper piece has discussed the validity or invalidity of any complaint.'[41] McGregor intended that the Commission's planned advertising campaign would be featured in all newspapers that agreed to allow it free space. A pamphlet offering guidance to those wishing to complain was being prepared for distribution in September to Citizens Advice Bureaux, law centres, libraries and public voluntary organizations.

At this stage McGregor's own contribution to the PCC's public relations campaign was to declare himself 'cautiously optimistic that the threat of statutory control has diminished'. (The Commission grappled inconclusively with the conundrum of 'defining privacy and justifying intrusion'.[42]) He pointed to a decline in the number of complaints about invasion of privacy. Tabloid editors, he judged, had become more responsible; and the crucial requirement was that a newspaper should not repeat the same or similar breach of the Code, especially relating to privacy. He remained confident that a Conservative government would see the advantage of continued self-regulation. 'As for Labour, I haven't met anyone who can tell me what their policy actually is. It changes depending who you talk to in the party.'[43] McGregor used the occasion of his St Bride's Tom Olsen lecture to warn of the 'tentacles of government' curling around every branch of life, and how they must be resisted by democratic pressure for freedom of information. He drew a sombre moral for the industry: 'A public which had demanded access to official information and records in order to criticize the behaviour and policies of governments has not been willing and will not be willing to tolerate a press which behaves as though it were exempt from criticism.'[44]

When it came to introducing the interim report to public and industry in September, McGregor, flanked by Patsy Chapman as chair of the Code Committee, again declared his cautious optimism. 'But what I can say is that we have no example of a newspaper against which a complaint was upheld subsequently reproducing the same breach of the code.' He judged that the first six months of the PCC indicated a 'calculated intention' on the part of editors to observe the Code; though Chapman was candidly ready to admit on behalf of the *News of the World* that 'I'm sure that at some stage we'll drop another clanger'.[45] The interim figures provided by the Commission showed that complaints had fallen compared with the Press Council's in the same period in 1990. Of the 479 cases actually dealt with,

70 were rejected as being outside the Commission's remit, 23 were disallowed on grounds of delay, 165 were held not to apply to a prima facie breach of the Code, 64 were dismissed as insubstantial, 14 were remedied before the processing stage, 52 were remedied by the Commission's good offices in bringing complainant and editor to conciliation, 73 cases were not pursued by complainants, and 18, involving 19 newspapers and one press agency, were adjudicated by the Commission, 11 of which were upheld. National tabloids were of course prominent in the sin-bin; but, as McGregor once remarked, there was 'a higher proportion of complaints about the regional Press than you would suspect in talking to people in the Newspaper Society'.[46] In the last full year of the Press Council, which accepted third-party complaints, 174 adjudications resulted in 82 rejections, 86 upholdings, and 7 partial upholdings.

These comparative Press Council figures were very apropos of the matter, as it happened. Louis Blom-Cooper, 'not worrying whether he would be accused of sour grapes',[47] took the opportunity at the end of 1991 to give the world the benefit of his opinions. He accepted that while it was 'far too early to pass judgment on the PCC's impact (if any) on the behaviour of the press, or the ethical standards of journalism', its adjudications were susceptible to 'provisional review'. His opinions were not flattering. From an eminent QC's point of vantage, Blom-Cooper detected that the Commission's adjudications suffered from being cryptic and inconsequent. He pounced on the careless phrase 'in which readers might be interested' in the Kinnock/*Today* case. The PCC in short, in Blom-Cooper's opinion, left the press with 'ambiguous standards by which to abide'; and thus left the press also 'with the perfect excuse to flout the Code of Practice, as well as the Commission's authority, when they have a mind to do so'. Blom-Cooper, however, departed on a more gracious note: 'with the issuing of better-reasoned adjudications in recent months, the PCC is now showing signs of promise that it may be able to develop a jurisprudence useful to both the newspaper industry and the public'.[48]

No doubt McGregor took this rap on the knuckles with the best grace he could muster – which was never much. Patsy Chapman saw the Commission's first year out in less captious vein: 'Nineteen ninety-one . . . and McGregor has us on the run.' She entertained *Guardian* readers with an insider's revelations about the methods and manners. While some papers thought it a 'tiresome body', most realized what was at stake. 'That's why almost all newspapers have co-operated in trying to stick to the rules and why ALL papers have published criticism against them, however much it hurts.' Chapman stressed that, 'despite the utterances of TV pundits and politicians with their own axes to grind, serious complaints against newspapers are pretty thin on the ground'.

> A few papers were caught with their pants well and truly down on matters of accuracy. There were several reporters who, when cornered, had 'lost their notes'. . . . And a tiny minority of local papers tried a few feeble fibs to get off the hook.
>
> My PCC colleagues have had passionate discussions about woofters and poofters, Pakies and Paddies, Jocks, Frogs and Chinkies. We have debated swear words and the difference between robust and colourful language in a tabloid versus robust and filthy (but presumably intellectual) language in the qualities. How would a law deal with such difficult f* * * * * * disputes, I wonder?
>
> We have pondered on where the public's right to know ends and privacy begins and we have come down hard on papers which have refused to correct significant mistakes and those who have persistently harassed grieving families. But my view, from inside and outside the PCC, is that the papers have tried desperately to do their best by their readers. Journalists are thinking harder than ever before about the way a story should be obtained, reported and projected.

Chapman mocked her own tabloid editorial style: 'Bimbo editor reveals all in secret press complaints shock!'[49]

There were, in fact, some genuine Press Complaints shocks at Salisbury Square by the end of 1991. On 20 December it was announced that the director of the Commission, Kenneth Morgan, was standing down at the age of 63. 'A replacement will not be appointed, but Mr Morgan will act as consultant.'[50] Ray Swingler, his deputy, had already departed in July, following a 'reorganization of staff' in which the old Council secretariat originally appointed from NUJ people were purged and replaced. Swingler had been the Council's general inquiries officer; and as a regretful Harry Roche of Pressbof pointed out, the PCC would no longer be doing that kind of work.[51] McGregor wanted to be a hands-on chairman and found Morgan's reluctance to accommodate him frustrating. There were many rows. Morgan had no rapport with the national press chiefs. They wanted to see a strong hand at the PCC getting a grip on newspapers. McGregor set about marginalizing Morgan. In March 1991 he brought across from the ASA Mark Bolland as his personal executive assistant and Enid Cassin as consultant. McGregor groomed Bolland, Canadian-born and bred in Middlesbrough and York University, to take over.[52] He was promoted in September to assistant director.

Within a couple of years from normal retirement, Morgan had assumed he would see out the Commission's probationary period, which would end with a review of its performance, probably in late 1992 or early 1993, when the political decision as to what to do about press regulation would be taken. Later, in a 'confidential report' obtained by the *Guardian*, it appeared that the former Press Council staff were dismissed for 'unsatisfactory work'. This was included confidentially in evidence given by McGregor to Sir David Calcutt in his review of the PCC's work, carried out between July and December 1992. To the *Guardian*'s revelations in 1993 Morgan reacted 'with surprise rather than shock at the disclosure that his former employer had secretly attacked his capabilities and disclosed his generous pay settlement to Sir David. "When you have been both general secretary to the National Union of Journalists and director of the Press Council nothing really shocks you." '[53]

It was essentially a question of procedural cultures. Morgan was an NUJ man. McGregor explained in the Commission's first annual report in May 1992: 'The procedures inherited from the Press Council did not satisfy the requirements of the Commission which have to be geared to a code of practice which the Press Council never possessed. The Commission have therefore been compelled to undertake a comprehensive review of procedures.'[54] After all, Blom-Cooper's recent critique had made essentially the same point. On Morgan's departure McGregor became effectively director as well as chairman, with Bolland promoted as deputy director, running the machinery very much with an Advertising Standards Authority procedural culture in mind.

McGregor's other concern at the back end of 1991 was the question of Andrew Morton's impending book about the marital problems of the Princess of Wales. As a book, it would be outside the scope of the Commission's responsibilities. But it would certainly be serialized in a newspaper, and would in any case open the door for a deluge of comment and speculation in the press. 'I told the then home secretary, Kenneth Baker', McGregor later recounted, 'of my anxieties in December 1991, and suggested that he might wish to consider how the palace press office could act to limit the damage. Later I also mentioned the situation to Mr [Gus] O'Donnell, the prime minister's press secretary.'[55]

The only way the damage could have been limited would have been by an industrial act of heroic self-denial on the part of the press. In the aftermath of the affair, which proved as injurious to his own and to the PCC's reputation as to that of the monarchy, McGregor speculated wistfully about the 'effects upon the monarchy, had the private life of the Prince of Wales, who became Edward VII, been subject to the same obsessive coverage by the media of his day as that experienced by his great, great grandson'.

One certain effect of such media exposure has been to destroy the institution of monarchy as Bagehot described it. 'Its mystery is its life', he said. 'We must not let in daylight upon magic.' The media has been a solvent that has eaten away the bonds of magic that used to bind the institution of monarchy together and sustained the deference and admiration in which citizens held it.[56]

PCC, Report No. 1, pp. 9–13 (edited)
Adjudication on Ms Clare Short, MP, v News of the World.

[Ms Short] complains that, after she introduced a Bill in parliament in 1986 about publication of what she regards as pornographic pictures, 'a campaign of vilification by The Sun' was also pursued by its sister paper. Ms Short says that the News of the World did this first by linking her with Tribune in a story about a small advertisement for 'naughty pictures' in that weekly and, later, by focussing attention on her in a story about the reported questioning by the police Obscene Publications Squad of a woman who had worked for her for a few months seven years earlier. The report was headlined 'Anti-porn MP's ex-aide quizzed . . . over porn!'. . . .

In the Commission's view these two stories raise an inescapable suspicion that the News of the World was pursuing its private interest against Ms Short to embarrass her in retaliation for her campaign against publication of page 3 pictures.

Whether newspapers should use, or should be allowed to use, such pictures is a familiar and legitimate argument which both sides pursued vigorously and properly. Much heat resulted. However, the Commission are satisfied that the News of the World went beyond legitimate argument about the issue and published articles which attempted to link Ms Short with pornography. She was dragged irrelevantly and unwarrantedly into the News of the World's story about the Tribune advertisement on the sole basis that she was a reader of that journal. Similarly, the paper connected her with her former employee in an unfair way designed to embarrass.

Ms Short's complaints in relation to these two articles are upheld.

Ms Short spoke of these and other matters in an adjournment debate in the House of Commons on 23 January 1991. She gave the House a detailed account of inquiries made by the News of the World into her private life, particularly about a man with whom she had a close friendship in the early 1970s.

She told the House that the man, John Daniels, had lived for some years at a house owned by her in Birmingham, as had also two of her sisters, her brother, a Chilean refugee couple, an American writer and others. Mr Daniels later went abroad but returned to Britain and was shot dead in 1979 in a car in Birmingham. His murderer has never been arrested.

Ms Short has complained that the story linking her with Mr Daniels was pushed to the press in an attempt to smear her by former officers of the West Midlands serious crime squad which she had criticised in Parliament. The Complaints Commission are not in a position to conclude, and cannot say, that the story was 'pushed to the press' by those officers or that smearing her was their motive. The editor has said that the material came from a freelance journalist and that it is likely to have emanated originally from a West Midlands policeman.

Miss Chapman told the Commission:

> *While the possible/probable motive of those who supply information is always a factor in considering whether a story be published, it is not, in itself, decisive as to whether journalistic enquiries should be made. If the nature of the information deserves proper scrutiny then it is legitimate for the Press to ask questions regardless of the source's motives. The day that ceases to be the case will be the day investigative journalism dies. In this case . . . the material we were given manifestly justified further investigation.*

Aspects of that matter are being investigated by the Police Complaints Authority on a complaint by Ms Short to the Chief Constable of the West Midlands. The Authority has released to the Press Complaints Commission a conclusion from its report by Assistant Chief Constable Clive Roche that there is no doubt that a large number of items of information published in the 27 January News of the World article about Ms Short and Mr Daniels are identical to information in police files of the investigation of his murder.

Clause 4 of the Code of Practice, agreed by editors, states that intrusion and inquiries into an individual's private life without her consent are not generally acceptable and publication can be justified only when in the public interest. The Code states that the public interest includes detecting or exposing crime, serious misdemeanour, or seriously anti-social conduct, protecting public health, and preventing the public from being misled. The 'public interest' is not whatever happens to interest the public. The Commission holds that it is crucial to maintain the distinction, especially in respect of people in public life.

The Commission recognises that circumstances in the private life of a Member of Parliament may bear on her conduct of that office or fitness for it. The Commission agrees that it is proper for such matters to be inquired into and published in the public interest. Mere passage of time, even of many years, does not necessarily diminish their relevance or the justification for publication in the public interest. Where there are no such circumstances and no such justification a Member of Parliament is entitled to the normal protection from invasion of her private life that Clause 4 provides.

In this case, the News of the World and Ms Short are at one in believing that a newspaper was justified in inquiring into that aspect of her private life of long ago. Ms Short has told the Commission that she accepts that her close friendship with someone who was later killed and shown to have serious previous convictions was a legitimate subject for scrutiny. In this context, the editor of the News of the World, Miss Patricia Chapman, told the Commission:

Given the fact that Ms Short is a prominent MP and a former Opposition Frontbench spokesperson, the . . . facts were obviously legitimate subject for press scrutiny and, possibly, for publication; the more so, since in the various interviews given by or on behalf of Ms Short about herself and her past no mention can be found of her close relationship with Mr Daniels or his murder.

The Commission agrees that there was a clear *prima facie* justification for inquiry by the News of the World to discover whether there were circumstances in Ms Short's private life which were related to the public interest. Such inquiries would not justify publication of a story relating to Ms Short and Mr Daniels unless the facts disclosed ought to be published in the public interest as set out in Clause 4 of the Code of Practice.

A reporter, Mr John Chapman (who is unrelated to the editor of the News of the World), visited Ms Short's first husband at his workplace. There is a conflict about what was said between them and who said it.

Ms Short complains that the paper asked her former husband hurtful questions and discussed with him the possible purchase of pictures taken of her long ago in a nightdress or, according to the paper's story, topless. Their marriage ended *de facto* in 1970 and *de jure* in 1978. She says that her former husband was intrigued by the approach and 'played along with it a little'. According to the newspaper, he offered to sell it photographs of which it had been unaware.

With its response to the complaint, the paper submitted a revealing memorandum about this incident, written by the reporter for its legal department. In the light of the memorandum, the Commission concludes that the News of the World's dealings with Ms Short's former husband were indefensible. The journalist discussed with him a number of matters which were irrelevant to any proper inquiry. Further, he knew (because he said so in his memorandum) that he was questioning someone 'who had been in and out of psychiatric institutions since the break up of his marriage and had even written threatening letters to Short'. An approach of this nature to Ms Short's former husband was a serious breach of the provision on Privacy in the Code of Practice and the newspaper failed to justify it. Ms Short's complaint in this respect is upheld. . . .

The Commission holds that it is particularly important for newspapers to be fair, and to be seen to be fair, when they are reporting or commenting on an issue in which they may be thought to be *parti pris*.

The News of the World was fully entitled to publish a reply to Ms Short's complaints against it. In doing so, it ought to have taken special care that it did not use the article as cover for the publication of irrelevant facts about Ms Short's private life which it could not otherwise justify in terms of Clause 4 of the Code of Practice. The newspaper has not sought to suggest that the information it possessed about Ms Short at the time when she made her speech in the House of Commons would have justified an article about her which was in the public interest.

The Commission holds that the News of the World misrepresented the nature of Ms Short's complaints against it . . .

Ms Short had not challenged the newspaper's right to investigate her relationship with Mr Daniels, but did complain about the manner in which it did so. Ms Short's complaints against the News of the World in this respect are upheld.

In its article and in correspondence with the Commission, the newspaper alleged that Ms Short had made a number of misleading and inaccurate statements in her speech to the House of Commons although it did not suggest that she deliberately gave a false account. Ms Short accepts that her recollection may have been faulty on one or two matters but asserts that she did not mislead the House of Commons in any way. . . .

The Commission does not accept that the News of the World can rely on this to demonstrate that Ms Short misled the House of Commons in her statements or in support of the justification for publication of the article. . . .

The Commission fully accepts that Ms Short made her speech in the reasonable belief, based on information from her ex-husband and her solicitor, that the News of the World was about to publish an article about her private life which could not be justified in the public interest and the contents of which it was unwilling to disclose.

The Commission also finds that the newspaper failed to let Ms Short know in advance of publication the allegations about her which its story contained, and thus gave her no opportunity to answer or comment on them. Even if, as it tells the Commission, it was unable to make direct contact with her, it could have given her the opportunity to respond by sending a facsimile message either to her or her solicitor detailing the allegations it was about to publish.

Ms Short's complaints that the News of the World broke Clause 1 on Accuracy and Clause 4 on Privacy of the Code of Practice are upheld. . . .

PCC Report No. 2, pp. 18–19.
The People

COMPLAINT

The Buckingham Palace Press Office complained on behalf of the Duke of York about an item appearing in The People. The substance of the complaint is set out in the adjudication.

ADJUDICATION

The People's treatment of a complaint by the Buckingham Palace Press Office on behalf of the Duke of York was in flagrant contempt of the newspaper industry's system of self-regulation.

The complaint is upheld as a clear breach of Clause 4 of the newspaper and magazine Code of Practice which condemns intrusions and enquiries into an individual's private life unless publication can be justified in the public interest, and of Clause 11 that journalists should not normally photograph children under 16 without the consent of their parents or other adults responsible for them.

On Sunday 14 July The People published two photographs of the Duke's baby daughter Princess Eugenie running naked in the high-walled garden of her home. They were taken surreptitiously without the knowledge or consent of her parents or other responsible adults.

It published the main picture a second time on 4 August eight days after the Commission had sent the editor, Mr Bill Hagerty, a complaint made on behalf of the

Duke. The Commission's regular procedure is, in the first instance, to give an editor an opportunity to reply directly to the complainant if he wishes.

When The People reprinted the photograph of Princess Eugenie, it also published a picture from a French magazine of the Duke running naked into a stream which had appeared in another English newspaper earlier that month. The People headlined the page 'Come on Andy . . . where is your sense of fun?' and invited readers to telephone different numbers to indicate whether they found either of the pictures offensive.

The People also published a leading article defending its action.

The editor seeks to justify publication by saying in his response to the complaint and in the leading article that these were charming, natural photographs of a little girl published good naturedly and affectionately. That is beside the point, as is whether they were offensive. They were an invasion of privacy. Editors commit themselves by the Code to abstain from invading privacy except where publication is justified in the public interest. There was no such justification here. However appropriate and unexceptionable such pictures of any young child may be in its family's album, their display in a newspaper after being taken secretly without consent is unacceptable no matter whose child is pictured.

The editor has said that the pictures were taken and offered to The People by a freelance photographer. The responsibility for publishing them lies with the editor.

In his reply to the complaint, the editor has argued that under English law anybody is free to take a photograph of anybody else. A main purpose of the Code adopted by editors and of the Commission set up by the industry, is precisely to avoid the need for a law of privacy by establishing agreed guidelines to which editors freely conform.

The People's further action demonstrated contempt for the complaints procedure and the Commission. Moreover, it was a breach of faith with other editors who honour the Code and support the procedure. In particular, by making capital out of the complaint by reprinting the picture and soliciting readers' views, The People deliberately undermined the complaints procedure.

The Commission was established following the Report of the (Calcutt) Committee on Privacy and Related Matters after the Government and Opposition gave the newspaper and magazine industry 18 months to demonstrate that self-regulation of the press would be effective.

The Commission emphasises that continuing breaches of the Code and contempt like that committed by The People in calculated disregard of the industry's assurances and intentions will inevitably lead to statutory intervention in the press.

CHAPTER THREE

'Getting perilously close to drinking-up time': last phase of probation, January–June 1992

'My concerns were not so much with the administration of the PCC, but with the circumstances surrounding its existence. It was set up by an industry in a panic. It puts us in an undignified and overexposed position. It followed too closely Calcutt's prescription and therefore runs the risk of leading us inevitably on to Calcutt's Phase 2, a statutory complaints body, if self-regulation goes wrong.'

Donald Trelford, editor of the *Observer*, in a speech to the Media Society,
5 April 1992

'Some people in the industry have forgotten the mess we got ourselves into only a few years ago, and recall fondly the old Press Council's role of promoter and protector of press freedom. I should be interested to see a list of the steps taken by the old Press Council to further their aim, but I fear that I should be looking at a pretty blank page.'

Sir Frank Rogers, chairman of the Newspaper Publishers Association,
UK Press Gazette, 13 April 1992

As the end of the Commission's probation time loomed in 1992, debate about its future became ever more entangled with the media exposure of the Waleses' and the Yorks' marriages and the exposé threatened by the Andrew Morton book. There was no chance whatever at this time of any collective act of self-denial on the part of the press. Such a thing became conceivable only after the chastening sequence of events after 1995 when Lord Wakeham negotiated his treaty with the industry over Princes William and Harry.[1] That in McGregor's time media exposure was a solvent eating away at the bonds of magic that bound the institution of monarchy was a cultural *datum*, not a consequence of deliberate choice. Here was another, paradoxical aspect of the irresolvable dilemma: the people most avid for the gossip were the people most avid for the institution of the monarchy.

An announcement was made in March 1992 that negotiations were to commence over the separation of the Duke and Duchess of York. 'The tabloids', as McGregor later recounted with infinite distaste, 'printed many long-lens colour photographs of [the] Duchess topless in a garden in the south of France being caressed by her Texan friend, John Bryan, described as her financial adviser.'[2] Clause 4 of the Code was taking heavy punishment indeed.

At Salisbury Square meanwhile the new managerial order settled into place. McGregor took over most of Morgan's former work, with Mark Bolland as his deputy. Bolland, as a practitioner of a smoother Advertising Standards style of administrative culture, was noted, and resented, by the NUJ. At its conference in May 1992, Paul Foot denounced the PCC as full of 'profs and toffs' who had 'ignominiously sacked' the NUJ's honest Kenneth Morgan.[3] Enid Cassin, the former director-general of the ASA, was retained by the Commission as consultant 'to speed up the complaints procedure and to give the Commission a new type of voice, one which is "open, fair, balanced and impartial"'. The Commission, the *Gazette*'s Jean Morgan noted, was now slimmer, more efficient financially (it was expected to come in considerably under budget this year), 'looking to turn round complaints more quickly' (preferably within four weeks) and 'is keen to continue its success in getting complaints resolved between editors and complainants without the need for a Commission investigation'.

The *Gazette* correspondent observed further that the Commission was setting out to make itself more accessible to the public and to convince decision-makers that it was fulfilling its role of making self-regulation work. Starting in January there would be monthly reports on complaints dealt with. Three thousand of these would be mailed to every editor in the UK, to MPs and members of the Lords, and to interested members of the public. Some 15,000 leaflets were being prepared for general distribution on how to make a complaint against a breach of the Code. Four thousand glossy 'Briefings' were to be mailed to 'people of influence' explaining what the Commission was and how it worked. And the Commission was about to launch a 'How to Complain' campaign backed by free advertising in newspapers.

All this bespoke an awareness that the PCC could not afford simply to trundle on as it had been. A year's experience in the job had made McGregor less confident than he had been in January 1991 that he could deliver self-regulation to public and Parliament. His line now, he said in an interview by Jean Morgan, was that while the newspapers, particularly the tabloids, were improving, he needed a longer probation than eighteen months. 'If we could have two years in which editors have got accustomed to following the Code of Practice, then we shall have an entirely new situation in the Press.' Given two years, 'attitudes *will* have changed; self-regulation will become instinctual'.[4] It was thought expedient also to make some play with the notion that the PCC was not unmindful of at least a residual role in defence of press freedom. It would not do to allow those with fond memories of the Press Council too much invidious leeway on this point. Now the *Press Gazette* recalled rather wistfully that 'In its early days, some PCC members told us that it was their intention that, once its basic procedures were bedded in, it would become more wide-ranging in its brief. It would become a body which, for instance, might campaign on issues of press freedom, even if this was not in the mind of David Calcutt QC when he set the PCC up.'[5]

The *Gazette* lamented that, as of March 1992, there seemed 'little sign of this happening'. Perhaps this was to ask rather a lot of McGregor's fledgling Commission. It could hardly yet be said that its procedures were comfortably bedded in. Undoubtedly McGregor did have a more wide-ranging brief ultimately in view; but such luxuries would have to wait until the ampler times of post-probationary press self-regulation. For the moment McGregor contented himself with preparing to do battle for press freedom on the 'hotline' issue. 'The Commission', he informed Frank Rogers of the NPA, 'will have no truck with prior restraint and have rejected, though not yet publicly, the Calcutt Committee's recommendation that they should operate a "hotline".' McGregor regarded 'any attempt to influence editorial judgement in this respect as an unacceptable infringement on the freedom of the press'.[6]

This was not a principle sustained absolutely. Sir David Calcutt observed sardonically in his review of the PCC's performance that defiance of his recommendation of Blom-Cooper's 'imaginative' hotline proposal did not preclude Lord McGregor's accepting telephone calls from MPs on behalf of constituents; and that in certain cases McGregor had intervened and spoken to editors prior to publication. Sir David further observed that while third-party complaints were not as a rule accepted by the PCC, they became acceptable when it was 'believed that issues substantially affecting the public interest were involved which had not been previously resolved by an interpretation of the Code, or where those parties were in some way representative of a person or body who might feel unable to make a complaint'. Complaints would thus be accepted from Citizens Advice Bureaux, from the Matthew Trust on behalf of mentally disabled people, and from MPs.[7]

These procedural variants would take time to bed down and become customary practice. A notable variant from Press Council practice at the time was the PCC's declining to take on the *Sun* over the 'poofters' issue. 'The Commission has taken the view', the reverend spokesman for the Lesbian and Gay Christian Movement was informed, 'that it is not able to proscribe the use of words which some might find objectionable.' The Commission found that there was no breach of the Code to consider. It was 'the language of the *Sun*'s readers, and we are not in a position to change that'.[8] This was pretty much to quote what the *Sun* had defiantly told Blom-Cooper in 1990.[9] This reminiscence was, as it happened, curiously apposite, as was the reference to the press freedom vocation. For Blom-Cooper had his own defiance now poised to loose at the Commission.

2

The timing factor was important. It was a matter not only of the PCC's probation running out in June. It was a matter also of the distinct possibility of the Conservative government's time running out in April. A general election was due to replace the 1987 Parliament. Could John Major pull off a victory to add to the three achieved by Margaret Thatcher? The odds looked against it. Labour under Neil Kinnock was ahead in the polls. A Labour government would have no reasons for gratitude to the newspaper industry at large. Proprietors and editors and journalists remembered what Roy Hattersley, Labour's deputy leader, had promised was in store for them.[10] It is in this context that the travails of the Commission need to be considered.

The tone was set in the fallout which enveloped the Commission in February in the wake of the Paddy Ashdown scandal. Somewhat as in the Clare Short case, the leader of the Liberal Democrat party was lined up by the tabloids as 'fair game' because exposure of an affair with a former secretary was held to reveal Ashdown's hypocrisy in posing as a happy family man. The *News of the World*'s evidence was a stolen document. Ashdown stopped publication with a swift injunction. The story eventually broke in a Scottish newspaper, immune from English legal restrictions. This gave the pot of furore an extra stir – to accusations of scandalmongering the tabloids retorted with scandalized grievance at the way the press was being muzzled by the growing readiness of judges to grant *ex parte* interlocutory injunctions.

Ashdown made no complaint; so the PCC was not formally involved in the matter. But its Clare Short adjudication, allowing that circumstances in the private life of a Member of Parliament might bear on conduct of that office or fitness for it, was much and indignantly quoted, particularly by other MPs eager to be in at the kill when the Commission's remit came up for review later in the year. It was an ugly reprise of the privacy question. Nor was it the only reprise of that question. *The Times* commented that 'the code of practice on privacy has certainly been tested over the past year – close to destruction in the case of Paddy Ashdown and in the numerous stories about royal marriages'.[11] 'Little has changed under the commission' was the *Guardian*'s tersely dismissive conclusion.[12]

McGregor felt obliged to rebuke newspapers for behaving as if they were still in the 'pre-Calcutt era'. He stressed the need for restraint in the run-up to the general election. If 'some sections of the press now turn themselves into little Kinsey reports on politicians and parliamentary candidates, then all the gains of the past twelve months will be lost'.[13] But all was not lost. The very vulnerability of the Commission incited the politician friends of self-regulation (mainly but by no means all Conservatives) to rally round. A question was also planted on 13 February for John Major: what was his policy on 'the freedom of the press'? Major, confronting a general election within weeks, responded obligingly.

> The government are committed to safeguarding the freedom of the press. They consider this is best served by responsible journalism and effective self-regulation. In pursuit of this policy the government have supported the recommendations of the Calcutt committee for a non-statutory Press Complaints Commission. We are committed to reviewing the effectiveness of those new arrangements later this year.[14]

'The future of the press' was, indeed, the leading feature of the keynote address later in February by John Wakeham, then at the Energy department and responsible for the co-ordination of Conservative party policy in relation to the general election. Wakeham accused the Labour party of planning an assault on the freedom of the press: to achieve those things hoped for from the Royal Commission the Labour government set up in 1974 but that never materialized in 1977 – a new order in the press industry shifting the balance of political influence towards Labour, to be capped by statutory regulation.[15]

This volatile mix of the coming review in relation to the coming election, spiced in the fallout from the Ashdown affair, offered critics of the PCC something of an imperative cue. It was taken with relish by Louis

Blom-Cooper. It took the form of an interview with Jean Morgan of the *Press Gazette* by way of preparing a piece for the *Index on Censorship*. Here the Commission was fortunate: neither the industry's trade paper nor a specialist journal had wide public resonance. And Blom-Cooper's axe-grinding penchant was notorious. Still, for all discounts applicable, here was an eminent public figure, former chairman of the Press Council, making a considered public statement on future policy on press regulation. If his message did not resonate widely, it might well penetrate to receptive benches in both Houses of Parliament.

In December, Blom-Cooper had allowed that it was too soon to assess the impact – 'if any' – the PCC had made on the chances of press self-regulation. Now, two months further on, he was in no doubt that such faint promise attributable then had faded entirely. 'A complaints system bereft of a philosophical and ethical underpinning', he declared, 'is likely to be no more than a collection of individual, unrelated decisions without a coherent code of professional standards.' The PCC looked, and acted, Blom-Cooper alleged, 'like the newspaper industry's protector, that may occasionally bark at its creator's misdemeanours'. Its 'cursory opinions, short on factual and legal analysis', left much to be desired 'in the light of the critical need to educate editors regarding precisely what practices are, and are not, journalistically acceptable'.

The necessary course, Blom-Cooper concluded, was to take press regulation out of the hands of the newspaper industry by abolishing the PCC and replacing it with a Commission on Press Freedom and Responsibility to be established by Parliament. Blom-Cooper held that 'the automatic assumption that it is in the Press's interest (and automatically the public interest) at all costs to stave off the introduction of legislation is only appropriate in relation to a press law that did not infringe on the freedom of the Press'. His press law would not so infringe. The Commission on Press Freedom and Responsibility would be a public body without obeisance to the newspaper industry and without being controlled by the government. Its members would be selected by an entirely independent Appointments Commission made up of members of the judiciary, the universities and other public walks of life such as the chairman of the BBC. It would be a small body with a professional staff, not all working journalists. Its powers would include the taking and hearing of evidence and the censuring of press misconduct by requesting corrections, a right of reply, and surrender of photographs. Its functions would not be restricted to dealing with complaints from members of the public with the object of maintaining standards of journalism; and it would initiate general inquiries as the Press Council did without waiting for a formal complaint. It would have its own code, not written by the newspaper industry. It would report to Parliament annually.[16]

The *Press Gazette* commented editorially that uncharitable people would see Blom-Cooper's project 'as the disgruntled sniping of a sidelined foe, but what he has to say is worthy of a more considered reaction'. There was the consideration that if the coming review told against the PCC, here was a blueprint conveniently available for parliamentarians to ponder. But also there was the consideration that keeping the government out of such a Commission might be difficult. Who was to appoint the appointers? Who would manage the debates on the Commission's report? What was not much evident at this juncture was a considered defence of the PCC. The *Gazette* itself praised faintly: 'Whatever else the PCC may be, it has lost almost entirely the investigative and moral bedrock on which the Press Council was founded.' And although the *Gazette* drew the line at legislation, it envisaged 'an even greater need' for a kind of body to represent the industry which the PCC was not: 'a body which argues a cogent position on a whole range of issues which are inextricably connected with the day-to-day business it performs'.[17] So much for the trade paper's defence of the trade's regulatory Commission.

That it was in need of defenders was made evident in a speech to the Media Society on 5 April by Donald Trelford, editor of the *Observer*, the senior Sunday quality then owned by the tycoon chief of Lonrho, R. W. ('Tiny') Rowland. Present at the occasion was Lord McGregor. Trelford's point of departure was the likelihood within days of a Labour government. That would mean the likelihood of imminent constraints on press freedom. Who would blame the Labour party for handing out to the press the same rough treatment it had been receiving from the press over recent weeks and months? That being so, it behoved the press to stop being defensive and to start thinking about coming to terms with the new power in politics. 'We should get ourselves ready not just to repel an attack or bend with the prevailing wind, but to enter a serious two-way debate with an agenda of our own.'

The kind of agenda envisaged by Trelford involved proprietors and editors accepting more constraints if such was Parliament's wish 'but only if the press is offered more real power in exchange – a Freedom of Information Act, and a review of the Official Secrets Act and the libel laws would be my opening demands'. At present, Trelford held, the press lacked authority. This void of public esteem allowed creeping encroachments by the state in new laws on contempt, official secrets, police and criminal evidence. Behind these encroachments were old Bennite threats and new Thatcherite threats, of which the apotheosis was the government's pertinacious 'lunacy' in attempting to suppress *Spycatcher*, the unauthorized memoir of a maverick former MI5 officer. 'More recently, when private members' bills were threatened on privacy and right of reply, we entered the downhill slalom which has resulted in the Press Complaints Commission, a defensive body if ever there was one.'

Trelford's reading of the case was that the PCC was the flabby product of flabby government. Ministers were afraid of alienating the press proprietors in the run-up to a general election; but the 'level of revulsion' in Parliament made it necessary that something should be seen to be done. The press allowed itself to be portrayed as a set of competing commercial interests, alien rather than essential to the needs of society. 'A prime example of the defensive technique at work is the Press Complaints Commission.' It accepts the Tory government's description of itself as 'the last chance saloon'. It projects itself as 'the press on probation'. It has abandoned a key objective of the Press Council as protector and promoter of press freedom and settled for a lesser role as fielder of readers' complaints. The new body's judgments have been swifter and more robust than those of its predecessor, but Trelford had the uncomfortable sense of complaints being rapidly dealt with on a pragmatic basis rather than on carefully argued principles and precedents offering a guideline to editors and journalists confronted with analogous situations in the future. 'The PCC's code of conduct is a classic woolly compromise, short on detail, begging more questions than it answers and totally inadequate as a guide for either the press or the public.' The composition of the Commission, moreover, a mixture of three national editors, regional editors and the great and the good, seemed to Trelford to invite criticism that it was drawn from the upper-crust and the self-interested. 'Are frantically busy tabloid editors the right people to sit in judgment on their peers?' It had, furthermore, failed to make its existence and authority known to the public and needed a much higher public profile if it was to inspire general confidence.

'That said, the PCC does appear to have had some effect in curbing the worst tabloid excesses, if only because the fear of legislation worries owners.' The great problem about the muck produced in the tabloids, Trelford was clear, was 'not that the public don't want this stuff, but that they do'. 'My concerns', he continued, 'are not so much with the administration of the PCC, but with the circumstances surrounding its existence. It was set up by an industry in a panic.' It was too much Calcutt's creation and therefore exposed the press to the risk of being led on inevitably to 'Calcutt's Phase 2, a statutory complaints body, if self-regulation goes wrong'. 'What the government and Calcutt effectively said was: "Here is a cliff we think you'll have to go over, but if you manage to walk along this narrow path, you may just avoid it." Lord McGregor and his supporters in the Newspaper Publishers Association were courting great danger in rising to this challenge, because it appears to leave them no escape if they fail.' On Trelford's agenda were ways of avoiding 'Calcutt's Phase 2' by pre-emption. 'The first need is a guarantee in law that freedom of expression is a valued human right in this country.' As well as a review of the Official Secrets Act, Trelford would include reviews of the Security Services Act as it affected the media, the broadcasting ban on Northern Ireland, the Neill Committee's proposals on libel, the Civil Service's 'routine abuse of the 30-year rule', denial of information on grounds of deportation, and the application of censorship in time of war.

A Labour government, Trelford speculated, might move towards 'some statutory Press Commission, answerable to Parliament', not just handling complaints but also defining the acceptable boundaries of taste, privacy and other areas where 'press freedom and responsibility' came into conflict with such issues as the revealing of sources and handing over unused film to the police. 'If the appointment of the Press Commissioners was genuinely independent of government, and if the government had first given binding and constitutional and legal guarantees for freedom of expression, a new and more acceptable situation would have been created in which an independent statutory authority could perform a valuable role.' Statutory controls might come about anyway, Trelford concluded, 'if the perilous experiment in self-regulation comes to grief '. It could do the newspaper industry 'no harm to be ready to set out the only terms on which we would accept it. We can't say we haven't been warned!'[18]

Trelford's declaration that a deal would need to be made with a Labour government was the first notable breaking of ranks in the self-regulated industry. It was also a breach of the unwritten industry code that the press must stand united against the outer, hostile world; that in the last resort the interests of stately quality broadsheets in press freedom were identical with those of grubby populist tabloids. This was not a point made explicit by Trelford; but heavily implicit in his argument was the presumption that the statutory deal with government might be a light touch of the whip to the broadsheets, but a flinging of the tabloids into the scorpion pit.

No doubt Lord McGregor, conductor of the 'perilous experiment in self-regulation', guide along the dangerously narrow path atop the beetling cliffs of Calcutt, listened to all this bracing critique with stoic resilience. Trelford could not be ignored in the way Blom-Cooper could. But on the other hand, the next few weeks would either usher in a Labour government or would not. If not, Trelford could be discounted, at least for the time being. McGregor contented himself with polite noises about there being much that Trelford said with which he agreed, together with somewhat plaintive explanations that the PCC's administrative difficulties had been inherited from the Press Council's 'method of working and its staff', and with a complaint at the failure of the press to mobilize support for the Commission. He denied that the PCC projected itself defensively. 'The point is that we had no alternative.' He was astounded at Trelford's questioning the role of tabloid editors in the PCC. He rebuked Trelford for the common error of ascribing the Code to the Commission. 'The Code is not the Commission's Code, it is the press's Code.' He rounded off with his own warning: it was either the PCC or statutory regulation.[19]

In any case, there would be no harm in wheeling out to the beleaguered PCC's aid heavyweight support in the form of McGregor's great friend and comrade-in-arms, Frank Rogers of the NPA. Without referring directly to either Blom-Cooper or Trelford, Rogers in the *Press Gazette* attacked the critics of the way the industry had 'moved forward to full self-regulation'. Rogers was sardonic on the Press Council's oft-proclaimed vocation to promote press freedom. He guessed that a list of its achievements in that sphere would produce a pretty blank page. He was particularly concerned to stress that the industry had never conceded Calcutt's view (not as a matter of fact exactly endorsed by Calcutt himself) that the body charged with handling complaints should not have a role to play in promoting the freedom of the press. 'For the PCC, freedom of expression is pre-eminent. Its Articles of Association require it to promote freedom of expression and the public's right to know, and to defend the press against improper pressure from government or elsewhere.' It was therefore vital, urged Rogers, 'that the method of maintaining the proper relationship between the Press and society is not in government action but in the Press itself'.

3

The constituencies returned the Conservative government to office, with a reduced but still adequate majority. There was great relief at Salisbury Square. McGregor declared himself very pleased at the press coverage of the election campaign. No complaints had been received. 'Of course there has been a great deal of partisanship but what do you expect?' McGregor was 'agreeably surprised that newspapers have not accompanied their political reporting with reporting about the irrelevant habits of the candidates'.[20] When a scandal did break, as in the case of Alan Amos (the Conservative MP who resigned following questioning by the police about an incident on Hampstead Heath) 'the reporting was done in a perfectly proper manner'.[21] A complaint was eventually lodged by the parents of Jennifer Bennett, a child who featured in a Labour party political broadcast about the National Health Service. McGregor had provisionally discounted a breach of the Code in this instance when a family in effect invaded their own daughter's or grand-daughter's privacy. 'Once members of the family had made statements to political parties and the politicians brought these statements into the public domain, it was perfectly proper for the Press to report them. Indeed, it seems to me it would have been improper for the Press not to report them.'[22] The parents' complaint was duly rejected.[23]

At Salisbury Square there was also a satisfying sense of achievement in a case involving a complaint against the *Hornsey Journal* over its coverage in 1991 of police raids in North London. The adjudication upholding the complain became a landmark: it was the Commission's first dealings with an issue of race. Its verdict insisted that 'circumstances required an ample apology for an article illustrated by seriously misleading photographs'. The Haringey Racial Equality Council extolled the adjudication as 'a significant success for more accurate reporting in our local press'.[24]*

Relief at Salisbury Square that John Major was still Prime Minister was, however, tempered by the fact that he had appointed David Mellor to the new National Heritage department (which had taken over responsibility for the media from the Home Office). It was Mellor who had coined the ominous quip about the popular press being in the last chance saloon.[25] It was Mellor who had seemed to nurse ambitions for a statutory all-media regulatory system. Still, as a BBC executive quipped to the *Press Gazette*: 'It could have been worse. It might have been Kenneth Clarke.'[26]

---

* See boxed adjudication, p. 84.

'If the Press is drinking in the last-chance saloon, David Mellor is the bartender.' Will he, asked the *Gazette*, press 'go' or 'destruct'? Privacy legislation seemed unlikely at this stage but remained a possibility. 'Despite the Tory tabloids' smear campaign against Kinnock, they have kept themselves more or less in order during the past eighteen months.' Brian MacArthur of *The Times* judged that 'a more powerful Press Complaints Commission has alleviated disquiet in Parliament – certainly on the Tory benches. Although Labour could complain about treatment during the election, there were no sex smears against either party.' Mellor was more problematic to call. 'Mellor has been described as a closet Hampstead liberal who disguised his true colours during Mrs. Thatcher's reign, but he is unlikely to go to the wall with a liberal issue like Press freedom.' As one Mellor-watcher put it: 'If he sees the Press are misbehaving themselves and there's a head of steam in Parliament, he'll go for it.'[27]

Received wisdom had it, however, that Mellor would certainly not press 'destruct'. *The Times*, contemplating the review of press self-regulation due to be undertaken under Mellor's aegis in the summer, deduced on 14 May: 'Signs throughout Whitehall and Westminster are that Mr. Mellor will choose to leave well alone.' The Press Complaints Commission was that day to publish its first annual report, 'and it is understood that Mr. Mellor will see no need to set up the government inquiry into press behaviour originally envisaged by the Calcutt committee'. The political world, *The Times* thought, had changed considerably since MPs on both sides of the Commons were regularly heard complaining about harassment by the press, invasions of privacy and inaccurate reporting. 'The real test was newspaper reporting during the general election campaign, which government sources suggest the industry passed. Conservative Central Office and Downing Street are understood to believe that self-regulation is working. The Labour party, although still smarting about Tory tabloids' biased election coverage, does not plan to press for statutory control.'[28]

The Commission was certainly more comfortable in this newly accredited Conservative political world. McGregor felt it prudent to warn the industry against complacency. He told Georgina Henry of the *Guardian*: 'I can't believe the press would be so foolish as to relax on a feather bed of thinking that what the government said some two years ago would be forgotten because it won't.'[29] One of the commissioners, Robert Pinker, previewed the statistics in the PCC's forthcoming annual report at the Guild of British Newspaper Editors' spring seminar in Birmingham. Pinker demonstrated that the debate on press standards had been over-coloured by allegations of misbehaviour by the national tabloids in the pre-Calcutt Committee era. As many complaints had been made against regional papers as against nationals. 'You cannot draw a firm conclusion about the propensity of different types of publication to publish material in breach of the industry's Code of Practice.' The overwhelming majority of complaints were about inaccurate reporting. The next biggest category were complaints about discrimination on race, sex and sexual orientation. 'Complaints concerning privacy made less than 10 per cent of the total.'

The message from the PCC, which upheld fewer than fifty complaints in its first year, was that it had not been inundated with complaints, and breaches of the Code had proved to be the exception rather than the rule. 'In general', as Pinker summed up, 'the PCC is satisfied that publications have observed the full adjudications in respect of complaints against them.' He was able to declare further that all newspapers and magazines had shown 'a creditable performance in the first year in which the new Code has been operational'. The figures supplied by the Commission gave Chris Oakley, chief executive and editor-in-chief of the Birmingham Post and Mail group, the opportunity to make the more polemical point that the low number of complaints about invasions of privacy 'gave the lie to MPs who had told the Guild that their mailbags were overflowing with allegations from constituents about breaches of privacy by the press'.[30]

It would have been in any case of the essence of the matter that McGregor should use the Commission's *First Annual Report, 1991*, published on 14 May 1992, to claim success for press self-regulation. In the circumstances of a more secure political atmosphere McGregor's claim took on a new plausibility. The report, he declared, 'contains evidence of their success in the parliamentary period which will end in July, 1992'. There was evidence that the industry's intention to change its habits was 'becoming a new reality'. McGregor was sure that 'the ethical standards embodied in the Code will now be observed cumulatively, expansively and irreversibly'. It was particularly gratifying to McGregor that the 'most pleasing and distinctive trait in our first year has been that interpreting and applying the Code of Practice has not polarised the Commission between the lay and professional elements. To the contrary, an easy working relationship has developed in which such a division is not easily visible.'

The outstanding conclusion to be drawn from the statistical data presented, McGregor considered, was the 'astonishingly small number of complaints made against newspapers in general and the popular national dailies and Sundays in particular'. He did cautiously allow, however, that it was not possible as yet to determine whether this low level of complaint owed more to public satisfaction with its press than to a low level of public awareness of the PCC. The Commission was, in any event, working to remedy the latter contingency. The 91 adjudications represented 6.5 per cent of the total complaints received (1,396). Fewer than half (43) were upheld. Just over half the total 'communications' were not pursued, on grounds of being outside the Commission's remit, disallowed for delay, involving no prima facie breach of the Code, or coming from third parties. In 387 cases (27.7 per cent) complaints were resolved through good offices directly with the editor concerned. Just on half the complaints were directed at the national dailies and Sundays. The *Sun* was the most adjudicated paper, with five complaints upheld and five rejected. Then came, in descending order of delinquency, the *Daily Mail*, the *Mail on Sunday*, the *People*, and the *News of the World* and the *Daily Star*; these two last being, of course, papers whose editors were on the Commission. McGregor made a point in the report of defending Chapman and Hitchen. 'Their presence on the Commission has been denounced as though they were publicans masquerading as loyal members of the governing body of a temperance association.' Only one complaint had been upheld in either instance; and Hitchen had earned credit for publishing new guidelines for his own staff on the *Star* on controversial matters such as invasion of privacy.

So bullish was McGregor feeling at this stage that he now contemplated the Commission's becoming sooner rather than later more proactive and expansive in its range of concerns and operations. He agreed, in an interview with Naomi Marks of the *Press Gazette*, that 'the climate was now right' to bring the issue of promoting press freedom 'further to the fore'. 'We weren't flagging this point to quite the same extent' in 1991, he explained, 'because at that stage I was much more concerned with the uncertain political future – to stress what was common between the PCC and the Calcutt Committee rather than identify the differences.' McGregor added that he had in view the PCC's playing 'an active role, particularly within Europe, in promoting Press interests'.[31]

Even more bullish was the atmosphere of rejoicing at the British Press Awards, the trade's mutual admiration event. 'Gunfight at the PCC corral' was the *Press Gazette*'s headline for it. Hugh Cudlipp's 'rip-roaring speech' was dedicated to 'those gunslinging tabloid editors who have begun to turn the Last Chance Saloon into a milk-bar': Patsy 'Get your Gun' Chapman, Kelvin 'Sundance' MacKenzie, Brian 'Butch' Hitchen, Bridget 'Snake Eyes'

Rowe, and 'Bronco' Bill Hagerty. Cudlipp's serious point was a post-election one: 'Since John Major had invested a considerable – perhaps even a very considerable – portion of his reputation in the Citizen's Charter and is lifting the veil of secrecy in Whitehall, he would need to be provoked beyond endurance now to favour legislation against the Press.' Calcutt Phase 2, in short, was no longer a threat. 'The loaded pistol pointed at the press following Calcutt was now returning to its holster.' Since the industry never regarded the threat as justifiable, the neutralizing of Calcutt merely signalled the moment when the industry 'should move onto the offensive'.[32]

There were those, such as Simon Jenkins, editor of *The Times* and former member of the Calcutt Committee, who felt that Cudlipp was too rip-roaring to be true, and that McGregor possibly risked over-stretch in his ambitions for the Commission. Jenkins's view was that Calcutt was broadly right in recommending that a body running press self-regulation would best confine itself to modest limits in its brief. Any body 'which regards as its prime duty the defence of Press freedoms', he pointed out, 'would find it difficult to convince an embittered claimant that its prime duty was to adjudicate properly'.[33] And, as to that, it was *The Times*, in its comments on the PCC's *First Annual Report, 1991*, which drew attention to the fragility of the Commission's situation. It was one thing to conclude that the message of the past eighteen probationary months was that 'the pact has held'. It was quite another to deduce from that rather brittle fact that the Commission's management of the industry's Code of Practice had conferred invulnerability on press self-regulation. Already there were indications that a private member's Bill would be introduced in the coming parliamentary session to enforce balance in press reporting and to limit cross-media ownership. Clive Soley, a veteran Labour scourge of the industry, wanted newspapers to be obliged to distinguish between 'news and views'. It was thought his Bill would have an 'excellent chance of being debated and tested'.[34] Soley's Bill, it so chanced, would be Blom-Cooperishly entitled Freedom and Responsibility of the Press. This was not because of any close connections with Blom-Cooper. Rather, Soley's Bill grew out of the work of the Campaign for Press and Broadcasting Freedom, started in 1979 by print union activists who set up their own Right of Reply Unit in the pre-Thatcher, pre-Murdoch heyday of union power in Fleet Street. *The Times* added a further pertinent observation. 'The Ashdown affair temporarily reduced the Code's privacy clause four to impotence. Nor is the Code likely to prove much use in defending royal privacy in coming months.'[35]

Report No. 7, March 1992
Hornsey Journal

COMPLAINT

Haringey Racial Equality Council of Turnpike Lane, London N8 complained that the
Hornsey Journal misleadingly and inaccurately implied that police raids in the Borough
of Haringey resulted in the arrest of black suspects, and the publication of two letters
and footnotes from the editor was not an adequate remedy in breach of Clause 1 of the
Code of Practice.

ADJUDICATION

Haringey Racial Equality Council, of London N8, has complained that the Hornsey
Journal misleadingly and inaccurately implied that police raids in the Borough of
Haringey resulted in the arrest of black suspects, and the publication of two letters, with
footnotes from the editor, was not an adequate remedy.

The raids were part of 'Operation Bumblebee' mounted by the police to demonstrate
their activity against burglars in Tottenham and Hornsey. To this end, the press were
involved to the extent that one reporter from the Hornsey Journal, another from its
sister paper, the Islington Gazette, together with one photographer accompanied dawn
raids by the police. The Hornsey Journal reporter accompanied officers from Wood
Green, the other reporter and the photographer went with the Islington group. No
photographs were taken in Haringey, where only one youth was arrested; photographs
which illustrated the article complained against in the Hornsey Journal were in fact of
three black men arrested in Islington.

The police recognise that the article and accompanying photographs caused grave
offence to black community groups, but strongly refute the suggestion that they were
part of a conspiracy to ensure that only black people arrested were photographed. The
Commission accept that the cause of the trouble was muddle not conspiracy.

When the issue was taken up with the editor, he published letters from the Haringey
Ethnic Minority Joint Consultative Council and Community and Police Consultative
Group, adding footnotes saying 'there was no intention to pinpoint a particular section
of the community as being responsible for the majority of burglaries in the area', and
regretted that this was the impression which had been given.

In his second footnote the editor said that the newspaper 'stands by its coverage of
what took place on the day in question'. The Commission hold that the circumstances
required an ample apology for an article illustrated by seriously misleading photographs.

In the Commission's view, the editor's response to the complaints did not amount to
an adequate remedy or correction and the complaint is upheld under Clause 1(i) of the
Code of Practice.

CHAPTER FOUR

'Damned for acting quickly and damned if we did not': McGregor impaled on the royals, June–July, 1992

'The recent most intrusive and speculative treatment by sections of the press . . . of the marriage of the Prince and Princess of Wales is an odious exhibition of journalists dabbling their fingers in the stuff of other people's souls. . . . The Commission have been distressed by this reversion by some newspapers to the worst excesses of the 1980s and are bound to state publicly that the continuance of this type of journalism will threaten the future of self-regulation just at the time it appears to be succeeding.'

Statement at the Press Complaints Commission, 1 Salisbury Square, by Lord McGregor, 8 June 1992

'I have decided to ask Sir David Calcutt QC . . . to undertake an assessment of how self-regulation has worked in practice since his Committee reported. His remit will be to assess the effectiveness of non-statutory self-regulation by the press since the establishment of the Press Complaints Commission and to give his views on whether the present arrangements should now be modified or put on a statutory basis.'

David Mellor MP, Secretary of State for National Heritage, House of Commons, 9 July 1992

Indications that a 'battle royal' had been raging between the camps of the disaffected Prince and Princess of Wales multiplied during 1991 and early in 1992. Neither Prince nor Princess, so *The Times* team of reporters ascertained, had built any formal links with newspapers. The Prince 'would have regarded it as beneath him to indulge in such sordid activity'; but he was nonetheless known to keep a sharp eye on the game.[1] Nor did the Princess telephone newspapers in person. But she was 'undoubtedly more than happy for her side of events to be given maximum exposure'. McGregor later recorded that he had 'picked up rumours that Princess Diana had been in touch with certain editors'.[2] But this did not lead him to doubt the efficacy of the attitude he had adopted a year earlier when he discounted Lord Rothermere's warning as an 'overstatement' of the case. He continued to see the problem as one primarily of press intrusion and speculation, and to see the Commission's role as 'attempting to protect the princess'.[3]

Throughout the early months of 1992 McGregor and, as it seems, therefore the PCC, continued unperturbed in this role. These were the months when arrangements for serializing Andrew Morton's *Diana: Her True Story* were concluded. An auction battle between the *Daily Mail* and the *Sunday Times* ended with the prize going 'out of the clutches of Rothermere into those of Murdoch'.[4] In conditions of intense competitive struggle to stem declining circulations it would be not only a question of the *Sunday Times*'s serialization but of many 'spoilers' that would be launched by its rivals. The imperative presumption at Salisbury Square that the Princess was in need of protection blocked all infiltrations of awareness that it might well be the PCC that was in need of protection.

One important explanation of the insulated innocence of McGregor and his colleagues is the faith they quite reasonably placed in the reliability of the information they had from the official Palace apparatus. If anyone knew about Diana, surely it must be her sister's husband, who happened also to be the Queen's private secretary, Sir Robert Fellowes? Among the things the Commission did not know was that the Princess regarded the Palace courtiers as her dedicated enemies. Behind the assurance retained in Fellowes and his Palace press colleague Charles Anson, it can be surmised, there lay powerfully reinforcing attitudes and prejudices. One, naturally, was about the 'usual suspects': delinquent newspapers and their atavistic instincts for journalistic feeding frenzy. It was perfectly plausible to account for the existence of the new problem from the history of their old behaviour.

But beyond that were deeper residues of sentiment which McGregor and the PCC shared with what was probably a majority opinion in the country. Like very many people of goodwill who valued the monarchy and who were appalled at the prospect of a dangerous crisis in its affairs, they preferred not to know the worst. This kind of sentimental evasiveness transmuted very readily into a muddled impression that the press must be the villain of the piece. Beyond that, again, would be the suspicion, once news of the serialization with the *Sunday Times* broke, that republican manoeuvres were under way. Murdoch, the proprietor, was of course much hated, not least for his republican professions. His editor, Andrew Neil, successor to Harold Evans's investigative tradition, was known to be an enemy to all that was identified as English establishment stuffiness. Neil in fact went to great lengths to verify Morton's sources. But the important thing was that Neil concluded that 'the sources directly reflected the Princess's views and her apparent wish to see the book serialized in the paper'.[5]

At the centre of McGregor's own sentimental evasiveness lurked a contradiction that later was to do himself and the Commission much damage. In 'attempting to protect the princess' McGregor was yet aware of rumours that she was in touch with 'certain editors'. Even with all discounts applicable, he could not in any case deny the fact, as he later put it, that 'the state of the marriage has been put in the public domain in part at least by the outward behaviour of the spouses, and it is therefore a legitimate subject within the public interest for report and comment by the press'.[6] In itself this was a perfectly accurate and sensible view of the matter. Had McGregor confined himself to sticking to this simple text and resisting all pressures upon him and within him to try to reconcile it with discrepant moral outrage about the manner and tone of 'speculative' reporting, he would have saved himself, his Commission and the cause of self-regulation an immense amount of discredit.

Why did he not? To have freed himself from this contradiction would have required of McGregor not only agile extrication from deep sentimental residues and strongly prevailing presumptions but also a readiness to face down public and political opinion precisely generated within those residues and presumptions. Being of a somewhat choleric humour, and prone to moral excitement within the frame especially of the politics of conscience, was no aid, in the circumstances, to the necessary agility. That he hated the way the monarchy's magic bonds were being shredded by 'relentless publicity' and 'irresistible scrutiny' is attested eloquently in the Harold W. Andersen lecture he delivered in December 1995 in the United States, sponsored by the World Press Freedom Committee. In that lecture he identified a new phenomenon bearing on the case: the way he felt himself and the Commission being pushed towards a signal intervention by the sheer force of outraged opinion. 'The Commission and I were put under powerful pressure by the public, by the churches, and by members of Parliament demanding that the Commission denounce these intrusions into the privacies of royal spouses in a collapsing marriage. The Palace press office was pleading informally for action by the Commission.'[7] The Archbishop of Canterbury called for something to be done. Georgina Henry in the *Guardian* reported pressure from 'the lay members and some regional editors to respond to calls from politicians for the commission to take a stance'.[8] David Chipp explained later in defence of McGregor that during the weekend before the statement was issued on behalf of the PCC 'he had been telephoned by contacts in both Houses of Parliament and in Whitehall to obtain a view about what the Commission intended to do'. The 'general feeling' as he understood it was 'that questions would be put to the Prime Minister on the Tuesday of the following week concerning privacy, right of reply and the need for a statutory body'. Chipp 'considered that only a rapid response from the Commission could have defused this situation'.[9] The stance the chairman had in view was plainly signalled to the Commission by McGregor's arranging an emergency meeting briefed by both Anson and Fellowes 'that the princess had had nothing to do with the book'.[10] By the Monday he 'judged that a failure by the Commission to have a public view on the reporting would have required the Government to dismiss the PCC as a tame and toothless body'.[11]

2

The critical moment arrived with the first serialization of excerpts from *Diana: Her True Story* in the *Sunday Times* on 7 June. Here were bald allegations of the Prince's taking a mistress, Camilla, wife of Brigadier Andrew Parker Bowles. Morton's book, recalled McGregor, 'gave a most unflattering and damaging portrayal of the Prince of Wales, detailing descriptions of the Princess's desperate unhappiness in the marriage, including her suicide attempts'. From then on, their relationship foundered 'on the front pages of every British newspaper'.

As the serialization date approached, 'other papers in competition with the *Sunday Times* ran spoilers in the course of which the industry's ethical code was frequently and grossly breached'.[12] The *Sunday Times* hardly came within the PCC's official purview. All it was doing was editing excerpts from a book being published with which the Commission had no business. What was in the Commission's official purview was the undoubted fact that the break-up of the marriage of the heir to the throne was 'a legitimate subject within the public interest for report and comment by the press'. On 8 June, the day following the first serialization, the *Mirror* blazoned a headline quoting Diana: 'I have not co-operated with this book in any way. All I want is to serve our country.'[13] In fact, as Morton later disclosed, she had personally annotated his draft text copiously.

What McGregor tried to do at Salisbury Square on that Monday, 8 June, was somehow to accept that such report and comment might be a legitimate message, while yet furiously blaming the messengers for delivering it.

The contradiction was not readily apparent because the language of his denunciation was so – in McGregor's own word – 'emotional' as to push the sensible bits to the margin. Some 400 outraged telephone calls and 80 outraged letters were pouring in. McGregor prepared what must be assumed was, in his own phrase, a 'carefully timed' scenario. He drafted a press statement for publication and invited a 'small group' from the Commission to consider it. This he had planned a week before. That small group consisted of Lady Elizabeth Cavendish, a personal friend and old colleague from the Advertising Standards Authority, and 'our two special editorial advisers', Sir Edward Pickering and David Chipp. Indications were that McGregor could feel secure in having the lay members of the Commission behind him. McGregor's tactic was that no active national editorial member would be given the opportunity to be awkward. His explanation later to the bemused Commission was that Pickering and Chipp had 'no immediate obligations to editors' and that Lady Elizabeth was the only commissioner 'with direct knowledge of the royal personalities concerned'.[14] Sir Edward appears to have been a largely silent, and thus consenting party to the proceedings. The Commission's acting-director, Mark Bolland, was of course present at Salisbury Square, but was not requested to attend this 'small group'. He thought McGregor's proceedings 'odd'. His absence was unfortunate: he would have put in a word or two about taking care.[15]

'We agreed', McGregor recounted, 'the following':

The recent most intrusive and speculative treatment by sections of the press and, indeed, by broadcasters, of the marriage of the Prince and Princess of Wales is an odious exhibition of journalists dabbling their fingers in the stuff of other people's souls in a manner which adds nothing to legitimate public interest in the situation of the heir to the throne. Such prurient reporting must add to the burdens borne by children whose lives are affected and greatly increase the difficulties for members of the Royal Family in carrying out their obligations to the public. The state of the marriage has been put into the public domain in part at least by the outward behaviour of the spouses and it is therefore a legitimate subject within the public interest for report and comment by the press. The industry's own Code of Practice affirms that the manner in which information is reported and the tone in which it is discussed often matter as much as the substance of the stories themselves. Frequently, the manner and tone of the reporting of the private lives of the Prince and Princess of Wales has beyond doubt been in breach of the Code of Practice. The Commission has been distressed by this reversion by some newspapers to the worst excesses of the 1980s and are bound to state publicly their view that the continuance of this type of journalism will threaten the future of self-regulation just at the time it appears to be succeeding.[16]

This statement was drafted and approved by people who thought they had reason to believe that the manner and tone which breached the Code were consequences of 'speculative treatment', not of accurate reporting; and who thought they had reason to believe the Princess innocent of collaboration or collusion in the Morton book. They had reason to believe, also, that they were under scrutiny from public, Parliament and ministers. McGregor thereupon took the precaution of once more getting direct confirmation that the Princess had not colluded.

As I had picked up rumours that Princess Diana had been in touch with certain editors, I telephoned the Queen's private secretary, in the presence of my colleagues, and read the statement to him. I mentioned these rumours about the Princess having spoken directly to editors and asked for an assurance that they were untrue. Sir Robert Fellowes gave me that assurance, which I accepted without demur, knowing that he was also the Princess's brother-in-law.[17]

McGregor also telephoned as many of the editorial members of the Commission as he could get in touch with. He later testified that the statement 'was not issued until there was a majority of Commissioners in agreement'.[18] Lord Colnbrook was the only lay commissioner to express reservations about McGregor's procedure. 'His calls exposed', according to Georgina Henry's account, 'not just a difference between some of the lay and press members, but a broadsheet/tabloid, national/regional split.' Max Hastings, editor of the *Daily Telegraph*, was 'unhappy about Lord McGregor's decision to issue a fierce condemnatory statement' because he felt this 'reflected visceral dismay rather than considered analysis. . . . As an individual editor I was not ashamed of venting my sentiments in public. But I was unconvinced that the regulatory press body should do so, unless a substantive issue within its remit could be identified.'[19] The national tabloid representatives in particular had good reason to call into question the issue of manner and tone in relation to legitimate public interest. The Code spoke not of manner and tone in any case, but spirit and letter; and questions of taste and decency had long been regarded as best left outside codification. No doubt the tabloideers resented words like 'odious' and 'prurient'. Although Brian Hitchen at the *Daily Star* did not publicly dissent from McGregor's condemnatory statement, his paper carried a front-page headline on 9 June proclaiming: 'It's all true – says Di's pal.' Patsy Chapman at the *News of the World* confirmed that day that she had told McGregor that his statement 'went too far'. She 'agreed only with the commission's view that it was a legitimate subject within the public interest . . . and that it was right to consider the effect on the children'. Chapman thought 'the statement smacked of the establishment closing ranks around the royals. . . . I think it is a story within the public interest and I can't understand the newspapers which are not covering this at all. We're talking about the future of the monarchy.'[20]

In the no doubt rather fraught mood of the occasion, it was not surprising that McGregor kept the industry component of the Commission at a distance, and in particular allowed the usual tabloid suspects no chance to talk him out of his intention to intervene boldly in a manner that would satisfy the Archbishop of Canterbury, the politicians and the decent-minded public. Hitchen and Chapman, after all, would be in the position of having to call either Fellowes or Diana a liar.

Two views, not incompatible, have been expressed about McGregor at this point. One is that the chairman was overcome by the sheer weight of the public and political pressure. The other is that he positively relished the release of moral excitement amid civic drama and media commotion. At all events he went to the front door of No. 1 Salisbury Square and read out his statement to the media throng. David Chipp recalls that looking over the draft gave him no qualms; it was while he listened to McGregor reading it out amid the scrum that he realized a disaster was in the making.[21]

3

Public response applauded the PCC's gallant deed. There was widespread misapprehension that it was an attack on the *Sunday Times*, 'leader of the republican pack'. Andrew Neil later described a 'haemorrhage of readers who simply did not want to know'.[22] Tony Newton, leader of the House of Commons, endorsed on behalf of the government the PCC's condemnation of the 'media speculation' about the Waleses' marriage. But, from the point of view of McGregor and the PCC, an entirely unwelcome paradox soon began to disclose itself amid the public plaudits. It became evident that the Commission's statement was being interpreted as a virtual acknowledgment by the press's self-regulatory body of the futility of press self-regulation.

The tone of Tony Newton's welcome of the statement led Geoffrey

Johnson Smith, member of the Tory 1922 Committee, to confide his trust that there would be no government witch-hunt against the press. He chided the PCC for muddling the distinction between 'stories where there is a legitimate public interest and cases of sensationalist presentation'.[23] Mellor's announcement in the Commons on 15 June positively dripped with unspoken menace: 'The statement issued by the Commission on 8 June has attracted much interest. We will be taking the Commission's views into account in the forthcoming review of press self-regulation.'[24]

Georgina Henry reported on 10 June that 'no one was going so far yesterday as saying that the commission, and the system of self-regulation, had been exposed as a sham, or that the row had shown the impossibility of achieving consensus within a voluntary body representing widely differing opinions'. Tabloids were split between those which appeared to be pulling back slightly and those – like the *Daily Express* and the *Sun* – which lambasted the PCC's statement.[25] Melinda Whittstock reported for *The Times*: 'Defiant tabloids yesterday hit back at the Press Complaints Commission's condemnation of newspaper coverage of the Prince and Princess of Wales with more screaming headlines, extensive inside reports and, in some cases, articles attacking the commission.' The *Sun* dismissed the PCC judgment as nonsense and accused it of 'confusing the message with the messenger'. The *Express* asserted that newspapers were 'merely doing their job in a free and open society'. Among the Commission's harshest critics was Andrew Neil at the *Sunday Times*. 'It's hard to work out what the Commission is really saying because the statement does so much damage to the English language that it is almost unintelligible.' Every hour that went by, Neil declared, 'we get more factual backup'. Neil could not believe that the PCC would want him to suppress a story which involved a suicide attempt by the Princess of Wales.[26] Hitchen's *Daily Star* headline, 'It's all true', was of course the leitmotiv of negative industry comment on the PCC.

To McGregor's extreme discomfiture, 'It's all true' was also the leitmotiv of a telephone message received from on high in the industry. McGregor recounted the story, and its aftermath, in his Andersen lecture.

Shortly after the statement had been published, I was telephoned by Andrew Knight, at that time Executive Chairman of Rupert Murdoch's News International, publisher of the *Sunday Times*. He told me that, to his certain knowledge, the Princess was in direct communication with some editors and suggested that I should look at all the tabloids the following morning because

Diana had arranged with some editors for photographs of herself and her children to be taken as she left the house of one of her friends who had been a principal contributor to Morton's book. Andrew Knight was right. The tabloids did indeed carry photographs of Diana and her children which, so editors told me, had been taken with the assistance of her security guards.

The Queen's private secretary was a victim of events and conduct that demonstrated his assurance to me to be unfounded. His personal integrity as a high official occupying a central position in Britain's constitutional arrangements had been impugned.

He and I had both been trapped in a web of manipulation. I was shocked and raised immediately this most damaging issue for the commission with a senior member of the Government, who spoke to Sir Robert Fellowes. Sir Robert apologized to me, though I had never doubted his good faith. His honour required him to offer his resignation to the Queen. It was not accepted. This episode was also a disaster for the Commission. The attempt to enforce the industry's Code of Practice in relation to the Royals collapsed in the ensuing ridicule. Members of Parliament used this incident as an argument for statutory legal sanctions against the press.[27]

A later statement from News International recorded McGregor's expressing his 'surprise' and then his 'shock and concern'. In due course he was to admit 'that the Princess of Wales had made a mockery of his attempts to protect her against the worst excesses of the tabloid press'.[28] The carefully staged visit by the Princess with her children to her friend Carolyn Bartholomew and the photographs of her leaving in tears amounted to, McGregor realized, 'a blatant attempt to win the sympathy vote'.[29]

'The actions of the Princess of Wales in this situation', as McGregor further recounted, 'seriously embarrassed the Commission and undermined the purpose of this carefully timed and emotionally phrased statement of their attitude towards the reporting of the state of this marriage.' Against this background and the likelihood that information would continue to be leaked to the press, McGregor concluded that the Commission had no alternative but to hold their hand for the time being. At the 'first opportunity' McGregor spoke to the Lord Chancellor and to Lord Wakeham, now leader of the House of Lords. Wakeham invited McGregor 'to repeat what I had told him to one of the Prime Minister's private secretaries, and subsequently spoke to Sir Robert Fellowes, who was then in Paris with the Queen'. On Fellowes's return and apologetic explanation, McGregor 'urged upon Mr Anson and Sir Robert Fellowes the desirability of their sending as formal complaints to the commission a selection of the large number of alleged factual inaccuracies about the royal family, taken from the press which they had sent to me'. Were the Commission to uphold a number of such complaints, it would be in accordance with their established policy to give guidance to editors in the form of an editorial in one of the monthly reports. 'This would enable the commission to tackle anew the problems arising from this type of reporting.'[30] The Palace decided against taking this precedent, and left the PCC empty-handed, and forlorn.

All this left the PCC vulnerable to criticism from the industry, possibly mutiny in the industry. Georgina Henry gathered that 'Lord McGregor's next step, if the reporting does not subside, will be to approach the newspaper proprietors asking them to step in. One Commission member said "it was a very dangerous situation for the Commission" . . . Another said "the consensus is under enormous strain".'[31]

It happened, with a certain comic untimeliness, that the Press Standards Board of Finance launched its *First Annual Report* slap in the middle of the turmoil, on 10 June. The substantial, though by now decidedly sidelined, point made by the chairman, Harry Roche, was that Pressbof saw no reason to accede to proposals that it establish a new body to perform the role of actively campaigning on issues of press freedom. The Board's view was that there was 'already adequate monitoring of such issues by existing organisations at the present time'. It was also the Board's view that all proposals for deals with the government by the likes of Trelford were unacceptable: 'any form of statutory control of the Press was anathema to a democratic society'. A Freedom of Information Act 'should be won on its own merits'. In the hectic circumstances of the moment all that Pressbof could do was to 'continue to demonstrate our commitment to the Code of Practice and our support for the PCC'. In that respect, added Roche, it was 'important that the industry takes due cognisance of the statement issued by the Press Complaints Commission on 8 June 1992 in relation to Press coverage of the Royal Family'.[32]

'Due cognisance' was indeed about as far as Roche could prudently go in the circumstances. A ringing endorsement would have hit quite the wrong note in the industry. A survey by the *Press Gazette* found national and regional editors alike seething about the 'appalling', 'confusing' and 'too hasty' PCC statement. Particular exception was taken to the way it was drafted by only a small number of Commission members. Stewart Steven of the *Mail on Sunday* thought it 'quite extraordinarily hasty'. What was the point of having such a body 'if at moments of deliberation that body is not brought together?' Mike Unger of the *Manchester Evening News* thought it 'an appalling statement because it was contradictory. In one paragraph, Lord McGregor was saying it added nothing to legitimate public interest, in another that it was a legitimate subject of interest. He can't have it both ways.' Unger thought McGregor seemed 'to be appeasing those Members of Parliament who want to hang the Press regardless'. In a slight twist to this theme, one 'top Fleet Street executive' judged the PCC statement uncalled for, but potentially valuable: 'The Tory party and Tory Central Office owes a debt. It may be a debt that has to be called in.'

Matthew Symonds, deputy editor of the *Independent*, was a little more sympathetic. 'The language was highly emotional, slightly curious and a little ill-judged. But I don't think anybody can sensibly deny the reporting of the Waleses' private lives has been entirely intrusive.' But Symonds also pointed to the 'confusing' nature of the statement 'combining moral outrage with recognition that it was a legitimate subject for public interest'; and thus unhelpful guidance for editors. An influential voice was that of Sir David English at the *Daily Mail*, who diagnosed McGregor's precipitancy through his 'confused and contradictory thoughts. He has produced what was in effect a judgment without a trial.'[33]

McGregor defended himself on grounds of the urgency of the Commission's need to act. There was no assertion of his statement's being 'carefully timed'. Nor was there any confessing that he had been trapped in a web of manipulation. That would come later. He stood by the statement, he insisted to the *Press Gazette*. Had it not been made, and quickly, 'we would have been blown out of the water'. There would have grown up, at an alarming speed, 'a political opinion in Parliament similar to that existing before the Calcutt Committee, seeking direct Governmental intervention in the Press. As a self-regulatory body we had to speak out in advance of Parliamentary questions and that was why the statement was produced at high speed.' David Chipp protested on behalf of the PCC: 'We were damned for acting quickly and damned if we did not.' McGregor believed that 'when editors are in a position to detach themselves from the intensities of competition, their consent to the action of the PCC and their support for what it is trying to do may be forthcoming'.[34]

Or maybe not. This was the defence of a badly shaken chairman. McGregor explained later, echoing Chipp, why he made no apology to the papers. 'After the event I found myself in an impossible situation, and, whichever way, I was in the position of being damned if I did and damned if I didn't.'[35] Recriminations peek out from behind the bland minutes of the Commission's meeting on 24 June. It was resolved that in future similar statements would be issued in the name of the chairman only and not on behalf of the entire Commission. Editorial members pointed to the potentially embarrassing position they would be in if seen to be agreeing to the wording of such a statement. That statement in any case had not the slightest effect in heading off an opinion in Parliament similar to that which in 1989 led to the Calcutt Committee. Labour backbenchers were calling vociferously by 10 June for statutory controls on the press. Clive Soley's Freedom and Responsibility of the Press Bill was sponsored by Mark Fisher, Bruce Grocott, Harriet Harman, Chris Smith, Glenda Jackson, Clare Short and the Liberal Democrat Charles Kennedy. Fisher derided self-regulation as having been 'made to look ridiculous in the past few days when the editors say they do not really mind what the Press Complaints Commission says . . . they are going to do it anyway'.[36] Demands for a privacy law took on a new life. Woodrow Wyatt, for all that he was a Murdoch columnist, extolled the French example. Manifestly the PCC had failed to protect the Princess of Wales's privacy. Circulation battles always took primacy over promises of good behaviour. The French, Wyatt observed, were 'amazed at what is published about the private lives of the royal family'; a book 'comparable to Andrew Morton's would not have appeared in France'.[37] (*Diana: Her True Story* went on to sell four million copies.) Mellor's tone, meanwhile, had lost nothing of its menace. He assured the Commons on 19 June that the government very much intended 'to review the effectiveness of press self-regulation over the period from 1 January 1991 to 30 June 1992'.[38]

Then the House of Lords galvanized itself into debate on 1 July. The chamber was awash with the same flood of outrage that had deluged Salisbury Square. Leading off, Lord Bonham-Carter contemplated the matter of the government's making up their minds 'whether the press had passed that "stiff test". It is even possible that our discussion may influence them.' The themes of that discussion were the villainy of Murdoch, the need for press legislation, the shameless political bias of newspapers, and the inefficacy of the PCC. There were noble lords who had illuminating things to say about the problem in social context. Baroness Birk pointed out that newspapers now reflected a 'greater liberation – some may call it licence – in society and the press. The two are interlocked.' The change could be seen not only in tabloids, but in the quality papers. It was a 'culture shock'. There were noble lords who defended the PCC. Lord Colnbrook, a member of the Commission, testified to the 'expert and very agreeable guidance' of Lord McGregor (who did not take part in the debate). Lord Thomson of Monifieth pointed out that the debate was, in practical effect, about the future of the Press Complaints Commission. He pleaded with noble lords to realize that the PCC was 'still in its early days. It is suffering a baptism of fire and should be given more time to prove itself.'[39]

Lord Stevens of Ludgate, chairman of United Newspapers and proprietor of the *Express* papers, denounced those 'as ever, who would like to exploit recent unease at some aspects of press behaviour to impose new restrictions'. Mr Soley's Bill in the Commons, Stevens asserted, was born out of 'exasperation' that a Conservative government had been re-elected because of their political supporters in Fleet Street. 'Above all that hangs, like a sword of Damocles, the power to turn the Press Complaints Commission into a statutory body.'[40]

This motif of the sword of Damocles was, rather like 'last chance saloon', to have a long and ominous life in public debate about the future of press self-regulation. There was another noble lord from the industry, however, inclined to discount omens. Lord Deedes, eminent *Telegraph* veteran, reminded their lordships of another kind of reality bearing on the issue of events:

> . . . at the risk of causing hurt looks from my own front bench, I see no likelihood of this government giving much encouragement to legislation which will antagonize the press. It is better to be blunt. The press did the government pretty well in the previous election. I make no bones about that. No government in their senses bite the hand they feel has fed them. For that and other reasons . . . this talk of legislation carries with it a great deal of bluff.[41]

No doubt advocates of self-regulation took heart from this refreshing whiff of healthy cynicism. They could take heart, also, from the wisdom received by the industry pundits that even if government was committed to a review of Calcutt's probationary period, it would be a low-profile bureaucratic committee affair, with any luck buried away in the recesses of the National Heritage department.[42]

Great, therefore, was the industry's shock and dismay at David Mellor's announcement in the Commons on 9 July.

> I have decided to ask Sir David Calcutt QC . . . to undertake an assessment of how self-regulation has worked in practice since his Committee reported. His remit will be to assess the effectiveness of non-statutory self-regulation by the press since the establishment of the Press Complaints Commission and to give

his views on whether the present arrangements for self-regulation should now be modified or put on a statutory basis. I have also asked him to consider whether any further measures may be needed to deal with intrusions into personal privacy by the press, and to make recommendations.

Sir David, added Mellor, was 'uniquely qualified to carry out this task'.[43]

Indeed he was: the point being that nothing was mentioned by Mellor indicating otherwise than that Calcutt would be solo, unimpeded by awkward colleagues. Back in April Donald Trelford had prophesied better, perhaps, than he knew: 'Calcutt Phase 2' was now in being, with a vengeance.

CHAPTER FIVE

Stay of execution, July 1992–January 1993

'"The last thing on earth this Tory government is about to do is countenance anti-press legislation", an old Conservative sage said to me the other day. "We are now simply in the business of gestures."'

Max Hastings, editor of the *Daily Telegraph*, former member of the Press Complaints Commission, in the *Guardian*, 13 July 1992

'The evil that men do lives on the front pages of greedy newspapers, but the good is oft interred apathetically inside.'

Brooks Atkinson, *Once around the Sun* (1951).*

Who would prove the truer prophet – Trelford or Deedes? Behind this question lurked ironies. A presumption widely nurtured in the nervous industry was that, after all, it was only the ructions set off by the Morton serialization that provoked ministers to have recourse to Calcutt. 'Left to its own devices', Max Hastings of the *Telegraph* thought, 'the Government would probably have chosen to do nothing at all. . . . But, unluckily for all concerned, the moment of decision coincided with the latest Fleet Street feeding frenzy.'[1] In its notorious statement of 8 June – which McGregor clarified as attacking the 'corpus' of press reporting, not any individual newspaper – the Commission had handed a sword to its enemies. An attempt to save press self-regulation by appeasing public opinion could plausibly be interpreted by that opinion as an admission of failure. An 'old Conservative sage' assured Max Hastings that 'the last thing on earth this Tory government is about to do is countenance anti-press legislation'. Ministers were simply 'in the business of gestures'.[2] All very well: but what about Mellor's alleged propensities to 'go for it' if a head of steam got up

---

*Prefatory epigraph chosen by Sir David Calcutt QC, *Review of Press Self-Regulation*, Department of National Heritage (Cm. 2135, HMSO, January 1993).

in Parliament? Hastings also reported 'Mac's' taking a much bleaker view of prospects than did Conservative sages. McGregor believed the threat of legislation on privacy remained very real, with widespread hostility to the press in the Commons translatable into action at any time. And the likeliest thing about Calcutt Phase 2 was that Sir David alone would recommend what he was prevented from recommending in Phase 1.

Already there was speculation that Calcutt was considering ways of giving the PCC 'more power'.[3] Precisely: power to impose a tougher code from outside the industry, power to fine, to compensate, possibly even to suspend publication. This had always been the great disciplinary attraction of statutory regulation, even if involving an apparatus of appeals and lawyers incompatible with existing self-regulatory practice. McGregor declared himself through clenched teeth grateful for Mr Mellor's 'prompt and constructive' decision, promising to give Calcutt 'all the information and assistance he needed' from the Commission.[4]

Peter Preston, editor of the *Guardian*, who had taken over from Hastings as a national editorial representative on the Commission, understandably took the most optimistic view feasible. Calcutt Phase 2 he considered 'a disappointment, but not surprising'. His analysis was that the current crisis in the industry was due entirely to the extraordinary circumstances of the royal story. Apart from that aberration, the tabloids had been 'mindful of the Code of Practice we agreed'. Preston trusted that 'when David Calcutt examines all these stories in detail he will conclude the same thing'. Patsy Chapman at the *News of the World* chimed in supportively that papers had done their best to improve standards. 'Many stories that would have just gone in unquestioned a few years ago have been stopped by various editors.'[5]

Preston judged that Mellor's unleashing Calcutt would result in 'a great deal of thoughtfulness on the part of the press'. The announcement, as the *Press Gazette* observed glumly, 'has not been greeted with joy in Fleet Street'. The *Gazette*'s own headline was 'Regulation rears its head'. Stewart Steven's expostulation in the *Mail on Sunday* spoke for the great majority in the industry: 'I feel there is absolutely no justification for putting the Press once more on probation.'[6]

Nor was it long before the industry turned to what the *Press Gazette* candidly called 'counter-attack'. The *Gazette* noted that Mellor's decision to leave the press to sober up 'languishing in the last-chance saloon' did not seem to have had 'a sobering effect on the nationals'. Whittam Smith, it was reported in the Lobby, had angered John Major with revelations in the *Independent* about Health minister Virginia Bottomley's earlier career as an unmarried teenage mother. Kelvin MacKenzie at the *Sun* and Andrew Neil at the *Sunday Times* took delight in adopting a holier-than-thou attitude to the virtuous Whittam Smith. Then there were further retaliatory backbitings between the *Observer* and the *Sunday Times*, presenting the broadsheet world in a deplorable light: playing, as the *Gazette* admonished, 'straight into the hands of the legislators'.[7]

Next came the turn of the National Heritage minister himself. Whatever the rights and wrongs of the Bottomley affair, to Bill Hagerty at the *People* Mellor was an irresistible target. Allegations linking him, ostensibly a family-man politician, to an actress were accordingly published. It was a matter of payment for information obtained by illegal phone-bugging. The Prime Minister declined Mellor's offer of resignation. John Major's anger at press behaviour once again, it was thought, had revived his inclination to push on with legislation to curb press intrusion into privacy. *The Times* diagnosed an old-fashioned sex scandal without any bearing on public interest; an exposé in which the *People* had 'done no favours to journalism'.[8] It transpired that there was an extra twist to the case: Mellor's decision to ask Calcutt to review press self-regulation was made at a time when he was aware that newspapers were investigating his affair with Antonia de Sancha. 'It left him compromised and the calls for his resignation eventually proved irresistible.'[9]

While 'most of the press was overdosing on the Mellor drama', McGregor called the Commission to an emergency meeting to consider what the *Observer* denounced as 'a disgrace to a free press'.[10] There was no complaint from Mellor himself, and the PCC's invitation to him to make one was refused. It was known that more revelations were to come from other papers. Some third-party complaints gave McGregor a case for proceeding. This time he was careful not to pronounce an outraged verdict before trial. What he found, however, was a Commission so divided that arriving at what he wanted and intended – using reserved powers to adjudicate on third-party complaints, especially in privacy cases, to deliver a swift and condign rebuke to Hagerty – was impossible. He would have had support from all or most of the lay members; but the case opened up dangerously for the PCC the prospect of a split on the lay/industry fault-line. Patsy Chapman flatly announced on her arrival at Salisbury Square that she would resign from the Commission if it found Hagerty in breach of the Code and without a public-interest justification. Her position was that it was the Clare Short case, so to speak, with knobs on. Chapman 'feared a ruling which would have made politicians seem untouchable'.

After three hours' deliberation, the Commission concluded that the Code was unclear in its definition of the public interest. A statement was issued unanimously declaring that in the case of politicians the public had a right to be informed about private behaviour 'which affects or may affect the conduct of public business'. Holders of public office 'must always be subject to public scrutiny'. Thus judgments about invasions of privacy 'must balance two sets of rights which may often conflict'. The Commission also decided that, in lieu of an adjudication, it would conduct a review of all its cases involving the privacy of public figures and consider whether to recommend to the Code Committee amendments or additions to the Code of Practice. It would consider also the working of privacy legislation in other countries. Findings would be presented later in the year to Sir David Calcutt.[11]

Chapman interpreted the Commission's avoidance of an adjudication as a vindication of Hagerty, but McGregor was quick to deny that the story had been found in the public interest. Chapman conceded that the *People* was neither praised nor blamed during the meeting. She did insist, however, that Hagerty's not being condemned amounted to 'a victory for the press in the battle with politicians. It is a blow for people in public life who think they can hoodwink the public with their double standards.' The Commission 'noted' claims in the *Sun* and the *Independent* that 'a senior cabinet minister' attempted to smear Paddy Ashdown, the Liberal Democrat leader, with untrue allegations during the general-election period. Hagerty's own reading of the case was that the PCC, by acknowledging that holders of public office must always be subject to public scrutiny, 'blew away the disreputable "blame the Press" tactics', and 'destroyed the appalling lie propagated by the great and not-so-good: that a privacy bill is necessary to protect the "ordinary people"'.[12]

In truth the rather dismayed PCC staff would, in the circumstances, have much preferred to do without these accolades conferred by tabloids at the expense of politicians. It was fortunate for McGregor and the PCC that their seemingly feeble performance in this episode escaped immediate parliamentary observation. 'No doubt', as the *Press Gazette* commented, 'its cautious response was influenced by the fact that Parliament is in recess and MPs are not in a position to rush privacy legislation through.' Indignant remarks from such as the Labour MP Joe Ashton gave adequate indication of what the predominant parliamentary attitude would have been to a PCC which appeared to have dodged its duty: 'as might be expected' from a body which included tabloid editors; which in effect gives approval to the tabloids' use of paid informers. 'If the cabinet does not now restore the rights of the individual against the press barons and their harassment of famous names', Ashton fulminated, 'then we might just as well accept that the press is more powerful than Parliament and close the latter down.'[13]

2

Day-to-day work at the PCC, as McGregor constantly had occasion to point out, was very little concerned with high-profile privacy disputes. On his retirement from the Commission, Max Hastings provided the *Guardian* with valuable insights into the Commission's interior life.

> I have been much impressed by the standard of debate on complaints at the PCC meetings. We have sat through hours of detailed argument about reporters' lost notes, alleged intrusions into personal privacy, suppressed misrepresentations of points of view. The only judgment we have made about which I have serious doubts . . . was the finding against the *Evening Standard* for publishing the Welsh address of Louis Blom-Cooper, which is anyway recorded in all the usual works of reference.[14] For the rest, I think the Commission has done pretty well.
>
> There is evidence that newspapers are seeking to abide by the agreed Code of Conduct, equally in their dealings with humbler citizens, who are the people who most need and deserve protection from press harassment and intrusion. The monthly agenda of the PCC is dominated by what one might call the usual, and predictable, list of tabloid suspects, with a cocktail of regional papers thrown in.
>
> But the overwhelming majority of cases that come before the Commission concern trivia. Does this reflect the fact that fewer heinous offences are being committed or that little of the real villainy reaches the PCC? I think the principal point is that, amid all the heat and dust about press behaviour, when individual cases are closely studied, by far the most serious problem is not one of privacy but of taste.
>
> Almost every day one newspaper or another publishes a story in a manner which arouses middle-class, middle-brow anger and contempt. But, in the overwhelming majority of cases, neither statutory nor non-statutory regulation can or should address the issues of taste which are at stake.

No parliament in the world, Hastings was convinced, 'can legislate against the British public's enthusiasm for fantastic daily fiction'. And for all his own revulsion at tabloid excesses, Hastings remained convinced that 'no workable and justifiable legislation on privacy is possible'. When privacy legislation was first mooted, Hastings was 'naïve enough to suppose that it would not affect the quality press. Our lawyers rapidly disillusioned me.' Because of the huge weight of material they carried, papers such as the *Daily Telegraph* would suffer more from privacy laws than their tabloid brethren – 'and crooks of every hue would profit mightily from the law's protection'.

Hastings concluded that 'the PCC today represents the least undesirable, most practicable form of press supervision we are likely to achieve'. He held strongly that editorial representatives should rotate regularly as members of the Commission. 'The PCC will quickly become discredited if any one set of editors is seen to be sitting in permanent judgment on their peers.' Hastings would be happy to serve another term in two or three years if the chairman wanted him. 'I doubt whether the Calcutt review will establish a case for any new government intervention to supplant the PCC.'[15]

There were others, such as David Newell of the Newspaper Society, who were a little more anxious. He thought it would be 'wholly wrong for the future regulation of thousands of publications to be put in the balance by several newspapers' coverage of the Paddy Ashdown, royal family, Virginia Bottomley and Mellor cases'.[16] What Newell did not realize at that point in early August was that before the month was out there would be yet another scandalous episode to add to his list.

3

An Italian freelance photographer (paparazzo), prowling the public lanes around the villa in the south of France where the Duchess of York and her friend and financial adviser John Bryan were staying, captured startling images of the couple's intimate relationship. These ended up on the desks of various European magazines and the *Daily Mirror*, via the good offices of the royal correspondent James Whitaker, on Sunday 16 August. Richard Stott, editor of the *Mirror*, held off printing the 'dynamite' photographs until the Thursday, ascertained Jean Morgan and Naomi Marks for the *Press Gazette*, because of an agreement with another publication to publish simultaneously. The Fleet Street consensus was that Stott had paid upwards of £75,000 for the rights.

Not in living memory had any national newspaper cranked up its presses for a lunchtime reprint, but those pictures caused such demand around the country that copies of the *Daily Mirror* were changing hands for up to £1.50. A massive print run had sold out swiftly and by 11.30 on Thursday morning the presses were rolling again to satisfy the extraordinary demand. If the public was any judge, there was no question of legitimacy. Editor Richard Stott was equally certain. This was not an issue of privacy but one of 'humbug'.[17]

When the story broke on 20 August, *Mirror* sales went up by 482,000 and by 573,000 the next day. On 22 August they were up 583,000: 'the biggest daily sales increase of any national newspaper in the history of Fleet Street'. On the Saturday the *Mirror* sales alone, without the Glasgow *Daily Record*, hit just under 3.7 million – 4.5 million including the *Record*.[18] 'Thanks a million, Fergie!' was the *Mirror*'s acknowledgment. Clive Soley observed later – apropos of his Freedom and Responsibility of the Press Bill, and with reference to the excesses stimulated by unbridled tabloid competition – that the *Sun* immediately hit back by publishing a tape of a bugged telephone conversation of the Princess of Wales – a tape which had been in the *Sun*'s possession for two years, but not published for 'a principled reason'. That principle dissolved in the maelstrom of the *Mirror* sales.[19]

Opinions varied in the industry on the rights and wrongs of the *Mirror*'s public-interest assertion. No complaint arrived at the PCC, though Bryan attempted by injunction to 'have the Commission act to stop publication, which it is not empowered to do'. McGregor was prudent in the matter. He did not see the Duchess as someone deserving and needing protection. Unwilling to prejudge any future adjudication, he took the view that 'I can't see that this will take us nearer or further from privacy legislation'.[20]

At Salisbury Square, nevertheless, the trauma of the deluge of public outrage over the Andrew Morton serialization had left its mark. Now promoted as director, Mark Bolland was determined that the PCC be on its toes to field the expected new surge of telephone calls and faxes from people appalled at the hounding of the Duchess. Bolland did not have newspapers delivered to his home but bought them from the same vendor every day. 'He knows something is up when I buy a copy of every single newspaper.' On this occasion Bolland 'did not need to spell out his order for the *Mirror*'.[21]

Bolland ordered his fourteen-strong team to be ready for action at the crack of dawn. McGregor himself joined this dawn vigil 'once he had fought his way through the army of television cameras outside his house in a quiet Hampstead street'. It took some time, however, for the 'remarkable' silence to end in a rush of 122 written and 127 telephoned complaints about both the photographs of the Duchess and the bugged tapes of Diana, but with no complaint from the parties directly concerned.

McGregor's prudence and discretion in not repeating his earlier performance led perversely to what the *Press Gazette* described as 'siren voices, mainly in the broadsheets, asking why it is that the Press Complaints Commission hasn't taken a stronger position on the royal farrago'.[22] The appearance of dodging rows with pugilistic tabloids undoubtedly, if quite unfairly, attached to the PCC. Hagerty and the *People* had got away with the Mellor bugging affair. Now Stott and the *Mirror* had got away with 'Fergie's pix'. (The *Sun*, however, did not get away with the 'Di tapes'; but that was down to Blom-Cooper, who, as chairman of the Committee for the Supervision of Standards of Telephone Information Services, 'pulled the plug', much to the outrage of the *Sun*'s assistant editor, Chris Davis: 'When Louis Blom-Cooper was chairman of the Press Council, we all knew he was an idiot and today he has absolutely surpassed himself.'[23])

McGregor was anxious naturally to avoid any widening of the lay/industry fault-line in the Commission. He was anxious particularly to keep the tabloids on board. He was, in the aftermath of his Morton serialization gaffe, in no position of strength to face down Patsy Chapman. He was helped at this juncture by Mellor's own weakness. Still clinging on in his own last chance saloon at the Heritage department, Mellor could hardly wield convincing threats. Reports were that he was expected to resist calls for a wide-ranging privacy law following the row over the photographs of the Duchess of York. 'After disclosures about his relationship with Miss de Sancha, he faces the delicate and potentially embarrassing task of dealing with the topic dispassionately.'[24]

In the end Mellor's role as regulatory decision-maker was unsustainable. After a desperate struggle to keep his career afloat, he had to scuttle by resigning in September. Peter Brooke took over at the Heritage department. The industry, meanwhile, was alarmed at the rather recessive figure being cut by self-regulation. Sir David could hardly fail to draw appropriate conclusions. This was not for want of scheming on McGregor's part. A lunch with a prominent Tory MP fuelled an ambition that a proposal could be put to the Prime Minister that 'the Palace press office should be reconstructed with Elizabeth Cavendish playing a leading role at the Palace end'. McGregor was further 'urged very strongly' that the PCC should 'get in touch' and 'lay ourselves out to charm' certain people at the Downing Street policy unit. 'Over to you', McGregor cheerfully wrote to Bolland.[25] The Palace press office intrigue was never likely to be a starter; but cultivation of the policy unit certainly proved a sound investment.* There were schemes also to pre-empt Calcutt with a signal stroke of virtuous self-denial: to strike a deal with Brooke whereby the Code would be amended to ban illegal bugging, trespass and intrusive, especially long-lens, photography – precisely the features most objected to in the Mellor case, the Diana 'Squidgy' tapes, and the pictures of the topless Duchess of York.

An initiative from the Association of British Editors suggested that editors confer to review the Code to take in the implications of electronic surveillance. Pressbof, keen to get something positive moving, backed McGregor's initiative in arranging a private dinner on 27 October at the Savoy Hotel. Present were Hayden Phillips, the permanent under-secretary at the Heritage department, and Paul Wright, head of its broadcasting and press division. McGregor, Pickering and Bolland represented the PCC. From the Pressbof board were Roche, Rogers and Newell, though in personal rather than institutional capacities. (Nisbet-Smith was unable to attend.)[26] '*The Guardian* understands', according to David Hencke's report, 'that the aim of the meeting was to start a dialogue between the ministry and the media.' Phillips was told that the newspapers would give a 'favourable response' to proposals to curb excesses provided the law was applied to everybody and not just the press; and would offer to open formal negotiations. The long and short of it was that the Heritage people did not take up the offer. Among other things, it is likely that they were unwilling to pre-empt Calcutt. At all events, that 'failure to take up the offer' was later 'viewed by ministers as embarrassing', since it fuelled the row between the government and the industry after the publication of Calcutt's report. Lord Wakeham, who chaired the Cabinet committee dealing with press legislation, was reported as 'angry that civil servants missed an opportunity to smooth over press relations'.[27]

Whether Pressbof at that point could actually guarantee tabloid willingness is a matter of conjecture. Possibly the Heritage people had well-founded doubts on that score. As things turned out it was advantageous for the industry to be able to demonstrate rejected virtue. But that was a long way off; and Calcutt was immediately at hand, assiduously assembling his evidence. At its August and September meetings the Commission chewed over what it should say to Sir David. McGregor planned to send a questionnaire

---

*The PCC contracted Research Surveys of Great Britain to produce a 'Survey of Public Attitudes' which found 'a great need for more and for better publicity'. PCC Paper No. 198, Commission Papers, October–November 1992. PCC, Chatham/219. See p. 371, fn. 26.

to all editors. What steps were they taking to familiarize their journalists and readers with the Code? The Commission pored over its draft submission.[28] Industry bodies earnestly pleaded their cause to Sir David. The Guild of British Newspaper Editors put it to him that he should not give 'undue weight' to the merits or otherwise of the grievances of five or six public figures. It was tough going. Nisbet-Smith recalled that giving evidence to Calcutt was like 'talking to a death's head'. Grahame Thomson told his Pressbof board that Calcutt regarded his 1990 report as 'holy writ and each departure from it is a heresy'. 'We had not', Thomson reported, 'expected to be grilled on the differences, paragraph by paragraph, between the Codes.'[29]

Industry submissions to Calcutt were, naturally, for the most part supportive of the PCC. The one major exception was that of the National Union of Journalists. 'The NUJ does not believe that the Press Complaints Commission has been a success.' In terms of providing redress for complainants 'it is by its own statistics less effective than the Press Council'. The NUJ found it 'unsatisfactory' that the PCC 'has not taken on the role of enquiring into and defending press freedom, that it apparently will not consider so many third-party complaints, and that its membership is dominated at present by present and past publishing executives'. The NUJ further submitted that it had 'little confidence that self-regulation can work', and advised that 'a new body may be required which would not be dominated by people responsible for unfair coverage in the first place'.[30] The NUJ was no longer the power it had been; but elements of its critique were now shared at large, and in particular were part of the Liberal Democrat party submission. While rejecting statutory regulation and privacy legislation, the Liberal Democrats urged that lay membership be made the majority on the Commission, that the industry members be more representative, and that proprietors take a more active role, within a wider shake-up of laws relating to the press.[31]

The superiority of the old Press Council to the new Press Complaints Commission featured also in the submission made by former Council figures, including Sir (as he now was) Louis Blom-Cooper and Kenneth Morgan. They rebuked the PCC for failing to install the telephone hotline, for refusing third-party complaints, for neglecting to initiate general inquiries into press coverage; but above all for renouncing the wider role of representing a 'more general interest of society in the behaviour of the Press'. In a personal submission Blom-Cooper advocated legislation allowing people other than those on the public payroll to take civil court action on having their privacy invaded. Sir Louis maintained that there was 'a right to be left alone'; and investigative journalism would simply have to take its chances.[32]

The Commission itself submitted what Melinda Whittstock in *The Times* described as a 'spirited defence of self-regulation'. It claimed that in the past eighteen months it had demonstrated 'the potentiality of self-regulation to protect people against the power of the press and the press against the power of the government'. (How impressed would Calcutt be by 'potentiality'?) It was no function of the press, submitted McGregor, 'to protect public figures from the consequences of their behaviour'. Citing statistics that revealed little evidence of any serious criticism from readers, the PCC drew attention to the low number of complaints about intrusion on privacy and harassment. 'In a powerful attack the PCC said it would be impossible to reconcile an individual's right to privacy with an individual's right to be informed.'[33] In the second part of its submission later in October the Commission argued that people welcome self-regulatory bodies because they are free, fast and without a 'legal ambience'. Its testimony did not lack candour. Freedom to act responsibly implied freedom to behave in ways which some might consider irresponsible; 'such behaviour by the Press is part of the price that a free society has to pay for liberty of expression'. A democratic press 'will never be a nice Press. This truth is inescapable, though to many unpleasing.'[34]

To all of this, as the Commission later complained, Sir David gave what seemed perfunctory attention. During his review of the performance of the PCC undertaken in 1992, McGregor accused,

> Sir David neglected to collect evidence of how it worked or what it had achieved. Indeed, he rejected the facilities we offered for putting his officials in our office to test our methods of enforcing the industry's self-regulating code of practice, and he agreed only reluctantly to meet members of the commission. In the event he declined to discuss their activities and restricted his conversation with them to the weather.[35]

(Brian Hitchen recalled that the 'eyeball to eyeball' buffet luncheon at Salisbury Square was the same day that the Waleses announced their - separation.[36])

It was resentment at what he perceived as Calcutt's air of hostile aloofness that prompted McGregor to write him 'a note that I promised as a summary of my oral evidence about what passed between Charles Anson, Sir Robert Fellowes and myself in respect of press reporting on the state of the marriage of the Prince and Princess of Wales'. That note McGregor addressed to Calcutt on 11 December. It was to prove the PCC's most effective way of sabotaging Calcutt's machine.[37]

4

As Sir David Calcutt assembled his evidence, Clive Soley's Freedom and Responsibility of the Press Bill made its prosperous way towards being granted a second reading on 23 October. Press self-regulation took on a beleaguered image. It was 'pointless for any of us to deny', editorialized the *British Journalism Review*, 'that self-regulation has not been a marked success'.[38] There were even internal problems with the PCC machinery. Beginnings of what proved to be a serious illness cramped Patsy Chapman's running of the Code Committee. McGregor reported the problems to Frank Rogers amid the preparations to confront Calcutt. McGregor and Pickering told Chapman that she would have to soldier on to see Calcutt out. Mark Bolland came to her aid with a draft statement for the Committee presentable to Calcutt.

McGregor's 'fierce defence' of self-regulation at a conference on media regulation reflected the sense of the press with its back to the wall. The dread vision was that of the statutory tribunal outlined in Calcutt's original report, with its 'formidable battery of powers'. McGregor pleaded the morally superior cause of voluntary self-regulation as against externally imposed disciplinary and privacy legislation. Newspapers had not had long enough to prove they could regulate themselves. 'You cannot hope to transform the habits of a whole industry within 18 months.' The extent to which the Code of Practice had been accepted by tabloid editors had 'already been quite remarkable'.[39]

The one kindly light amid the encircling gloom was Peter Brooke's pronouncement in his speech at the Conservative party conference in Brighton in October. He pledged that on press freedom he would consider 'calmly and deeply'. All the issues would be carefully examined when he received Calcutt's report. He would not be influenced by 'hysterical calls for censorship'. It must be remembered 'that in a democracy a free press is a crucial foundation of all our freedoms'.[40] Here one can almost hear echoes of Lord Deedes and Max Hastings's old Conservative sage. On the other hand, many Tory MPs, as the *Press Gazette* gathered, believed the government had missed an opportunity to crack down on press intrusion after Calcutt's first report by not enacting the recommended legislation on placing surveillance devices, taking photographs and recording on private property without the owner's consent. One solution favoured by MPs was to introduce a new trespass law which would cover all three kinds of intrusion. 'That would stamp out the worst abuses, like bursting into the hospital bedroom of Gorden Kaye, bugging David Mellor's telephone or crawling through undergrowth to get pictures of Fergie having her toes sucked', as one Tory MP put it.[41]

This would make an attractive political agenda. It might well chime in with Calcutt's new recommendations. If so, Brooke might be hard put to stem the parliamentary flow. A conceivable way to stem it could come from Brooke's resisting pressures in the Commons by politely blackmailing Pressbof and the Code Committee into pre-empting legislation by incorporating the trespass and surveillance proposals in an amended Code of Practice. There were voices in the industry who warned that to outlaw modern technological tools like tape and camera would seriously handicap genuine investigative journalism. Brooke might sound solid enough, but 'in this age of political U-turns only an ingenue would yet heave a sigh of relief', said the deputy editor of the *News of the World*, Paul Connew.[42]

Certainly, at the back end of 1992, the pre-Calcutt Phase 2 report period, there was no lack of reasons for the newspaper industry's forebodings. Two parliamentary committees, one on Soley's Freedom and Responsibility Bill, the other a National Heritage select committee chaired by the Labour MP Gerald Kaufman, were taking evidence on press misbehaviour. 'Their two reports', warned Sheila Gunn for *The Times*, 'and the anger among some MPs at the coverage of the royal family will put pressure on Sir David Calcutt QC to recommend statutory legislation in his review of the press.'[43] McGregor, Patsy Chapman and Peter Preston appeared before the National Heritage committee to put the PCC's case – to little avail. Alan Travis reported in the *Guardian* Kaufman's declaring that 'nothing he had heard convinced him of the Commission's effectiveness'.[44]

A series of seminars hosted by law firms in association with *The Times* offered little cheer to the industry. John Rubinstein's account reported a debate on privacy legislation involving Blom-Cooper, Lord Williams of Mostyn, Richard Shepherd MP and Simon Jenkins: 'The press is not in the Last Chance Saloon. It is in the doghouse.'[45] The same conclusion could be drawn from discussion in later seminars on curbing press abuse, including schemes for legal arbitration as well as privacy law. Lord Bonham-Carter urged a scheme to give 'muscle' to the PCC by requiring newspapers to lodge a bond annually with it, to be forfeited in case of misconduct.

'Public pressure for the newspaper industry to set up machinery to compensate victims of press misconduct or inaccuracy', Frances Gibb reported in *The Times,* 'is growing in the build-up to Sir David Calcutt's second report in the new year on press self-regulation.' Without action from the industry, 'pressure for legislation to curb invasions of privacy in the aftermath of the "Dianagate" and David Mellor affairs may prove irresistible'. The press, after all, was not adamantly as one on the issue. The *Independent* as well as the *Guardian* inclined favourably to some measure. 'Even more curiously', as the *Press Gazette* pointed out, 'the *Sunday Telegraph* and the *Observer* have argued both for and against.'[46] Even Simon Jenkins declared himself 'strongly critical of the PCC: this has not worked as envisaged by Calcutt'. It had failed to react appropriately to public exhortations about recent breaches of the Code; it had not set up a hotline; it did not entertain complaints from third parties.[47]

The announcement of the formal separation of the Prince and Princess of Wales added an extra intensity to the atmosphere in Parliament of 'common loathing towards the tabloid newspapers whose "invasions" of palace privacy had allegedly precipitated a crisis'.[48] This loathing manifested itself notably on the Soley and Kaufman committees, where opinion unforgivingly held that the newspapers were largely responsible for undermining the royal marriage. Michael Shea, former press secretary to the Queen, in a series for *The Times* on 'The palace, the press and the people', asked: 'When are people going to stand up and say: "Enough"?' The PCC remained 'emasculated, wringing their hands in the wings. We await Calcutt.'[49]

The industry, awaiting Calcutt, defended itself. The *Press Gazette* organized a 'What the editors say' splash, giving them an opportunity to support the Commission. Bridget Rowe of the *Sunday Mirror* offered a hint of more tactical industry thinking: 'If Calcutt considers that there are specific examples of journalistic behaviour which could still be regarded as unjustified, then they could be taken into consideration with a view to modifying the Code of Practice by which we all live.'[50]

Andreas Whittam Smith's approach was to point to the weakness of the government's position in relation to the press. Since the summer ministers had been on the defensive following the ERM debacle, the backbench rebellion over Maastricht, the furore over pit closures and the controversy over the Matrix Churchill case about illegal arms exports to Iraq. After the Matrix Churchill scandal, 'they don't have the moral standing to tell the press how to behave'. There was no question, Whittam Smith was clear, 'that the tabloid press frightened the government out of proceeding with a Privacy Bill. Major's earliest retreat was over that.' It left the press 'in control of the field as far as current affairs are concerned'. Together with Whittam Smith's insistence that press standards had improved since the introduction of the Code, and with both the PCC's statistics and his own post bag showing that the public was not vastly distressed by press behaviour, government weakness vis-à-vis the press would neutralize both Soley and Calcutt.

That was the confident view of things which the *Press Gazette* asserted at the end of 1992.

> At the beginning of last year the politicians were making all the running. By saying often enough that the public was deeply concerned about the Press, it almost became true. At the end of [this] year, that situation has begun to be reversed.
>
> Clive Soley's Bill is beginning to look doomed but there is still Calcutt to worry about. For a moment there, however, it wasn't the Press in the Last Chance Saloon so much as the truth, and Calcutt would do well to balance the importance of shackling the Press, which time and time again has been proved right on stories about which it has been most severely criticized, against the benefits of weeding out the occasional transgression.[51]

But those in the PCC and Pressbof who were allowed the privilege of a preview of Calcutt's draft report with a view to correcting inaccuracies did not emerge quite so nonchalantly. McGregor and Bolland appeared for the Commission; Roche and Thomson for Pressbof. 'We were all appalled', reported Thomson, 'by the surrounding observations which were highly critical and unbalanced.' Very little of the PCC's evidence had been considered. Two chapters were 'so pejoratively selective' that 'we would not be making any comments'.[52]

5

Calcutt Phase 2 appeared in January 1993. Sir David's *Review of Press Self-regulation* was delivered to Brooke at the National Heritage department on 8 January and was in the public domain the following day, leaked to the PCC by a mole possibly in the department itself. For his literary epigraph Sir David chose an extract from the American essayist Brooks Atkinson's *Once around the Sun* (1951): 'The evil that men do lives on the front pages of greedy newspapers, but the good is oft interred apathetically inside.' Evil, greed and apathy were apt keynotes for his assessment of the newspaper industry's performance in self-regulation since 1 January 1991.

> The Press Complaints Commission is not, in my view, an effective regulator of the press. It has not been set up in a way, and is not operating a code of practice, which enables it to command not only press but also public confidence. It does not, in my view, hold the balance fairly between the press and the individual. It is not the truly independent body which it should be. As constituted, it is, in essence, a body set up by the industry, and operating a code of practice devised by the industry and which is over-favourable to the industry.[53]

Sir David recommended as a remedy the constitution of a statutory Press Tribunal as set out in his Privacy Committee's report of 1990, and as supplemented in his present review. The dread vision had come to be.

CHAPTER SIX

Calcutt strikes again – and misses: January–November 1993

'The government accepts that the Press Complaints Commission, as at present constituted, is not an effective regulator of the press. It is not truly independent and its procedures are deficient. Sir David's detailed analysis of these shortcomings is compelling. We also recognize the strength of the case . . . for a statutory tribunal with wide-ranging powers. At the same time, we are conscious that action to make that body statutory would be a step of some constitutional significance, departing from the traditional approach to press regulation in this country.'

Peter Brooke MP, Secretary of State for National Heritage, House of Commons, 14 January 1993

'Journalism is a rough old trade, and long may it continue to be so.'

Gerald Kaufman MP, House of Commons, 10 June 1993

Great was the lamentation and wringing of hands in the industry as the dread vision of Calcutt disclosed itself. Well-sourced leaks in the *Guardian* and the *Independent* had accurately predicted 'dire reprisals for the press'. Calcutt had indeed gone solo – almost certainly his initial great mistake. Had he consulted former colleagues, he might have hit nearer the bullseye of acceptability by the government.

Calcutt cited six instances upon which he founded his verdict of the PCC's failure and its necessary demise: the *Sport*'s contempt when it refused to publish an adjudication; the *People*'s contempt in the Princess Eugenie case; the PCC's handling of the Morton serialization affair; and its feebleness in the Ashdown, Bottomley and Mellor scandals.

The Press Complaints Tribunal as prefigured in 1990 would be presided over by a judge or senior lawyer appointed by the Lord Chancellor. He would sit with two lay assessors drawn from a panel appointed by the Heritage secretary. Its duties would be to draw up and review a code of practice; to restrain publication of material in breach of the code; to receive complaints (including third-party complaints) of alleged breaches of the ode; to inquire into those complaints; to initiate its own investigations in the absence of a complaint; to require a response to its inquiries; to attempt conciliation; to hold hearings; to rule on alleged breaches of the code; to give guidance; to warn; to require the printing of apologies, corrections and replies; to enforce publication of its adjudications; to award compensation; to impose fines; to award costs; to review its own procedures; to publish reports; and to require the press to carry, at reasonable intervals, an advertisement to be specified by the tribunal indicating to its readers how complaints to the tribunal could be made.

Legal representation would be permitted, with a right of appeal; but the waiver against recourse to the courts would be reintroduced, as the 1990 report envisaged. The 1990 recommendation for three new criminal offences for press intrusion was re-recommended; with, additionally, a civil tort of infringement on privacy. Calcutt recommended further that the Data Protection Act of 1984 be amended in relation to misrepresentation or intrusion, and that legal restrictions be imposed on press reporting relating to minors and the interception of telecommunications.

All this was designed, Calcutt insisted, 'to make a positive contribution to the development of the highest standards of journalism, to enable the press to operate freely and responsibly, and to give it the backing which it needed, in a fiercely competitive market, to resist the wildest excesses'. It was not designed to suppress free speech or to stultify investigative journalism.[1]

Outraged protests from the industry predictably poured forth. Editors declared their 'total opposition'. Kelvin MacKenzie of the *Sun*: 'We're not going to have some clapped-out judge and two busybodies deciding what goes into our paper.' Lord Rees-Mogg warned that the state would use any extension of its power for unsavoury ends. Sir Frank Rogers of the Newspaper Publishers Association lamented a return to state regulation which had last existed in 1695. For the Newspaper Society David Newell denounced a regime more draconian than that applied to the broadcast media, calculated to enhance the power of the state and weaken the rights of citizens. The privacy laws, grumbled others, would prove a 'villains' charter'. Lord McGregor vehemently rejected the allegation that the PCC had failed as a self-regulatory body. 'If the Calcutt recommendations on the press are as they have been reported,' he announced, 'I am terrified – terrified because I grew up in a democracy and I wish to carry on living in one.'[2] A satirical piece by Brian MacArthur made the point that Calcutt would have had the editors who reported the royal marriage debacle fired; yet they were accurate. What then?[3]

This was precisely the point McGregor, in his own way, seized upon. In his 'note' to Calcutt on 11 December,[4] a few days after the announcement of the separation of the Prince and Princess, he gave an account of his interviews with Mackay and Wakeham and one of the Prime Minister's private secretaries in the aftermath of his abortive statement of 8 June. McGregor then disclosed: 'I told ministers that, if the Commission were criticized for a failure to deal effectively with the reporting by the press of the publication of Mr Morton's book and related matters, I should be prepared to issue a public statement containing a narrative of events.'[5]

Calcutt's treatment of the PCC – described by the *Daily Telegraph* as 'savagely critical' – certainly constituted such an incitement. McGregor was clearly outraged that Calcutt – 'a lawyer', as he witheringly termed him in his Andersen lecture, 'whose dislike of the press is matched only by his distrust of self-regulation' – had ignored the redeeming implications of his narrative for the Commission. What McGregor narrated was the story of how he had liaised with the Palace early in 1991, how he had persuaded himself to believe the Palace rather than Lord Rothermere, how he planned the announcement of what he thought was a careful and well-timed, if a little emotional, rebuke to the press at the crisis of the Morton serialization, of how sickening awareness came upon him that both the Palace and the Commission had been deceived by the Princess, how he had related these matters to senior ministers, how the Queen's private secretary had apologized to him and had offered his resignation, and how the PCC had been stranded high and dry, an object of mockery by its own industry – an industry which, for all the public abuse heaped upon it, had done its job well.

As it happened, McGregor had no need to issue his narrative of events. His note included in Calcutt was indeed the prime reason why a PCC mole – who could it have been? – leaked the report before its publication. Victimhood was the readiest antidote to savage criticism. It served the interests also of people at the Heritage department who feared that a 'turning' by John Major in Calcutt's direction could lead to a 'battle royal with the press'.[6] This fear was reciprocated at the Downing Street Policy Unit, with which the PCC by now was on usefully intimate terms. The scoop was handed to the *Sunday Telegraph*. Frank Rogers, who engineered the affair, did the rounds on Saturday night to alert the other Sundays. Brian Hitchen was also in on it. It was, as Mark Bolland recalls, 'wonderful drama'.[7]

With David Hencke to the fore, the *Guardian* was the first daily off the mark and published the leaked document in full on 12 January,

followed immediately by all the other papers, to general public astonish-
ment. They seized immediately on the implications of McGregor's story
compromising Calcutt's position. The *Times*'s media team took the point
the next day: the leak had 'effectively killed the prospect of statutory
control of the press'. McGregor announced his regret at the publication in
advance of the report 'of a small part of the evidence the Commission had
submitted to him'; and his regret particularly at Calcutt's including
McGregor's account of his conversation with Lord Rothermere, which he
had requested be omitted. Yet for all that, when being interviewed about
his 'sadness' at the Princess's 'mockery' of his attempts to protect her
against the tabloids, McGregor 'expressed quiet satisfaction over the
damaging impact the leaking of his letter to Sir David Calcutt had on the
campaign to muzzle the press'.[8]

2

Several developments took shape amid that 'damaging impact' on the
prospects for statutory regulation of the press. One consequence of
McGregor's revelations was a backlash against Diana for her manipulative-
ness. Her image 'as an innocent victim of the media', as George Jones
reported for the *Daily Telegraph*, had been 'badly dented'. McGregor added
the consideration that the Prince was entirely absolved of any suspicions
that he had been a party to briefing the press about his marriage, and held
that the Princess 'had in practice been invading her own privacy'.[9] This was
a doctrine which in due time would come to figure largely in the PCC's
interpretative repertoire.[10]

Certainly Calcutt was well upstaged long before official (and hurried)
publication on 14 January. A cartoon by Brookes in *The Times* the day before
depicted Diana pulling a rug from under Sir David. All this could only be
encouraging to Patsy Chapman and the Code Committee. They were
planning to get in ahead of Calcutt by amending the Code to cover
clandestine bugging devices and interception of telephone calls.[11] This,
after all, had been on the agenda ever since the fallout over the Mellor
scandal and the rejected initiative to strike a deal with the Heritage department the previous October. There was, as it happened, extra topical
immediacy in the matter. A Murdoch magazine in Australia had published
a full transcript of a bugged intimate conversation between the Prince of
Wales and Camilla Parker Bowles. Both the *Mirror* and the *Sun* followed up
with edited extracts. The industry was fortunate in the circumstance that

its, and the Prince's, guilt in 'Camillagate' was somewhat offset by the Princess's innocence now being at a discount.

Then there was the impact that Calcutt's draconian heavy-handedness had on other critics of self-regulation. Both Soley and Kaufman found Calcutt indigestible; too concerned, in Kaufman's words, to protect the privacy of public figures 'in the palaces of Westminster or Buckingham'. Geoffrey Robertson held, as ever, that the industry had only itself to blame for the 'inevitable conclusion' by Calcutt that self-regulation had failed. 'The industry has for many years sought to fob off demands for a privacy law by financing portentous voluntary bodies – the Press Council, and then the Press Complaints Commission – which are little more than confidence tricks that have failed to inspire confidence.' Yet Calcutt, argued Robertson, compounded the problem rather than remedying it. 'The press cannot be improved by state-appointed censors.' Calcutt's proposed tribunal and his criminalizing of press intrusion were equally misconceived. 'Privacy will not be protected by sending journalists to jail, and press freedom will not be safe in the hands of a government-appointed tribunal issuing on-the-spot injunctions and directing publication of insincere apologies.' Having thus demolished Calcutt, and being once more of immense service to the newspaper industry's system of self-regulation in spite of himself, Robertson could only envisage hopefully a 'new settlement between the press and the public' coming out of political debate on Calcutt, leavened by awareness of the need to enact the European Convention on Human Rights to which, since its inception, Britain had been a signatory.[12]

If dissension among critics of press self-regulation was now exposed by Calcutt's impact, dissension among ministers was not less likely to obtain. Amid reports that MPs on all sides were recoiling from 'vengeful endorsement' of the Calcutt proposals, there was speculation about splits in the Cabinet over the government's next move. There was embarrassment at McGregor's disclosures about the extent of awareness among leading politicians as to what was afoot. Both Kenneth Baker and Gus O'Donnell denied they had been briefed by McGregor in December 1991 as relayed by McGregor. But there was no doubt that Mackay and Wakeham, the chairman of the Cabinet home affairs committee, had been alerted by McGregor in June 1992. However, when asked in the Commons when he was first apprised of the contents of McGregor's note to Calcutt, Major replied: 'when it first appeared in the national press'. Kenneth Clarke, the Home Secretary, made the same reply.[13]

On 13 January, Major chaired a two-hour Cabinet to consider how to handle Calcutt. It was, after all, very strong medicine. The 'signals from Downing Street', according to Michael White of the *Guardian*, were that 'although some ministers, including Mr Major, have privately expressed considerable irritation with press conduct, there is widespread caution about the known pitfalls of press censorship'.[14] Philip Johnston's report for the *Daily Telegraph* was that 'ministers were said to be unanimous in their opposition to a statutory tribunal', but they were thought to favour some kind of privacy legislation.[15]

No doubt the words of one 'top Fleet Street executive' in June 1992 about the Tory party's owing a debt that might have to be called in remained applicable to the case. So did the words of Lord Deedes in the Lords on 1 July 1992, and those of the 'old Conservative sage' (assuming him to be other than Deedes) reported by Max Hastings on 13 July.[16] Clive Soley alleged that newspaper editors were deliberately firing 'warning shots across the bows' of the Cabinet. There had been, he was sure, 'evidence for some time that newspapers at a senior level were going to go "nuclear" on the government if they went down the Calcutt road or supported my bill'.[17]

The ultimate fortunes of the Soley Bill and the forthcoming report of Kaufman's National Heritage committee gave ministers plausible markers in the middle future to delay making risky decisions. Opinion at the *Daily Telegraph* was that the Princess's complicity in the Morton book made it hard for the government to use the royal family as a 'stalking horse for legislation against the press'. So did the disclosure that the Queen's private secretary apologized to the PCC for misleading it over the Princess's involvement.[18] Major was known to loathe the press generally and the tabloids in particular, but consensus in the industry was that he would back away from state regulation but take up the privacy issue and insist on the industry's stiffening the Code of Practice.

In Cabinet the difference was split accordingly between Calcutt's and the industry's definitions of press freedom. Peter Brooke announced in the Commons on 14 January that the government accepted that the PCC 'as at present constituted' was not an effective regulator of the press. It was not truly independent and its procedures were deficient. Sir David's detailed analysis of those shortcomings was compelling. Ministers also recognized the strength of his case for a statutory tribunal. 'At the same time we are conscious that action to make that body statutory would be a step of some constitutional significance, departing from the traditional

approach to press regulation in this country.' The government wa
tant so to do. A more persuasive case would need to be made
coming to a final view the government would want to take into account the
debate on the private member's Bill brought in by Mr Soley. Ministers
would also take into account the report of the inquiry into privacy and
media intrusion which the National Heritage select committee had set in
train. As far as the PCC was concerned, it followed that the government
would expect 'reform' in respect of its independence from the industry and
improvement in its procedures.[19]

Thus press self-regulation, having been let free by Calcutt in 1990 in 'one
final chance to demonstrate that it can put its house in order', now in 1993
escaped, in its disorderly house, his condemnatory clutches. But the
industry would have to pay the price of this second emancipation. That
price would be stiff. The pressures from now on would be more onerous
and intense than they had been in the second half of 1990. Then the industry had been largely left to its own devices. Now it would have the government breathing down its neck. There were limits to the credit the industry
could call on from its account with the Tory party. As Sir Frank Rogers put
it on behalf of the NPA, 'modifications to the self-regulatory system will
be the subject of dialogue with the Government'.[20]

3

In the matter of amending the Code of Practice, things were already far
advanced. The Code Committee's plans to get in ahead of Calcutt
were being circulated to the five industry bodies contributing to Pressbof.
There were consultations between Pressbof, the Code Committee and the
PCC. The Commission set up its own review of Calcutt.[21] A meeting of
twenty-one editors and senior newspaper staff representing every national
newspaper – a gathering hailed in the House of Commons as 'historic'[22] –
met on 22 January under the auspices of the NPA to pronounce ritual
anathemas on Calcutt. Its more urgent purpose was to endorse proposed
changes to the Code to provide safeguards against eavesdropping and
bugging, and to endorse arrangements for a lay majority on the PCC to
underline its independence from the industry.[23]

The lay majority decision was very much an industry management move,
via Pressbof, to placate government. It was not liked, and never has been
liked, by editors and journalists. As Roy Greenslade pointed out, there was
a déjà vu effect: shades of the old Press Council. Editors decried the move

as a 'terrible mistake'. 'Only professionals', protested Stewart Steven, now editor of the London *Evening Standard*, 'know what is what and why certain things happen.'[24] This was but the first instalment of the stiff price being paid by the industry for self-regulation's emancipation.

Pressbof itself promptly issued its own counterblast to Calcutt: *The Press Responds: Strengthening Self-regulation*. Harry Roche drew attention to the fact that the PCC had been established with an editorial majority in compliance with Calcutt's original recommendation. It had nonetheless operated with entire independence. But now, to meet any misconceptions as to that independence, the Commission's membership would be altered to assure a lay majority consisting of eight non-press members, seven editors, and an independent chairman. To meet further misconceptions, Roche also drew attention to the fact that the Commission had always given itself discretionary power, in appropriate circumstances, to accept third-party complaints and to hold oral hearings. Membership of the Appointments Commission which appoints the Commission's members would be increased from three to five. Three of these would be independent members who, along with the chairman of the PCC, would thus be in a clear majority. The Pressbof chairman would in fact be the only industry member on the Appointments Commission.[25]

In the matter of the Code of Practice, Roche conceded that while it was an essential element of self-regulation that the industry should be responsible for it, it was essential that the Code had the confidence of the public. 'For this reason, in future, the Commission itself will be asked to ratify the Code and any subsequent changes to it. A procedure has been introduced to resolve any potential differences as to the content which may arise between the PCC and the industry.' (The arrangement was that the Commission could accept or reject proposed amendments or additions to the Code, but not negotiate about them. A right of negotiation was later conceded.[26]) Changes covering the use of bugging devices and long-range cameras, and dealing with the long-running problem of 'jigsaw' identification of unnamed children, had been agreed. A new clause covering definition of public interest was also under examination. These would be promulgated together, after ratification by the PCC.

The PCC, Pressbof disclosed, was also to get extra funding to speed up its procedures and to set up its own telephone helpline to provide a new service to members of the public seeking to contact the PCC for assistance where they feared the Code had been breached or was about to be breached. 'The helpline will provide instant basic information about the publication or news agency concerned and give the name, address, telephone and fax numbers of the relevant editor so that the complainant may be speedily put in touch.' This was a half-way gesture on the issue of the hotline so often urged on the PCC. Roche's unspoken point was that prior restraint was not to be a feature of the helpline facility.

Patsy Chapman's Code Committee approved and adopted changes in the Code dealing with secret bugging devices and eavesdropping on telephone calls. Chapman announced that they would also consider a further amendment to control intrusive photography.[27]

Pressbof's *Press Responds* was a retort to Kaufman's National Heritage select committee, whose dismissive report came out on 25 March, as well as to Calcutt. The PCC's submission was given as short a shrift by Kaufman as by Calcutt. The two most significant testimonies otherwise submitted to the select committee were those of Calcutt himself, and a storming performance by the *Sun*'s roustabout editor, Kelvin MacKenzie. Calcutt urged that newspapers be given no more 'last chances'; the 'newspaper industry's bluff had to be called'. Were the government to go down the route it had indicated, Calcutt protested, 'I fear we are in danger of having an even weaker Press Complaints Commission because they will have no sanction worth the name'.[28] MacKenzie teased and mocked the committee on privacy ('Shall I tell you that if we had US privacy laws we could publish the name of every single MP named in the Lindi St Clare file? – every one of their alleged sexual peccadillos and you couldn't claim one penny. So all this is nonsense about wanting US privacy laws – you guys must be mad.'). His most telling evidence was his defence of the PCC and the Code; and the tenor of his submission, behind the bravura, was almost apologetic. 'I think it would be fair to say that the spotlight is upon us in a way which would make it foolhardy to do anything which would attract more opprobrium than already exists.' MacKenzie revealed that at the *Sun* the Code of Practice was 'part of the handbook and part of the contract'. 'We have tried very hard – very, very, very hard – to make sure we stick within this code. . . . If you made a fundamental error which I thought was against the spirit of the code, you'd just be fired straight out.'[29]

It was indeed noteworthy that the populist editor of the most notorious tabloid should have asserted that the industry's Code was included in contracts of employment. For this very issue was at the head of an agenda of 'other steps' that Roche and Pressbof had in mind, following the Calcutt and National Heritage reports, to raise as matters requiring action or clarification for industry response. It was also held to be of significance that MacKenzie was shortly afterwards moved up in the Murdoch empire and replaced at the *Sun* by Stuart Higgins.

All this activity would no doubt be very helpful to the industry when it returned accounts of progress made to Brooke at National Heritage at the end of March. A problem was that, among the 'series of nods, winks and smoke signals' by which Brooke was telling the industry what he wanted it to tell him, was his desire that a system of sanctions – fines or compensation – should be imposed on contumacious newspapers. The industry was bound to resist this as unworkable. Another difficulty was Brooke's heavy hints that 'a new PCC chairman more acceptable to the Government than Lord McGregor' be provided. John Major had made it clear to certain editors that he believed McGregor had 'gone native'. The industry, for all its bad memories of last summer, was by no means yet prepared for so drastic a recourse. And there were indications that Brooke might turn awkward on the hotline issue. 'The question is', as the *Press Gazette* put it, 'to what degree is Peter Brooke asking for more than he would settle for, and how is the report of the Heritage Committee hearings at the end of the month likely to influence his views?' Brooke was known to be quite taken with the committee's notions about a super-ombudsman. Industry bodies were talking earnestly. 'We are beginning to get a clear idea of what is being asked of us', Dugal Nisbet-Smith of the NS announced, rather nervously.[30]

Among the things Brooke clearly asked for at the Newspaper Press Fund occasion was a code of practice to match Calcutt's original 1990 model. Brooke drew invidious attention to eleven areas in which the industry's Code had departed from Calcutt's rigorous text. He waved sticks but he also proffered carrots. The National Heritage committee report offered him plenty of sticks. It rejected Calcutt but proposed in Calcutt's place a complicated hybrid scheme of state ombudsman and voluntary press commission, both armed with stringent powers to fine and enforce corrections and right of reply, together with a privacy law. Ministers found this mix rather too much of a big stick; and the PCC thus gained an area of doubt among its enemies and a slight edge of advantage in its negotiations with Brooke.

No doubt McGregor would have widened that edge of advantage had he managed successfully to raise the Commission's profile in his attempt to exploit the 'Camillagate' tape scandal. Even before the tape was published, the Palace had pressed McGregor for 'a much harder approach to the general question of intrusion on privacy'. The Commission, having received ten letters from complaining third parties, invited the Prince and Mrs Parker Bowles to participate in an inquiry into the publication of the tape of their telephone conversation. The Prince declined the offer, suggesting instead that the Commission conduct its own investigation into the wider issues of news reports based on bugging and other forms of intrusion. Mark Bolland explained that before the Commission made a decision to investigate possible breaches of privacy 'we need to find out if the individuals involved are prepared to co-operate. In cases involving personal matters, people have a right to silence if they do not want the matter investigated.'[31] With the Palace as well as the government looking over his shoulder McGregor felt he could hardly leave the matter there. At the Commission's regular monthly meeting on 27 January, publication of the tape was deplored. The question of whether to proceed with an inquiry as a matter of public interest was debated. In the end, after a four-hour meeting which also included its formal rebuttal of Calcutt, the Commission restricted itself to calling for legislation to clarify the law on bugging.[32]

4

The image of hand-wringing ineffectiveness projected itself once more. Cartoonists mocked the PCC's rejected pleadings. Editors concerned defied the 'Camillagate rap'. At the annual *What the Papers Say* awards on 19 February, McGregor went out of his way to redress matters by excoriating Calcutt and boasting – perhaps in deliberate defiance of Major – that he had 'gone native over the liberty of the press'.[33] By this time it had become publicly observable that within the frame of the government's finding nothing in Calcutt, Soley or Kaufman's Heritage committee with which to replace the PCC, and therefore being forced back on to the alternative of making the PCC something rather different from 'as at present constituted', the question of its leadership became increasingly a matter of speculation. Brooke had put the point to the industry chiefs. Roger Gale, an MP and a member of the NUJ, put the point in the Commons, as 'members of the press ordered the last drinks in the last chance saloon', that a revamped Press Complaints Commission, under a new chairman and with many more lay members, might eventually prove to be the way forward.[34]

Then Stephen Castle, political correspondent of the *Independent on Sunday*, reported flatly that McGregor was to 'step down at the end of the year as the newspaper industry attempts to salvage self-regulation'.

The Press Standards Board of Finance . . . has made it clear that Lord McGregor's contract, which ends in December, will not be renewed. Although his record has not been criticised by members of the funding body, which met last week, the Labour peer's position is regarded as politically untenable and a successor is being sought. . . . The issue may be discussed this week when the board meets Peter Brooke. . . . It requested the meeting to outline some of the changes it proposes for the commission in response to the Calcutt inquiry.[35]

Castle suggested that the front-runner replacement was Sir Gordon Borrie, former director-general of Fair Trading and chairman of Labour's commission on social justice: 'someone with a proven record as a regulator and [who] has fewer links with the press than Lord McGregor'. Lord Colnbrook, one of the original Commission members, was another prospective candidate, said Castle.

The source of Castle's information was his own editor, Ian Jack, a member of the Code Committee, where, presumably, McGregor's future was a matter of speculation. 'So why', inquired a diary note, 'Coded practices', in *The Times*, 'after just four months, is Ian Jack, editor of the *Independent on Sunday*, resigning from the Code Committee . . . ? Could Jack's resignation have anything to do with a story in the *IoS* earlier this month which suggested that the position of Lord McGregor . . . has become politically untenable and that he would be replaced at the end of the year?' Indeed it did. Harry Roche, incensed at the gross indiscretion, wrote pungently to the *Independent on Sunday* stating that Pressbof was not looking for a successor to Lord McGregor, whom they did not regard as 'politically untenable'. The letter was published, as Jack admitted, in truncated form. 'A lively private correspondence between the two men duly followed', as the *Times*'s diarist recorded. 'Jack duly resigned. Don't you just love self-regulation?'[36]

It was a curious circumstance that the day after the Stephen Castle piece in the *Independent on Sunday*, there was a splash by David Hencke in the *Guardian*, for many years Roche's professional perch. This disclosed that in October 1992 the PCC along with Pressbof observers had offered National Heritage a ban on illegal bugging, trespass and intrusive photographs; an offer rejected by the department.[37] This splash was as timely for McGregor as it was embarrassing for ministers. And McGregor now had, if fortuitously, Roche's formal public backing; which almost made being the object of invidious public comment worthwhile. Still, that invidiousness never quite evaporated; and it persisted in the surmise that Jack and

Castle might well have saved McGregor's skin. At the PCC there was a feeling, in any case, that McGregor lacked the energy to move on decisively. Possibly this marked the early symptoms of the serious illness which would see him in hospital for a major operation at the end of 1993.

However that may have been, there were other, bigger players on the field. Roche and his Pressbof directors met Secretary of State Brooke with his Under-Secretary Hayden Phillips and four other Heritage civil servants on March 9. The Pressbof board offered ten proposed improvements in the self-regulatory mechanism. Grahame Thomson noted gnomically: 'These were received placidly. There was no confrontation. The questions which were asked were significant and the questions which were not asked possibly more so,'[38] Heritage was not going to cause waves.

Then there was another big player, Lord Rothermere. He had lately been very active and prominent as a defender of the industry from the evils of Calcutt, Soley, Kaufman and the excessive manipulation of Brooke. But he had not, it may reasonably be deduced, much admired McGregor's handling of the Morton serialization crisis. The sharpness of his correction of McGregor on a matter of interpretation of McGregor's subsequent 'narrative of events' attests to a somewhat unsympathetically impatient attitude on Rothermere's part to the beleaguered PCC chairman.[39]

Rothermere at this time was also party to the most consequential new appointment to the self-regulatory apparatus other than McGregor and Bolland themselves. If the Code Committee had recently been the scene of Pressbof chiefs slapping down editorial gossips, it was also now the scene of Patsy Chapman's withdrawal. She was under too severe strain and needed release.[40] The emerging replacement was Rothermere's star editor, Sir David English. Having made his brilliant reputation as the saviour and reviver of the *Daily Mail*, English became also chairman and editor-in-chief of Associated Newspapers. There were two sides to English's fame in the industry. On the one hand he was the 'artful dodger'; on the other he was the only man in the industry comparable for force and influence with Rupert Murdoch.[41]

Rothermere saw English, it can be surmised, doing for self-regulation what he had done for the *Daily Mail*. With McGregor seemingly tottery, and Bolland hard pressed to keep the PCC show on the road, English would come in to provide the necessary dynamism and stiffening. The Code Committee chairman was ex officio a member of the Commission: English would thus have two bases of operation. Though somewhat tainted in the eyes of many by his chequebook journalism in the Yorkshire

Ripper affair, English suffered no rebuff from Pressbof; and his appointment was made public on 23 March.

Over the next few months English settled in to get to grips with the
reworked Code of Practice. There was the backlog of the ambitious
Pressbof *Press Responds* agenda to deal with. In May new self-imposed rules
for self-regulation were announced in the matters of journalists identifying
themselves in relation to public interest guidelines about subterfuge. There
were to be restrictions on the use of long-range cameras and with 'jigsaw'
identifications of young victims of sex offences. These were presented to
the public with a flourish at a press conference by English and Peter
Preston of the *Guardian*. There would be refinements of the provision
relating to harassment. The new lay majority, now in place, meant the
unwilling departure from the Commission of David Chipp. Pickering also
ceased to be a member of the Commission but his presence was retained
as a non-voting consultant. The public helpline service was duly launched
by the PCC. In this climate of amenability McGregor had 'helpful and
encouraging' conversation with Hayden Phillips of the Heritage department on the 'unworkability of the schemes emerging from the Heritage
select committee'.[42] Within the Commission, however, the amenities were
sometimes wanting. There were furious wrangles among the editorial
members over the *Daily Mirror*'s serialization of bugged tape conversations
of Charles and Diana published in James Whitaker's *Diana v Charles*,
reminiscent of the 1992 Morton episode. Lady Olga Maitland claimed in
the House of Commons to have been given 'vivid descriptions of almost
farcical behind-the-scenes scrapping at the PCC'. Meetings, she informed
the House, 'now last for four or five hours, with editors wrangling and
discussing complaints'. She assured the House that Sir David English,
known to her of old since her days at the *Express*, was 'as tough as hell,
which is just as well given his present role as chairman of the PCC's Code
of Practice committee'.[43]

Lady Olga offered these remarks in defence of self-regulation and the
PCC to the debate on 10 June on the report of the Heritage select
committee on privacy and media intrusion. Though the debate was
voluminous and lively, the report, like the Calcutt report, was for the most
part already effectively sidelined. John Major, speaking a month earlier at
the AGM lunch of the Newspaper Society, gave 'as broad a hint as possible
before publication of the post-Calcutt White Paper that the Government
will back the process of self-regulation in the press'. He pledged not to 'do
violence to freedom of speech in this country'. He welcomed the recent

PCC measures to strengthen self-regulation, but warned: 'We will keep a particularly close eye on how effectively and widely the new measures are implemented.' Under questioning, Major made clear that while he rejected Calcutt's prescription for statutory press regulation, he accepted his recommendation for privacy legislation.[44]

This left Brooke, winding up the debate in the Commons on 10 June, with little to say beyond undertaking that the government's response to the Heritage committee's report would 'take into account the totality of the industry's response' to its recommendations as well as to those of Calcutt. Which question he immediately begged by adding: 'The important fact is that the press has responded to the public concern evidenced in pluralist ways.'[45]

The one feature of the Heritage committee report that did take on life despite industry deprecation, however, was its recommendation of a statutory ombudsman appointed by the Lord Chancellor to oversee the press self-regulatory process, with powers to fine and award compensation. To the industry in general and the PCC in particular this looked like governmental regulation, if not by the back door, then by a side window. To Brooke it was a way of mollifying disgruntled backbenchers who resented the newspaper industry's evading yet again healthy statutory discipline. Government whips had made sure Soley's Bill was talked to death. A gesture was expedient. Brooke made a point of the ombudsman scheme at the Conservative party conference in October, like tossing a bone to growling dogs. McGregor, with full industry support, threatened to resign if Brooke tried to bolt an ombudsman on to the existing mechanism. Brooke tried to mollify the industry on the other side by arguing that it 'could be achieved by investing the Press Complaints Commission or some part of it with an ombudsman's powers'.[46] The PCC would have to find a way of neutralizing this persistent initiative.

5

Pressbof's *Second Annual Report, 1992–1993*, produced on 23 August, reflected a mood in the industry of guarded optimism about the general shape of things. The worst threats to press self-regulation embodied in Calcutt, Kaufman and Soley had been baffled. The privacy legislation question was dormant for the present, awaiting the government's White Paper – which might well be a long way off. Reforms to the Code had been set in place. 'The last year has seen the PCC fully recognised as an independent complaints authority.' Lord McGregor's initial three-year appointment as an independent chairman was to end on 31 December; and Roche expressed himself 'very pleased that he has accepted our invitation to continue as chairman for a further year'. Of routine issues, the problem of harassment or 'doorstopping' continued to be an 'area of adverse public perception'. In such situations 'there will, of course, be radio and television crews alongside the press journalists and photographers. The Code Committee is in dialogue with radio and television authorities seeking a common approach to the problem.' The momentum of self-regulation would best be maintained by the industry's acknowledging its commitment to the Code and to the authority of the PCC at regular intervals, and by ensuring that copies of the Code were issued to all editorial staff and, wherever possible, referred to in contracts of employment.

One element in the dialogue between Pressbof, the Commission and the Code Committee in the wake of the Calcutt and Heritage reports was the question of equipping the Commission with what were conventionally termed 'teeth'. Their absence was the point of focus uniting all the critics of self-regulation. If the teeth recommended by Calcutt or Kaufman or, for that matter, Soley were anathema to the industry, and if notions of industry-funded fines or compensation were equally deplored as invidious and divisive, what else? If it came to tabloids, both English and Pickering had direct lines to Rothermere and Murdoch respectively. Here perhaps might be a way forward. The idea, after all, was not new. It had been one of Blom-Cooper's more offensive demands on the industry in 1990 that 'in appropriate, serious cases where the Council itself rather than a complaints committee adjudicates against the conduct of an editor, it should invite the proprietor or publisher to recall the commitment he has given to uphold the Council's principles, and ask what he intends to do about the conduct of his paper in the future'.[47]

That proprietors were the last resort in saving the industry from itself was an old cry, redolent of despair.[48] The times now were not exactly times of despair, but they were not exactly times of good hope either. The idea of getting proprietors to agree to form a kind of strategic reserve in the rear of the self-regulatory lines seemed in the circumstances of 1993 to have a future.

The idea of incorporating the Code into journalists' handbooks and contracts of employment also seemed to have a future. The council of the regional Newspaper Society had already given a lead in this direction. Its head of employment affairs, Sandy Park, had written to regional chief executives that 'adherence to the code of practice' was 'a key component in demonstrating to the Government and the public at large that the present self-regulatory system is working'. The Society 'strongly recommends that you consider incorporating a clause requiring adherence to the code into the employment contracts of all your editors and journalists'.[49] A possible problem here would be the NUJ, which had had its own code of conduct since 1936. There was of course the issue of ensuring that any changes in conditions of employment be introduced by consent. As things turned out, this was not a difficulty.[50] But also there was the larger question of the NUJ's position in relation to the Pressbof-funded self-regulatory system in general. The NUJ had not forgiven Calcutt for abolishing the Press Council and replacing it with the Press Complaints Commission; until, that is, they rejoiced at his urging that the PCC be abolished and replaced by statutory arrangements. The NUJ had testified keenly to all relevant inquiries against the self-regulatory status quo and the PCC.

The one thing that survived the death of Soley's Freedom and Responsibility of the Press Bill was PressWise, a version of a victim-support body to promote understanding of the press, and to advise, guide and sustain those who found themselves at the sharp end of inaccuracy and harassment. It was initiated by Mike Jempson, NUJ activist, former Labour party press officer, and Soley's press adviser. PressWise initially saw itself as a kind of counter-PCC, independent of a proprietor-dominated industry as embodied in Pressbof, and also able to offer advocacy on behalf of complainants. In due course there would develop a cautiously co-operative relationship with the PCC. PressWise would prepare complainants for the PCC; and the PCC would send complainants who needed preparation to PressWise.[51]*

If Harry Roche's Pressbof was the private, in-house face of the industry's self-regulatory apparatus, David English now emerged as its smiling public-relations face and master of ceremonies in the arts of displaying skills whereby the industry so well defended itself. A smooth operator, English was the perfect antidote to McGregor's professorial manner. 'The Commission', McGregor advised, 'should take immediate action to correct the Whitehall policy, exemplified by the Lord Chancellor's Paper, of ignoring the existence and achievements of the PCC.'[52] English was the man custom-designed for this task.

---

*Based in Bristol, PressWise, a not-for-profit limited liability company, published in 1995, updated in 1996, *Press Complaints Commission: History and Procedural Reform.*

In these months McGregor had relatively little to do with problematic or landmark cases. The Commission refused to entertain complaints from Merseyside politicians about press comment on the Jamie Bulger killing. It wisely declined demands from thousands of indignant Michael Jackson fans that the PCC investigate press treatment of allegations of child sex abuse against their hero. McGregor warned newspapers that any payment to two women freed from a Bangkok jail after convictions for heroin smuggling would be in breach of Clause 9 of the Code. The problem here was, as the *Press Gazette* pointed out, that while newspapers could not buy stories from criminals, others could: 'book publishers, film producers, TV producers, and, for all we know, T-shirt manufacturers'.[53]

The salient case in point of payments to criminals for their stories that came before the PCC at this time was *Hello!* magazine's financial arrangements with Darius Guppy, the jailed insurance fraudster, and his wife. The Commission's adjudication in this instance of third-party complaint (almost inevitable in such cases) took on an instant reputation as the 'PCC's toughest ever'. '*Hello!* gets hammered!' was the *Press Gazette*'s headline.[54] The magazine committed its greatest crime against the Code, perhaps, not so much in its chequebook journalism as in its chequebook journalism's being so politically untimely. 'Newspaper editors were understood', Jon Slattery reported, 'to be furious about the Guppy interview appearing at a time when the Government is looking at ways to regulate the press, and the general condemnation at Westminster of cheque-book journalism.' What was a matter of more consequence ultimately was that in a rider to that adjudication the Commission found that the magazine's behaviour was 'so contrary to the requirements of the Code that this breach of Clause 9 will be taken up with the publishers'.[55]*

In October 1993, however, the big question for press self-regulation seemed to be not the chequebook issue so much as what preparations needed to be set in place in anticipation of the looming government White Paper, which would reveal to the industry what measures to protect the right of personal privacy were going to be imposed on it. There was the recent affair of the Director of Public Prosecutions, Sir Allan Green, being exposed by the *Mirror* for cruising prostitutes in King's Cross. As with the Mellor case, Max Hastings expostulated in the *Telegraph* about careers wantonly destroyed. A strategy seminar in London comprising senior editorial staff from broadcasting and national and local press considered a pre-emptive strike against

---

* See boxed adjudication, pp. 133–4.

the government. Arranged by the Association of British Editors, the Guild of British Newspaper Editors and the International Press Institute, with Mark Bolland of the PCC in attendance, the seminar was advised by ABE chairman James Bishop that the government was having problems getting its White Paper together. A programme was agreed to 'scoop the politicians' by producing a counter 'White Paper' in defence of self-regulation.[56] A prominent ex-journalist who did concede the need for legislation to protect individual privacy, Sir Bernard Ingham, Margaret Thatcher's former press secretary, called on the government to stop agonizing about its White Paper. At the annual dinner of the Institute of Journalists at Leeds, Ingham urged ministers to consign Calcutt to the dustbin, leave matters of taste to the market, and 'conclude by giving the press a ringing endorsement'.[57]

Within a few days all such innocent preoccupations were overtaken by a crisis that almost blew self-regulation apart.

Report No. 20, August–September 1993
Hello!

COMPLAINT

Ms Marika Huins, of Compayne Gardens, London NW6, complains about a feature in the 5 June 1993 edition of Hello! magazine which interviewed Darius Guppy, currently serving a prison sentence for fraud, and his wife. The complainant said that Hello! magazine is known to pay large sums of money to those it interviews and the complaint is raised under Clause 9 of the Code of Practice.

ADJUDICATION

The magazine said that 'no payment was made in connection with this feature which breached Clause 9'. The Commission sought confirmation from Hello! that this reply was not evasive. The Commission made repeated attempts by telephone and writing to obtain an answer from the magazine.

Three months later, Hello! apologised for the delay which they said was due to changes of staff and to absences on holiday. A new editor told the Commission that payment had been made partly to the agency from whom the feature had been purchased and partly to a relative of Mr and Mrs Guppy nominated by the agency. The editor said the magazine had not understood that Clause 9 would cover 'someone who had been convicted and imprisoned and thus had ceased his criminal activities' and apologised if they had breached the Code. In the Commission's view, this affected misunderstanding of the plain language of Clause 9 amounted to a calculated flouting of the rule observed by all other publications.

The magazine's delay in responding to the Commission and its initial evasiveness when it did are so contrary to the requirements of the Code that this breach of Clause 9 will be taken up with the publishers of Hello!

The complaint is upheld.

CHAPTER SEVEN

'MGN has thrown a hand-grenade at us': the Princess Diana gym photos affair, November–December 1993

'The dubious honour of being the arch-buffoon went to Lord McGregor.'

Daily Mirror, 8 November 1993

'This has been a bad business but the whole of the press has stuck together and I do believe we have strengthened the PCC. It may seem hard to see that at the moment, but we have made the *Mirror*, after tremendous defiance and contempt, climb down and recognise the authority of the PCC. That means they are on-line now and won't step out of line again.'

Sir David English, *UK Press Gazette*, 15 November 1993

The primal elements in the affair were two. The first was that at various times in April and May 1993, the owner of the L.A. Fitness Club in Isleworth, west London, where the Princess of Wales kept fit, one Bruce Taylor from New Zealand, smitten by the beauty of Diana and by the prospect of making money, fixed a hidden camera in the ceiling of the gym and captured several images of the Princess at exercise. Rumours about the existence of these photographs had the Princess's security, the police, and the Princess's personal trainer at the gym on the alert over the next few months.

The second element was that in May 1993 sales of the two most popular tabloids, the *Sun* and the *Daily Mirror* – 'no fiercer battle in Fleet Street' – were slumping in the depressed post-ERM times.[1] The *Sun* was scraping the barrel with a 'royal scoop' of an alleged transcript of an argument between the Prince and Princess of Wales. At the *Mirror* there were fond memories of the 'Thanks a million, Fergie' scoop of a year before but the present reality was slashings and sackings by the Mirror Group Newspapers' chief executive, David Montgomery.

Enter the egregious Taylor with his precious cache. The *Sunday Express* claimed virtuously to have refused them. The *News of the World* turned them down. The mood at Murdoch's News International empire was one of rather chastened caution. That had very much been the theme of Kelvin MacKenzie's testimony to the National Heritage committee: being in the spotlight and not wanting to do anything that would incur more opprobrium than already existed.[2] The White Paper, after all, was thought to be looming. Nor would the industry welcome being embarrassed by a gross indiscretion of privacy intrusion at such a delicate juncture. And News International journalists, as MacKenzie had disclosed, were already having the Code incorporated into their contracts.

The *Mirror* was not so chastened. And it was trailing the *Sun*. And it had got away with the 'Fergie pix'. Still, there were long and cautious editorial conferences at MGN. The pictures were indeed sensational; everything the *Sunday Mirror* and the *Daily Mirror* was to say about them was true: 'delightful, charming and radiant pictures of the most famous, the most photographed woman in the world'.[3] The Princess actually smiled in most of them, for all the world as if she were posing. That was what most struck Charles Wilson, MGN's managing director.[4] And of course – this was very material to MGN's defence on the issue of privacy – she was arguably not in a private place; she was in the middle of a busy gymnasium. Wilson questioned the *Sunday Mirror*'s editor Colin Myler closely about the legality of their origins and how they had arrived at the paper. What Wilson did not realize, and was not informed of, was that the cameras had been hidden.[5]

The *Mirror*'s editor, David Banks, took up the story.

The photographs, neither distasteful nor offensive but flattering and beautiful, were taken some months ago, without collusion or inducement from Mirror Group Newspapers, by the owner of a gymnasium which anyone may join. They were taken using a hidden camera. They were taken without the consent or knowledge of the Princess.

Our Code of conduct prevents intrusion into an individual's private life without his or her consent, including the use of long-lens photography to take pictures of people on private property.

It goes on to define private property, as it affects this case, as 'any private residence . . . garden or outbuildings, in addition, hotel bedrooms (but not other areas in a hotel) . . .'.

In my submission, a long lens is the moral (or otherwise) equivalent of the hidden camera, normally rendering its operator invisible to the quarry; a gymnasium which anyone may join and which, in the course of her membership the Princess shared with thousands of assorted members of the general public, can never be classed as a private place; the Princess, in using equipment on view to the outside world through several windows and in the company of so many Kens and Barbies, can never have regarded the exercise room as her private domain.

Odious indeed may have been the role of the man who activated the lens shutter, but. . . .

No one now appears to doubt the independent prior existence of these photographs. They were shown to at least one other newspaper. They were always going to appear somewhere, if not in Britain then abroad . . . but they came to the *Mirror*. . . . They came, we saw, we published, and were damned.[6]

The MGN managers came to two conclusions: juridically, a plausible case could be made out that the Code would not be breached in the matter of privacy, and that in any case there was a 'public interest' defence about the laxity of the Princess's security; pragmatically, that if MGN did not publish, someone else would. Possibly the fact that the parliamentary session had ended on 5 November was a material consideration. Only David Montgomery could make the final decision. The 'canny Ulsterman' had no high respect for McGregor and his Commission, and was certainly willing to take another Fergie run across its bow. He was widely credited for clinching a £100,000 deal for the gym photos.[7] But there is the possibility that in the end it was his eager editors who persuaded Montgomery into the venture.

Thus it was that on 7 November the *Sunday Mirror* loosed on the world 'the most amazing pictures you'll ever see', splashed in colour across pages 2, 3, 12, 13 and the centrefold, of the 'People's Princess' in a variety of fetching gymnastical attitudes. Colin Myler was quite clear that his 'Di Spy Sensation' would 'spark a new Royalty storm'. But he and his *Mirror* colleague Banks seem genuinely to have been taken aback by the fury of the storm they conjured. Reports that the Princess was considering legal action to secure an injunction to restrain further publication – 'Diana Puts Boot In'[8] – seem 'to have caused shock'. Myler was deeply apologetic on 14 November for having misread her likely response to pictures that were intended as a loving tribute. An MGN spokesman insisted that the pictures were 'harmless and charming and taken in a public place'. It was not expected that they would cause the Princess distress, but since they apparently had done so the *Mirror* would make no further use of them without adequate notice.[9]

Enter Lord McGregor. He had seen the *Sunday Mirror*'s spread that day. His telephone never stopped ringing. The media pack scrummaged. What he should have announced was something along the lines of there being on the face of it question of press intrusion on privacy to consider which the

Commission would be called together promptly to investigate, even were there no complaint; and that the MGN people must expect to be interrogated rather severely on their interpretation of the Code of Practice; but that meantime there must be no prejudging the case.

What he did, however, was to storm out in front of the media gaggle and fulminate in 'his angriest public outburst since the *Sunday Times* serialised extracts from Andrew Morton's biography of the Princess of Wales', that publication of the photographs 'was in flagrant breach of the letter and the spirit of the newspaper industry's code of practice', and that this breach 'constitutes dishonourable conduct for which there can be no excuse'. He also invited advertisers to show their displeasure at the *Mirror*'s 'unethical and outrageous behaviour'. He dismissed the paper's security defence as the 'most hypocritical justification for a breach of the code I have ever heard from an editor'. Remembering the recriminations after the Morton affair, McGregor described this as a 'personal statement'. The Commission, he added, would adjudicate shortly. Anticipating what might appear in the *Daily Mirror* on the following day, McGregor further added: 'I shall expect the Mirror Group to avoid any further publication of these improperly obtained photographs.'[10] In the course of this furious harangue McGregor waved the *Sunday Mirror* in front of the eager press and TV photographers, thus ensuring maximum diffusion of its offence.

News International applauded this ban on the *Sunday Mirror* as an outlaw. Andrew Knight declared unctuously that 'all editors feel outraged by this flagrant breach of privacy. There is no possible excuse.' The broadsheets registered fear and loathing. Peter Brooke, on BBC Radio 4's *The World at One*, spoke more in sorrow than in anger. It was a sorry blow to self-regulation, a very nasty jolt to everybody. 'It makes it that amount more likely that legislation will come forward.'[11] Downing Street deplored the *Mirror* intrusion, saying that 'it brought into sharp focus the powers of the Press Complaints Commission to regulate'. Mo Mowlam, Labour's shadow National Heritage minister, announced that statutory controls were more likely now that the press had begun to 'break ranks over self-regulation'. McGregor's call for an advertising boycott was understood to be endorsed by several companies.[12]

2

Whatever executives at MGN may have thought of the plausibility and viability of their case on the Code and public interest, McGregor's astonishing condemnation without trial let the company off the hook. That it was a personal statement counted for nothing. That it included incitement to an advertising boycott counted for everything: it was so totally out of order. It placed MGN in a position of commanding tactical advantage. MGN immediately unleashed Banks to fill the *Mirror* the following morning with the harmless and charming images, and a front-page headline, 'We love Di!' Banks had some invective for people not loved. 'Led by Lord McGregor of the Press Complaints Commission, who was being egged on by our jealous rivals, a rag-bag of MPs rushed to spew out indignation on radio and TV. Rarely has there been such an extraordinary display of hypocritical opportunism.' It was ludicrous to talk about privacy invasion – 'there is more privacy on a polo field'. Once the photos were taken it was 'absurd to pretend they would never be seen by the public'. The public-interest defence was real, MGN insisted. What of the IRA? What was witnessed yesterday, Banks concluded, 'was the British establishment in full pompous flight'; and the 'dubious honour of being the arch-buffoon went to Lord McGregor'.[13]

At this point, on all previous form, Sir David English should have stepped forward and uttered a call to order. It was English, after all, who in the Morton serialization case had pointed to McGregor's pronouncing judgment without trial.[14] The extraordinary thing is that he uttered only a half-call to order. First he echoed McGregor: 'Publication of these photographs is a flagrant breach of the Code. The attempt at justification is monumentally hypocritical.' Then he talked proper procedure: 'The Commission must have an urgent meeting to see if the *Mirror*'s defence is sustainable. If not, it must condemn it and all its executives in the strongest language.'[15]

Why this half-cocked equivocation? Doubtless Sir David did not wish to challenge or embarrass Lord McGregor. Also, it can be assumed, events had caught him off-balance. He was now self-regulation's accredited ambassador to Whitehall. On 8 November the *Press Gazette* reported his speech at the Guild of British Newspaper Editors' gala dinner. Speaking as the industry's man in the corridors of power, Sir David reassured the Guild that the government's White Paper on the press might be further delayed and in any case would not contain threats to self-regulation. 'All that I've heard is that we aren't going to have a compulsory ombudsman or massive fines.' Sir David believed that 'wiser heads in the Government had prevailed' and removed much of the menace. 'I just feel that these threats are going to disappear by the time that White Paper turns up.' One of the reasons it had been held up was that the 'wiser heads have decided that self-regulation should be given time to demonstrate it is working'. The PCC, he declared, was 'now respected by editors and was "light years" away from the Press Council, which we held in contempt'. Most of the attacks on the press, whether by Calcutt or by people on the Heritage committee, were based on the excesses of newspapers that 'none of us in this room would really consider newspapers. I am talking about the *Sunday* and *Daily* [*sic*] *Sport* and papers like that. Everybody is in danger because of what they do. It is incredibly important that we get this over to MPs. It is absurd that they don't actually understand, or choose not to understand, the difference between the working press and the publications owned by Sullivan.'[16]

Almost every word in that speech had become, in the circumstances of 8 November, heavily loaded with dramatic irony. English had been about as comprehensively contradicted by events as it was possible to be. It was stunningly disconcerting. One Commission member was reported as groaning, 'the timing is a disaster. MGN has thrown a hand grenade at us.' And McGregor had, unbelievably, replicated his Morton serialization gaffe. Why? No doubt partly because the timing was so compelling. McGregor had the politicians not just looking over his shoulder but breathing down his neck. There was the argument that when push came to shove for press self-regulation, the political priority was imperative. Then on top of that was McGregor's notoriously choleric humour. Words like 'rumbustious', 'bluff manner', 'robust defender', 'immense energies' were much in the air among the commentators. So also was the rider 'but many editors fear he may soon be a spent force'.[17] *Private Eye* had its own rumbustious interpretation of the episode. It protested that 'someone ought to complain to the PCC about the astonishingly smooth ride given by the media to the irascible chairman'.

> McGregor was ennobled by the late Labour Government, but his weakness is aristocracy, and especially royalty, whom he adores. The strongest influence in his life is Lady Elizabeth Cavendish, for 40 years a lady in waiting to Princess Margaret, who worked with him for ten years in the Advertising Standards Authority and moved with him to the PCC (along with many others).
>
> Any humiliation of royalty sends McGregor into paroxysm of righteous indignation, which explains his two recent outbursts in which he ignored his colleagues, his regulations and procedures by flouncing into the media and spouting his rage.[18]

The 'private-eyeness' of *Private Eye* always requires a certain discounting; but here it was cutting pretty close to McGregor's bone.

There were reports that the Princess might take the 'unusual step' of making a formal complaint to the PCC, something only one member of the royal family, the Duke of York, had so far done. Charles Anson, the Palace press secretary, discussed the matter with McGregor; the Commission later denied that it had invited a complaint. The Princess in fact opted for an injunction from the courts and then sued for damages. The Commission was to meet in emergency session on Wednesday 10 November. One 'senior commissioner' put it about that 'the Mirror Group is in danger of becoming the pariah of the newspaper world'.[19] The Mirror Group took him at his word. David Banks announced on BBC radio that MGN would dispense with the Commission's services and go it alone.

On 9 November the *Daily Mirror* issued a manifesto. Noting that the 'motley crew' of the Commission were to meet next day, the *Mirror* asserted the simple principle of justice, that an accused is not to be found guilty without fair trial. 'We believe our case is unanswerable.' But it could not be put because of the machinations of the *Mirror*'s commercial rivals. 'Their tool is the hapless Lord McGregor, seen and heard spluttering his outrage yesterday at every opportunity.' Self-regulation had been turned into a farce, an 'unfair, unrepresentative charade that has been used to pillory us'. The Press Complaints Commission had 'lost all credibility under Lord McGregor's chairmanship'; and accordingly Mirror Group Newspapers, which included the *People* as well as the two *Mirrors*, withdrew 'with sorrow' from the self-regulatory system under the Commission's supervision.[20]

If publishing the Diana pictures was a hand-grenade thrown at the Commission, this was a nuclear torpedo. Though Banks was the herald of repudiation, the MGN decision seemed to have David Montgomery's hallmark stamped on it. He represented faithfully the MGN tradition of distrust of the PCC as serving Murdoch's manipulative interests. The notion of McGregor as a hapless tool of MGN's rivals was pure Montgomeryese. In any case, in the situation MGN was in, attack was much the best form of defence. The *Sun* immediately accused Montgomery of 'slipping a noose around the neck of the press'. Roy Greenslade, a former *Mirror* editor, judged that the whole business, photographs and all, reeked of Montgomery – 'it does not reek of Banks or Myler. Neither has the power to put things in the other's paper: they are run as totally different entities.'[21]

For a major national newspaper group, affiliated to Pressbof through the NPA, to withdraw its presence (and its money) immediately put the future of the PCC in particular and the industry's system of self-regulation in general into high jeopardy. 'Princess to sue Mirror group as press complaints body totters', blazoned the *Guardian*. Peter Preston: 'I do not see how it is possible to operate a system of self-regulation without one of the major groups taking part.' David English: 'If self-regulation is to work everyone has to accept it. If the *Mirror* doesn't come back, it seems to me the Government will have to put something all-embracing over all of us, so we will all be chained because of the Mirror's lack of responsibility.'[22] Sir David Calcutt understandably had some pertinent comments to offer on BBC Radio 4 on the *Daily Mail*'s [*sic*] attitude of total contempt (one tabloid, at a certain distance, being much like another). The 'arch-buffoon' insult to McGregor intrigued him. 'One wonders what future there is for self-regulation if that is the way they treat their own Press Complaints Commission. If the PCC is now to be treated in this way by an important, significant journal, you then have a real problem, as I see it, for self-regulation.'[23]

Quite. Even before the MGN torpedo, McGregor's chairmanship was in a seriously wounded condition. The advertising boycott indiscretion mightily annoyed the industry and Pressbof. After a foray by McGregor gesticulating to the media from the doorstep of No. 1 Salisbury Square, Mark Bolland said to a group of journalists in McGregor's office: 'Humpty Dumpty has just fallen off the wall.' Could all Pressbof's horses and Pressbof's men patch him together again? For if they could not, self-regulation was sunk. Robin Young reported in *The Times* that the withdrawal of the Mirror Group 'appears to threaten a shootout' at the 'last chance saloon'.[24] Simon Jenkins thought it all a terrible pity: John Major and most of his colleagues 'have been searching for excuses not to legislate against the press'. This was 'partly because they are scared of the newspapers, partly because they know that privacy makes a dreadful law'.[25] But unless MGN could be got back on board, a press law there would be, like it or not.

3

What chances of pulling MGN back on board? There was the small print in the MGN manifesto. MGN would of course adhere, as it always had done, to the Code of Practice, which in any case it insisted it had not breached in the Diana photos affair. It withdrew from the self-regulatory apparatus 'with sorrow'. 'There may come a time', the MGN statement allowed, when the PCC 'behaves with the decency and dignity which newspaper readers deserve. Until then, the *Mirror* can have no part.' English, chairman of the Code Committee, had used the words 'come back'. Given that the torpedoed McGregor was beached on his beam-ends, it was clearly up to English to take on the role of mediator and smoother of ruffled feathers. Harry Roche and the Pressbof people would naturally have every interest in helping reconciliation: the whole point of their existence depended upon it.

The man with most leverage in the background was Sir Edward Pickering, consultant for the Commission. As executive vice-chairman of Times Newspapers he was Rupert Murdoch's man in the corridors of Wapping. He it was who alerted Murdoch to the serious implications of the crisis. If self-regulation was not patched together again, a great hole would be left where the public standing of the newspaper industry in the UK used to be. The government would have no choice but to fill it. There was no question of any new version of press self-regulation on the models of 1953 or 1990. It would be statutory regulation on the models of Calcutt, Soley, Kaufman or whatever. Probably a mixture of all three; or perhaps something along the lines of a comprehensive broadcasting and press media regulatory regime.

David English conducted the negotiations. 'I spent many hours talking to Rupert', he told the *Press Gazette*, 'who told me, "I agree we need to get them together".' McGregor was 'happy to have me as intermediary and so was the PCC'. Jean Morgan reported for the *Gazette* how for 48 hours the lines between Kensington and Holborn Circus were rarely silent as English grappled telephonically with Montgomery. 'There was no easy rapprochement, say sources. It took a call from News International boss Rupert Murdoch in the USA to persuade Montgomery to call English ... and even then it appears that bringing MGN back on board the Commission was an uphill task.'[26]

One problem, as English defined it, was that David Montgomery 'did not appreciate how much the climate of opinion about the press had changed and how important it was that the code be obeyed'. 'I think he has seen that now, and will see that his journalists and his staff will carry on with it.' In turn, Montgomery made no secret of the fact that he deeply distrusted David English. The other part of that problem was that Montgomery was being cajoled on the part of the owner of the *Sun* and the *News of the World*, MGN's deadly rivals. The essence of English's negotiations was to turn that great impediment to advantage. As *bona fides* he had the fact, after all, that News International had turned down the Diana photographs. 'It was important,' English recounted, 'that Montgomery and the *Mirror* apologise to McGregor on a personal basis because we on the

PCC respect McGregor so very much. Eventually I did persuade David Montgomery that it would be in everyone's interest if the *Mirror* were to make a decent and gracious apology. And that was the breakthrough.'

English also outlined what he would be telling Peter Brooke at National Heritage. 'This has been a bad business but the whole of the press has stuck together and I do believe we have strengthened the PCC. It may seem hard to see that at the moment, but we have made the *Mirror*, after tremendous defiance and contempt, climb down and recognise the authority of the PCC. That means they are on-line now and won't step out of line again.'[27]

Andrew Culf's report for the *Guardian* set out the terms of the reconciliation. The Mirror Group rejoined the PCC 'and gave the kiss of life' to the system of self-regulation. 'In an agreed statement MGN said: "We now withdraw any criticism that we have made of the PCC and apologise to the chairman for any remarks he may have found offensive."' McGregor in turn withdrew his remarks urging advertisers to boycott the *Mirror*. This 'proved enough to secure the agreement'. MGN had wanted him to urge rival newspapers to abandon their criticism, but settled instead for his comment that he trusted 'all newspapers will create an unprejudiced environment in which future complaints will be heard fairly'.

For its own part MGN announced: 'Following conversations with other publishers, MGN believes editors will now accept this advice to desist from attacks based on obtaining commercial advantage, or on vindictiveness. It is now recognised that a newspaper should be condemned and punished only after a hearing is concluded and a complaint upheld.'

In a brief statement after its meeting on 10 November, the Commission welcomed the return of the Mirror Group to its fold. In fact, as Jean Morgan reported, the Commission was 'bewildered at the time it took to get a response from Mirror Group which they expected at 4.10 p.m.; it finally came at 6 p.m.'. There could, in any case, be no adjudication on the issue while court proceedings were under way; which, in the fraught circumstances, was just as well for the PCC. Peter Preston, one of the editorial members of the Commission, declared that it was 'a good meeting and we have made some positive progress. The task now for everyone is to move on.' David English, credited by common consent as the architect of the double apology, stressed that 'Mirror Group editors and journalists will be obliged to stick to the code of conduct which the industry has hammered out.' That Code prohibited the taking and publishing 'of anyone's picture on private property without their permission'. The whole industry recognized that this kind of invasion into personal privacy could not be tolerated.[28]

4

In the aftermath there was recrimination among the Mirror Group journalists. The majority of those to whom the *Press Gazette* spoke felt that publication of the 'spy in the ceiling' picture of Diana was a mistake. 'More particularly, they felt their company had handled badly the ensuing outcry from politicians, some of the public (since sales of both the *Sunday Mirror* and the *Daily Mirror* were up by 100,000 copies, not all could have been outraged), and the Press Complaints Commission.' If McGregor was an 'arch-buffoon', as one of the Group's senior journalists said, 'there was buffoonery on this side too', mainly from Banks. MGN's 'huffy' withdrawal from the PCC also came under criticism. 'If they thought what they had done was justifiable, they should have stood up and said so. It was crass foolishness to have left the PCC because there was some criticism.'

> There was strong feeling that it was one man, chief executive David Montgomery, who called the shots over publication of the pictures. But Montgomery was quoted in Thursday's *Daily Mail* as saying: 'I am not the editor of the newspaper. There is a fine line in some of these decisions and people from time to time get these decisions wrong or they misjudge the reaction to them.'[29]

In any event it was Montgomery who had ultimately to accept responsibility. But the MGN managers could well justify their 'huffy' withdrawal from the PCC on the grounds of its chairman inciting an advertising boycott. This had astounded many commentators. Simon Jenkins admonished: 'such backstairs pressure on editors, whether through proprietors or advertisers, is not in the PCC's constitution'.[30] David English raised the question with Mark Bolland as to whether, by acting *ultra vires* of the PCC's articles of association, McGregor had rendered his chairmanship invalid. Roy Greenslade was more outspoken about McGregor.

> In spite of the PCC lacking sufficient sanctions to deal with a rogue newspaper group, it was not his place to hand down a sentence of commercial death. To use another legal phrase, he was obviously acting *ultra vires*. So astonishing was his passionate performance that the same piece of 'boycott' footage was used on every news bulletin throughout Monday. But did he honestly think he was helping to pressure *Mirror* to back down and apologise? If so, he was sadly mistaken. He achieved just the reverse – he gave Montgomery the excuse he needed to duck the substantive issue (invasion of privacy) by complaining about the PCC having prejudged the case.

And McGregor's 'boycott' intervention gave Montgomery grounds for withdrawing from the PCC, 'precipitating a crisis for the carefully crafted edifice of self-regulation'. A PCC chairman, Greenslade went on, should act like a diplomat when problems like this arise, 'and not be the cause of the problem'. Nor was this his first such misdemeanour. In the circumstances Greenslade found it 'disheartening that Lord McGregor's contract as PCC chairman was renewed recently'. McGregor's 'contribution to the unfolding of last week's events', Greenslade concluded, 'was so ill-advised I now believe the time has come to consider his future in the post'.[31]

Pressbof now most certainly would have begun thinking along those lines. But there were more immediate problems to see to. What the industry could fairly say to the politicians was that, after all, the fact that one gross indiscretion had almost blown its self-regulatory system apart attested more convincingly then anything else could to the seriousness with which the system was now taken. Politicians generally chose not to take that point. Peter Brooke told the Institute of Public Relations that in the last four days the Press Complaints Commission's voluntary Code had 'clearly failed'. The government, he warned, was still committed to examining the scope for civil and criminal remedies to protect personal privacy. The screw of polite blackmail was given another turn. The press, in effect, was being put on renewed notice that it faced restrictions if it was unable to make the 'quantum leap' needed to transform self-regulation in a way that was 'credible and carries conviction'. As Alexandra Frean reported for *The Times*, Brooke 'implied that the press had not quite drunk their last drink in the "Last Chance Saloon" although they had caused a nasty mess by knocking over the bottle'.[32] Roger Gale, chairman of the Conservative backbench media committee, was less forgiving. 'You cannot have an organisation dropping out of the PCC at will. You cannot have the chairman of a Commission prejudging an issue one day, and indicating that perhaps he was wrong the next, and convince the public that this is anything other than a self-serving organisation designed to meet press interests and not the interests of the public.'[33]

That was all very true; and it was the sort of commentary on the 'bad business' which set off a scramble in the industry to make 'quantum leaps' and jump through hoops and generally to display eager readiness to make self-regulation credible and carry conviction. A meeting of the Commission on 24 November considered the question of a 'Privacy Commissioner'. The feeling was that there existed 'undoubtedly a political need to emphasise the importance that the Commission attached to privacy and establish more defined procedures for dealing with complaints in situations requiring swift and decisive action'. McGregor was unhappily aware that his marginalization was now under way. The meeting 'also took the view that the industry should give further consideration to the possibility of the self-regulatory system having a sanction to be deployed against editors who are responsible for extreme and deliberate breaches of the Code of Practice'.[34] Murdoch's intervention with the MGN chiefs undoubtedly gave decisive impetus to the idea of bringing proprietors and publishers forward on an agreed basis of contention in moments of crisis. McGregor wrote, 'as instructed', to Pressbof seeking views as to 'possible sanctions that might be imposed by the industry upon editors in gross or deliberate breach of the Code'. The chairman conveyed also the Commission's proposal that it might 'avoid the harassments of *Mirror*-type situations by creating a special procedure under the aegis of a new Privacy Commissioner for dealing with privacy cases generally and any other breaches of the Code which may lead to public or political outcry'.[35] In doing so the chairman conveyed a virtual abdication of direct responsibility.

There was also, concomitantly, support for getting all editors to have the industry's Code of Practice written into their contracts, 'meaning their jobs would be at risk if the Code were breached'.[36] Alexandra Frean followed up the issue: the editorial contract measure 'marks the industry's first response to Peter Brooke'.[37] National newspaper editors could be sacked if they break the Code of Practice, headlined the *Press Gazette*, if the Press Complaints Commission wins agreement with proprietors to ensure that the Code is written into contracts.

With McGregor being eased toward the margin, it was English more than ever now who made the running for the PCC: the real beginning of the English-Bolland axis which would keep the Commission steady for the remainder of McGregor's incumbency. It was English who led the way on how a voluntary ombudsman for the press could work and make recommendations to the PCC. This was something Brooke had suggested. '"We certainly can't ignore it", said Sir David.'[38] It was English who set about winning agreement with the proprietors on the contracts issue. Some newspapers, notably those in Murdoch's News International group, had already started to include the Code in journalists' contracts. But it was editors' contracts that really mattered. 'As national papers are usually the offenders in such high-profile breaches of the Code', wrote Sally Weale for the *Guardian*, 'the PCC wants national editors signed up first. Most are

understood to have expressed their support for the move, including MGN.'
A PCC statement announced: 'The newspaper industry is now committed
to the progressive incorporation of the PCC's Code of Practice into the
individual contracts of all journalists and editors.' Peter Preston applauded:
'This is a positive step which will remind all national newspaper editors how
vital the Code is, not just in honour, but in hard practical terms. I think
many will welcome it.' It would also give editors 'some protection against
any pressures from above – commercial pressures – to break the Code'.[39]

In reality, as far as journalists' contracts in general were concerned,
'encoding' was always more of a propaganda point, with which the industry could impress public and politicians, than a practical issue. Given formal
professions of commitment to the Code by publishers and given that
editors' contracts were redrawn to incorporate the Code, the legal position
was that it was 'implied' in journalists' contracts.

It was English also who took the lead in opening negotiations with the
Palace. It would be well to put something in the hole left by the collapse of
the understanding between Fellowes and Anson at the Palace and the
Commission, in the welter of McGregor's *Sunday Times* serialization
debacle. The last time there had been a formal Palace/industry understanding was in 1981 over Diana's pregnancy. One option gaining ground,
Alexandra Frean reported, was for editors 'to meet representatives from
Buckingham Palace to discuss the issue of media intrusion'. Preston, for
the editors, thought that since the Palace was obviously so concerned, such
a move would be 'constructive'. English thought it would in any case be
'cosmetically good'. The first step would be to get editors pinned down
contractually to the Code of Practice. This English would be recommending to the Code Committee. The Palace would then have protection from
'maverick editors' tempted to defy their publishers.[40]

5

Pinning editors contractually to the Code had important implications. It
inserted legalism into what had been a voluntary arrangement. This in turn
raised the premium on the Code's clarity and practicality. Editors were
starting to put this point to English. One of them, John Dale, editor of
Britain's biggest women's weekly, *Take a Break*, pointed out that the privacy
Clause 4 was confused. 'Surely what matters is not whether it is private
property, but whether it is a private view.' As the Code stood, editors would
be forced to run impossible checks on general location shots of streets or

crowd scenes which could include some people on private property. English's advice was that editors would be unable to publish a picture of someone on private property without their permission, even if they were clearly in the public view. Dale responded that this would cover someone mowing their front lawn but visible from a public footpath, or people photographed in the forecourt of Buckingham Palace. 'Do we need the permission of everyone in, say, a wedding reception picture? If ninety-nine agree to publication, would one disagreement prevent it?' Dale called for reconsideration of Clause 4. 'We seem to have become obsessed by this issue of property. There is a danger of over-reacting and being stampeded into self-censorship rather than self-regulation.'[41]

Here was a crucial point on the long trail through the industry's self-regulatory system wherein the Code of Practice was transformed gradually from Patsy Chapman's model of 1990, which placed emphasis on editorially convenient flexibility, to the Wakeham model of 1998, boasted as the 'toughest in Europe'. Comment on the European dimension of the privacy problem in the wake of the Diana gym photos affair made much of the French *droit à l'image*. In France, as Charles Bremner pointed out, those photos would have led to the certain conviction of both photographer and publishers. The Duchess of York and John Bryan had won more than £80,000 from *Paris Match*. It was a matter essentially of celebrities fighting off paparazzi within a culture of decorum and a climate of conformism in which the private lives of politicians and notabilities were accepted as being out of bounds.[42] As the Commission never ceased pointing out, privacy complaints were a very small part of its business; essentially, again, celebrities fighting off paparazzi. The problem was that in Britain any legislation on privacy or any tweaking of the industry's Clause 4 confronted a press culture neither decorous nor conformist.

The whole issue of the Palace, the press, and privacy came to the fore again in December, with the announcement from the office of the Princess of Wales that she intended to withdraw from most of her public duties because of what she regarded as the intolerable intrusions of the media. David English immediately announced that, as the Princess completed her final round of public engagements, 'all of us now feel that there is more than just the privacy of the Princess of Wales at stake'.[43] He announced also that, as chairman of the Code Committee, he was going to keep a close eye on future newspaper stories about Diana; and as chairman of Associated Newspapers, on stories in the *Daily Mail*, the *Mail on Sunday* and the *Evening Standard* in particular. 'If she makes a public statement or public appearance we'll report it, but we won't be using cameras to take photographs of her in her private property or her private life. That's a terrible intrusion', he declared. When royalty were on skiing holidays, English argued, the national press should be given one picture call and then 'we should leave them alone and not chase them across the slopes every minute of every day'. (But reporters and photographers should be at hand 'in case there's a horrendous accident'.) The Code Committee, English emphasized, had 'drawn editors' attention in the past to the fact that they should not buy or use freelance photographs that intrude on someone's privacy'.

> It is the editor's duty to check the provenance of the pictures and, if it breaks the Code, he shouldn't use it. I hope we will cover Princess Diana in the future with a great deal of responsibility and by carefully adhering to the laid-down agreements under the Code. If we stick to that, her privacy won't be intruded upon. In marginal areas it's a matter of common sense and some understanding.[44]

By now there was the question also of Prince Edward and his friend Miss Sophie Rhys-Jones. The Prince asked the press in an open letter to respect their privacy. There was as well the case of the 'lamentable' lapse of Bridget Rowe, editor of the *People*, in publishing a 'snatched' photograph (taken from up a tree) of the wife of the Yorkshire Ripper relaxing in her garden. The PCC was able to round off 1993 satisfactorily with a 'brickbat' adjudication dismissing Rowe's public-interest plea. The PCC reminded editors that they were required to ensure as far as possible that material accepted from non-staff sources was obtained in accordance with the Code.[45]*

These matters were possibly in the minds of MPs asking Peter Brooke questions about what assessment he had made of the current operations of the Press Complaints Commission and what he intended to do about it. His answer was that the government had not made their final assessment; but they were agreed on the desirability of self-regulation being maintained 'if it possibly can be'. To Soley's point that there was need to give the PCC 'real teeth, as the Advertising Standards Authority has, so that it can enforce factual accuracy, just as the ASA enforces accuracy in advertising', Brooke responded with guarded blandness. 'There is agreement among observers that the improvement in the work of the PCC regarding accuracy and the speed of its response to complaints has been notable in the past two years.

---

* See boxed adjudication, p. 153.

Much of the attention centres on the privacy cases.' It was important to ensure that we do not produce, Brooke added, 'a machinery more cumbersome than that we are seeking to improve'.[46]

'Cumbersome' was instantly decoded in the industry as meaning 'statutory'. 'Threat of press curbs recedes', rejoiced *The Times*.[47] The *Press Gazette* focused on Brooke's 'measure of praise' for the PCC.[48] It was little enough; but in the wake of the horrendous month of November 1993 it seemed a lot.

Pinning editors contractually to the Code had implications also going beyond inserting a legal element into voluntary arrangements and consequent questions of the Code's clarity and practicability. The horrendous month of November 1993 gave rise to a paper drafted by Bolland, 'Review of Press Regulation', PCC Paper No. 477 (which eventually became PCC Paper No. 506, December 1993). In effect, this was an exploration of possible measures to fill the gap left by McGregor's shrinking authority. 'The Commission requires (a) a sanction imposed upon editors in gross and deliberate breach of the Code that will be accepted by politicians and the public as a deterrent and (b) an approved and well-advertised procedure for dealing with (i) privacy cases generally and (ii) any other breaches of the Code which lead to a public and political outcry.' McGregor, painfully aware of their implications for his own position, was very reluctant to move in these directions. In his letter of 25 November to Harry Roche at Pressbof, written 'under instruction' from the Commission, McGregor had pointed to the need for Pressbof to amend the PCC's articles of association to give it greater flexibility in handling complaints and responding to criticisms which might arise were the impending White Paper to lead to further government pressure. The 'recent difficulties with Mirror Group Newspapers have highlighted yet again the need for the Commission to be free to raise complaints of their own motion against publications and to pronounce on general issues relating to the Code of Practice'.

With this Pressbof had no great difficulties (pointing out snootily that it had already, on 14 September 1992, advocated the same procedure). With the privacy commissioner proposal it also concurred, suggesting the 'political advantage in making the designation "Privacy Ombudsman"'. It was the Commission's proposals as conveyed by McGregor about sanctions to be imposed by the industry upon editors which gave Pressbof pause. 'In terms of sanctions, the Commission have instructed me to ask Pressbof to give further consideration to the possibility of the self-regulatory system having a sanction to be deployed against editors who are responsible for extreme and deliberate breaches of the Code of Practice.' After his traumatic collision with the MGN chiefs, the last power McGregor wanted to be invested with was to set proprietors or publishers on their editors. He much preferred that the blood be on Pressbof's carpet. The Commission felt, he urged, that it was 'Pressbof, and Pressbof alone, that is in a position to decide what will be practicable in this respect for the industry'. The Commission envisaged continuing to determine complaints under the Code but being able 'in extreme circumstances' to ask Pressbof to consider 'whether it would be appropriate to ask publishers to initiate disciplinary proceedings'. The Commission felt that this would be a 'proper division of responsibility' between itself and Pressbof.[49]

At this Pressbof baulked. Such a sanction would be outside its mandate and in any case 'natural justice obligations' would 'necessitate a very full consideration of each such request of the PCC'. Pressbof had an even lower opinion of several sanction ideas floated by McGregor: 'one lay member' urged 'performance bonds' of a sufficient sum to hurt (£500,000 in the case of the *Mirror*); a general fund to award compensation to success-ful complainants; compulsory contributions to charities. But Pressbof had the wit to counterpropose that in the rider to a recent *Hello!* adjudication 'there would appear to be a form of precedent for action by the PCC'. Pressbof envisaged that the Commission should be prepared 'to issue similar riders on the following lines: "The breach of the Code is of such seriousness that the matter is being drawn to the attention of the publisher in order that the need for appropriate disciplinary action may be considered." '[50]

Thus neatly hoist on his own petard, McGregor chewed on this at the Commission's meeting on 22 December. The chairman remained notably unenthusiastic. Everyone was getting rather impatient. Behind the scenes Roche was known to be ready to shove if push did not suffice. McGregor capitulated. The minutes of the 32nd meeting of the Commission included the item: '*Disciplinary Action*. The Commission agreed to Pressbof's sugges-tion that the Commission should attach a statement recommending that publishers consider the need for disciplinary action to follow peculiarly adverse adjudications.'[51] McGregor retreated forlornly to hospital and major surgery.

Report No. 21, October–November 1993
The People

COMPLAINT

Ms Sonia Szurma, of West Yorkshire, complains that The People published a photograph of her on 29 August 1993 that was taken without her permission in circumstances which breached Clause 8 of the Code of Practice. The photograph was published with an article headlined 'Revealed at last . . . it's the changing face of Mrs Ripper'.

Ms Szurma told the Commission that, having gone into the garden at the rear of her house to relax in the sunshine, the sound of a camera attracted her and she saw a man up a tree in the field adjoining her house taking photographs.

The complaint was put to the editor who was asked to reply within seven days. She replied after two weeks following a reminder, saying the picture was not commissioned but was taken by a freelance. She said the newspaper could not be held responsible for the circumstances under which it was taken, but justified the publication of the photograph in the public interest as it showed the strain on Ms Szurma following the imprisonment of her husband for the so-called Yorkshire Ripper crimes.

The Commission believe that the manner in which the photographs of Ms Szurma were taken and published undoubtedly breached Clause 8 of the Code, which states clearly that individuals should not be photographed on private property without consent unless the enquiry is in the public interest. (Private-property is defined in the Code as any private residence together with its gardens and-outbuildings.) The Commission are unimpressed by the editor's attempt to justify the publication of the photograph in circumstances in which no public interest was served. Further, the Commission find lamentable her failure to accept responsibility for the manner in which the photograph was taken and remind editors that they are required to ensure as far as possible that material accepted from non-staff members is obtained in accordance with the Code of Practice.

The complaint is upheld.

CHAPTER EIGHT

Exit McGregor, enter Wakeham, 1994

'For, as a result of a quite unintended consumer-test, I have come to feel that for the average punter the PCC is the best news since Caxton. In the storm of furious emotion when a newspaper does you down, it serves as a shock-absorber, a buffer, an emollient Jeeves. It is a restorative nip of tonic justice. It keeps you off the hard stuff of writs and suits. . . . They ought to get a Nobel prize.'

Libby Purves, *The Times*, 6 April 1994

'A PCC that is appointed not to improve the standards of the press but to insulate it from the risk of legal regulation does not deserve to work – whatever the disadvantages of statutory control. For its creation was a fraud. Wakeham's appointment is just the most recent extension of the calculated attempt to calm Parliament. It will not work: too many backbenchers have passed the point at which they might have been mollified by Good Old John. . . . The proprietors have backed the wrong horse.'

Roy Hattersley MP, *Guardian*, November 1994

The Commission entered its fourth year as custodian of press self-regulation rather in the condition of walking wounded: limping but mending. Peter Brooke 'spurned every invitation to step over the PCC's front door and see it in operation'.[1] But still his interest was to speed its convalescence with a kind of menacing solicitude. He exploited its recent travails with ever more flourishing of carrots and sticks. 'In the field of adjudicating on accuracy', he declared to the Institute of Public Relations, 'the PCC has shown itself to be increasingly effective.' But the Code had failed on privacy. 'In terms of privacy the press must do better. It may now be time for the press to consider the establishment of a voluntary ombudsman to adjudicate on matters of privacy, with the power to recommend correction and compensation.'[2] The carrot was this concession of a voluntary ombudsman; the stick was that self-regulation must be equipped with 'teeth'.

There was lively speculation as to who might be the ombudsman to be equipped with these fangs. The *Guardian*'s guide to runners and riders was

Lord Howe, former Chancellor and Foreign Secretary, 6-1; Professor Pinker of the PCC, 5-2; Sir Timothy Raison, former Home and Foreign Office minister and chairman of the Advertising Standards Authority since 1991, 15-1; Baroness Dean, former general secretary of the Graphical, Paper and Media Union, now on the PCC, 25-1; and Sir David Calcutt, 100-1. For the Commission in particular, the most invidious aspect of the matter was that, whether statutory or voluntary, an ombudsman would be what the Heritage committee defined him as: 'a bulwark . . . against the inadequacies in the way the Press Commission operates or in which news-papers respond to its adjudications'.[3]

McGregor's threat to resign rather than accept the humiliation of the Commission's being formally confirmed as inadequate chimed in with the industry's strong reluctance to accept any ombudsman scheme with powers to fine or compensate which would be funded by the industry through Pressbof. 'Many would prefer', as Andrew Culf reported for the *Guardian*, 'to take their chances with a statutory body imposing fines of up to £5,000 – which, if the self-regulatory body had collapsed, would be regarded by some as a cheap licence fee to print sensational circulation-boosting material.'[4] The advantage to the industry of some kind of ombudsman would be his being able to 'defuse the kind of high-profile time-bombs' like the Diana gym photos or the 'Camillagate' tapes which had 'so undermined the commission's efforts'. The disadvantage of the ombudsman schemes on offer would be a further undermining of the Commission's status and effectiveness. Calcutt later reproached the industry for its self-regulatory fixation on the ombudsman issue. 'In whatever way the press may present it, self-regulation appears to be the limit to which the press itself is prepared to go, and initiatives suggested by others which con-template even a modest degree of statutory support receive a uniformly hostile press reception, often bordering upon paranoia.'[5] The industry response to this, as articulated by the *Press Gazette*, was that having a modest degree of statutory support was like being to a modest degree pregnant.[6]

The question for the industry was: did it want to continue with the status quo and McGregor? The answer was that after only three years' experience it would seem premature to make changes. McGregor, moreover, had good friends in Pressbof, among them notably Frank Rogers. McGregor's contract was extended for a further year, to 31 December 1995.

Brooke thus had to contend with the fact that the industry would not budge on the matter of self-regulatory 'teeth'. David English stated very firmly the editorial view that compensation awards were unacceptable: they would 'lead to thousands of false claims'.[7] The industry would stick with the PCC. Brooke's bluff, in effect, was being called: his options were either to revert to a statutory ombudsman, which would quite probably lead to a general collapse of the PCC and perhaps the whole Pressbof apparatus, or to accept the logical alternative – a self-regulatory ombudsman within the PCC framework.

That was how the matter was eventually resolved in January 1994. Professor Robert Pinker, academic protégé and old ASA colleague of McGregor, was designated 'privacy commissioner'. Reputed an 'arch-conciliator', Pinker would be empowered to initiate his own investigations in cases of intrusion. But there was no question of fines or compensation. Alexandra Frean in *The Times* observed that with this appointment the Commission 'clearly hopes that the new measure will bridge the "confidence gap" between itself and Downing Street'.[8] Jon Slattery in the *Press Gazette* asked: 'Is a privacy commissioner the last piece in the jigsaw to stave off Government intervention?' He interpreted it candidly as an 'attempt to torpedo any plans by the Government to impose a press ombudsman'. The Commission improved the shining hour by announcing that it would abrogate its self- imposed restriction on following up most cases in the absence of a complaint; and that it would recommend that the Code of Practice be written into the contracts of all editors of national newspapers. With Pinker's appointment 'the PCC hopes it will no longer appear so mealy-mouthed or inactive when the next outcry over privacy breaks'. Pinker would undergo television training to prepare for his new 'high profile role of responding to the media'. McGregor, Pressbof trusted, would thus be kept out of harm's way. Pinker indeed turned out to be a very effective privacy commissioner. But for Pressbof that was a happy accident rather than a policy decision.[9] His real job was to deflect media attention away from McGregor. That was the crucial bonus in the overall PCC package. One Commission member, Slattery reported, said: 'The PCC has answered criticisms of it by the politicians point by point. This appointment is in some ways the final piece of the jigsaw.'[10]

In reality, what was crucially the final piece of the jigsaw was a bald announcement arising out of the Commission's meeting on 22 December after Pressbof's rebuff.[11] Rather unregarded in the turmoil of events, this policy statement was to have in due course highly important consequences. 'In January 1994 the Commission announced that it would in future bring instances of severe or calculated breaches of the Code of Practice (whose terms are incorporated into the conditions of employment of members of staff of many newspapers) to the attention of publishers.'[12] Bringing forward the publishers, like bringing forward Pinker, was part of a policy both of bridging the gap between the PCC and Whitehall, and filling also the hole left by McGregor's sagging authority. Harry Roche later designated the 'additional facility' of having the proprietors to resort to as an 'important sanction'.[13] The crucial January meeting of the Commission was presided over by Pinker. McGregor was recovering in hospital from a serious operation.

2

Having got away with its self-regulatory privacy commissioner, there was a feeling in the industry that the worst might well be over. The joint Association of British Editors, Guild of Editors and International Press Institute propaganda project of an 'alternative White Paper' was going ahead.[14] Peter Brooke did indeed announce on 7 March that he hoped to produce the real thing 'shortly'; but indicated that there were difficulties about the proposed criminal and civil legislative remedies for intrusion on privacy.[15] Jon Slattery observed that 'in the present climate' there were those in the industry emboldened to believe that the government 'will be keen to keep putting off the publication of the White Paper and give the PCC and its new privacy commissioner more time to prove that self-regulation works'. "Can you see the government wanting to publish a paper to do with regulating the press after this week?" asked an industry insider. "The press would crucify them".'[16]

Media pundits were indeed speculating now that 'until recently at least the press have been losing the argument'; but there were signs lately that the tide might be turning against the politicians.[17] The Stephen Milligan scandal, in which the Conservative MP accidentally strangled himself in the course of exotic sexual experiments, certainly gave the press a field day at the expense of the politicians. That David Mellor should then choose this moment to come forward with a plea for mutual respect between press and politicians was very much a sign of these times. 'Perhaps now is the time for fraternising in no-man's land', Mellor suggested at the *Press Gazette* British Press Awards at the Savoy Hotel. He admitted that his own crash had been the result of carelessness. He regretted the present lack of respect 'between the two great organisations of the state – a free press and the Government and MPs'. There should be 'tension, yes, but contempt, no'.[18]

Tension was evidently getting to the Prime Minister. '"Draconian curbs" on the press too much for Major' was the keynote of a report by Philip Webster for *The Times*. A rethink, it seemed, had been ordered on the long-awaited government plans to tighten press regulation. The White Paper due to be published in March had been 'torn up amid signs that the effort to lessen press intrusion has run into serious difficulties'. Major and Brooke wanted Lord Chancellor Mackay to rewrite his proposals. The Cabinet's home affairs committee, chaired by Wakeham, 'had proposed a draft White Paper giving citizens the right to sue for breach of privacy', with Mackay and Kenneth Clarke in favour and the Home Secretary, Michael Howard, playing a waiting game. But a 'serious split' had developed, and the committee was asked to try again. Wakeham himself was still of the pro-self-regulation opinion he had declared in 1992. Major in any case thought the proposals should be in the form of a consultative Green Paper and that a 'public interest' defence be incorporated. His message to Mackay was that a civil tort on privacy was worthless if not accessible to ordinary members of the public: which was the case since the legal aid system was currently a cost-cutting target for the Treasury chief secretary, Michael Portillo. And some ministers were 'wary' of introducing tough regulation proposals in the run-up to the local elections. Professor Pinker's appointment as privacy commissioner was welcomed.[19]

Here indeed was cheering news for the industry, even if there were still editors who doubted that the PCC would ever achieve credibility with the public. One such, Derek Jameson, formerly of The *News of the World*, the *Daily Express* and the *Daily Star,* citing two cases of intrusion on privacy, asked a Guild of Newspaper Editors' conference at Birmingham: 'Are we to believe that these newspapers wouldn't do exactly the same thing next week or next month?' Yet it was another sign of these times that Jameson was challenged by Chris Rycroft-Evans, assistant editor of the *Sun*.

The Press Complaints Commission works because all editors are now concerned about what they put in the paper. Readers will not believe it and the Establishment will not believe it, but editors are very, very cautious about what they put in the paper. The PCC is a young institution and it's growing. I think we have got to try and convince the Establishment that what we need is more time. Two years down the line, the PCC will be a lot more effective than it is today. They've got to allow us to give it a chance and the only way we will be given the chance is by being a little more careful, a little more cautious and a little more responsible – not words I like using very much, I must admit.[20]

This was significant testimony. It related back to News International's stance at the end of the 1993 Diana gym photos affair, and was to relate forward to a News International case in 1995 that became celebrated for a different reason in the PCC's history.[21]

Meanwhile, the Commission went about its business. In a landmark ruling at the end of March 1994 the Commission rejected a complaint by British Nuclear Fuels against articles in the *Daily Star* critical of safety arrangements at the company's reprocessing plant at Sellafield. To uphold the complaint, the Commission explained, would have been tantamount to supporting the company's arguments on nuclear energy and preventing a free discussion of important issues of public policy. The Commission was not competent to have an opinion on the technicalities; and in any case accepted that the very essence of a newspaper was to be 'partial in circumstances in which they would not deceive anybody that they were reading a partisan account'. Peter Hill, editor of the *Star*, pointed to the importance of the case: 'This is the first time the commission has ruled on the press's right to be partial.' Tabloid newspapers 'do more to overturn stupid decisions and laws than any other section of the media'.[22]*

More troublesome was the question of 'jigsaw' identification of children who were victims of sexual abuse: the idea being to protect them both then and in later life from undeserved notoriety. The Code Committee had earlier included a formula to cover this problem: any press report of a case involving a sexual offence against a child might identify the adult concerned but not the child; the word 'incest' where applicable should not be used; and care should be taken that nothing in the report implied any relationship between the accused and the child. The difficulty arose from the different standpoints of reports in different media and different kinds of newspaper, allowing separate items of information to be 'jigsawed' together. In this respect local and national papers had 'opposite instincts'. Local papers featured news about the accused; national papers featured details of the occurrence. A classic case of 'opposite instincts' led to a complaint to the Commission by the weekly *Andover Advertiser* against the *Mail on Sunday*. Because of the rather full information given by the national, the local paper was almost entirely blocked in its reporting. The PCC's director, Mark Bolland, told a Newspaper Society/Guild of Newspaper Editors' law seminar that the Commission might use its new powers of raising complaints to police this part of the Code.

---

* See boxed adjudication, pp. 173–4.

David English had spent many months securing agreement among the different media on a codified resolution of the problem. Faced with the *Andover Advertiser* complaint, together with other instances of jigsawing, he conceded that the Code Committee had been too optimistic in supposing that this very complex issue had been satisfactorily resolved. A 'process of education' among editors and journalists would be needed. English called together the Code Committee secretary Grahame Thomson, BBC controller of editorial policy Richard Eyre, Charles Morrissey of ITN, Press Association News broadcasting editor Neil Williams, and Geoff Elliot of the NS and editor of the *Portsmouth News* 'to press home the Code ruling to every newspaper and broadcasting outlet in Britain'.[23]

3

It was as a by-product of the Milligan scandal that the Commission dealt with a complaint from the journalist Libby Purves against *Today*, which concocted a 'vast and lurid double-page' from the fact that she used to go out with Milligan when she was a student. Her experience of the PCC's procedures led her to think of having a T-shirt made 'with one of those fey red hearts on it signifying I Love the Press Complaints Commission'. Her account in *The Times* was a paean of unreserved praise for the 'miraculous effect' of the PCC's treatment of her complaint, for the unfailing politeness and helpfulness of its staff, for their 'Herculean' attempts at mediation. 'They respond promptly to every communication, shuttle faxes and letters to and fro between the parties, and exude their Jeevesian air of sympathy without bias. . . . for the average aggrieved punter, the PCC is the best news since Caxton'. In the 'storm of furious emotion when a newspaper does you down', the PCC served as a 'shock absorber, a buffer'; it was 'a restorative nip of tonic justice'. It kept you off 'the hard stuff of writs and suits'. And, unlike a lawsuit, the whole thing was over in seven weeks. Purves summed up: 'They ought to get a Nobel prize.'[24]

Unstinting 'praise where it's due', as the *Press Gazette* commented, was no doubt gratifying to the embattled Commission; but in a statistical world of 'consumer satisfaction' such anecdotal evidence is insignificant. Moreover, by the very nature of its procedures, the PCC practically guarantees a predominant quantity of customer dissatisfaction. As the Commission pointed out in its *Review* of its first three years in 1994, more than a third of complaints received were rejected from the outset as not raising prima facie a breach of any clause in the Code of Practice. On top of that was the policy of not entertaining third-party complaints except in special circumstances involving a major public-interest element or in privacy cases. Then there were complaints not proceeded with as being out of time or withdrawn by complainants. From 1 January 1991 to 31 December 1993, the Commission rejected or disallowed 3,490 complaints on these various grounds (including 589 withdrawn). It processed in the same period 1,050 complaints, of which 806 were resolved by conciliation and 244 adjudicated upon. Of those adjudicated, 104 were upheld and 140 rejected. The quotient in bald figures of presumably satisfied to possibly dissatisfied customers thus comes out at 910 to 3,630: that is to say, only 25 per cent of complainants could reliably be designated as satisfied with the result.[25]

This brute statistic more than anything else gave plausibility to the incessant denigration of the PCC as a tool of the industry. In fact, investigation showed that the dissatisfaction rate among complainants was much lower than these raw figures would suggest; but it was still high.[26] Only a few days after Libby Purves's ecstatic endorsement Clive Soley, in debate with Robert Pinker at an NUJ conference, reiterated his indictment of the PCC: 'A body funded by the newspapers, set up by the newspapers and still so overwhelmingly represented on its board by editors, will invariably put market interests first. . . . A market-driven press is not going to give us press freedom.' What was needed, Soley insisted, was an independent body to arbitrate disputes between readers and press. All Pinker could do in reply was to assert that the PCC *was* an independent body. Its lay members, now a majority, had never felt their independence compromised.[27]

It was an argument that Pinker and his fellow lay commissioners could never convincingly win, for all that the condemnation by Soley and his fellow critics of press self-regulation was a non sequitur. That the industry had created Pressbof, which in turn created the PCC in order to fend off statutory regulation of the press, was a transparent fact, never cloaked, never denied. But it was not necessarily the case that it followed that the PCC could not be other than a fraud or confidence trick. That the PCC might in practice be fraudulent or in some other respect deeply inadequate was of course always a possibility. But that would be a matter of contingency, not necessity. There was no essential or integral contradiction between the PCC's being created to insulate the industry from statutory regulation and its being given the job of improving press standards. That the newspaper industry, and especially its national tabloid component, was market-driven was another transparent fact. Arguably, it was the worst way of getting press freedom – except for all the other ways. In any case, it did not necessarily preclude achieving a viable system of press self-regulation broadly satisfactory to both industry and public. The industry had a powerful motive for achieving precisely that. Again, whether that motive would reliably outweigh market motivations was another question of contingency.

The industry's trade paper, the usually well-informed *Press Gazette*, apropos of what it described in April 1994 as the 'excellent conference' organized by the NUJ on journalistic standards, made the point that a new element in the self-regulatory equation was beginning to assert itself: proprietor power. The change, the *Gazette* was sure, had already begun. 'Pressure from within the industry for improved self-regulation has come from the very top. Very late in the day in some cases and only, you might think, through enlightened self-interest.' But the success of the PCC thus far – 'and it must be judged on balance a success' – was due largely to the fact that 'proprietors have put their full weight behind it and insisted that their editors do so'.[28] The Commission had already announced in January its intention to bring instances of severe or calculated breaches of the Code to the attention of publishers.[29]

That proprietors should now come forward to reinforce self-regulation was unquestionably a calculation of enlightened self-interest. The intermediaries between the proprietorial Olympus and the self-regulatory mechanism in the field were those industry eminences with a special relationship to the gods: notably Sir Edward Pickering and Sir David English. Murdoch's démarche to the MGN bosses in 1993 set the scene and gave the tone. Something of that tone had already been discernible in Kelvin MacKenzie's disclosure about the Code's being written into handbooks and contracts.

Harry Roche's Pressbof *Annual Report*, in July 1994, attested that something on these lines was now afoot. 'I tire of critics who repeat the cliché that the PCC has no teeth', he declared. 'The obligation to publish with due prominence an adverse adjudication – and see it published by one's competitors – is to the professional more punitive than a financial penalty. The additional facility whereby the PCC may, in appropriate circumstances, ask a proprietor/publisher to consider disciplinary action is also an important sanction.'[30]

4

Bringing up the big guns in the rear of self-regulation's defensive placements added great extra fire-power to the Commission's weaponry. Pinker was now the man out in the PCC's front line. Bolland and English had their grip on the interior lines of command. McGregor, in his bunker, never did, as it happened, have occasion to summon up the big guns. There was disquiet at the PCC as to whether now he could nerve himself to do so. Pressbof briefed Spencer Stuart and Associates, a leading firm of London headhunters, to come up with a successor in good time to prepare himself or herself to replace McGregor at the expiry of his contract at the end of 1995. Pressbof's brief listed seventeen criteria desirable in a chairman 'not connected with newspaper or magazine publishing', 'sympathetic to self-regulation', and of 'unsullied ethical and moral reputation'. They included someone with access to both politicians and civil servants, who was 'articulate and literate', 'cool and collected', who had 'experience of dealing with the media', and who had a 'good television presence'.[31]

While Spencer Stuart delved amid the public talent – knowing quidnuncs, as Alexandra Frean observed, talked of a shortlist including Baroness Dean and Professor Pinker from the Commission, Lord Skidelsky, Sir Clive Whitmore, Lord Windlesham, Viscount Runciman and Lord Rodgers[32] – the PCC pressed on amid its alarums and excursions.

Was a deal reputedly being hatched by the *Sun* with the exiled Ronnie Knight, allegedly involved in the £6 million Security Express robbery in 1983, in breach of the Code barring payment to people engaged in crime? 'The Commission, which has toughened up its act to demonstrate the effectiveness of self-regulation', as Andrew Culf noted in the *Guardian*, 'is acting under new powers which allow it to initiate investigations to ensure the code of practice is upheld.'[33] Then there were the long-lens photographs of Prince Edward kissing his friend Sophie Rhys-Jones at Balmoral. Charles Anson complained to the PCC on the Prince's behalf against a gaggle of tabloids. The Commission upheld the complaints; but found some of the culprits recalcitrant. Stuart Higgins of the *Sun* failed to see that he had been at fault, especially in view of 'intense speculation about the possible length of the Prince's bachelorhood'. Richard Stott of *Today* was also inclined to resist. Behind this recalcitrance was the embarrassment for both Anson and McGregor of Prince Edward's getting cold feet and attempting to abort the complaint. He did not wish, he told Sir Nicholas Lloyd, editor of the *Express*, 'to be a ping-pong ball between the palace and the PCC'. Sharp divisions, it was suspected, were exposed within the royal household; and revealed also were the lengths to which the royal family, shaken by scandals, was prepared to go to remain on good terms with the tabloid press.[34]

A ping-pong game of insults traded between McGregor and Calcutt enlivened the debate. McGregor took the opportunity of the Commission's Review to comment on the many ways Calcutt's report was 'particularly flawed'.[35] Calcutt hit back in his Child and Co. lecture at the Council of Legal Education by pointing scornfully to McGregor's performance in the Diana gym photos affair.[36] McGregor retaliated with more grievances about Calcutt's rudeness to the Commission and how in any case his conclusions about the implications of present cover-price circulation wars were devoid of evidence to support his case.[37]

This diverting game ended abruptly with the eruption on to the scene of the furore over the methods used by the *Sunday Times* in its investigation of certain Conservative MPs accused of accepting cash payments for asking questions in the Commons. The *Sunday Times*, under its acting editor John Witherow, conscious of its reputation for adventurous investigative journalism, had used subterfuge to trick MPs into betraying themselves. One of the members, Graham Riddick, complained to the PCC about entrapment by a journalist posing as a businessman. The paper pleaded public interest justification. Here was a press sting with a vengeance against the politicians. Conservative MPs furiously denounced the *Sunday Times* for contempt and demanded that the PCC keep its nose out of the Commons' affairs and leave the matter to the House committee of privileges. Riddick attempted to withdraw his complaint on the grounds that it would preempt the committee's investigation. The Commission went ahead, and came up with an adjudication in favour of the *Sunday Times*.[38]*

In the 'cash for questions' affair the Commission seemingly scored well. In judging that Riddick's complaint 'raised an important issue of public interest on which it ought to offer its verdict'[39] the Commission gained kudos from the industry while not lending colour to the standard accusation that it was the industry's puppet. The Prime Minister's 'back to basics' strategy was in tatters and his government discredited. Peter Brooke had been replaced as National Heritage secretary by Stephen Dorrell, who was 'well-liked by journalists and seen to be on the left of the party'. The industry line was that he would be less of a taskmaster than Brooke.[40] But the industry worry was that while a weakened Conservative government was less likely to be a meddlesome threat to press interests, a Conservative government in terminal decline opened up the prospect of a Labour government in its place, with Hattersleys and Kaufmans and Soleys rampant. Possibly it was this kind of thinking and the consequent notion of an expedient touch of neutralizing trim that led Murdoch, in August 1994, to speculate publicly that he 'could even imagine supporting Tony Blair'.[41]

---

* See boxed adjudication, pp. 174–5.

5

In his Pressbof report in 1994, Harry Roche felt he had fair cause to endorse the Commission's own verdict on its performance: 'Press self-regulation has emerged stronger as a result of intense scrutiny over the past three years. With the backing of the industry, the Commission will now continue to build on the accomplishments that have already been achieved.' Roche added his own encomium: 'The industry must be grateful to the members of the PCC under the dedicated leadership of Lord McGregor for the way in which their responsibility is discharged.'

What Roche did not then count upon was McGregor's perverse aptitude for converting a matter of no concern for the PCC into a crisis about its future. The matter arose out of what the *News of the World* hyped as a 'royal sensation', and headlined 'Di's cranky phone calls to married tycoon.'[42] Piers Morgan, the editor, claimed he had 'one of the great scoops', and was scornful of the decision of the *Daily Express* not to run the story. Jean Morgan reported for the *Press Gazette* that the *Express's* proprietor Lord Stevens, after consulting his editor, Sir Nicholas Lloyd, 'wanted to see the Princess's side of the story put and see that his newspapers did not indulge in "idle speculation"'.[43]

The fuss turned out to be one of the great non-scoops; but that was later. Members of Parliament, smarting over the *Sunday Times's* exposure of the 'cash for questions' scandal, saw an opportunity to castigate the press for idle speculation and scandalmongering at the expense of the Princess, and what was the PCC doing about it? McGregor was woken at 7 a.m. on Monday 22 August by Radio 4's *Today* programme. The BBC had wheeled on as prime castigator of the press one of the more irate MPs, Sir Ivan Lawrence QC. There was nothing particularly that McGregor needed to say beyond pointing out that no breach of the Code seemed to be involved, that it was a matter for the police, and that were there to be a complaint, it would duly be dealt with. But he allowed his choler to be incited by the BBC. He was told that on the programme would be MPs commenting on what would be presented as 'one more flagrant example of press intrusion into people's privacy'. McGregor rose to the bait. 'Unwilling as I was to expose myself in that way', he told the *Gazette*, 'I said yes, I would take part because of the MPs.' It was almost as if he saw in Sir Ivan Lawrence QC a version of his bugbear Calcutt.

That McGregor defended the *News of the World* as not being in breach of the Code, that he explained that were the Princess to complain, Professor

Pinker would investigate, and that he accused the broadcasting media of stirring up animus against the press, were not in themselves exceptionable or damaging. What caused the damage was intrinsically trivial. There was a tragi-comical 'silly season' aspect to the affair. 'I went on the programme', McGregor recounted, 'and I very foolishly answered one question honestly: Had I read the *News of the World*? I said, "No, I hadn't", but I had read summaries of the story which Mark [Bolland] had told me accurately represented the story, and it was for that reason that I did not trek out to buy one. I had accurately informed myself of its contents before opening my mouth.'[44]

In that instant McGregor hopelessly wrongfooted himself. He exposed himself and the PCC to derision. The derision was unreasonable, but it stuck. After what the *Press Gazette* described as a 'stumbling performance', McGregor's efforts in later interviews to repair the damage caused by his gaffe served only to give it more notoriety. Colleagues on the Commission were said to be 'exasperated by Lord McGregor's performance over the Princess Di/phone pest affair'. They felt that by 'shooting from the hip' in interviews he had unnecessarily dragged the Commission into the controversy. They thought he had made a mistake in going on the *Today* programme, quite apart from being foolishly truthful. He should have kept the PCC clear of a story with which at the time it had no need to concern itself. 'They are angry that Lord McGregor rushed to judgment without consulting them. It is felt the PCC chairman has learnt nothing from earlier debacles, such as his outburst that advertisers should consider boycotting the Mirror Group following the publication of the Princess Di gym pictures.' A successor to the PCC chairmanship was being sought to take over from Lord McGregor at the end of next year, added the *Gazette*. 'It is thought that process could now be accelerated.'[45]

That point had already been made by Andrew Culf in the *Guardian*: 'Lord McGregor's days as chairman of the Press Complaints Commission appeared to be numbered'. Several members of the Commission were privately expressing concern that 'a wave of interviews on television and radio' had transformed 'a legitimate story about the state of mind of the Princess into another trial of press self-regulation'. Michael Fabricant, a Conservative MP and a member of Kaufman's Heritage committee, announced that McGregor should consider resigning after insisting on *Today* that articles about the Princess did not breach the Code, 'despite admitting that he had not read the original story in the *News of the World*'. Fabricant returned to the attack on Radio 4's *World at One*: 'First of all there is no case to answer, and then he says, well he hasn't actually read the article. . . . I really do think the PCC, if they are going to maintain any level of credibility, should reconsider the position of Lord McGregor and I think he should reconsider his own position.'[46]

One of the criteria stipulated by Pressbof to the headhunters seeking McGregor's successor was 'cool and collected'. McGregor had just given a striking demonstration of how necessary those qualities were for press self-regulation and how deficient he was in them. McGregor told the *Guardian*: 'I have no intention of resigning unless my colleagues on the commission tell me I no longer possess their confidence.' Fabricant he dismissed as a well-known detester of the PCC making a silly point. McGregor admitted he had been foolish to take literally the question about whether he had read the *News of the World*. 'I had, of course, read two summaries and discussed it with my colleagues who told me it did not come within shouting distance of a breach of the code.' Grahame Thomson, secretary of Pressbof, declared supportively: 'We have full confidence in Lord McGregor. You should not react on the spur of the moment to situations like this.'[47]

But the knives were out. Other 'leading newspaper figures described the peer's intervention as a public-relations disaster which could damage the industry's standing with the government in the lead-up to publication of a White Paper on the press in the autumn'.[48] Roy Greenslade was particularly scathing in *The Times*: 'Another right royal gaffe.' Had Lord McGregor 'put his foot in it for the last time?' Greenslade thought McGregor's explanation that he had 'no machinery for obtaining copies of the *News of the World* throughout the hours of darkness on a Sunday night' beggared belief. Greenslade nominated Pinker to take over without further ado. 'He was appointed at the beginning of the year specifically to counter criticisms of Lord McGregor and the PCC. Since then the London School of Economics academic has stayed out of the limelight and proved an effective defender of self-regulation. Even he, however, cannot defend Lord McGregor from himself.'[49]

6

All this was very formidable and, for McGregor, tragic. A man of enormous attractiveness and erudition, 'the Professor', as Lady Elizabeth Cavendish admiringly called him, or 'Mac', as other friends and colleagues knew him, had undermined his own position irremediably by a kind of incontinence of what in many respects were his best traits. The irony of this latest gaffe being, in contrast to those of 1992 and 1993, one in which he defended the press and attacked the politicians, served only to aggravate the tragic element.

That aggravation intensified with McGregor's reluctance to accept that the end had come. He was 73 and not in the best of health; but he had another year to go on his contract. His stumbling performances in the media could be discounted, after all, as matters of mere cosmetic public relations. They should not be allowed to outweigh his substantial achievement in making the PCC a going concern. But the consensus in the industry was that he had become too much of a liability. The 'silly season' business took on an emblematic status quite at odds with its triviality. McGregor might have hoped that that Sir Frank Rogers of the NPA would see him safe; but, for all his liking for 'Mac', Rogers had run out of patience with his vagaries. Behind Sir David English loomed Rothermere, thumbs down. MGN naturally would not lift a finger. No major industry group had any interest in keeping McGregor afloat. The word went down to Harry Roche at Pressbof to accelerate the headhunters' quest and find a replacement by the end of 1994. Roche had the distasteful task of persuading the distressed McGregor to abandon his contractual claim and offer his resignation. A settlement was agreed on 9 November.

As lame-duck chairman McGregor presided over a few more barren months. Demoralization at Salisbury Square was such that no annual review for 1994 was assembled. The issue of what the government planned to do about press regulation had seemingly lapsed into quiescence. On 3 November Stephen Dorrell ritually answered a ritual question about the by now almost mythical White Paper: it would certainly not land on McGregor's desk. There were a few technicalities to attend to. Action was needed to end the manipulation by celebrities and public figures whose public relations agents 'set up' photo opportunities for their clients to gain publicity but then objected to any picture being taken which they did not control. This would necessitate changing the rules covering photographs on private property. These changes would also involve tightening up the rules governing consent. The PCC was anxious to establish under what circumstances it would be considered unreasonable for subjects to withhold consent for a photograph's being published.[50] Pinker presented to the Commission's meeting on 28 September a paper elucidating some difficult points in the change of the rules about photography on private property.

Sputterings from the 'cash for questions' scandal were still to be heard. Neil Hamilton, a former junior minister, denied asking questions in the

House in return for money from the Egyptian owner of Harrods, Mohamed Fayed. Claiming to be a victim of media blood-lust, Hamilton denounced the PCC as 'a sheep in wolf's clothing'. He urged its replacement by a more balanced body with greater power. He accused the press, both broadsheet and tabloid, of undermining the nation's institutions and being 'only too prepared to destroy anything in its sights'.[51] One of the last items to engage McGregor's no doubt somewhat jaded attention would have been the controversy over the naming of an £18 million National Lottery winner by *Yorkshire on Sunday* and the *News of the World*. Was there an invasion of privacy? Was there a public-interest justification? Or was it a matter simply of what interested the public? Jack Straw, the Labour MP, had lodged a complaint with the Commission. It would not be for McGregor to deal with.

The one issue of substance to land on McGregor's desk in these latter weeks was the question of the *Guardian* and Jonathan Aitken, Financial Secretary to the Treasury and Cabinet minister. The editor, Peter Preston, a member of the Commission, was investigating the financial relationship of Aitken to a Saudi Arabian business partner. To this end he wanted a copy of Aitken's bill at the Ritz Hotel in Paris, where he stayed in 1993 at the same time as the Saudi. Mohamed Fayed, the owner of the hotel, would not hand over to another party private information about a guest at his hotel. But if he were to receive a request for a copy of the bill purporting to come from Aitken himself, he would supply it. Accordingly Preston forged Aitken's name on Commons notepaper requesting a copy of his bill, faxed it to the Ritz, and received from Fayed a fax of the bill. Preston's defence of his 'cod fax' was that there was 'no other way forward' in the *Guardian*'s investigation of Aitken, which was a question of first-rate public interest. Fayed had 'cast-iron protection'. And, 'crucially, the fax itself was designed, if discovered, to direct all flak at the *Guardian* itself'. 'I rehearse these facts and arguments', Preston told McGregor, 'for you only to show, I hope, my concern for the Code of Practice. Whether anyone agrees or not, I was very anxious that we did nothing I believed ethically wrong. And I still do not think that we did.'[52]

There were some who disagreed. Complaints were promptly lodged at the PCC against the *Guardian* and Preston 'who appear to have committed forgery and impersonation in their eagerness to attack a government minister.'[53] McGregor's response to Preston's explanatory letter was initially sympathetic. An arguably analogous precedent did exist. The Commission had upheld the use of subterfuge for the purposes of investigative journalism in the 'cash for questions' affair. Preston indicated to McGregor his readiness to resign from the Commission if the chairman deemed it appropriate. McGregor assured him that that would not be required. Later that day, however, the chairman's soundings revealed that 'some lay members were opposed strongly to . . . Preston's continuance as a member'. McGregor told Preston late that afternoon that 'a sufficient number of his lay colleagues were so opposed to his actions as to make his position on the Commission uncomfortable'. Preston thereupon with some asperity immediately confirmed his resignation.[54]

The PCC was faced with four possible courses of proceeding. It could invite Aitken to make a complaint, and proceed accordingly; and if Aitken declined, not proceed at all. It could consider the matter on a third-party complaint basis, as raising an important issue of principle or public interest. It could deal with the issues raised otherwise than by a complaint under the powers granted to the Commission by 53. 1(a) of its Articles of Association which states that it shall be a function of the Commission to consider and pronounce on issues related to the Code of Practice which the Commission in its absolute discretion considers to be in the public interest. Or it could note Preston's letter of 1 November without further comment. The relevant clauses of the Code appeared to be Clause 17, on confidential sources, or Clause 7, on misrepresentation. The matter was placed before the Commission for discussion and consideration.[55]

7

As it happened, that was as far as McGregor needed to take the case. The item foremost on his personal agenda early in November would have been Pressbof's choice of his successor. This turned out not to be Pinker or indeed any of the touted favourites. In the industry's eyes Pinker was assumed to be too like McGregor: a professor, an academic, brought across by McGregor from the ASA. Baroness Dean, also on the shortlist, was held to be unacceptable to some managements because of her trade-union background. The selection committee, consisting of Roche, Nisbet-Smith and Grahame Thomson, were looking for someone at home in the inner corridors of power and influence. The coming White Paper might prove a tricky obstacle to surmount. Spencer Stuart and Associates came up with a candidate supremely well qualified on the political-governmental side of the criteria they were charged with meeting. The committee settled eventually for Lord Wakeham of Maldon, former Conservative Chief Whip,

Leader of the House of Commons and Leader of the House of Lords; and, specifically, chairman of the Cabinet's home affairs committee. His appointment was announced on 9 November. It was 'understood within Pressbof and the PCC that Lord Wakeham was considered easily the best candidate' for the £75,000 three-day-a-week job, contracted for three years from 1 January 1995.

Harry Roche, however, was not at all happy with that outcome. A man of *Mirror* and *Guardian* culture, he was eventually knighted by Tony Blair. For all Wakeham's merits and qualifications, he was famously one of Margaret Thatcher's paladins, her supreme 'fixer'. He had, moreover, privatized electricity during a spell at the Energy department. But on the other side of the political equation was Wakeham's reputation as a 'safe pair of hands'; and his roles as whip and leader of both Houses attested to a capacity for managerial arrangements with opposing parties. In the Commission Wakeham had an influential advocate in David English, who appreciated the advantages available to the PCC from Wakeham's fund of credit in Westminster and Whitehall. It was English in effect who neutralized Roche's hostility. There was also the consideration that in 1992 Wakeham had gone out of his way to proclaim his adherence to the cause of press freedom and self-regulation.[56] That episode was well-known to the PCC and Pressbof (Wakeham had sent a copy of his speech to McGregor). But to the industry at large it remained in obscurity. Most accepted Alexandra Frean's reading of the case for *The Times*, that Wakeham had no established reputation as an advocate of press freedom. 'Indeed, he chaired the Cabinet's home affairs committee, which produced the much-delayed White Paper recommending the introduction of privacy legislation.'[57] It suited Wakeham himself to endorse that reading of his past: that it was precisely chairmanship of that committee, and the tearing up of its White Paper with Lord Chancellor Mackay's privacy legislation scheme, that began his conversion to the merits of self-regulation. In fact Wakeham was playing a subtle game. His time as minister responsible for co-ordinating government policies from 1990 to 1992 had educated him in the merits of self-regulation, but in 1994 he preferred to let that pass. The aborted White Paper was technically Wakeham's responsibility; but it did not represent his own will or desire. His tactic now was to make a virtue of his necessity then. Better to come to the job ostensibly as someone needing to be convinced.

On announcing Pressbof's confirmation of Wakeham's appointment on 21 November, Harry Roche – still unhappy, but outgunned – emphasized that it had the 'overwhelming support of senior publishers'. McGregor made his bow gracefully: 'I know . . . that the values of freedom of expression are central to his whole outlook and will be allied to his unsurpassed administrative and political experience in furthering press self-regulation.'[58] It was undoubtedly that experience which so recommended Wakeham to the publishers. In Brian MacArthur's words, 'they have chosen a practised Tory politician with easy access to Whitehall and Downing Street'.[59]

A practised Tory politician was not likely to be welcomed with universal acclaim either in the industry or by the public. Labour party spokesmen were predictably cool in their response to the news of the PCC chairman-to-be. Chris Smith, the shadow Heritage secretary, protested at the Wakeham 'job'. 'I very much doubt if he will have the robust independence which is essential in this very important role. It is another job for an ex-Conservative minister, when what we need is someone who holds the public's interest first and foremost.' Wakeham sent, as Smith put it, the 'wrong signals'.[60] Roy Hattersley was more polemically forthright.

The idea is simple enough. John Wakeham – Margaret Thatcher's fixer and troubleshooter – will be immensely reassuring to Tory backbenchers who believe newspapers have got above themselves; at least until the next election press legislation will be postponed by the assurance that 'if you give John a chance, he'll get it right in the end'. That is the reason for the Wakeham appointment. . . .

A PCC that is appointed not to improve the standards of the press but to insulate it from the risk of legal regulation does not deserve to work – whatever the disadvantages of statutory control. For its creation was a fraud. Wakeham's appointment is just the most recent extension of the calculated attempt to calm Parliament. It will not work: too many backbenchers have passed the point at which they might have been mollified by Good Old John. . . . The chance of avoiding legislation would be much improved if the PCC produced a convincing 'public interest criterion', supported newspapers that respected it and brutally condemned those that did not. That would involve defending the press against powerful vested interests – the *Sunday Times* over the payment-for-questions scandal and the *Guardian* in its pursuit of ministers' business connections. It would also require public assault on those newspapers that intrude into the lives of the quiet majority who are entitled to be left alone. I cannot see Lord Wakeham performing either of these tasks. As a result, the PCC will be further diminished. The proprietors have backed the wrong horse.[61]

Report No. 23, January–February 1994
Daily Star

COMPLAINT

British Nuclear Fuels, of Risley, Warrington, Cheshire, complains that two articles in the Daily Star, headlined 'Temple of doom' and 'Countdown to tragedy', on 20 and 21 September 1993 respectively contained a number of serious inaccuracies, in breach of Clause 1 of the Code of Practice.

The articles concerned safety at Sellafield and transportation of nuclear waste, and the first, 'Temple of doom', contained:

(i)   statements on the part of the newspaper that the quantity of nuclear waste stored at the plant was sufficient 'to create ten disasters like Chernobyl' and 'enough to make Britain the nuclear dustbin of the world', as other countries, knowing its dangers, were 'only too happy to pay a fortune to dump it at the other side of the world';

(ii)   claims by the newspaper that it was the first to have access to certain parts of the plant;

(iii)   references to the necessity for workers to wear full-body PVC suits and masks when working in contaminated areas (the journalist was 'protected only by a white coat and flimsy cotton shoes');

(iv)   a statement that some 'nuclear waste lies around unmonitored' and that there was inadequate storage space and that the long-term aim was to 'bury it deep underground and forget about it';

(v)   a reference to a 'leaked secret document', indicating the large amount of intermediate level waste stored at the plant;

(vi)   a statement that 300 workers were recently evacuated after a leak, necessitating an immediate top-level inquiry;

(vii)   a description that in order to prove the nuclear waste area was safe, by allowing access to the newspaper representative, it first had to be 'cleaned' to make it less dangerous;

(viii) a statement that contamination stretched 85 miles along the Cumbrian coastline;

(ix)   a statement that British Nuclear Fuels said 'Thorp will get the go-ahead, despite all the objections, because it will make a fortune for all concerned'; and

(x)   an assertion from pressure groups that 'the deadly krypton gas pumped from the new plant will kill at least 10 people a year'.

The second article, 'Countdown to tragedy', was illustrated by a photograph of an alleged crash test captioned 'Crash test: the nuclear flask survived this test in 1983 – but critics say it proved nothing'. The newspaper acknowledged and regretted that the photograph was not of a British Nuclear Fuels experiment but pointed out that the text alongside the photograph was supplied by BNFL, describing the experiment and its safe outcome. The article contained:

(a)   statements that 'lethal nuclear waste is being moved through highly populated areas of Britain';

(b)   a suggestion that 'nuclear bosses and British Rail chiefs do not want the public to know' particular routes and that if 'just one flask broke open it would release enough radioactivity to kill 1,300 people'; and

(c)   the suggestion that there is 'talk of transporting the deadly material by air'.

During the investigation the Commission was provided with a large volume of press cuttings, extracts from government papers and other material produced by both parties, and also photographs and extracts from the complainants of their own publication, BNFL News; evidence from both sides of what was a complicated, technical and often emotional issue.

ADJUDICATION

In considering the complaints from British Nuclear Fuels the Commission have been careful not to inhibit the vigorous debate and reporting of an issue which is primarily a matter of public policy. The Commission also recognise that conflicting and seemingly equally convincing technical evidence is offered by proponents of the many arguments about the safety of nuclear electricity generation. The concern of the Commission is to uphold the right of the press to be partisan on such issues while ensuring a clear distinction between comment, conjecture and fact. Where statements are presented as matters of fact capable of objective assessment, they are required to conform to the Code of Practice's tough provisions on accurate reporting.

In this particular case, the Commission are of the view that the reports in the Daily Star are so clearly championing well researched concerns about nuclear power that no reader could possibly conclude that they were an impartial account of the arguments on each point. In effect, the complainants are asking the Commission to support their arguments about nuclear energy, as set out in their publication, BNFL News, against the concerns raised by the Daily Star. It is not the role of the Commission to make such judgements for the benefit of any party in a debate about a matter which is essentially one of public policy, to be decided through argument by democratic and elected institutions.

Even if the points which the complainants have asserted to be inaccurate and which can be assessed objectively were proven to be inaccurate, the Commission consider that they did not bear significantly on the substance of the article and therefore was not in breach of Clause 1 of the Code.

The complaint is rejected.

PCC Report No. 25, May–July 1994
The Sunday Times

COMPLAINT

Mr Graham Riddick, MP for Colne Valley, complains that information contained in an article in The Sunday Times of 10 July headlined 'Revealed: MPs who accept £1,000 to ask a parliamentary question', was unfairly obtained through subterfuge. He maintained that such information was readily available elsewhere and raised his complaint under Clauses 7(i), 7(iii) and 18 of the Code of Practice.

The article described how a journalist posed as an investor interested in buying a firm. He offered the complainant £1,000 to table a question in the House of Commons to the Secretary of State for Social Security about any work done by the firm (the name of which had been invented) for the Department.

Mr Riddick has since told the Commission that as the House of Commons has established a Committee of Privileges to consider issues relating to this matter he does not wish to proceed with his complaint.

The Commission is the appropriate body to decide whether The Sunday Times has breached the PCC's Code of Practice and it sees no conflict with the role of the Committee of Privileges in so doing. The Speaker of the House of Commons has informed the Commission that she does not see any conflict between an adjudication by the Commission based on the provisions of the Code and any investigation by the Committee of Privileges.

The Commission has the power, of its own motion, to raise or continue the investigation of any alleged breach of the Code and it considers that Mr Riddick's complaint raises an important question of public interest on which it ought to adjudicate.

The Sunday Times told the Commission that it undertook this investigation after being told by a prominent businessman that it was common practice for MPs to be paid to table questions in Parliament and the 'going rate was £1,000'. The newspaper's receipt of this information coincided with rumours which it had picked up in the House of Commons that MPs were being paid for putting down questions. The newspaper believed that an investigation into these matters was in the public interest and considered that a debate about the question of payment to MPs and their consultancies was timely. The propriety of any such payment seemed to the newspaper to be unclear. Erskine May's 'Parliamentary Practice' indicates that the receipt of payment by MPs for tabling questions may be a breach of privilege, yet payment appears to be permissible if MPs record any financial relationship with outside parties within a set period. An examination by the newspaper of thousands of parliamentary questions appeared to confirm their suspicions but not to offer exact proof. The newspaper contended that the use of subterfuge was the only method by which the matter could be investigated.

ADJUDICATION

The Commission accepts the newspaper's explanation for its behaviour. The subject matter of the article raised issues of serious public interest which the newspaper had a right to pursue. In all the circumstances of this case, the Commission considers that the subterfuge used was justified as the only effective investigative tool available by which the information concerned could be obtained.

CHAPTER NINE

'We are not out of the woods quite yet': Wakeham takes over, January–July 1995

'I am convinced that if legislation were ever to be introduced, it would not be because the PCC had failed the public. It would be because we made a mistake in our handling of one or two of those issues which aroused great controversy. That will not happen during my chairmanship. . . . these problems will be an opportunity to strengthen our standing: nothing else.'

Lord Wakeham, speech at the British Press Awards, 4 April 1995

'When the history of how newspapers saved themselves from statutory legislation after ten years in the dock before Whitehall and the House of Commons is written, the defining moment may well be seen to have occurred in May 1995.'

Brian MacArthur, *The Times*, 18 July 1995

To most people in the newspaper industry Wakeham was something of a mystery. Evidently he had convinced the selection committee and Pressbof that he was their man; but he had no 'form' in the way McGregor had. As the *Press Gazette* remarked, journalists would not be able to look up Wakeham's statements on the press to find out what his views were. 'He was not given to making many.' That was not Wakeham's way. Journalists could, of course, have checked with the Energy department's press release of 28 February 1992[1]; but that was not their way. A parliamentary correspondent told Jon Slattery of Wakeham: 'He was one of the most successful manipulators of the media before he went to the House of Lords. And it would be counter-productive, wouldn't it, if you are manipulating the press quietly, successfully, on your own, to say things about the press that would alienate them?' According to others at the lobbies Wakeham was 'genial, persuasive, approachable' and liked to give titbits to selected journalists to persuade them that they were 'on the inside of what was going on'. His first act on taking over the leadership of the Lords in 1992 was to stop the weekly

briefings of the handful of national newspaper and broadcasting journalists who covered the doings of the Upper House. Instead, he spoke to
journalists individually – 'usually friendly journalists'.[2]

A talent for quiet manipulation was not a surprising attribute in a successful Tory Chief Whip; nor in a successful Leader of both Houses of
Parliament. Woodrow Wyatt recorded of Wakeham in 1988: 'As Leader
of the House he adores all the intrigue and manipulation which has to go
on to get the business through.'[3] In pretty well all respects he is a quite different man from Oliver McGregor. His predominant humour is phlegmatic.
His initial professional training was in accountancy. He likes sailing yachts
and racing horses. McGregor looked upon the newspaper industry grandees
with a certain academic awe. Wakeham, a man at ease with power and the
manners of power, takes them as seriously as he finds them. He made a
point of giving the false impression that he had no passionate convictions
or prejudices in the matter of press freedom on libertarian first principles.
Critics among his former colleagues would say of him: 'He's got absolutely
no vision at all. He only ever asks how instead of why.'[4] This was very much
Wakeham's manipulative public line on entering into his chairmanship.
He readily confessed to having been a willing member of a government
which committed itself to some measure of statutory press regulation. He
insisted that his withdrawal from that commitment was entirely pragmatic.
'Whilst we were looking at the details it was quite clear that it is very much
more difficult and not necessarily a very effective way of achieving what I
think can be achieved from self-regulation.'[5]

Lord Wakeham's line in beneficial humbug, thus, is that he became a
successful defender of press self-regulation essentially out of the
experience of having been an unsuccessful regulator of the press. 'After
fifteen years in Government I came to the job well aware of the difficulty
involved both in balancing the public's right to know with the right of
individuals to privacy, and in ensuring accuracy in reporting. I also came to
the job with an open mind about the PCC.'[6]

This was a circumstance important for the PCC in several respects. It
gave Wakeham bona fides which offset quite natural public suspicions
about the tendency of Tory grandees not to wish to offend the press
magnates. It gave Wakeham an advantageous stance upon which he could
argue his case against advocates of statutory press regulation. And it gave
reassurance to the industry. As the *Press Gazette* put it, 'it seems highly
unlikely to us that Lord Wakeham would have taken the job and publicly
committed himself to maintaining self-regulation if he did not believe

there was already a fair wind for it. And he certainly would not have come if privacy legislation was imminent – there would hardly have been a job afterwards.' Thus Wakeham's arrival came at a time, as it seemed to the *Gazette*, 'when we should be feeling more confident after our miserable spell in the Last Chance Saloon'.[7]

This was also the feeling at Salisbury Square. That the new chairman should apparently come in with an open mind about the prospects of the PCC, and that he should rather flaunt his taking on the job 'on the basis of such scepticism',[8] bespoke a refreshing change from McGregor's evangelism. It would be a relief to work for someone without illusions and with a *politique* cast of mind ('I'm not the old Press Council. It's not our job to go campaigning everywhere. But because I probably have a bit of influence, I try to use it in the right direction.'[9]). It was, in its way, reassuring to the PCC staff that Wakeham should assert with seeming candour that he 'remained to be convinced about the independence and effectiveness of the Commission', that he would give the job his best efforts, but that were he to conclude that self-regulation could not be made to work, he would declare this publicly and recommend an appropriate statutory alternative. 'I had first to ensure', as he stated later, 'that the Government, the public and the House of Commons – and in that order – thought that the PCC was a serious organization doing a reasonable job.'[10]

Another thing reassuring to Bolland and his team was that Wakeham arrived with clear notions of what needed to be done. This later became dignified as the 'strategic plan'.[11] It consisted firstly of demonstrating the Commission's independence of the industry by heavyweight new appointments 'of stature and clout' both to the Appointments Commission and to the PCC itself. Secondly, Wakeham would 'win back authority by avoiding off-the-cuff comments and speaking only when the PCC had an agreed position'. Thirdly, Wakeham had observed 'how tenaciously tabloid editors fought back when they were about to be criticised', and he determined 'to get editors themselves to take the PCC seriously'. Finally, Wakeham wanted to imprint press self-regulation on the public consciousness as the normal, everyday reality, and to banish statutory controls from the political agenda.

Tactical means to these strategic ends consisted essentially in finding in Bolland an executive talent with whom he could work smoothly and effectively, and in employing with Bolland managerial techniques to avoid time-consuming and formalistic consultation with the Commission and to arrive at agreed positions speedily by the gently coercive manipulations characteristic of the whips' office. This regime suited Bolland perfectly. As Roy Greenslade later observed, 'none of the mud thrown at McGregor stuck to Bolland'.[12] A good working relationship with Bolland linked Wakeham to Bolland's colleague David English. Wakeham had every reason to respect English's talents and his crucial importance in the mechanism – though he was often wryly amused by English's vanity and his thirst for a peerage.

After having acquainted himself with the Commission and its staff, Wakeham immediately set about acquainting himself with the industry at large in a 'comprehensive round of meetings' in London, the regions, Scotland and Northern Ireland, which was expected to last until the end of February. David Banks, now editorial director at MGN, expected that Wakeham would 'give us a rough ride, but he is a sound appointment'. He saw Wakeham as 'fair-minded' and with no reputation for favouritism to the press: 'he will be no one's poodle'.[13] At his Mirror Group consultations Wakeham was impressed with the usefulness of the supportive role Charlie Wilson could play outside the Commission: as important in its way as Pickering's role inside. Many of the industry chiefs Wakeham conferred with in these rounds he of course already knew; but he was determined, as the *Gazette* understood, 'to re-establish and lay down contacts which will enable him to do his job properly'.[14]

His first executive contact with the Pressbof apparatus other than the PCC itself was to take his place on the Appointments Commission, still consisting of Harry Roche and Derry Irvine, to select new members for the PCC. The people of 'stature and clout' whom Wakeham had in mind were a very senior, lately retired civil servant conversant with the corridors of bureaucratic power, and major representative figures from each of the main political parties. The mandarin he got, Sir Brian Cubbon, had headed first the Northern Irish Office and then the Home Office. Having been pipped as head of the Civil Service, Cubbon was a catch of the first rank for Wakeham. Sir Brian quickly established himself as the key new lay commissioner within Wakeham's inner 'cabinet': English, Pickering and Charlie Wilson being the industry people.

On the Labour party side Wakeham wanted Peter Shore, formerly one of Harold Wilson's henchmen; but Shore was booked up with the Nolan Committee dealing with the 'arms to Iraq' affair. Wakeham had been a great friend of John Smith, the late Labour leader; it was a gracious gesture to invite his widow, Baroness Smith of Gilmorehill, to join the Commission. Among Liberal Democrats of stature and clout Wakeham at first hoped for the eminent barrister Lord Lester of Herne Hill QC (Wakeham did not share McGregor's animus against lawyers), but was gratified eventually to secure Lord Tordoff, the Liberal Democrat leader in the Lords. It was with his plan for a Tory of stature and clout that Wakeham came adrift.

One of the things the industry thought it knew about Wakeham was that, in the *Press Gazette*'s words, his presence at the PCC would 'subdue the wilder forces of reaction on the Conservative back benches'. What Irvine (the shadow Lord Chancellor) was not prepared for was Wakeham's nomination of Sir Bernard Ingham for the slot. 'Lady Thatcher's voice and mind reader', 'scourge of journalists and famous for his blunt Yorkshire speaking', as David Hencke of the *Guardian* put it,[15] Ingham's role as Thatcher's press secretary put him almost exactly in the same category of ex-Thatcherite fixer and troubleshooter as Wakeham himself, with a bonus reputation for pugilistic abrasiveness. Wakeham's motive was that these were precisely the qualities needed to make tabloid editors sit up and take the PCC seriously. Irvine felt strongly that this was one reactionary step too far. Besides, what was needed was a lay member; and while Ingham was strictly eligible under that rubric, his journalistic past and current role as columnist on the *Express* was held fairly to rule him out. Wakeham argued that Ingham would be balanced politically by the other, uncontroversial, appointments. He got strong support for Ingham from Stephen Dorrell and grudging acquiescence at first from Roche, but strong resistance from Irvine, seconded by Chris Smith. Irvine's position was that, with Ingham, there was no comparing like with like. A good deal of nobbling occurred, stretching down to prominent Ingham-haters among the Tory 'wets' who leaked privy information to Labour friends at the *Mirror*.

The wrangling went on through February into March. In the end Wakeham had to give way. 'In view of your implacable approach', he wrote crossly to Roche, 'which I fear has set back the cause of a truly independent Press Complaints Commission, I do not think it right for me to continue to advocate his membership at the present time.' Ingham, convinced that he was the target of a Leftist plot, at least had the satisfaction of revealing that the Appointments Commission was itself unconstitutionally appointed; which set the embarrassed Pressbof scurrying to rectify the anomaly. In the event, a well-respected industrialist, Sir Denys Henderson, chairman of ICI, and the vice-chancellor of Exeter University, Sir Geoffrey Holland, were added to the newly regularized Commission to lend it gravitas.[16]

Many found the Ingham business disturbing. How could so reputedly shrewd a politician as Wakeham have so misjudged his ground? The

Association of British Editors, the lobby group of two hundred senior media figures including several national editors, diagnosed that the PCC was in 'a parlous state of flux'. Roy Greenslade, Pinker's earlier champion for the chairmanship, while allowing that 'it might seem harsh to attack a chap barely two months into a new job', thought nevertheless that Wakeham's activities 'demand critical attention'.

> The PCC is the cornerstone of the press's continually shaky hold on to the right to self-regulation. So it should be above suspicion. It should be seen to be impartial. It should enjoy the confidence of politicians of all parties and, of course, it must maintain credibility with the public. Yet Wakeham's record since acceding on January 1 is hardly conducive to enhancing the PCC's reputation.
>
> The former Tory minister succeeded Lord McGregor, a legal academic who was clearly viewed as impartial, if mildly eccentric and often inept. McGregor's only other job was the uncontroversial and press-related chairmanship of Reuters trustees. Wakeham, in spite of collecting £75,000 a year for three days a week at the PCC, is taking on jobs galore and becoming the subject of stories in papers he is supposed to regulate. In January, he took up a £20,000-plus non-executive directorship of merchant bank N. M. Rothschild, moving centre stage in the controversy over jobs for the boys. Six weeks later he was voted on to the British Horseracing Board's industry committee and is tipped for the chairmanship next year. Wakeham's first PCC decision – to draft Sir Bernard Ingham as a lay member – calls into question his judgment and impartiality. . . . But so far no politician has questioned Wakeham's own suitability. It is time they did.[17]

Greenslade presumably missed Hattersley's dismissive critique back in November. In any case, the signals for Wakeham were at danger. He seems to have read them accurately. At all events there has been no record since of any comparable misreading of the signs.

2

Foremost among the cases held over from 1994 was the *Guardian*/Jonathan Aitken issue. It was decided that the PCC would investigate 'of its own motion, two relevant matters'.

> First, the PCC intends to consider whether the terms of its Code of Practice are such that it permitted the *Guardian* to manufacture a letter on House of Commons notepaper purporting to come from Mr Aitken's office for the specific purpose of providing such a letter to the Ritz in case any question arose as to the source of the *Guardian*'s information concerning this bill. Secondly, the

Commission will consider, as a more general issue, the length to which newspapers are permitted to go in order to protect their source of information. It may be that the Commission will wish to give general guidance to editors on this matter.[18]

An adjudication on these points by the Commission would have been a most significant landmark document. But Aitken opted to seek redress in the courts. The Commission's terms of reference, as Bolland explained to the relevant third-party complainants, 'do not permit it to adjudicate on matters which are the subject of court proceedings'. In consequence, the Commission decided that it could not proceed in the matter.[19] Aitken, armed with what he described as 'the sword of truth' against 'the cancer of bent and twisted journalism', went ahead to perjury and disaster. In its way, it was a classic instance of the benefits of sticking with the PCC and keeping clear of the courts.

Keeping in with his late colleagues in government was a matter much on Wakeham's mind. Stephen Dorrell was giving disturbing signs of wanting to do something. Clive Soley asked: 'Is the Secretary of State saying that we really have reached the stage of drinking-up time in the last chance saloon?' Dorrell's answer was 'No; I am saying we are thinking about it.'[20] It was not a question of any imminent privacy legislation. 'I should make that clear', one leading brief assured the industry, 'by saying this is a John Major-style of decision. It is a decision *not* to decide to do anything about it.' There had been no White Paper. There was no draft Bill. There was no legislation posed for the current session. There was no likelihood of its coming in for the following session. And by then it would be 'perilously near to an election'.[21] What was on Dorrell's mind, it transpired, was the notion of the industry's setting up a compensation fund for victims of press intrusion on top of the £1 million with which it funded Pressbof's existing machinery. Dorrell also planned to revive the idea of the Commission's establishing a hotline giving complainants the opportunity to get in ahead of publication.

Dorrell raised these issues with Pressbof at a meeting on neutral territory in a London hotel. He had some encouragement. There was, according to Jean Morgan of the *Press Gazette*, 'a school of thought in the industry which regards the compensation fund as the "least worst" of the options'. Harry Roche, however, was not of this school; nor were any of his colleagues. He had no great problem getting the money to keep the PCC and the other organs going; but he knew there would be resistance to paying a compensation premium. It would be divisive. The regional press and national broadsheets would resent having to pay for national tabloid exploits. Editors would resist being fined by fellow editors, often commercial rivals. Wakeham pointed out that this would trigger costly legal battles. Every variety of opportunistic rogue would try to cash in. David Newell, deputy director of the Newspaper Society, objected that a compensation scheme confused the legal system with press self-regulation, and was 'likely to snarl up and delay a system we believe is working well'. Terry Quinn, editor of the Glasgow *Daily Record*, mocked the proposal by announcing that he planned to demand compensation for intrusion on time and resources wasted on investigating spurious complaints against his paper for the PCC. 'As for the hotline', the *Press Gazette* observed, 'that was dumped as impractical two Secretaries of State ago.'[22]

While Dorrell's initiative waned, Wakeham prepared to relaunch his chairmanship after the Ingham imbroglio with a major statement at the British Press Awards on 4 April at the Hilton Hotel. At this 'big annual event in national newspaper journalism', Wakeham found himself in the 'odd position' of applauding the *News of the World* when its 'newsroom hack' Gary Jones won the Reporter of the Year award. Yet he pledged himself to making the self-regulatory system so secure 'that no one will want, or be able, to put anything better in its place'. His tactic still was to exploit his reputation as having no self-regulatory 'form'. 'As one who was involved in government looking at these issues – the gamekeeper before he turned poacher – I am only too aware that the press in the 1980s came perilously close to the flames.' Moreover, for all that the setting-up of the PCC by an 'historically diverse and fiercely competitive industry' was a 'logistical and political triumph', and the development of the Code of Practice immensely impressive, each of the inquiries that scrutinized press self-regulation between 1991 and 1994 found it wanting. 'We are not out of the woods quite yet.'

How to escape from the cycle of crisis that had from time to time engulfed the PCC? Wakeham's diagnosis was to build up confidence among both politicians and public in the ability of the Commission to perform its 'core function'. On this score Wakeham was confident that, with some seventy complaints coming in every week, of which the vast majority were resolved in a matter of weeks, sometimes days, the Commission was performing well. 'Ordinary people *do* believe that we are working better than ever before – and they are voting with their stamps.' The second requirement was to make sure that core effectiveness was not wrecked overnight by 'another crisis of our own making'.

This was code for avoiding McGregor's doorstep outbursts. At his first meeting of the Commission in January 1995, Wakeham stressed the importance of the Commission's not commenting 'on any current or ongoing matter until it had taken evidence and properly considered its adjudication'. It was vital that the Commission 'regained its credibility and authority as a judicial investigative body'.[23] The *Gazette* had earlier made the point:

> Lord McGregor's habit was to say what he thought and it was his downfall. Lord Wakeham's style has always been to offer a straight bat in public and to do his work behind the scenes. This will help enormously when he faces the inevitable barrage of microphones, tape recorders, television cameras and urgent inquisitors.[24]

At the Press Awards occasion Wakeham set out a wider frame of reference for the virtues of calmness and consistency.

> I am convinced that if legislation were ever to be introduced, it will not be because the PCC has failed the country. It will be because we made a mistake in our handling of one or two of these issues which aroused great controversy. That will not happen during my chairmanship. As they inevitably occur, these problems will be an opportunity to strengthen our standing: nothing else. And, as Ben Jonson once told us, it will often happen that short-term squalls 'are best answered with silence', rather than with reactions in the heat of the moment which leave our standing diminished.

This concept of opportunistic exploitation of critical issues for the PCC was to prove Wakeham's most important contribution to the ways and means of press self-regulation.

The third and final requirement diagnosed by Wakeham was defence of the PCC's independence.

> The PCC will not survive if it ever becomes common currency among public and politicians alike that it is merely a public relations exercise by the press to stave off statutory regulation. Political history is littered with gimmicks. We are not one, but perceptions can be as real – and as deadly – as facts. The Commission's continuing independence from the press must therefore be unyielding.[25]

Wakeham was now in a position to demonstrate the weight of independent lay membership of the Commission by announcing the appointment of Baroness Smith and Lord Tordoff, together with Lady Browne-Wilkinson, senior partner in a major firm of solicitors, and the eminent mandarin

Cubbon. Lay majorities were now in place in both the Commission and the Appointments Commission.

Thus fortified, Wakeham prepared for his second foray in unfolding what he called 'the Wakeham contract with the press', scheduled for the Scottish Press Fund gathering at Glasgow later in April. Events got in ahead of him. First there was Piers Morgan's exposé in the *News of the World* of the irregular private life of Richard Spring MP, aide to Sir Patrick Mayhew, Northern Ireland secretary. This was the eighth resignation from John Major's administration, and the seventh since the launch of the unlucky 'back to basics' project at the Conservative party conference of 1993. A hubbub of predictable cries for privacy legislation arose once more in Parliament, especially as it appeared that Spring had been the victim of entrapment and bugging. Arguments that a privacy law would make the public suspect that politicians were legislating in their own interests were drowned in the din. Woodrow Wyatt, a Murdoch columnist in the *News of the World* as well as an extoller of the way these things were managed in France, urged that legislation was needed 'if the red-blooded are ever again to take high-profile jobs'. Morgan had 'as good as asked for a privacy law'.[26] Gerald Kaufman reminded the world that his Heritage committee had supplied a privacy blueprint. 'We are still waiting. Ministers keep saying the response will come soon. But nothing happens.'[27] At the *News of the World* Morgan was perfectly placed to plead that the revelations against Spring were consistent with the government's own 'back to basics' definition of the public interest.

The *Sunday Mirror* could plead the same justification in the case of its destruction of the career of the deputy governor of the Bank of England, Rupert Pennant-Rea, who was discovered 'in flagrante' on the Bank's premises. But there was a twist in this tale, bespeaking certain selective scruples existing in the tabloid world. The *Daily Mail* originally had the Pennant-Rea story, but in deference presumably to Sir David English's exalted role in the apparatus of press self-regulation, it was handed to the *Sunday Mirror* 'on a plate'.[28] *Private Eye's* comment on the Spring affair was possibly more to the point than it realized at the time:

If a privacy law is introduced, it will be largely thanks to the antics of the gorm-less Piers Morgan, editor of the *News of the Screws*. Even Woodrow Wyatt, the paper's 'Voice of Reason', felt the exposure of Richard Spring was a scoop too far.

Woodrow Wyatt is a close and influential friend of Rupert Murdoch. But Murdoch also makes millions out of the *News of the Screws* weekly invasions of privacy. So which way will the Digger jump?

Murdoch has a long record of adjusting his behaviour to ingratiate himself with governments in the countries where he operates. . . . Besides his wife is known to be embarrassed by the sleazy reputation of some of his titles. So he could placate British politicians (and Woodrow Wyatt and Anna Murdoch) by sacking Piers Morgan and promising that the *Screws* will clean up its act. If so, however, the paper's circulation might well plummet, depriving the Digger of much-needed cash.[29]

For the moment, it was enough that Dorrell and Wakeham spoke 'in concert' as Tory backbenchers 'bayed' for privacy legislation. Dorrell made it clear he was not so minded. Wakeham told the *Press Gazette* that neither front bench was keen on legislation. 'It's the task of the PCC and the industry to make that system of self-regulation so successful that nobody can seriously want to pursue the statutory option.' But that would depend on total commitment to the Code by the press.[30] And the particular point made by Wakeham at the Scottish Press Fund occasion on 21 April was to stress that as long as editors exploited the public interest provisions in the Code as 'loopholes', that commitment was less than total and left the press vulnerable to the 'pontification of some broadcast journalists and the baying in the ranks of illiberal liberals, predictably calling for privacy legislation'. The PCC needed to ensure that editors did not flout the authority of the Code 'by defending stories as being in the public interest when they did not involve issues of genuine public concern'. For by this time Morgan's reckless splash in the *News of the World* early in April of a story about Countess Spencer, Diana's sister-in-law, was beginning to rebound upon him. Whereas in the Spring and Pennant-Rea cases the victims had preferred not to complain to the PCC, in this case a complaint was promptly lodged.

At Glasgow, Wakeham referred to 'a number of stories – some broken since I spoke in London' which had raised sensitive questions and 'brought into sharp focus the issue of what constitutes a "public interest" defence'. In the wake of these 'squalls which have rocked the boat of self-regulation', Wakeham commented that 'the *Guardian* was kind enough last week to say that . . . "the spotlight turns on Lord Wakeham". So it does.' In the matter of editorial humbug about the public interest, Wakeham promised, the Commission would be 'stinging in its criticism'.[31]

3

For Wakeham the orbits of events, circumstances and possibilities had moved into a favourable conjunction. Squalls rocking the self-regulatory boat set the scene. The spotlight was on him. An editor of a major national tabloid had recklessly exposed a vulnerable flank. Here was scope for opportunistic exploitation of a critical issue such as Wakeham had outlined in his British Press Awards speech: 'these problems will be an opportunity to strengthen our standing: nothing else'. Above all, here was scope for signal recourse to the big gun the Commission had armed itself with: appealing to a proprietor or publisher to consider disciplinary action in cases of 'severe or calculated breaches of the Code of Practice'.

The offence committed by Morgan at the *News of the World* was to publish a story over the first three pages of its 2 April edition, headlined 'DI'S SISTER-IN-LAW IN BOOZE AND BULIMIA CLINIC – ROYAL EXCLUSIVE', garnished with a long-lens photograph of the Countess Spencer in the grounds of the clinic. Her husband, Lord Spencer, Diana's brother, complained on the Countess's behalf to the PCC on grounds of breaches of the Code relating to privacy (Clause 4), hospitals and similar institutions (Clause 6) and harassment (Clause 8). Morgan's motive (and that of Bridget Rowe of the *People*, who was also involved[32]), apart from the circulation boost, seemed to be dislike of the 'hypocrisy of the arrogant Lord Spencer'. Aware of his vulnerability, Morgan then offered a rather half-hearted apology, in which he disclosed that 'careful consideration' had been given to publication of the picture 'for we knew that it could be in breach of our own Code of Practice'.

The significance of the case lay not so much in the prompt adjudication which upheld all the complaints[33]* as in the equally prompt despatch of a draft of it to Rupert Murdoch in New York with a covering letter from Wakeham invoking the 1994 'additional facility'. The circumstances were held to be appropriate: a breach, or breaches, of the Code so gross as to warrant rebuke more condign than the Commission's most 'stinging criticism'. Wakeham told Murdoch that the *News of the World* needed to review its application of the public interest clause in the Code dealing with intrusion on privacy and the use of subterfuge. He stressed that the published photograph of the Countess was in 'flagrant breach' of the Code.[34] It can be surmised reliably that the way was cleared for this procedure by the invaluable Sir Edward Pickering. *Private Eye* had asked: 'So which way will the Digger jump?' The Digger jumped on Piers Morgan.

'Murdoch blasts his "young editor who went over the top" after press body attacks NoW's countess coverage' was the *Guardian*'s headline on

---

* See boxed adjudication, pp. 196–9.

the report of the 'humiliating public rebuke' administered to Morgan, summoned by his proprietor to New York. Joanna Coles reported Morgan 'reeling from such a public dressing-down':

> Piers Morgan was not expecting it. When he breezed into his office yesterday morning he had no inkling that the Press Complaints Commission had already been in touch with his boss, Rupert Murdoch. He knew, of course, the PCC's adjudication was due sometime in the next 10 days but the timing took him by surprise. So did the severity of the adjudication. He had already murmured to colleagues that he thought he had got away with it.
>
> Perhaps, he had thought, a moist rebuke over the photograph, a gentle word in the ear from Lord Wakeham. Not a bit of it. He left his office basking in the humiliation of a very public dressing-down and a warning that he had better pull up his Argyll socks. He was very upset.
>
> By contrast, two miles away, Lord Wakeham . . . was very cheerful. He was basking in the knowledge that at last, the commission had been seen to pull its socks up so high they almost covered its knees. It was the first time the PCC had sent a letter to a publisher and the response was gratifying. 'I think Mr Murdoch is to be congratulated for taking such a strong line', said Lord Wakeham. 'I think papers are taking the code increasingly seriously.'[35]

After being informed of the Commission's ruling in a letter from Lord Wakeham, as Alexandra Frean reported, 'Mr Murdoch said yesterday: "While I will always support worthwhile investigative journalism as a community responsibility, it is clear that in this case the young man went over the top."' Murdoch added that News International, which also owned *The Times*, 'would not tolerate its papers bringing popular journalism into disrepute'. Morgan announced in a separate statement that he accepted full responsibility for the story and had sent 'sincere apologies' to Lady Spencer.

Things might have been worse for Morgan. Wakeham told Murdoch that, as well as the Spencer affair, the Commission wanted to investigate how the *News of the World* got hold of its material about Richard Spring's private life. The investigation had to be dropped on Spring's declining to agree to it.[36] Soon afterwards Morgan was only too ready to be poached by MGN to become editor of the *Daily Mirror*.[37]

Clearly the episode was an immense boost for Wakeham and the Commission. Wakeham had exploited his opportunity to optimum effect – the first of a series of such exploitations. For the first time the Commission and its chairman had been in the critical spotlight of favourable public attention. For the first time it had demonstrated that it was equipped with teeth that could bite. There was a fair chance that the Spencer case might prove to be the turning point in the PCC's fortunes. There were knowledgeable observers of the press scene who endorsed that interpretation. Charles Wilson wrote glowingly of 'Wakeham's pivotal move' which revealed a PCC 'powerful, independent, and effective'.[38] 'When the history of how newspapers saved themselves from statutory regulation after ten years in the dock before Whitehall and the House of Commons is written', commented Brian MacArthur, 'the defining moment may well be seen to have occurred in May 1995.'[39]

4

On Monday 22 May Wakeham breakfasted in London with Murdoch. 'Your support for what we are trying to do at the PCC', he told the proprietor, 'is of very great importance to me and I am extremely grateful.'[40] Wakeham was now in a strong position to give leads for the future. One of the first was to tell the *Press Gazette* that the PCC must rewrite the definition of public interest so there can be no doubt as to what it means – 'and not whatever an editor might believe interests the public'.[41] Another was to set going a debate about opening up the Code Committee to lay members of the Commission. Lay input, Wakeham calculated, would make the Code more acceptable to the public, especially when it came to redefining the 'public interest' defence in privacy cases. The Commission's ratifying role at present consisted in simply accepting or rejecting amendments or additions proposed by the Code Committee. Wakeham envisaged the Code Committee's status being raised 'to that of the Commission itself and of Pressbof, the industry funding body'. For all his vanity, David English was not likely to be easily softened up by this kind of sop to his Committee's status. He thought Wakeham's initiative 'a very interesting idea, and one I want to ponder on and then discuss with my fellow editors'. For the moment he was content to point out that the Code was 'a professional Code and it has to be set by members of the profession'.[42]

For all that the PCC had performed creditably in the spotlight of public and parliamentary scrutiny, its critics for the most part remained as vociferously unappeased as ever. Wakeham had wrangled earlier with Joe Ashton MP, one of the Heritage committee members. The Commission, Ashton accused, could never be 'a really independent ombudsman so long as it has members of its jury with a vested interest in "not guilty" verdicts'.

Neither can it be a professional body or industry watchdog like the BMA, or the Law Society, or even the Football Association, when it refuses to introduce self-imposed sanctions to fine, or suspend those who bug telephones, plant tape recorders, act as *agents provocateurs*, break embargoes, ignore agreements not to print photographs of rape victims, or pay for pictures of women with their legs in the air in gymnasiums, or use methods of entrapment to gain 'evidence' which would be immediately thrown out of any court of law.

Wakeham would soon be in a position to answer at least Ashton's ultimate accusation – 'what is even worse, rogue editors know it, and laugh at it' – by citing the recent hammering of the *News of the World* and the fact that Piers Morgan was not exactly laughing. But, confronted before that hammering with Ashton's formidable indictment, Wakeham had to concede that 'we still have a long way to go to convince some legislators that the PCC can fairly hold the balance between the public and the press'.[43]

Among such eminent and influential critics of press self-regulation, Geoffrey Robertson QC had not modified his long-held conviction that the PCC was 'a fraud and a confidence trick'. At a 'Publish and be Damned' conference at the London College of Printing presided over by Roy Greenslade, Robertson and others grappled with the Commission's delegate, Robert Pinker. One of the Labour party's media spokesmen, Graham Allen MP, condemned the PCC for its failure to take the initiative in investigating the murky background of the Richard Spring affair: this, alleged Allen, 'highlighted its weaknesses'. Allen raised an important issue of PCC procedure. Could it be justified in instigating an investigation against the express wish of the victim concerned? Pinker was there to draw attention to the awkward possible implications. Greenslade later had occasion to describe them as 'nightmares'.[44]

As ever, Robertson could be relied on to do good service to self-regulation by his polemical skills in demonstrating how much worse the cures being proposed would be than the disease. He forecast that the Commission would get more powers, such as power to enforce compensation payments in lieu of any privacy legislation: a case assuredly of cure being worse than disease. All Professor Pinker had to do was agree and dilate on the improvements in the Commission's handling of privacy cases over the last couple of years.[45]

Robertson in fact was an accurate forecaster, at least as far as the Labour front bench was concerned. Lord Irvine, member of the Appointments Commission as well as shadow Lord Chancellor, came up with a scheme to equip the PCC with a compensation fund for victims of invasion of privacy. He told the Fleet Street Lawyers' Society: 'There are strong advocates of a new wrong of invasion of privacy. That can be warded off only by effective self-regulation.' Irvine allowed that the PCC's reforms in 1993 and early 1994 had been important, but he would 'welcome a definitive report on how widely the Code of Practice has been incorporated into journalists' contracts, as the PCC has urged'. And the principal weakness of the PCC remained: its shortage of punitive sanctions. 'I would urge the press to introduce a compensation scheme to be administered by the PCC as the most cogent means of persuading the public that self-regulation really works.'[46] In its mocking dismissal of Irvine's 'nonsense' – 'the moment that the PCC undertakes to fine its members, and to decide the size of that fine, is the moment self-regulation starts to collapse' – the *Press Gazette* nonetheless confirmed the accuracy of Robertson's forecast: that is, the government's White Paper in response to Calcutt and to the National Heritage committee was soon to be published, and would almost certainly include recommendations of which Irvine's float was a foretaste.

In the run-up to this event the PCC's work, quite apart from the Countess Spencer/*News of the World* affair, was not without incident. An instance of 'jigsaw' identification led to the Commission's upholding a complaint against *The Times*.[47]* Ironically, as the *Press Gazette* observed, the *Times*'s report was published on the same day that David English and representatives of the BBC, ITN and ITV were telling the Home Office minister David Maclean what the industry was going to do to prevent jigsaw Code breaches. Maclean, according to English, was 'impressed and thought the industry was doing its very best in complex circumstances but could not guarantee that the Director of Public Prosecutions would not take action if children were involved'.[48]

The politicians were not best pleased when the *Mirror*, the *Sun*, and *Today* breached the clauses in the Code on harassment and intrusion by publishing stories which 'intruded in a serious manner into the confidential medical affairs of a private citizen and the grief of his immediate family' on the death from Aids of the nephew of Tory MP Peter Lilley. The *Mirror* complied with Lilley's request that his nephew's name not be published, but held that the public was entitled to know if a relation of a senior Cabinet minister was dying of Aids. The Commission rejected the papers' public-interest claims and upheld Lilley's complaint.[49]

---

* See boxed adjudication, pp. 199–200.

This was precisely the kind of problem Wakeham thought should be attended to in his projected revision of the public-interest guidelines in the Code. 'The way the Code develops has to be thought through', he told Jean Morgan. 'Nowhere do we define what is private life. It is a good question.' There were examples from either end of the spectrum. Some were instances of legitimate inquiry because the person concerned was a public figure. 'On the other hand, there are times when it is clearly not. But the real world is in the middle.' Wakeham suspected that, in the end, 'we will never be able, and rightly so, to remove the element of good professional judgment by editors on whether or not publication is going to be justified'.[50]

Then an important precedent was established by the PCC when Wakeham decided to reopen the file on the *Sunday Times*'s exposé of the 'cash for questions' politicians, which had involved issues of subterfuge and entrapment. Having considered the findings of the Commons' privileges committee, the Commission reviewed its handling of Riddick's complaint and concluded there had been a discrepancy in the evidence submitted by the newspaper. Sir James Spicer, a Tory MP, rejoiced: 'This is good news. Every member of the committee felt that the conduct of the *Sunday Times* had not been properly investigated by the PCC.'[51] The Commission had also proceeded improperly by continuing with the case after Riddick had withdrawn his complaint.

This was both good procedure and good politics for the PCC. Relations with the National Heritage department were now, as the *Press Gazette* understood, 'very good'. From the beginning of 1994 Dorrell had made it clear that the press would continue to be self-regulatory for the foreseeable future. There was no consistent push for regulatory controls from the dithering John Major. Dorrell had at one time worked for Wakeham at the whips' office. 'He and I worked extremely closely together', Wakeham acknowledged, 'but that does not mean we always see eye to eye.' On occasion Wakeham was prepared to be quite ruthless in imposing his political weight and authority to keep juniors like Dorrell in line. That Wakeham's fingerprints might be traceable on much of the documentation coming through the latter stages of the department's White Paper is a reasonable conjecture. And he had accomplices here in David Newell of the NS and David English.

When Virginia Bottomley took over from Dorrell in June, Wakeham welcomed yet another of his former pupils. 'I gave her a great deal of encouragement in her career when I was chief whip', he later told Brian MacArthur. 'She's very level-headed and sensible.'[52] No doubt Wakeham had reason to find her most level-headed and sensible in her approach to the White Paper drafts she inherited from Dorrell. For public consumption Wakeham wrote to her on 19 June welcoming her as a co-worker in the field of press freedom and conveying the great strides being taken by the PCC in making the Calcutt and National Heritage committee recommendations supererogatory. But for all his forceful manipulation behind the scenes, he took care publicly not to seem to take his former colleagues for granted. And it was ever expedient to keep the industry on its toes. His view, as he told Jean Morgan, was that neither government nor opposition front benches 'particularly want to bring in statutory regulation'; but both could do so. 'The majority of their supporters on the back benches still want to see it. The press should not underestimate the forces who want statutory control.' It was still too early to say whether self-regulation was working. But in any case Wakeham reminded the industry that it would never be possible or desirable to resolve totally the tensions between government and the press.[53]

5

Those tensions were again evident when Virginia Bottomley finally unveiled the government's responses to the Heritage select committee's recommendations in its White Paper, Privacy and Media Intrusion, on 17 July. Industry response was, on the whole, one of relief. David Newell, for the Newspaper Society, declared it 'much better than expected'. The PCC 'is supported as against statutory regulation in a more unequivocal way than ever before by the government. They've backed off a statutory agency with controls over the press, backed off the criminal law suggestion, backed off the tort of privacy.' The only area of discussion opened up was 'how the PCC should evolve over the years in terms of its composition, the Code and the issues of sanctions and the compensation fund, where the government would like to see further development'.[54]

Jon Slattery reported 'much cheering in the Last Chance Saloon' when the White Paper revealed that ministers had abandoned any legislative plans for the press. Disgruntled Labour MPs complained that the last chance saloon had been given 'a substantial extension of its drinking hours'. Bottomley was much heckled during her statement in the Commons. 'Senior backbenchers could hardly believe their ears.' At one point she was interrupted by a storm of protest that she was ignoring public concern. There were jeers from the Tory benches: 'You're giving in to the Fourth

Estate.'[55] Jill Sherman reported in *The Times* that MPs across the political spectrum were angered by the government's lenient treatment of the media after more than two years of delay over recommendations for statutory control by Sir David Calcutt. Bottomley's point of departure was in effect to echo Peter Brooke's initial response to Calcutt in January 1993. A statutory body to regulate the press, she declared, would be 'a very significant step on a path we have no wish to travel'. A 'free press is vital to a free country'. The difficulties in defining the scope of a privacy law were 'formidable'.

There was a consensus in the industry that, while Virginia Bottomley made the announcement, 'the paper had the stamp of Stephen Dorrell all over it – leave well alone'.[56] In truth, the stamp of Wakeham was even more clearly traceable.

The rituals of 1993 were now again also to be reworked. Bottomley threatened that 'legal measures should not be ruled out'. Industry feeling, however, was that ministers were no longer in the strong post-election position they had enjoyed in 1993, when their polite blackmail had to be taken seriously. Now, 'given the amount of wolf-crying since the Last Chance Saloon opened its doors for business, few editors are taking the threat seriously'. But where the rituals really mattered was that, while the industry in general was let off, the PCC in particular was going to be presented with the bill.

On the face of it, that bill was quite formidable. In her explanatory response to Wakeham, Bottomley stressed that 'sanctions are a crucial issue'. Ministers had been impressed by the increased authority of the PCC following its strong ruling over the Countess Spencer/*News of the World* affair. 'I am not clear', Bottomley however continued, 'what further action, beyond a reprimand, a proprietor may take against an editor who is in blatant breach of the Code. Should not proprietors consider dismissal in appropriate cases, and the Commission make recommendations to that effect?' Then it emerged that Dorrell's old partiality for a compensation fund was still on the agenda: very much as Irvine had urged on behalf of the Labour front bench. Then also it appeared that the old 'hotline' scheme was still alive.

None of these matters was likely to prove contentious. The Commission's recommended sacking of editors was no doubt quite agreeable to Wakeham but was never likely to be countenanced by the industry which, for practical self-regulatory purposes, meant Pressbof. Even were it legally feasible (which it was not) it would have been an entirely inappropriate power to be wielded by a voluntary lay-majority body such as the PCC. The main thrust of the White Paper's impact on the PCC was Bottomley's insistence that the Code of Practice needed radical overhauling. It tilted too much in the direction of the public's 'right to know'. It was set up and controlled by a committee consisting exclusively of editors. Bottomley made it clear that the arrangement was 'not best calculated to reassure the public about the committee's independence from the industry'. She suggested that the PCC's director, Mark Bolland, should henceforth act as secretary to the Code Committee and that it should include a 'lay element' and 'input from the public'. Could it have been that over these proposals to marginalize Roche, Grahame Thomson and Pressbof, Mark Bolland's tell-tale fingerprints were perhaps most insidiously detectable? The Code needed tightening in the clauses dealing with privacy, public-interest justification, and intrusion into grief and shock. Bottomley suggested also that the Commission should publish fuller summaries of adjudications, so that journalists and the public could get a clearer idea of the reasons behind them. She recommended that the Commission consider greater use of oral hearings. Her parting shot was that incorporation of the Code into journalists' contracts should be extended to freelances.[57]

With certain of these administrative and Code reforms Wakeham was already perfectly in tune. He could respond quite readily that amending and tightening the Code would be the PCC's priority over the next three months, with special emphasis on 'what is considered by many to be an area of weakness – the mechanism by which the Code is reviewed'. This would be another instance of opportunistic exploitation of problems. Immediate obstacles were that neither Roche nor Thomson had any intention of letting Bolland take over the secretaryship of the Code Committee: while Roche and Wakeham had settled down to a perfectly amicable working relationship, there remained little love lost between their respective satraps Thomson and Bolland. And Sir David English disliked very much the project of diluting the profession's control of its Code of Practice. Lay membership had infiltrated the Commission, as it had the Press Council. But infiltrating the Code Committee was another matter.

To Harry Roche at Pressbof it was clear that he faced an uphill task with the industry so cool on the compensation fund scheme. News International, the country's biggest national newspaper publisher, while supporting self-regulation, had 'expressed reservations about such a fund in the past'. Roche announced that 'we could probably quite readily agree with one or two of the Secretary of State's proposals, but others would be more difficult'. The compensation fund would be counterproductive, Roche suggested, because

it would clog the wheels of self-regulation. Lawyers would inevitably be involved, and 'the next thing is you build up a backlog'. And given that the industry would never accept the prior restraint censorship inherent in the hotline, its apparent attractiveness diminishes considerably. Roche's parting shot was that hitherto he had extracted £1 million and more a year from the industry without difficulty – the implication being that the money to fund self-regulation was not an unconditional resource.[58]

These were polite responses from the industry's self-regulation grandees. The *Press Gazette* treated 'poor old Virginia' and her 'latest climb-down' with even more contemptuous mockery than it had inflicted on Irvine.[59] In Fleet Street the reaction was reported as 'not so much a sigh of relief as a shrug of the shoulders'. *The Times* commented that 'Damocles' sword works only when it is hanging over your head: the sword which the Heritage Minister rattled on Monday evening had been gathering dust in a Whitehall drawer for so long that editors doubted that it could ever do them real harm'.[60] Wakeham permitted himself a measure of gratification. The position adopted by the government, he observed at the Commission's meeting on 26 July, 'represented a considerable triumph for the press and the Press Complaints Commission, as for the first time ever the Government had recognised the fundamental efficacy of the PCC'. The 'damaging analysis' of Calcutt 2 'had finally been overcome'.[61] Still, for all his own thankfulness that at long last the government had opted to carry on with press self-regulation, and that the Commission would have a new standing and prestige from this endorsement, Wakeham could not yet rejoice that they were quite clear out of the woods.

Report No. 29, March–April 1995
News of the World

COMPLAINT
The Earl Spencer complains that in publishing a story covering the first three pages of its 2 April 1995 edition the News of the World unjustifiably intruded into the privacy of his wife in breach of Clauses 4 (Privacy), 6 (Hospitals and similar institutions) and 8 (Harassment) of the Code of Practice.

Earl Spencer has informed the Commission that the complaint is made on behalf of his wife and with her consent.

The story was headlined 'DI'S SISTER IN BOOZE AND BULIMIA CLINIC . . . ROYAL EXCLUSIVE . . . Earl Spencer's ailing wife has secret therapy' and reported that 'Victoria Spencer, 29, is suffering from bulimia . . . is also believed to have a drink problem' and was being treated in a private addiction clinic. The article went into considerable detail about the circumstances of Countess Spencer's alleged problems and featured, on the front page and again on page three, a photograph of Countess Spencer walking in the grounds of the clinic. The photograph had clearly been taken using a telephoto lens without her permission and was captioned 'BATTLING: Victoria in the clinic grounds . . . SO THIN: Victoria walks in the clinic's grounds this week'.

After the publication of the story Earl Spencer issued a statement to the Press Association in which he condemned the intrusion he alleged his wife had suffered. He said that Countess Spencer was a private individual and he could see no justification for the publication of this story in terms of Clause 18 (Public Interest) of the PCC's Code of Practice. He argued that if anybody needed privacy and freedom from harassment it was a person suffering from psychological disorders.

The associate editor of the newspaper responded to the complaint on behalf of the News of the World.

He argued that Earl Spencer was a public figure whose privileges by birth made him open to a degree of public examination. He claimed that Earl Spencer was no stranger to publicity in the press and had on many occasions encouraged media interest in his home and family in return for fees or publicity. He cited a number of examples in this respect, arguing that Earl Spencer had by putting his family in the public arena on so many occasions waived their rights to privacy. With regard to the issue of the Countess's health the associate editor drew the Commission's attention to two particular matters. First, he referred to an item in the social diary column of Harpers and Queen magazine dated August 1993 which reported on '*an evening of music and champagne in aid of the Eating Disorders Association*' in which the writer claimed that Countess Spencer had attended the evening as a guest of honour with her husband and had told her in a private conversation that she '*had suffered from the condition for many years*'. The second was a reference to the Daily Mail dated 5 August 1993 containing an interview with Earl Spencer about his family estate. This stated that Earl Spencer '*revealed that Lady Spencer worked part-time at St. Andrew's Hospital, Northampton, where she voluntarily helps young girls suffering from anorexia, which plagued her own teenage years*'.

In its edition of 9 April, the News of the World published a lengthy editorial piece headlined '*Hypocrisy of the arrogant Earl Spencer . . . His privacy can be invaded – for cash*'. Towards the very end of this piece the editor wrote '. . . *we openly admit that we did take a photograph of [Earl Spencer's] wife from a public road outside the grounds in which she was walking at the time. Careful consideration was given to the publication of that picture for we knew it could be in breach of our own Code of Practice. If it caused offence or distress to Lady Spencer, we apologise to her. But one reason we carried it was to prove our story was true. For Earl Spencer has a rather disturbing tendency to lie through his back teeth when the press he so loves to manipulate uncovers less than complimentary stories about him.*'

The newspaper maintained that Countess Spencer's illness had been put firmly into the public domain by her actions and those of her husband and she was not entitled to rely on the privacy provisions of the Code of Practice. It claimed that the clinic was not a hospital but a health centre offering no medical treatment and having no doctor on the staff.

Clause 6(ii) of the Code states that '*The restrictions on intruding into privacy are particularly relevant to enquiries about individuals in hospitals or similar institutions*'. In the view of the

Commission, the '*similar institutions*' referred to in Clause 6 clearly include the type of clinic involved in this case.

Two further matters arise in relation to the PCC's Code of Practice: the specific question of the publication of the photograph of the Countess in the grounds of the clinic and the more general issue of alleged intrusion into her privacy raised by the publication of the story by the newspaper.

The photography of individuals on private property without their consent specifically constitutes harassment under Clause 8(ii) of the Code unless such action can be justified in the public interest under Clause 18.

In the absence of such public interest justification, the Commission does not accept that the publication of a photograph taken with a telephoto lens of an indisputably unwell person walking in the private secluded grounds of an addiction clinic can be anything other than a breach of the Code. The Commission notes the 'apology' published to the Countess as part of the newspaper's comment on her husband but does not accept that this can reasonably be seen to remedy the complaint or exculpate the newspaper from a failure to observe the Code in the first place. The contention that the newspaper published the photograph to demonstrate the veracity of the article is rejected by the Commission, which concludes that the newspaper is guilty of a serious breach of one of the most unequivocal parts of the Code of Practice.

The Commission has no doubt that matters of health fall within the terms of an 'individual's private life' described in Clause 4 (Privacy) of the Code. On Earl Spencer's complaint of intrusion into privacy the Commission therefore considered whether Countess Spencer was entitled to be protected from any intrusion into her privacy in the face of the newspaper's arguments to the contrary.

In arguing that the Countess's privacy had not been invaded, the newspaper made allegations concerning the Earl's character and his attitude and behaviour towards the press.

ADJUDICATION

While the Commission considers that the Earl's past relationship with the press and his admitted planting of false information published in the News of the World on 7 May affects the extent to which he may now be entitled to privacy in respect of particular aspects of his own life, it does not believe that this necessarily leaves the press free to report on any matter concerning the Countess. The fact that Earl Spencer may have sought publicity in the past cannot reasonably be taken to mean that, henceforward, every aspect of the private affairs of his wife is a matter which the press has a right to put into the public domain. In the view of the Commission, this must apply particularly to matters affecting her health and psychological well-being. The magazine diary piece cited by the newspaper is, in the view of the Commission, an insufficient basis on which to build a case that the Countess had opened her illness to public scrutiny or that there is a public interest justification for the articles and photographs printed. The Daily Mail article put forward was an interview with the Earl containing a passing comment about the Countess's health in the past.

To justify the intrusion of which the complaint is made the newspaper is required under the Code of Practice to demonstrate that publication was in the public interest.

The newspaper has failed to offer any sufficient argument to sustain its position on this point.

The complaints are all upheld.

The Commission takes a particularly serious view of this matter. The article by the newspaper was not justified as being in the public interest under Clause 18 of the Code. This breach was compounded through a flagrant breach of Clause 8(ii) by the publication of the photograph of the Countess in the private grounds of the clinic.

In January 1994 the Commission announced that it would in future bring instances of severe or calculated breaches of the Code of Practice (whose terms are incorporated into the conditions of employment of members of staff of many newspapers) to the attention of publishers.

In accordance with this statement, the Commission has referred its adjudication in this case to the publisher of the News of the World.

Following the Commission's adjudication on the complaint from Earl Spencer against the News of the World, Mr Rupert Murdoch, Chairman of News International plc, issued the following statement:

'While I will always support worthwhile investigative journalism as a community responsibility. it is clear that in this case the young man [the editor] went over the top. Mr Morgan has assured me that his forthcoming apology to Earl and Countess Spencer on this matter is sincere and without reservation.

I have no hesitation in making public this remonstration and I have reminded Mr Morgan forcefully of his responsibility to the Code to which he as editor – and all our journalists – subscribe in their terms of employment. This company will not tolerate its papers bringing into disrepute the best practices of popular journalism which we seek to follow.'

Later that day a statement was released from Mr Piers Morgan, editor of the News of the World:

'I have read carefully the PCC adjudication and accept their ruling without reservation. The decision to publish the story and the photograph of Countess Spencer in the grounds of the clinic was mine and mine alone and I take full responsibility. I am sending my sincere apologies to the Countess Spencer for any distress that our actions may have caused at an obviously difficult time for her.

Mr Murdoch has made his feelings on this subject very clear to me and I am determined that, as he says, the News of the World will strive to maintain the best practices of popular investigative journalism within the agreed parameters of the PCC's Code of Conduct.'

Report No. 30, May–July 1995
The Times

COMPLAINT

Mr J A Hazzledine, of Chester, complains that children who were the alleged victims of an indecent assault were identifiable through jigsaw identification due to a breach of Clause 13 (Children in sex cases) of the Code of Practice by The Times on 1 May 1995.

The Times responded immediately to the complaint, apologising fully for an irrefutable breach of the Code. The newspaper told the Commission that as soon as the breach was realised, a memorandum was sent reminding those in charge of all departments of the paper of their obligations to work within the Code.

ADJUDICATION
The Commission regrets this serious lapse by The Times and expects the editor to ensure that the procedures put in place to prevent it recurring are effective.

The complaint is upheld.

CHAPTER TEN

'I think we have turned the corner with the PCC',
July–December 1995

'Sadly, the Government has lost its nerve in protecting privacy. . . . it will not do to leave it to Lord Wakeham's Press Complaints Commission.'

Woodrow Wyatt, *The Times*, 1 August 1995

'PCC now *recognized* for the first time as an authoritative, credible, and independent body capable of doing a good job. *This was not the case before the beginning of the year.*'

Lord Wakeham, note for speech to the board of the Newspaper Publishers Association, London, 4 October 1995

The two 'defining moments' that shaped for the Commission the turn of events in 1995 – Rupert Murdoch's jumping on Piers Morgan at the *News of the World* and Virginia Bottomley's White Paper – had passed. How could it be ensured that their definition remained impressed upon the future? Murdoch was already taking his own steps into the future. Tony Blair, the Labour leader, accepted his invitation to address News Corporation executives on Hayman Island, off the Queensland coast, on the theme of 'Cross-media Ownership: Labour's considered response.' Blair's speech, it was observed, 'did appear to curry favour in the Murdoch camp'. (Which is more than the Conservatives had managed. Wakeham, after his breakfast with Murdoch on 22 May, was perforce apologetic: 'As for developments on the question of media ownership we at the PCC have no view. You will know from our conversation that I am concerned the government may not have got it quite right.'[1]) Whatever the implications of this 'Great Press Hijack' for the Conservative party or the Labour party – was Blair 'selling his soul or sealing his premiership?'[2] – a future Labour government neutralized on the issue of press self-regulation could only be beneficial to the PCC.

The existing Conservative government, already so neutralized, was the subject of much angry comment. 'Sadly, the Government has lost its nerve on protecting privacy', lamented Lord Wyatt. 'Perhaps it fears, in view of its small majority, that such a controversial law would not pass. But this is a cross-party matter, and it will not do to leave it to Lord Wakeham's Press Complaints Commission.' Having dismissed the recommendations of both Calcutt and the Heritage committee, the government 'preferred to rely on the optimism of Lord Wakeham'. This, Wyatt was sure, was a most unsafe procedure. To the proposed new sanctions for the PCC 'a suitable reply from innocent bystanders is "ha ha"'. Wyatt cited recent scandals which gave the lie to the cosy exchange of compliments between Bottomley and Wakeham: witness Mike Atherton the cricketer, Liz Hurley and Hugh Grant the film stars, and Sir William Greenbury, chairman of the committee on executive remuneration, who had decided to withdraw from public life. 'Soon only the brazen and the bloodless will be willing to endure the media pillory.' The Prime Minister's son was being continually harassed. 'Not a dickie-bird from the PCC.' There would have to be a privacy law eventually. 'Why not now?'[3]

More grist for Wyatt's mill turned up later in August, with Piers Morgan at the *News of the World*, according to *Private Eye*, 'thrilled with his scoop' about Will Carling, the England rugby captain, and his affair with Diana. 'So thrilled, indeed, he ran another five pages on the subject a week later, embellished with copious quotations from love-letters Carling sent to a girl-friend four years ago.'[4]

Two counter-measures from the industry reflected its concern at the hostility represented by Wyatt both in Parliament and public opinion at the way press self-regulation could plausibly be mocked as 'velvet-gloved raps on the knuckles by the well-meaning Lord Wakeham and his futile PCC'. Murdoch, it was 'widely rumoured', 'believes Piers Morgan has delighted us enough and may soon invite him to seek alternative employ-ment'.[5] In September Morgan moved across to MGN to edit the *Mirror*. For much the same reason, Murdoch had promoted Kelvin MacKenzie on from the *Sun* in 1994.

Wakeham's counter-measure was his second proactive move after his request for Murdoch's intervention in May. Both he and David Eng-lish foresaw a political storm erupting if press intrusion marred Prince William's arrival at Eton and his life at the college. Wakeham was in touch with Charles Anson at the Palace press office. English had inside knowledge that pupils at Eton and locals were being lined up by some newspapers to supply stories about the Prince when he began his schooling in September. English, so the *Press Gazette* had it, 'is believed to have warned that the PCC should act before the whole issue blew up and derailed press self-regulation'. It was Wakeham's particular opportunistic twist to the affair to exploit the circumstance that in July the Commission had upheld a complaint from a parent in Accrington whose son had been approached as he was leaving school by a reporter from the local paper asking for information about other pupils, in breach of Clause 12 of the Code.[6]*

In a speech at St Bride's Institute, Fleet Street, on 23 August, Wakeham offered historical insights into the 'schizophrenic' relationship, veneration alternating with contempt, between the monarchy and the press in the nineteenth century. The point of his address was to make a case for press responsibilities as well as rights in respect of reporting the royal family. 'Next month Prince William starts a new school. Prince William is not an institution: nor a soap star: nor a football hero. He is a child: in the next four years – perhaps the most important and sometimes painful of his life – he will grow up and become a man.' Prince William, Wakeham insisted, was entitled to the same protection from media intrusion as was any other child. He 'must be allowed to run, walk, study and play . . . free from prying cameras'. Last month the Commission upheld a complaint from a parent in Accrington. 'What goes for a child in Accrington goes for a child in Eton.'[7]

This was unbeatable populist copy. As the *Press Gazette* commented, Wakeham was an astute politician, and his Accrington gambit was a 'shrewd move'.[8] Virginia Bottomley promptly applauded this proactive initiative. 'This is an early step in what I expect to be a continuing process in the drive to place greater importance on individual privacy.' Buckingham Palace welcomed the speech as a 'timely intervention'. 'Fleet Street royal pack growls as it is called to heel' was the *Guardian*'s line.

Alexandra Frean reported for *The Times* that editors of tabloid newspapers understood Lord Wakeham's concerns. 'Privately, however, some said they had arrived at a gentleman's agreement with the Palace . . . "We have agreed not to harass him. But if stories are brought to us from outside, we will work with the Palace and they have agreed to be more forthcoming than usual", one editor said.' Stuart Higgins of the the *Sun* and Tessa Hilton of the *Sunday Mirror* undertook to co-operate. David English seconded Wakeham's declaration with his own letter to national newspaper editors. A sour note came from Jacob Ecclestone, assistant general secretary of the NUJ, who accused Wakeham of acting as 'a public relations agency for

---

* See boxed adjudication, pp. 212–213.

the Royal Family'.[9] And there was what the *Press Gazette* called a 'justifiable fear' that, were anything newsworthy to happen to Prince William, it would be left to the Palace press office to decide whether anything should be released to the media. That office 'is not seen by royal correspondents as always the best judge of what makes a story'.[10]

Moreover, as with the affair of Murdoch's swoop in the Spencer/*News of the World* case, high-profile coups in press self-regulation involved correspondingly high risk. The industry could see that the future of self-regulation was in effect being 'gambled on the behaviour of the national tabloids'.[11] At the St Bride's Institute Wakeham had pointed to the opportunity for the industry 'to show its maturity'.

> When the issues are so clear cut, if we fail we have only ourselves to blame for the consequences. But if we succeed – when the temptations are undoubtedly so great – no one will ever again be able to cast doubt on the ability of the press to regulate itself. That is a prize well worth fighting for.[12]

2

As 'gangs of forelock-tugging hacks and snappers jostled outside Slough grammar for the arrival of Prince William',[13] the Commission could reasonably feel assured that the Accrington gambit had indeed proved a shrewd move. The Prince of Wales signified his gratitude for Sir David's backroom expertise. The industry rather preened itself that 'for once, after Calcutt and the threat of Government White Papers, it is the press which is taking the lead in regulation', with Lord Wakeham charging in and setting the agenda.[14] Virginia Bottomley's telling the Newspaper Press Fund in London that more work was to be done before MPs and the public were convinced that the industry could effectively police itself was only to be expected. She was under pressure on the one side from Tory backbenchers angry at her refusal to crack down legislatively on newspaper excesses, and on the other from her need to keep up her own pressure on the newspaper industry.

That need was soon advertised. The pot of scandalous press behaviour bubbled away in these weeks with rumours of papers buying up witnesses in the forthcoming trial of Rosemary West, widow and alleged accomplice of Fred West, the Gloucester serial murderer. There were demands that the law on contempt of court be sharpened. That the PCC now enjoyed a commanding new standing is evident from the *Press Gazette*'s urging that, with the pressure now on the Attorney-General, it was time for a concerted effort to thrash out the whole problem of contempt, 'and a solution might be for the Press Complaints Commission to become involved'. After all, the PCC 'showed over its pre-emptive warning to newspapers to respect Prince William's privacy while he is at Eton that it can act on behalf of the press, rather than just react when a problem blows up'.[15]

For Wakeham and his PCC colleagues it was gratifying to see that an important point was being taken. Problems, nonetheless, kept threatening to blow up. Alerted by PressWise to growing concern about journalists' behaviour and persistence in seeking background information from relations of victims in the West case, the Commission circulated confidentially to all editors on 27 September that they be especially mindful of the Code of Practice bearing on the problem. Possible breaches of Clause 9 on payment for articles could spill over into breaches of Clause 8 on harassment and Clause 10 on intrusion into grief or shock.

Before long Wakeham would be signalling concern at the way newspapers were handling their reporting of the West trial and the Commission eventually would initiate investigation. But in these latter months of 1995 the predominant mood at the PCC was one of having at last got on top of the intricacies of regulating the press. At the meeting of the Commission on 27 September, 'the chairman again noted the publication of the Secretary of State for National Heritage's landmark statement about the Press Complaints Commission. This was generally held to be a defining moment in the PCC's history as it was the first time the government had recognized the fundamental efficacy of self-regulation in its present form.'[16] When Wakeham and Bolland introduced themselves to the national newspaper chiefs at a luncheon hosted by Frank Rogers at the NPA offices at Southwark Bridge Road on 4 October, they were no longer the embarrassed supplicants of former times. To the assembled representatives of the Telegraph Group, News International, the Guardian Media Group, the Mirror Group and Associated Newspapers, Wakeham spoke as a confident chief to chiefs. His theme was that the Commission was 'now <u>recognized for the first time as an authoritative, credible and independent body capable of doing a good job. *This was not the case before the beginning of this year.*'</u> The challenge now was to deal with the Bottomley 'suggestions for the way forward': there was the hotline, the compensation fund, the tougher Code, the different way of reviewing the Code, more publicity, oral hearings, dismissal of editors for breaching the Code, and so forth. The method of dealing with these would be to 'move energetically but slowly'. In Wakeham's view, with an improved perception of the PCC's independence and with a refreshed lay membership, 'the system as it is works well and I find it difficult to see that any significant changes are necessary at the present time'. However: '<u>MUST</u> avoid any further crunch points of confrontation between DNH and PCC/industry – all politicians want press controls to stop being an issue.'[17]

Later that October, Wakeham used the occasion of the Harold Macmillan lecture at Nottingham Trent University to set his sense of the Commission's new authority, credibility and independence within a wider frame of explanatory historical reference. His title, 'Away from Damocles,' expressed his belief that allusion to the sword of Damocles best represented the febrile and dangerous relationship that had existed between the press and the body politic in Britain for the greater part of a decade. The natural and even desirable tension between those who exercise power by popular mandate and those who scrutinize that exercise on behalf of the mandatory people had in recent years become stretched to breaking point. 'It cannot be right for a relationship so fundamental to democracy to be conducted in the brawling atmosphere of the last chance saloon.' As a democrat and as a former politician Wakeham declared 'but one central aim as chairman of the Press Complaints Commission: to remove the sword of Damocles – that is, the threat of statutory controls and privacy legislation hanging over the head of the fourth estate – which has been souring the crucial relationship between politicians and the press over the last ten years; and put the regulation of the press beyond the bounds of day to day political debate'.

Wakeham had a vision of Britain's public life returning 'to those Elysian times where press and Parliamentarians maintain a robust rather than sullen regard for each other, where their relationship is one of mutual respect rather than mutual threats'. (Wakeham, it seems, particularly had in view the exemplary precedent of Lord Palmerston's assiduous leader-writing for his friend Algernon Borthwick's *Morning Post.*) He saw the decision of the Secretary of State for National Heritage not to introduce privacy laws or statutory regulation as 'a watershed for the PCC'. It signalled that 'we are beginning to emerge from the troubles of recent years – to regain that neutral ground that had existed for generations beforehand'.

The story was not over yet. 'A series of unwise stories from the newspapers could blow us off course; the pressures of an impending election could again make politicians more nervous about their relationship with the fourth estate.' Wakeham now judged the chances of such derangements 'increasingly remote'. In January 1996 the Commission would arrive at its fifth birthday. 'We still have a good deal of work to do. Damocles' sword hangs in the background and though the debate about press regulation – if not yet dying – is looking increasingly sickly, there is still some way for the PCC to go.' He would shortly be announcing plans for changes in Code supervision and for bringing the Commission's procedures in line with criteria set out in the Citizen's Charter.[18]

In the matter of changes in the administration of the Code Wakeham had the advantage over English. Wakeham deployed the argument he had rehearsed to the NPA: avoidance imperatively of 'further crunch points of confrontation' with National Heritage. The argument as deployed to English was about the feeling that the 'voice of the public', as represented by the Commission, had not been heard loud enough in the framing and reviewing of the Code of Practice. Input to the Code Committee by the Commission would give 'substance and transparency' to supervision of the Code within the self-regulatory mechanism. The industry's ownership of the Code would remain 'sacrosanct'. Bringing the 'experience and authority' of the Commission to bear on the procedure of reviewing the Code, thus leading to a 'true partnership between the press and the public' ensuring that the Code's authors were genuinely held to account by the PCC as well as the press, would in no way detract from the 'entirely professional basis' of the Code. So Sir David English was assured. He and his Committee managed, notwithstanding, to fend off the worst of what was smudged with the fingerprints of Wakeham and Bolland in the Bottomley White Paper. Grahame Thomson saw Bolland off in the matter of the secretaryship of the committee. Thomson would continue to combine the Code job with the secretaryship of Pressbof. Thus an equilibrium within the self-regulatory apparatus would be maintained. What English could not avoid conceding was that Bolland be admitted ex officio to the Code Committee as non-voting observer, and that Wakeham be accorded the same courtesy should he ever have occasion to attend. Roche's fingerprints conceivably could be traced all over that concordat.

This, it was calculated, together with rather cosmetic 'performance indicators' and 'user-friendly' literature conformable to John Major's Citizen's Charter criteria, would be enough to pacify the government. Wakeham would move energetically as far as the business of the PCC was concerned, but slowly in matters of structure and mechanics. There was no need, he told the Commission on 27 September, to 'rush at the various proposals – they should each be dealt with one at a time and a position on each developed and fortified'. He was now confident enough about the 'watershed'

to begin flourishing the word 'success' – if only, as at the annual conference of the Chartered Institute of Journalists in November 1995, to warn
against complacency in the industry. 'There is much more we have now
to do to make our success permanent.'[19] This was also the theme of
Wakeham's talks with industry representatives (including his old colleague
Sir Norman Fowler) in Birmingham, and in Cardiff. 'I think we have turned
the corner with the PCC', he told Fowler, 'and the support that I continue
to receive from the press will be vital to ensuring that success can be made
permanent.'[20]

3

One of the contributions from the industry to that end of making the
PCC's success permanent was an attempt by the Code Committee in
November 1995, in deference to a recommendation put forward by the
Secretary of State, to include under Clause 4 a definition of privacy.
Definitions formulated by the Calcutt Committee and the Heritage select
committee (with added preamble) were provided as inspirational prompts.
Even so, the Code Committee found the task beyond it. 'The Committee
at that time', as Thomson later minuted, 'decided not to insert a definition
in the Code, believing that any definition could restrict the rights of the
public and possibly restrict the scope of the PCC. The importance of
the spirit of the Code was emphasized by the Committee.'[21]

Wakeham had been confronted a little earlier by a determined effort on
the part of Diana to contribute to the debate on privacy. Having indicated
her wish to meet the chairman of the PCC, the Princess was invited in
September by Sir Gordon Reece, famed as Margaret Thatcher's image-
maker, to a small private dinner party at his house, to which the Wakehams
also were invited. Amid the social pleasantries the Princess argued strongly
for privacy legislation. Wakeham demurred, with all the standard reasons.
It was an entirely amiable occasion. The Princess made no hint of any
public initiative being in her mind.[22]

As things turned out, both Wakeham's dinner-table demurral and the
Code Committee's baffled unwillingness to define for the regulation of
journalists a concept slippery and elusive enough in the hands of lawyers
or legislators, soon proved at that juncture oddly, and ironically, appropriate. The crux was the question of famed victims of invasion of privacy
deciding to invade their own privacy. It was announced that the Princess
was to be interviewed on BBC's *Panorama* on 20 November. Wakeham's

proactive antennae were instantly alerted. He was worried about possible indiscretions on the part of Diana. The main reason for his worry was the example set by Prince Charles in the ITV television interview he had given in June 1994, which accompanied Jonathan Dimbleby's *The Prince of Wales: a Biography*. In that interview the Prince complained about media intrusion. But at the same time indiscreet personal confessions were elicited from him. Wakeham's proactive initiative was prompted as much by regrets about Charles as it was by anxieties about Diana. He decided to make a public statement in general terms, naming no names, but making the point that if people allow their private lives to be blazoned in the media, they are not well positioned to demand protection for their privacy. He faxed his inner 'cabinet': Pickering, Newell, Pinker, English, Cubbon. David English, whose impatience with Diana's erratic behaviour was now manifest, put the *Mail on Sunday* at Wakeham's disposal on 19 November.

The *Mail on Sunday* understood that Wakeham was 'unhappy with the Princess's decision to give the interview'. Indeed he was; but his intent was to steer Diana away from repeating Charles's mistake. At the end of a standard disquisition on the problematic relationship between the monarchy and the press in which no individual was specified, Wakeham concluded:

> At the end of the day, privacy is an inalienable right for us all – for you and your children and for the Royal Family and their children. And which the PCC is there to uphold. But that privacy can be compromised if we voluntarily bring our private life into the public domain. Those who do that may place themselves beyond the PCC's protection. And must bear the consequences of their actions.[23]

Panorama normally attracted some five million viewers; on this occasion more than 21 million in the UK and many millions more throughout the world ogled this 'remarkably frank interview' which was 'infinitely more revealing than had been expected'. It is not known whether the Princess had any clear preconceived notions in her mind as to what she intended to say. She disparaged the royal family and the Palace officials (whom, along with her own private secretary, she had not informed of her intention). She questioned the Prince of Wales's fitness for the throne. She admitted adultery. She pleaded for a public role as 'queen of people's hearts'.

Wakeham's proactive counter-manipulation has to be read in the context of what the *Mail on Sunday* had reason to believe was his unhappiness at the Princess's proceedings. Unavoidably, in the circumstances, what was in effect a signal to take care took on the appearance of a rebuke. Ironically, it was the very sensational nature of what she said that gave, retrospectively, a confirmatory sense of rebuke to his words. In the longer, and ultimately more important, run, Wakeham had in effect done an anti-McGregor: he publicly pre-empted an erratic public demonstration by the Princess; he did so in the coolest conceivable manner; and he had the advice and consent of his core Commission and Pressbof.[24]

Amid the uproar over Diana was a lesser, but audible, uproar over Wakeham. Appearing to deliver rebukes to the queen of people's hearts was not a popular office. There were those in the industry who resented the scoop for one of English's papers. There were those who feared he had 'opened the gate to journalists' and 'lent encouragement to the tabloids'.[25] There were those who were scathing about the 'protection' so far accorded the Princess by the PCC: 'about as much use as a paper hat in a monsoon'.[26] Louis Blom-Cooper accused Wakeham of prejudicing, in the eyes of the public, the independent and impartial judgment of the Commission which he chaired.[27] None of this censure stuck. The abiding impression on the public mind was one of proactive clear-headedness contrasting well with the media frenzy. Wakeham could hardly have made the point he wanted to make better than by the way he chanced to make it. A reactive statement from Salisbury Square would have conjured up the old hand-wringing image. It was a point, moreover, that came to have a bearing on adjudications in future cases of complaint over intrusion on privacy.

With the Diana frenzy in full spate, the PCC found itself enveloped also in a massive fall-out on the 'payments to witnesses' problem in the aftermath of the gruesome Rosemary West trial. It was known that Lord Wakeham 'expressed private concern over the way newspapers handled the reporting of that trial'.[28] Private concern was made public on 22 November with a tough press release about 'serious allegations' on which the PCC had been 'maintaining an extremely close eye'. At its meeting next week, the full Commission 'will be considering this matter and the issues it may raise for the PCC and the Code of Practice'. Scandalized accounts abounded of huge sums changing hands. The police were anxious that a future high-profile trial might collapse under the weight of evidence tarnished and witnesses discredited by reckless chequebook journalism. The Lord Chancellor and the Attorney-General ordered inquiries to determine whether there were grounds for changing the law of contempt to criminalize such payments. Clause 9 of the Code was subject to much criticism for what was held to be ambiguous wording. It was a senior police officer, familiar with time-honoured practices (which included the soliciting of chequebook-flourishing journalists by police officers) who pointed to the difficulties of tighter controls. 'Would it apply just to witnesses who were to give evidence? Or would it extend to those who have already given evidence? Would it extend to relatives, friends and colleagues of witnesses?'[29]

The Commission debated the question on 29 November. It affirmed that full scrutiny by the press of high-profile trials was in the public interest. But what more precisely it could affirm was not then apparent. The cardinal point was to ensure that no payment should to any degree be likely to affect the outcome of a trial. Wakeham would write to all national newspaper editors seeking their views. There would be consultations with 'industry experts' on what was 'one of the most crucial and difficult areas confronting the press'. A review committee would report to the Commission in January. 'We think it needs looking at', announced Wakeham, 'to see if it can be clearer.' Meanwhile the Commission took care not to make any public statement interpretable as prejudging specific allegations against chequebook-touting newspapers in the West trial in case complaints were made.[30]

A problem for the PCC was that thus far it had received no complaint about payment to a trial witness. In the nature of the case such complaints were bound to be third-party. The only precedents and case histories lay back in Press Council times. Then it was David English who led industry resistance to demands from lawyers that chequebook journalism should be stamped out.[31] Now the lawyers were at it again. Lord Dixon-Smith raised the question in the Lords on 20 December. Lord Wakeham thought it opportune to attend. It was his first appearance there as chairman of the PCC. His position was that to prejudice the administration of justice was no part of press freedom. Together with Lord Chancellor Mackay, Lord Irvine, the Home Secretary and the Attorney-General, he was examining the case for further legislation on contempt. 'My task', he explained, 'is to seek to make press self-regulation more effective. However, it may not be right to expect a self-regulatory body to seek to enforce procedures designed to protect the legal system.' Some might well conclude that those were matters for the courts, the Attorney-General or ultimately, if the law was failing, for Parliament. But Wakeham insisted that it would be no remedy for the law's failings to bring in legislation to ban payments by newspapers to court-case witnesses. The remedy would be for the PCC to administer a tightened Code of Practice for the industry in the light of the lessons of the Rosemary West trial. He pointed out that payments to witnesses were justifiable in certain circumstances. These could sometimes be beneficial to court proceedings. Journalists with inside information obtainable only through chequebooks were often very helpful to prosecuting authorities.

Wakeham suggested to their lordships that the solution would be to add a three-point protocol to the Code of Practice 'for the press to ensure that where newspapers and magazines, having given proper consideration to the public interest, have financial dealings with potential witnesses, they must take every possible step: first to demonstrate that there is a legitimate public interest at stake involving matters that the public have a right to know; secondly, to ensure that no dealings have influence on the evidence that those witnesses may give; and, thirdly, that the payment or offer of payment to any witness who is actually called in proceedings should be disclosable to the prosecution and the defence'. Transactions must be 'transparent and open to scrutiny'. Wakeham did not offer to guarantee to their lordships – who in any case made clear their scepticism about the remedial powers of press self-regulation and its Code of Practice – that he would be able to negotiate a satisfactory protocol; but he would make 'a determined attempt'.[32]

On that note of defiance on hostile parliamentary terrain, Wakeham concluded his first year as chairman of the PCC. Did the claim he had made to the industry people in Birmingham early in November stand? Had the PCC indeed turned the corner? Was 'success' as a 'permanent reality' attainably in view? The Press Complaints Commission, he told the Warwick University Law Society, had just passed its fifth birthday, which would be marked by a party in London. 'Nevertheless I do not intend there should be too much time for celebration. We still have a good deal of work to do.'

Report No. 30, May–July 1995
Accrington Observer & Times

COMPLAINT
Ms Mary Livesey, of Accrington, Lancashire, complains that her 15 year old son was approached as he was leaving his school by a reporter from the Accrington Observer & Times who was seeking information concerning other pupils, in breach of Clause 12 (Interviewing or photographing children) of the Code of Practice.

The editor responded that on the morning of 4 July the newspaper had received 'a strong tip-off' that a party of school pupils had been sent home early from an adventure weekend because of bad behaviour and it was thought some of those responsible might have been expelled. Seeking to justify the approach to the pupils the editor said:

'As we clearly did not have sufficient information at that stage to contact the school directly about the allegations, it was decided that a reporter should speak to pupils leaving the school at the end of the day with the sole intention of asking them to point us in the right direction, ie., by giving us names of people who were actually on the trip.

'Our reporter spoke to a few of the oldest-looking pupils, one of whom was Mrs Livesey's son. She did not realise that all 16-year-olds had already left the school after their exams.'

ADJUDICATION

The Commission viewed this justification as demonstrating a clear breach of the terms of Clause 12, which provides that children under sixteen should not be interviewed or photographed on subjects involving their personal welfare in the absence of or without the consent of a parent or other adult who is responsible for the children. Further, and more specifically, children should not be approached or photographed while at school without the permission of the school authorities.

In this case, the complainant's son was approached leaving school premises and asked about matters which plainly involved the personal welfare of children at the school. The editor may have wanted more facts before approaching the authorities about the rumour of expulsions from the school – but the questioning of minors was not an acceptable method of gathering such information. The complaint is upheld.

CHAPTER ELEVEN

Self-regulation 'delivering the goods'? A deceptively auspicious interlude, January–August 1996

'Do you want to read Nick Leeson's account of the collapse of the former Barings Bank? Probably. Do you want to know how Darius Guppy perpetrated his fraud? Maybe. Do you want to have an intimate account from Peter Sutcliffe about his murders? I hope not. Do you want any of these people to benefit financially from their crimes? No.'

Mark Bolland, director of the PCC, speech to the Newspaper Society, 5 March 1996

'[Privacy] legislation would mean that the rules the courts applied would carry the imprimatur of democratic approval. But if legislation is not forthcoming, cases will arise in which the need to give relief is obvious and pressing, and when they do arise, I do not think the courts will be found wanting.'

Lord Chief Justice Bingham, *UK Press Gazette*, 31 May 1996

The Commission entered 1994 in the condition of walking wounded: limping but mending. It entered 1995 more limping than mending but with the advantage of a new broom at its head with a reputation as a sweeper-up of problems. It entered 1996 for the first time in what might fairly be described as good fettle. Wakeham's 'strategic plan' seemed to be working. In an address to the Newspaper Society, the PCC's director Mark Bolland allowed modestly that the Commission had 'recently permitted themselves a moment or two of reflective satisfaction'. The statutory controls that seemed inevitable five years ago – indeed only fifteen months ago – had now receded into the background. Their spectre remained, of course, as a warning against complacency. But, 'that said, the industry has – in my view – crossed the Rubicon'. The White Paper of July 1995 marked a 'watershed' for the Commission and for the industry. 'It signalled a cessation of threats and hostility which we now have to seek to make *permanent*.'[1]

The *Annual Report, 1995* which the Commission published at the end of

January seemed to symbolize a new dawn of confidence. In his introduction Wakeham recalled his initial scepticism about the Commission's prospects when he took on the job; his 'remaining to be convinced about the independence and effectiveness of the Commission'. Now, 'a year into it, no such doubts remain in my mind. Even more importantly than my own views, the Government and the main political parties also came finally in 1995 to accept that self-regulation is working – and working well.' The Commission had been taken off probation. Speaking on Radio 4's *The World at One* on 31 January Wakeham 'hailed a year in which . . . the body had proved its independence and ability to bite'. He was convinced self-regulation was delivering the goods. 'I want in 1996 to build on this success.'[2]

There was nothing in the *Report* of any statistical significance. Established patterns persisted. Of 2,508 complaints received – a rise interpreted, naturally, as evidence of the PCC's higher profile and growing public confidence – only 476 were deemed investigatable. Of these 413 were resolved or withdrawn. The vast majority related to matters of accuracy. Adjudications upheld 28 complaints and rejected 35. National dailies and Sundays figured in 15 of the complaints upheld. Among the routine figures one stood out: the helpline telephone service for members of the public seeking advice on how to complain, or believing themselves to be involved in forthcoming newspaper reports breaching the Code, was now getting an average 120 calls a week.

The industry, in short, was defending itself well. The Commission deserved well of it. The fact that a Harris poll commissioned by the magazine *Parliamentary Monitor* found that 85 per cent of Conservative and 90 per cent of Labour MPs wanted some form of privacy legislation[3] counted for relatively little. One of press self-regulation's most consistent and effective advocates among senior journalists, Brian MacArthur of *The Times*, came forward to render thanks. He recalled Wakeham's early days when figures on the Left such as Hattersley predicted that the industry had backed the wrong horse. 'Yet a year on, Mrs Thatcher's "fixer" seems to have fixed it yet again. Within 12 months the issue that has dominated the relationship between Fleet Street and Westminster for more than a decade . . . seems to have been decisively resolved in favour of self-regulation.'

He arrived with a strategic plan and one by one he ticks off the items on his agenda from a year ago. . . . It was the Murdoch endorsement, according to Lord Wakeham, which finally persuaded the Government that the PCC was 'serious and for real'. . . . As a former Chief Whip, he also knows when to be brutally frank with editors and ministers, as he has, and when to lay on the charm, as he does. With the PCC helpline . . . he has used these skills to warn editors privately when they have been in danger of trespassing against the code. He has also visited editors and encouraged them to ring him when they have doubts about the ethics of news stories, a service which several have used.

At the *Sun*, the verdict of the editor, Stuart Higgins, is that Wakeham has done a very good job without being intrusive. 'His office has worked closely with me and senior colleagues when things were a bit touch and go. Our regular conversations have dramatically reduced the number of complaints, with the vast majority being resolved without being upheld.'

A few editors still worry that a political appointment has set a bad precedent for the PCC. Lord Wakeham points out that he was appointed by the newspaper industry and not the government. 'Nobody could point to a single act or statement that would seem to indicate the slightest party bias.'[4]

2

All very well and good, no doubt. But, as Andrew Culf pointed out in the *Guardian*, publication of the Commission's report coincided with a 'growing row' over its decision to reject complaints from Julia Carling, wife of the former England rugby captain, that the *Sun* had invaded her privacy.[5]* Back to business. Controversy over what the *Press Gazette* headlined 'short shrift for Carling' was among the issues raised with Wakeham on the *World at One* radio interview. His response was that if people encouraged details of their private lives to come into the public domain, it was 'not unreasonable for newspapers to comment'.[6] Under further pressure he denied that the case signalled a free-for-all to the press. He wrote to Virginia Bottomley, as Alexandra Frean in *The Times* reported, defending the PCC's decision. He was concerned that the case had 'given rise to mis-statements and misunderstandings that needed to be corrected'. The Commission had not given carte blanche to newspapers to publicize the private lives of people in the public eye. Wakeham pointed to the precedent of the Diana affair with *Panorama*: people compromise their right to privacy in such ways. To the argument by Carling's lawyers that the PCC adjudication would 'further encourage media excess in relation to so-called public figures', Wakeham pointed to the 'bizarre result' of people in the public view being

---

* See boxed adjudication, pp. 229–30.

free to give information about their private lives for the purposes of self-publicity, and yet being able to stifle reporting on the same facts on the ground that a breach of privacy had occurred.[7]

As well as alluding to the precedent of the Diana *Panorama* instance, Wakeham alluded also to a forthcoming adjudication concerning the television presenter Selina Scott. Her complaint was that the *News of the World* had invaded her privacy by running an inaccurate account alleging an affair fifteen years before. Scott's complaint was upheld in what amounted to a deliberately counter-Carling adjudication.[8]* On the theme of 'timely warnings to all those who would milk the media lest they become stuffed with cream',[9] Mark Bolland dilated to the Newspaper Society on these symmetrical adjudications: 'I think it is most fruitful to compare the cases of Selina Scott and Julia Carling.' The principles applied to the Selina Scott case provided the framework of the Commission's consideration of Julia Carling's complaint. The tests 'the Commission apply in these cases are clearly set out in the text of the adjudications; and the lesson for certain celebrities is "don't grumble if the press pursues your particular publicity angle on yourself"'. There was a lesson in all of this also, Bolland added, for certain members of the royal family – 'particularly those with the divorcing tendency'.[10]

Two other cases involving privacy engaged the Commission's attention at this time. The first was a revisit to the case of Ian Brady, one of the Moors murderers. In July 1993 the *Sun* had published a long-lens photo of him at Ashworth maximum security hospital. Brady complained and the *Sun* pleaded a public interest justification which the Commission accepted.[11]†

The interest in this case was Brady's being granted legal aid to apply for a judicial review of the Commission's ruling. As Brady's solicitor pointed out, the case raised questions on privacy and the press which had never before been considered by a court. 'This is a real test of the mettle of the PCC and the code of practice. They may have to consider changing their rules.'[12] Brady's written application for review was rejected, as was later the plea on his behalf before Mr Justice Jowitt in the High Court. Wakeham declared himself pleased that the court had 'expressly confirmed that the PCC approaches in a correct and fair manner its application of the press's privacy code'. He was even more pleased when Brady's appeal was disallowed by Lord Justice Woolf in very much the same commendatory terms.[13]

The further interest in the affair consists in the question as to whether the PCC is in any event subject to the High Court's jurisdiction on judicial

---

* See boxed adjudication, pp. 228–9. † Ibid., pp. 233–4.

review. 'For tactical reasons', as Mark Bolland disclosed, 'on the advice of our lawyers, we fought the Brady case on its merits and on the assumption that we were susceptible to judicial review.' At some point in the future the question of the Commission's susceptibility will need to be decided. Were a court ever to be of the view that an applicant has an arguable case for a review of a PCC adjudication, the Commission would want to contend that it is not subject to judicial review because it was privately, not governmentally, constituted. The Commission was not created by statute, statutory instrument or royal prerogative, and its de facto powers have not been woven into any system of statutory regulation.[14]

That was the Commission's position as of March 1996. The implications then beginning to come into view – of the incorporation of the European Convention on Human Rights for the press and privacy with respect both to UK law and practice and the jurisprudence of the European Court of Human Rights at Strasbourg – would soon create even larger vistas of uncertainty for the Commission.

Larger vistas were not, however, the keynote of the second privacy case attended to by the Commission, in February 1996. This was a matter not of formal complaint and formal processing. The Duke of Edinburgh, using an 'old-style analogue' mobile telephone in speaking to a friend in December 1993 about the 'soap opera' in view now that the Queen had announced her wish for the Prince and Princess of Wales to divorce, had been intercepted and the tape passed into the hands of the *Sun*. Its treatment, and that of the *Daily Mirror* in following up the story, was, by the standards of former times, restrained. Ostensibly, it was a story about insecure mobiles. The Palace press office 'put Royal concerns to the Commission privately'. The Commission in turn put its concerns to the papers in tones more of sorrow than of anger. 'Dukegate' had little in common with Diana's 'Squidgygate' or 'Fergiegate' and then 'Camillagate', all back in 1992. The Commission, feeling that it could not stay silent in the absence of a complaint, took the view that while it was 'not a clear-cut case that the newspapers had broken the Code', they were nonetheless getting close to the margins. The Commission invited the editors involved to review their procedures. '*Sun*'s royal scoop gets yellow card', was the *Guardian*'s apt headline.[15]

3

Behind the scenes the Code Committee grappled both with the privacy question and the 'payments to witnesses' and 'payment to criminals' questions. Virginia Bottomley's Privacy and Media Intrusion White Paper had, after all, recommended to the industry that it should incorporate the main elements of a privacy tort into its Code. The Committee had failed in November 1995 to agree on a formula. David English returned to the problem in January 1996 of defining privacy more clearly in Clause 4 for which Wakeham was pressing. The Committee was faced with a definition based on the draft Privacy Bill: 'An individual's private life includes personal information, communications and documents covering (a) health or medical treatment, (b) marriage, family life or personal relationships, (c) sexual orientation or behaviour, (d) political or religious beliefs, and (e) personal legal or financial affairs.'

English would have none of it. 'I am sure that such a definition would be totally unacceptable to the Committee and I am not convinced that the inclusion of any definition would be helpful.' The Calcutt Report of 1990 charged the proposed PCC, English reminded his Committee, with two prime responsibilities: dealing with complaints of unfair treatment and unwarranted intrusions into privacy. 'In many ways it might have been preferable for the industry to have only a two-sentence code of practice enshrining these points, leaving it to the PCC to adjudicate on what it considered unfair treatment or unwarranted intrusion.' It was far too late to return to such primitive simplicity. But English insisted that 'attempts to be specific in the Code may encourage a search for loopholes and may well preclude complaints which do not fit into a prescribed definition'.

English recalled also that Calcutt's twin prescription for the PCC was based on the Broadcasting Act 1990 and that was the precise charge for the Broadcasting Complaints Commission. 'I have discussed the question with the chief executive of the BBC and he was quite confident that the BBC would not wish to have a definition or privacy. He was confident that the BBC "knew" what constituted an unwarranted intrusion and he immediately cited one case which he considered was incapable of being fitted into any definition.' English believed that editors and journalists 'knew' as well as BBC executives what must be an unwarranted intrusion and that the PCC was fully capable of adjudicating on the basis of the existing Code. 'It is not our aim to provide the equivalent of statutory protection.' English suggested that the Committee take no action on this point.[16]

Payments to witnesses, and the 'cash for criminals' angle to it, however, was not so readily brushed under an intuitive carpet. The Commission had on its agenda a complaint that the *Daily Mail* breached the Code by agreeing to publicize *Rogue Trader*, a book by Nick Leeson, whose huge losses had toppled Barings Bank, in return for serialization rights. The complainants – rival newspapers, among them the *Daily Express* and *The Times* – claimed that the *Mail* was attempting to get around the Code. A comparable recent instance, where the *Daily Mirror*, after clearing with the PCC, had withdrawn from a deal with Darius Guppy, had put Clause 9 of the Code under scrutiny. Wakeham made clear to English his anxiety as to the public unease on the 'cash to criminals' aspect and the need for clarification. The Commission had virtually no case law to work on. English agreed to call a special meeting of the Code Committee. 'I think the clause is completely out of date. I have looked at the provenance of it and it goes back to some grandiose announcement of the old Press Council around the time of the Ripper trial.'[17]

The options available were to exclude editors paying for stories, to 'take the clause apart line by line and re-examine it for meaning, and more for ethics,' or to abandon the clause altogether. 'Is it the job of the Code Committee or the PCC', asked English, 'actually to take a moral stand on this?' This notion that the Commission had no business judging decisions on the morality of paying certain people for stories was common enough among journalists. English threatened: 'The special meeting of the committee will certainly rewrite the clause. We may even revoke it.'[18] This latter was not an option, however, which Wakeham felt would be prudent in the interests of self-regulation. The judges concluded that no serious harm had come to the West trial from payments to witnesses, but they remained unhappy about media buy-ups. Wakeham reassured them that the self-regulatory mechanism would be adequate to the task.[19] Having failed to get a grip on the Code Committee, he planned to set up a lay-majority PCC Code sub-committee, consisting of himself, Sir Brian Cubbon, and Lady Browne-Wilkinson, with a token industry representative, to strengthen what he called the Commission's 'independent voice'.[20] To preserve the protocol he had outlined in the Lords in December, which put particular obligations on editors in the matter of payments to witnesses, Wakeham was prepared to use his sub-committee to 'intervene forcefully', as Bolland informed Cubbon. Lord Wakeham would also attend the next Code Committee meeting, 'and intends to back it up with strong language'.[21]

The upshot, after consultation with the industry, was a two-pronged Clause 9, one for witnesses and one for criminals, together with the protocol, realized finally in a revised Code in November 1996. Wakeham's undertaking to the Lords of a 'determined attempt' was fulfilled. English, for his part, had the satisfaction of the Commission's rejecting the complaint against the *Daily Mail*'s arrangement with Nick Leeson.[22]*

4

Another case revisited was that of the *Sunday Times*'s subterfuge and entrapment of MPs in the 'cash for questions' affair of July 1994. The Commission conceded that there had indeed been procedural errors in the handling of the case and that crucial parts of the evidence submitted by the newspaper were flawed. The initial adjudication was thus overturned.[23] On the other hand, the Commission upheld in principle the right and duty in certain circumstances of investigative journalists to entrap public figures by means of subterfuge; the *Sunday Times* was justified in its purpose, if not in its methods. The Commission's 'clarification' was judiciously ambiguous. David Hencke interpreted the 'overall tenor' as a blow for the Commons privileges committee.[24] Roy Greenslade thought it 'a setback for press freedom'.[25] Wakeham could feel that he had got it just about right.

Getting the next case concerning issues of general interest just about right was in some ways harder, some ways easier. In September 1995 *Business Age* magazine ran a feature on 'The Rich 500'. Its estimate of the Queen's personal wealth at £2,200 million was held by her and her advisers to be grossly exaggerated. It was a delicate political matter at a time when the Queen's eligibility for income tax was a public issue. Having failed to get the magazine to retract or correct, her press secretary, Charles Anson, complained to the PCC on 9 October under Clause 1 of the Code on breaches of accuracy. The issue turned on the immense complexities involved in such an assessment as between what was personal to the Queen and what was invested in the Crown, and the necessity of applying to it expert and painstaking research. The Commission upheld Anson's complaint on the grounds that the magazine presented speculation as established fact and failed adequately to check its facts and made errors which were not properly addressed.[26]†

Peter Kirwan, editor of *Business Age*, came back at the Commission in the *Press Gazette*. He allowed that 'overall, the PCC's task was unenviable'. It lacked the resources to tackle issues arising from sophisticated financial journalism. 'Wisely, the PCC refused to formally criticise *Business Age*'s £2.2bn valuation of the Queen.' Yet it criticized the magazine for not

---

* See boxed adjudication, pp. 234–5. † Ibid., pp. 235–9.

carrying out exhaustive research. But exactitude remained impossible because of Palace secrecy and archaic royal financial structures. The monarchy's finances remained 'a riot of legal imprecision'. 'Our legal advice', declared Kirwan, 'is that, in such situations the PCC could be vulnerable to judicial review.' Kirwan acknowledged the Commission's welcoming his attempts to open a rational dialogue with the Palace press office. 'So far, so good.' But if the Palace now intended to complain, logic demanded that it must also explain. The PCC's ruling, he held, 'avoids the real issues'. Moreover the PCC had 'opened the floodgates to complaints from all kinds of secretive and unusual institutions', for example offshore companies, which feel that journalists have valued their assets too aggressively. 'For City editors, this spells trouble.'[27]

Apart from the fact that floodgates were not opened, much of the thrust of Kirwan's counter-complaint was fair comment. The Commission had no choice but to avoid the 'real issues'. But to allege, as Kirwan did, that the Commission ruling 'effectively chills discussion of the royal finances' was both a non-sequitur and too flattering.

In these days Wakeham was on the road. At a lunch to mark the 1995 Race in the Media Awards, organized by the Commission for Racial Equality, he appealed for more complaints on Clause 15 of the Code, binding editors to avoid 'prejudicial or pejorative references' to a person's race or colour, and also to refrain from publishing such details about a person, unless directly relevant to the story. Very few substantive complaints under the discrimination clause come before the Commission, Wakeham told his audience. He supposed this was because 'some readers still do not believe it worthwhile complaining to us. I came here today to tell you that those who think this could not be more wrong.' Every complaint upheld, he explained, 'sets a precedent and adds to our body of case law'. In the absence of substantive complaints which raise a real breach of the Code, it was difficult to gather such precedents.[28] Speaking a few days later in the City of London at a dinner of the Worshipful Company of Stationers and Newspaper Makers, Wakeham extolled the way the press had moved 'light years from the contentious days of ten years ago', and cited the maturity and responsibility of its reporting of the 'mind-numbing events at Dunblane'. He observed also of that same maturity that self-regulation had to be judged 'by what doesn't appear as much as by what does'. That the press and the Commission co-operate, draw from case law, and work together in interpreting the Code *before* some stories are published was the hallmark of maturity. 'It is the silent part of our work. But it is real nonetheless.'[29]

All the more reason to draw attention to recent lapses in the matter of photographs of Prince William at school. Some papers had begun to stray into 'grey areas around the dividing line between the freedom of the press and its duty to respect the privacy of a child'. Wakeham was ready, if necessary, to look into the mechanics of how Buckingham Palace and the press were co-operating over legitimate coverage of landmarks in the life of a future king. 'It was always accepted that the Palace would arrange access for the media to report moments of key interest during Prince William's time at school – and it is important that this accord is effective and remains in place.' And an area to which the Commission would be turning its attention in coming months was that of the paparazzi. Wakeham hoped that 'the press will continue to think carefully before purchasing photographs which serve no legitimate purpose from some freelance photographers whose very presence may occasionally constitute harassment under the Code of Practice'.[30]

5

Amid consideration of what might be called such conventional self-regulatory concerns, the Commission was beginning to have its attention directed at quite new and unconventional questions. The first and most important of these related to the government's reluctance to embark on privacy legislation. This brought to the forefront the provision of a right of privacy in the European Convention on Human Rights. The British government was a signatory to this Convention at its inception in 1951. It followed that there was presumption that Parliament would intend to legislate consistently with the Convention. But in the absence of such legislation British nationals had to plead their cause at the European Court at Strasbourg.

In the notorious Gorden Kaye scandal in 1990, which did so much to discredit the then press self-regulatory system, the court regretted that it had no power to take action against the *Sunday Sport* for gross intrusion on Kaye's privacy.[31] There were judges who held that the court in this case had misdirected itself, and that it was perfectly feasible for courts in the UK to build up a common law on privacy as had been done in the United States. Would the judiciary be ready to move in this direction of 'judge-made' privacy law? Or would the Strasbourg model offer readier prospects? It was a notable event for the press in 1996 that, even though the PCC had upheld Lord Spencer's complaint on behalf of his wife, he was taking her case to

Strasbourg, where, as a PCC position paper put it, 'some jurisprudence may emerge' to oblige the British government to bring in a privacy law.

What was coming into view now was a swell of opinion wanting to move beyond merely Parliament's not legislating incompatibly with the Convention to Parliament's incorporating the Convention holus bolus into UK law and practice. There was a pro-privacy law, anti-press self-regulation angle to this, but in general the motives were much wider and deeper, especially in the Labour and Liberal Democrat parties. But in any case it was an issue in which the newspaper industry was bound to take a very serious interest. That incorporation would take place sooner or later seemed inevitable. No party could be against human rights. The Labour party was committed to incorporation. The practical issue for the newspaper industry was: would the UK courts develop human rights jurisprudence conservatively or adventurously? Article 8 of the Convention guaranteed a right to privacy. Article 10 guaranteed a right to freedom of expression. In what direction would the balance tilt? 'If the Convention is incorporated', the Commission paper further pointed out,

> its effect on the Code's article 4 on privacy – whether in its present form or elaborated as recommended by the government – is difficult to predict. Those seeking a quick, free remedy and an apology would presumably still complain to the Commission, while those who wished to see the newspaper penalized would go to court. If a complainant went to the Commission and the courts, the newspaper might not want to co-operate with the Commission for fear that disclosure of its case to the Commission could prejudice its case in court (the Commission does not normally adjudicate on a case which is sub judice).[32]

The industry already considered it had reason to be deeply suspicious of the ambitions of the judiciary to get a privacy law one way or another. 'The judges are going to tell journalists what to do', screamed the leader headline of the *Press Gazette* on 31 May. The new Lord Chief Justice, Sir Thomas Bingham, threatened that while privacy legislation was preferable as carrying the 'imprimatur of democratic approval', were such legislation not forthcoming, cases would arise in which the need to give relief was 'obvious and pressing', and Sir Thomas did not think the courts would be 'found wanting'.[33] The *Gazette* protested against this 'breathtaking assumption of power without accountability'. 'Wigocracy' was the cant industry term for it. The judiciary's obvious retort to this was to quote Stanley Baldwin in 1931 on the theme of the prerogative of the harlot.

Thus it was in 1996 that the two great extra-parliamentary powers in the

land affronted one another. The issue and its implications had a long way
to go before any resolution would become discernible. For the moment,
the industry had detected menace in yet another unaccountable power:
the Data Protection Registrar. It was Sir Frank Rogers, chairman of the
Newspaper Publishers Association and the European Publishers Council,
director of the Telegraph group, member of Pressbof's board, who
sounded the tocsin for press freedom. 'How many editors and journalists
are aware', he asked in the *Press Gazette*, 'that three Governmental officials
are establishing privacy legislation by the back door and without any discussion in Parliament?' These officials were the Data Protection Registrar,
Elizabeth France, and her deputy and her legal adviser. 'They have a
history', Rogers accused, 'of interpreting data protection in terms of individual privacy despite the obvious serious damage to press freedom.' Were
their aspirations to be realized, Rogers warned, journalists' investigative
and writing skills would be seriously inhibited. Editors and journalists
should be concerned because a new European directive, for the first time,
guarantees citizens '*in particular their right to privacy with respect to the processing
of personal data*'. In the current UK Act there was no mention of privacy. In
her various statements France claimed for herself 'a privacy function well
beyond her data protection remit and an influential political role'. It was
unacceptable, Rogers argued, 'for a public official to consider that her role
is political rather than administrative'. Parliament had not vested her
with any powers or duties to influence either national or international
thinking on privacy. 'She says she wishes to be Privacy Commissioner
rather than Data Protection Registrar.'[34] Rogers pressed his case to a
receptive Commission.

What should be of great concern to every journalist, Rogers urged, was
the Data Protection Registrar's stated objective of turning sensible data
protection legislation into a personal privacy charter. 'The Registrar has
made some sweeping assertions that journalists may be failing to comply
with current data protection legislation and will have continued compliance
difficulties in the future. She has used these allegations as a vehicle to attempt
to persuade press representative groups to hold discussions with her to seek
remedies for unspecified and unsubstantiated assertions.' If there were con-
flicts between individual privacy and press freedom, it was for the registrar
to demonstrate that data protection legislation was a more effective remedy
than current libel laws and Press Complaints Commission procedures.
'Every editor, every journalist, every press organization in the land should
vigorously and persistently challenge what the Registrar is proposing.'[35]

Rogers was seconded vigorously by Brian MacArthur, who pointed out that it was the Data Protection Act of 1984 that Robert Maxwell's lawyers advised him to resort to.[36] The four major media organizations – the Newspaper Society, the Newspaper Publishers Association, the Periodical Publishers Association and the BBC – all responded in like terms to the Home Office consultation paper on the EU directive. Wakeham made his own contribution on behalf of the Commission by 'responding frigidly' to an approach by France, who consistently avowed herself misrepresented and misunderstood. She proposed to Wakeham on 10 July that the Code of Practice should include guidelines to journalists on how to comply with the Data Protection Act. She suggested a meeting to 'discuss how the PCC interprets the Code, how the Code might be seen to relate to the 1984 [Data Protection] Act, and whether the Code is one which I could properly encourage under . . . the Act'.

Wakeham, irritated that the Registrar should have addressed her letter to the House of Lords rather than to Salisbury Square, responded stiffly that the Code could not be supervised or negotiated by anybody else 'beyond the press' but the PCC. His tone was that of magisterial put-down. He counter-proposed a meeting between the registrar and the PCC's senior officers, including its privacy commissioner, Professor Pinker, but subject to the Home Office's consultation process being completed. France replied in disappointment that she was particularly alert to the 'sensitivities you indicate and was hoping simply for the sort of relationship I have with bodies such as the Advertising Standards Authority and the Code of Banking Practice Review Committee'.[37] This was not, as yet, to be. 'Dog', the *Press Gazette* gossip columnist, commented: 'The DPR feels misunderstood. Dog wonders how wilful this misunderstanding is.'[38] Two other powers in the land, lesser but not less proud, affronted one another.

Something of a sense of representing an industry embattled with insidious forces sapping at its bastions is evident in Wakeham's address to the American Chamber of Commerce (UK) at its Independence Day luncheon on 4 July. They had the First Amendment to the Constitution providing that Congress should make no law abridging the freedom of speech, or of the press. In the absence of constitutional safeguards the British press had always had to defend itself within a tradition of freedom no less libertarian than that of the US but subject always to the supremacy of Parliament and therefore to the need to fend off parliamentary propensities to abridge. It was the PCC, Wakeham suggested, as guardian and supervisor of the Code of Practice, which ensured 'that the essentials of press freedom are maintained and that in practice our laws observe the spirit of the First Amendment'.[39] This was morale-boosting at its most boostful.

6

During the early months of 1996 the divorce settlement was negotiated between the Prince and Princess of Wales. Its terms were announced on 12 July and the marriage officially dissolved on 28 August. The Princess was no longer to be styled Her Royal Highness, but Diana, Princess of Wales. (There had been a 'quickie' divorce for the Duke and Duchess of York in April.) The reputation of the monarchy in general and the Prince in particular was at its lowest ebb since pre-Victorian times. Andrew Alderson reported for the *Sunday Times* in May that the Prince of Wales had recruited a new aide 'to help him win the media battle against his estranged wife over their impending divorce'. Mark Bolland, director of the Press Complaints Commission, was 'finalising a deal that would see him join forces with Commander Richard Aylard, the Prince's private secretary'.[40]

Bolland's five years at the PCC, the *Press Gazette* reported, 'are seen as having given him a unique insight into the British press'. It was thought 'he will have a major role in attempting to rebuild the Prince's public image'.[41] There was certainly a general consensus in the industry that Bolland had performed well. He and Wakeham, as Roy Greenslade observed, formed the 'smoothest of diplomatic teams to guide the PCC, and the newspaper industry, into calmer waters'.[42] Wakeham was well placed to recommend Bolland to the Prince as a man who was second to none in his grasp on the ways of the media.

As Bolland prepared to move to St James's Palace as the Prince's deputy private secretary and media strategist, Wakeham was looking for a replacement. It was an opportunity also for a review of the Commission's administrative structure and procedures. Wakeham was never in doubt as to his own choice as Bolland's successor. During the 1987 general election campaign, the Central Office man who every morning briefed him as Chief Whip and then Margaret Thatcher was Guy Black. ('Make her laugh', was Wakeham's invariable adjuration as Black went in to see the Prime Minister.) Wakeham and Black thus went back a long way. Then in 1989 at the Department of Energy Wakeham, who was responsible for the presentation and co-ordination of government policy, appointed Black as his special adviser. Wakeham knew that Black could handle the job and that they would get on as a team.

A brilliant product of the Peterhouse history school in Cambridge, Black had since worked impressively for the lobbying company Westminster Strategy and then the public relations concern Lowe Bell. 'I know Lord Wakeham well and I've known Mark Bolland for many years, so in a way I've had a tangential relationship with the way the Commission has developed', he told the *Press Gazette*.[43] The difficult and sensitive aspect of the matter for Wakeham was Black's Central Office provenance. There could well be objections to a cosy Conservative party job. (Black for a time had been a Conservative councillor in Brentwood.) As counterweight arguments Wakeham could point to evidence of Black's undoubted diplomatic and managerial skills in the lobbying and public relations world which were skills analogous to those of the whips' office rather than of ideological partisanship, and to his own success in allaying the many doubts voiced in 1994 about his own appointment to the chairmanship. Black, moreover, was in good standing with the Union of Communications Workers for having been instrumental, while at the Lowe Bell PR concern, for having almost singlehandedly blocked privatization of the Post Office. Wakeham's fix was to split the directorship and ease Black into a lower-profile role as secretary of the Commission and director of policy and public affairs. Bolland's former assistant director, Susan Roberts, another importation from the Advertising Standards Authority, was to be director of complaints.

Black arrived just in time to see the end of calm times.

Report No. 31, August–October 1995
The Sun

COMPLAINT
Mr Charles Kaye, Chief Executive of the Special Hospitals Service Authority, of London W14, complained that a report headlined 'Well-fed face of evil child murderer Ian Brady' in The Sun on 26 July 1995 was illustrated by photographs of Ian Brady inside a hospital building which constituted an invasion of his privacy, in breach of Clauses 4 (Privacy), 6 (Hospitals) and 8(ii) (Harassment) of the Code of Practice.

The complainant objected to the publication of photographs showing Ian Brady standing in front of a window in Ashworth Hospital, which had been taken with a long range telephoto lens from outside the perimeter of the hospital.

ADJUDICATION
The provisions of the Code of Practice upheld by the PCC which relate to the privacy of individuals in hospitals or similar institutions are designed to prevent distress and

unwanted publicity for those who, because of their illness, may be in a vulnerable position. However, as well as being a patient at Ashworth, Ian Brady is also a notorious child murderer – a matter in itself which justifies scrutiny of him in the public interest – and the Commission noted that the indistinct photograph of him published by The Sun was only able to be taken as he was in a position from which he could be photographed.

In the particular circumstances of this case the Commission took the view that the publication of the photograph of Ian Brady was not a matter which warranted censure under the Code.

Report No. 32, November–December 1995
The Sun

COMPLAINT

Mrs Julia Carling complained through solicitors, Messrs Stitt & Co., of London EC4, that The Sun newspaper intruded into her privacy in breach of Clause 4 (Privacy) of the Code of Practice (i) by publication on 12 and 13 October of an interview given by a former boyfriend about them, (ii) by publication on 13 October 1995 of details of her dinner appointment with her hairdresser and (iii) by publication on 14 October 1995 of the Franklin cartoon showing the complainant with her hairdresser gesturing towards her husband, and a 'Deidre's photo casebook special' giving a cartoon-like sequence of alleged conversations between the complainant and her husband concerning his friendship with the Princess of Wales. The complainant also alleged that the newspaper endeavoured to obtain a story from her through intimidation in breach of Clause 8 (Harassment) of the Code by offering her a sum of money to sell her own story to the newspaper prior to publication of the interview with the former boyfriend, allegedly implying that if the complainant did not sell her story then the former boyfriend's material would be used. She also complained of harassment in that she was telephoned one night at midnight by a representative of the newspaper. The Commission was also asked to consider a complaint raised under Clause 1 (Accuracy) of the Code in that the 14 October edition of the newspaper contained a further article, 'Now Julia is taking a pop at Carling!', wrongly stating that she would be recording a version of the song 'Stand by your man' which had subsequently been corrected, but in the complainant's view insufficiently promptly, on 28 October 1995.

On 12 and 13 October 1995 The Sun published several articles regarding the complainant's personal life and marriage. These included interviews with a former friend, Mr Carl Pickford, who gave a detailed account of the couple's former personal relationship. The complainant's solicitors pointed out that they had written to the editor of the newspaper in advance of the articles appearing objecting, on the complainant's behalf, to the publication of personal details involving her some five years previously. They said that their client did not consent to any intrusion into her private life whether in respect of her relationship with Mr Pickford or otherwise. The solicitors claimed that the circumstances surrounding the publication amounted to harassment in breach of Clause 8 of the Code. The complainant had earlier rejected the editor's offer to pay her a substantial amount of money for her story and the solicitors asserted that it was implicit from the offer that the Carl Pickford articles would not be published if Mrs Carling agreed. This, they said, constituted unfair pressure on her.

The solicitors also alleged that Mrs Carling had been harassed by a telephone call at midnight by a Sun reporter.

In response the newspaper denied that there had been any breach of the provisions of the Code relating to privacy in respect of Mrs Carling. It justified publication of the articles by reference to interviews (a selection of which were enclosed) given by Mrs Carling over the previous few years. The newspaper alleged that she had been happy to publicise personal details of her past, her marriage and her relationship with former boy-friends, said that she had sold a detailed and exclusive interview about a crisis in her marriage and then subsequently given interviews about it. It suggested that on the back of these interviews about her private life she had publicised, bolstered and built-up her career as a television presenter and part-time fashion model. In particular it referred the Commission to previous articles in which she had talked about her relationship with a former boyfriend, Mr Jeff Beck.

The newspaper provided the Commission with a copy of the letter to Mrs Carling from the editor offering to publish an exclusive interview with Mrs Carling and said it could clearly be seen that there was nothing sinister in it. The newspaper confirmed that a message was left on Mrs Carling's answerphone at midnight on 10 October 1995 for the purpose of asking her for a reaction to a story in another newspaper which was running the following morning. Since her answerphone was switched on the newspaper contended that the inconvenience to her must have been minimal.

In response, the solicitors acting for Mrs Carling analysed the selection of articles and interviews provided by the newspaper. They claimed that nearly half of them were plainly not interviews at all and that most of the rest came about either as a direct result of Mrs Carling or her husband's contractual arrangements (including those which obliged her to obtain publicity) or by a desire on her part to stop further press specula-tion about her personal affairs. They accepted that she had on occasions 'given limited and innocuous details' about her private life but said that this could not provide the press with 'carte blanche' to intrude into every aspect of her private life especially where she had objected and withheld consent to publication. They alleged there was no conceivable justification for a disturbing telephone call to Mrs Carling at around mid-night for a reaction to a story appearing in another newspaper the next morning.

ADJUDICATION

In carrying out its functions the Commission is charged with a duty to have regard, inter alia, to freedom of expression and the public's right to be informed of matters of public interest. This may include cases where one side in an otherwise private relationship between two parties gives an account of that relationship. In taking a view as to whether breach of privacy, as defined in Clause 4 of the Code, has occurred, the Commission may take a number of factors into account including the extent to which the parties involved have already put matters about their private lives into the public domain, or otherwise have consented to publication, expressly or by implication.

In this case the newspaper did not attempt to justify its story as being in the public interest for any of the three distinct reasons specifically set out in Clause 18 of the Code. However, Clause 18 provides that in any case raising issues beyond these reasons the Commission will require a full explanation by the editor of the publication involved seeking to demonstrate how the public interest was served. Had the newspaper contended that Mrs Carling had put matters involving her personal life and relationships into the public domain by continued interviews and statements about them, most latterly in respect of her own marriage. If she did so she could not complain when newspapers published articles about the same subject to which she did not consent.

In the view of the Commission, persons who put matters involving their private life into the public domain may not be able to claim the protection of the Code when articles are published without their consent, and which seek to comment on, contrast or clarify the information given by the information provided by the persons concerned. Although the Commission accepted the contention of Mrs Carling's solicitors that a number of the articles produced by the newspaper were not relevant to any proper consideration of the matter, the Commission took the view that Mrs Carling had clearly placed details of her past and current relationships into the public domain by virtue of articles and interviews designed, in part, to enhance her image, promote her career and in pursuance of her contractual obligations to publicise herself.

The matter does not end there because the Commission also needed to consider whether the degree of intrusion represented by the articles concerned was fair in all the circumstances. The Commission has previously made it clear that the fact that a complainant has sought publicity in the past or put matters concerning his or her private life into the public domain cannot reasonably be taken to mean that henceforth the press are entitled to publish articles on any subject involving complainants or their families. The Commission accepted that in its frankness and personal detail, Mr Pickford's interview went beyond the revelations made by Mrs Carling in respect of her past and current relationships. However, the Commission came to the view, having regard to matters set out above, that the newspaper was entitled to publish the articles concerned which directly concerned the same areas of her personal life as placed in the public domain by Mrs Carling, and that such publication did not therefore breach the privacy provisions as defined by Clause 4 of the Code.

Having considered the offer letter from the editor to Mrs Carling the Commission did not consider that it could be considered as constituting intimidation or harassment within the terms of Clause 8 of the Code. Neither did it find that the conclusions reached by Mrs Carling's solicitors about the intention and effect of the letter could be made out by any surrounding circumstances.

Nor did the Commission regard a single telephone call made to an answerphone asking for a comment as constituting harassment by the newspaper within the terms of the Code.

Given the findings to which the Commission came, as set out above, it did not regard the publication of the cartoon and 'Deidre's photo casebook special' as constituting a breach of the privacy provisions of the Code. The newspaper told the Commission that the 'casebook' is frequently used in the case of real life personalities. While understandably distressing to Mrs Carling, the Commission found that both items went no further than to attempt to comment humorously on matters which could properly be regarded as already being in the public domain.

The complainant's solicitors said that the story about Mrs Carling having dinner with her hairdresser Mr Galvin was an intrusion into their client's privacy made without her consent. She had not engineered the attendance of the media at the restaurant and the fact that photographs were taken outside the restaurant could not, and should not, be a licence to publish details of Mrs Carling's every movement and engagements over the pages of the newspaper. They invited the Commission to find that this further conduct, taken cumulatively with that referred to above, was another example of harassment of Mrs Carling.

The newspaper denied that there had been any breach of the privacy or harassment provisions of the Code. It provided the Commission with statements from two photographers involved who said that they had remained at all times on the public highway and had taken pictures of Mrs Carling after she emerged from the restaurant and was clearly aware of their presence.

It was not disputed that Mrs Carling had no part in arranging for photographers to be present outside the restaurant concerned and the Commission accepted that she did not consent to pictures being taken of her afterwards. The newspaper article itself was largely descriptive of her evening out and contained a short interview with Mr Galvin who denied that he and Mrs Carling were dating. Applying the test set out above, the Commission found in all the circumstances that publication of the article and photographs was not a breach of Clause 4 of the Code, but related to matters already in the public domain since Mrs Carling had herself issued a statement in relation to her own marital situation, and both she and her husband had given interviews about it over a period of time. While the Commission sympathises with public figures who may be pursued by photographers and newspapers in circumstances where aspects of their private lives and relationships have been publicised in part, by their own action or statements, it did not conclude that there was any harassment in this instance on the part of the photographers concerned who had remained on the public highway and had not intruded into the restaurant itself.

The solicitors for Mrs Carling also complained that the newspaper had not dealt promptly with the publication of a correction in relation to a statement that Mrs Carling would be recording a pop song. The Commission found that the newspaper accepted that a correction ought to be published within a few days but that a further delay occurred because of disagreements between the newspaper and the solicitors concerned about the nature and prominence to be given to the correction. Having regard to all the circumstances the Commission found that the newspaper was prompt in accepting that an error had been made and the length of time taken to publish the correction was not unnecessarily long.

All the complaints were rejected.

Report No. 33, January–March 1996
News of the World

COMPLAINT

Ms Selina Scott, of London, W8, complained that a front page and inside story in the News of the World dated 23 July 1995 inaccurately and wrongly claimed that she had had an affair over fifteen years ago on the Isle of Bute with a named man, an interview with whom formed the basis of the article.

She also complained that the newspaper story intruded upon her privacy without any public interest justification. Ms Scott's agent was quoted at the end of the article as saying that Ms Scott had not seen the man for years and that she failed to see what relevance the story had to Ms Scott now. The complaint was raised under Clauses 1 (Accuracy), 4 (Privacy) and 18 (Public interest) of the Code of Practice.

The newspaper provided the Commission with a sworn affidavit from the man which claimed that he and Ms Scott had had a sexual relationship which ended in 1979 and also a copy of a letter which she had written to him in July of that year (partially extracted in the article) in which she congratulated him on his engagement to be married. They also provided a transcript of a taped interview and a further telephone interview with the man as well as a transcript of a telephone conversation which a reporter had had with Ms Scott's agent.

ADJUDICATION

In adjudicating on this matter the Commission found itself in obvious difficulties in investigating the factual basis for a story many years old which was strongly disputed by one of the two people involved. The Commission has no power to examine Ms Scott or the man concerned under oath or to compel the attendance of other witnesses who might be able to provide information to assist in corroborating or denying the allegations or factual background set out in the article.

In cases of this sort where the Commission feels that it is not in a position to make an informed judgement on the truth or otherwise of the facts concerned, it may restrict itself to finding whether the newspaper had, or had no, sufficient and reasonable grounds to print the allegations made and whether it had taken all or any reasonable steps to check whether such allegations had any basis in fact.

In carrying out its functions the Commission is charged with a duty to have regard, inter alia, to freedom of expression and the public's right to be informed of matters of public interest. This may include cases where one side in an otherwise private relationship between two parties gives an account of that relationship. In taking a view as to whether a breach of privacy, as defined in Clause 4 of the Code has occurred, the Commission may take a number of factors into account, including the extent to which the parties involved had already put matters about their private lives into the public domain; whether the newspaper had tried to corroborate the facts concerned; the extent to which a right of reply may have been afforded, as well as any other relevant factors.

In this case the Commission did not accept that the affidavit from the man concerned, the letter from Ms Scott or a transcript of a conversation with her agent constituted any or any sufficient material to justify a breach of the complainant's privacy in describing a matter which may, or may not, have occurred over fifteen years previously. No attempt appeared to have been made by the newspaper to check some of the background facts or to question independent witnesses on the Isle of Bute who might have a knowledge of the matters described.

The newspaper, in support of its argument that there had been no unwarranted intrusion into the complainant's privacy, supplied the Commission with numerous cuttings from various newspapers and magazines featuring articles by Ms Scott or interviews which she had given since 1984 about herself and her career. The Commission did not find that any of these were of such a nature as to disentitle the complainant from a degree of privacy concerning the reporting of events in her life a considerable time before. Nor did the fact that the newspaper attempted to contact the complainant before publication for her comments, or its offer to publish her own account thereafter, alter the balance of the degree of privacy to which the complainant was entitled in the circumstances.

To the above extent both complaints under Clauses 4 and 18 were upheld.

Report No. 33, January–March 1996
Daily Mail

COMPLAINT

Mr Hugh Gordon of Johnsfield, Duns, Berwickshire, complained that a series of articles in the Daily Mail from 12 to 16 February 1996, serialising a book by Nick Leeson, was published in breach of Clause 9 (Payment for articles) of the Code of Practice.

The complainant objected to the serialisation of a book by a man serving a jail sentence for fraud and enquired what payment had been made for the story since he believed that the articles were in breach of Clause 9 of the Code.

The newspaper responded that they had not paid anyone – including Nick Leeson, his lawyers or any trust on his behalf – for the serialisation rights to the book. They stated that publication was in the public interest in order for readers to know how one man brought about the downfall of Barings Bank. The newspaper had, they said, advertised the series on television, as they did with other book serialisations.

ADJUDICATION

While the Commission noted that the newspaper had not made a payment for the serialisation rights to the book, the payment for television advertising might be construed in this particular case as a breach of the spirit of the Code since its effect might be to benefit Mr Leeson through royalties obtained from increased sales of his book. In this instance, however, the Commission accepted, on balance, that the information provided as to the collapse of Barings was of legitimate public interest sufficient to justify the way in which the newspaper dealt with the matter.

The complaint was rejected.

The Commission notes that the newspaper and magazine industry's Code of Practice Committee is presently reviewing Clause 9 of the Code and will draw this decision to their attention.

Report No. 34, April–June 1996
Business Age

COMPLAINT

Charles Anson, Press Secretary to the Queen, complained that an analysis of the Queen's personal wealth and that of other members of the Royal Family included in a feature entitled 'The Rich 500' in the September 1995 issue of the magazine, Business Age, was inaccurate and misleading in breach of Clause 1 (Accuracy) and Clause 3 (Comment, conjecture and fact) of the Code of Practice.

Each year Business Age publishes a lengthy article about the personal assets of people who the compilers regard as the richest 500 individuals in the United Kingdom. The editorial to the September 1995 edition described 'The Rich 500' as 'our definitive guide to wealth in Britain . . . And our research is exhaustive.' A column explaining how the list was compiled states that it 'details individual and not family wealth'. The magazine said that it made a judgement in each case as to the portion of family or trust wealth to allocate to individuals who are ranked according to the total estimate of their wealth made by the compilers.

In the issue concerned the magazine explained why the Queen with an estimated wealth of £2.2bn, had risen in one year from 72nd to 1st place in the list. It said that in the previous year it had 'looked at what the Queen might walk away with in the event of a successful republican revolution. This consisted of her non-landed assets, valued adjust £158m. This year, we have decided on a figure fourteen times higher. This is certainly not attributable to investment success. In fact it is mostly a matter of legal argument'. The magazine said that while assets readily identifiable as the Queen's private and personal wealth such as racehorses, stocks and bonds and bank deposits had been the basis of its valuation in the previous year, it had added in a large number of other assets which it had now attributed to the Monarch personally. These included some of the art treasures, jewellery and palaces belonging to the Crown. The magazine added, 'As we have discovered, royal retainers are willing to go to remarkable lengths to minimise estimates of the Monarch's personal wealth . . . Nevertheless our verdict stands.'

Mr Anson disputed much of the analysis in regard to the Queen's wealth. He said the assessment which had been made, as well as much of the accompanying discussion, was both inaccurate and misleading. He claimed that Business Age had chosen not to check any of its material with the Palace Press Office before publication and enclosed copies of correspondence passing between the Press Office, the Director of Media Affairs for the Royal Collection Trust and Business Age. He disputed the suggestion that there was concealment in connection with the Royal Finances and said that Buckingham Palace had answered over 60 Parliamentary Questions on the subject; a press conference on the matter had been held in 1993; Palace officials had given over five hours of evidence on the financing of the occupied Royal Palaces to the Parliamentary Accounts Committee; and in addition, 15,000 copies of the Palace's Royal Finances booklet had been distributed in the last couple of years.

The Buckingham Palace Press Office also made a large number of factual and other criticisms of the magazine article. The main point was that the overall estimate of The Queen's wealth included inalienable assets such as the occupied Royal Palaces, the Royal Art Collection and most of the Queen's jewellery which, contrary to the magazine's contention, cannot be disposed of as the Queen wills but are regarded as heirlooms to be passed on in due course to her successor. Buckingham Palace pointed out that such items are held in trust by the Queen as Sovereign and Head of State and not as an individual. The Royal Palaces were no more the Queen's personal property than the White House or the Elysée and their contents belong to President Clinton or President Chirac. A number of complaints were made by the Palace about the accuracy of figures given in the article in relation to other members of the Royal Family, the Duchy of Lancaster, the Crown Estates and Royal Palaces. With reference to the Civil List the magazine had confused amounts provided as parliamentary annuities to meet official expenses, some of which were repaid by the Queen to the Government.

The Director of Media Affairs at the Royal Collection Trust had written to the magazine to deny that works of art in the Royal Collection, including 600 Leonardo sketches, were included in the Queen's personal wealth. He stated that the Queen does not personally own the Sevres porcelain collection, the Royal Library or, with the exception of some personal papers, the Royal Archives.

In responding to this initial correspondence on a large number of factual points in late September 1995, the editor of Business Age said that the magazine had tried to work with a difficult legal – and sometimes extra-legal – structure of ownership. In attempting to address those difficulties – primarily the question of inalienability – the magazine had exercised legitimate powers of interpretation. At a more detailed level he set out a number of major queries in response to the information given about the royal jewels, the occupied Royal Palaces and other important areas of concern which, he felt, needed to be answered before the manner could be resolved. Notwithstanding these, he said that the magazine's view still was that the Queen merited her position at the top of its list.

The editor said it was true that Business Age had not contacted the Palace Press Office during its investigation nor had there been any attempt to approach the appropriate officials in the Royal Household for information. The magazine's researcher had explained that, 'It has been [the Palace's] invariable practice for the last two years to direct media enquiries about the Royal wealth to a pamphlet which is two years out of date and which contains inaccurate and obsolete figures. The possibility of consultation with the three officials [mentioned] has not previously been offered to me or my researchers. Between 1988 and late 1993, it was [Palace practice] to decline to discuss Royal Finances with any journalists.' The editor did however accept that it might well be that the magazine's description of the Royal Finances as 'one of the most carefully cultivated mysteries' was a little harsh given the current climate of openness.

Solicitors acting for the magazine and the editor said that Business Age was happy to consult with the Queen's Press Secretary, 'and any other person he may nominate in the course of its research into "The Rich 500" of 1996'. They also said that their clients would be happy to co-operate in a fair and proper investigation and adjudication of the complaint. After being given a number of extensions the magazine delivered a reply including an explanation of how the figure of £2.2bn had been reached.

In correspondence, Business Age's solicitors raised a number of procedural matters with the Commission. They suggested that the manner should only proceed after a measure of disclosure from the Palace had been provided and an opportunity given to their clients to present their case, examine the complainant and tender expert evidence after its experts had been given the facility to inspect and value properties and other assets associated with the Royal Family. They also asked to be able to cross-examine the author of a letter (a copy of which had been provided by the Palace Press Office) who had personally written the previous year's article on the Queen's wealth.

ADJUDICATION

The Commission rejected all these requests. While the PCC is prepared to consider oral submissions, expert evidence and cross-examination where appropriate, the approach set out below does not, in its view, require any procedural change from the normal practice of considering complaints only on the basis of the written documentation submitted. In considering the complaint the Commission did not consider the letter mentioned above as being of any assistance to it as the author appeared to have no current knowledge of how the magazine arrived at its conclusions and the basis for the calculations adopted.

While complainants may be required to supply necessary information to satisfy the Commission that a complaint is well founded, the PCC did not accept the solicitors' contention that their clients and their representatives should be able to conduct a roving expedition into the facts and background. Such a course might not only cause inconvenience and expense to complainants but would allow newspapers and other media to print speculation under the guise of being factually correct as a means of flushing out information if a complaint was subsequently made. This cannot be right. It must be for the publication concerned to satisfy the Commission that either its statements are true and accurate, or that there is a reasonable factual basis for the material printed.

The Commission had considered carefully the approach which it should adopt in this case. The PCC is concerned not to inhibit investigatory journalism in the public interest, nor does it wish to criticise proper speculation by the press about matters which are unclear. Mr Anson did not contend that any investigation into the Queen's wealth was not a manner of public interest but he did argue that the magazine's conclusions had been reached without properly checking the facts with the relevant people concerned, were riddled with inaccuracies and presented supposition as authoritative fact.

The Commission accepted the magazine's contention that there were complicated matters of a legal and factual nature which may be the subject of legitimate discussion and argument in any assessment of the Queen's wealth. The Commission was pleased to note that the magazine had agreed to consult with the Buckingham Palace Press Office and others during the course of this year's investigation and trusted that this may enable the differences between the two sides to be narrowed. In considering the current complaint the Commission confined itself to a consideration of whether the magazine's claim that its research on the subject was exhaustive was justified and whether it may have indulged in speculation disguised as fact and without checking its conclusions with the relevant officials at Buckingham Palace.

The Commission considered that in increasing the total figure from £158m in 1994 to £2.2bn for 1995 the magazine should clearly have explained the basis on which the new figure was calculated. Only a limited breakdown was given in the magazine article without a clear description of how the final figure has been reached. However the magazine had supplied the Commission with a lengthy document together with a number of appendices which sought to set out the basis of the figures selected. The Commission agreed with a contention made by the Buckingham Palace Press Office that if there was insufficient information and understanding on which to base a valuation of the Queen's personal wealth this should have been reported, rather than presenting purely speculative numbers as established facts. The Appendix to this adjudication addresses in more detail the basis for the conclusion set out above.

Mr Anson had alleged that the editor and his colleagues took a conscious decision not to contact the Press Office before publication because they did not want their headline points and assumptions challenged or refuted. This had been vigorously denied by the editor. The Commission considered that in increasing its previous estimate to one four-teen times larger, the magazine ought properly to have checked the basis of its new figure with the relevant officials, even if it did not ultimately accept any comments made.

The magazine's explanation of why it had not consulted the Press Office set out above was challenged by Mr Anson who pointed out that numerous press briefings on Royal Finances had taken place during the period mentioned by the editor. Further, a booklet on Royal Finances had been widely distributed to the media. The editor replied that his previous statement was in the circumstances 'somewhat troublesome for us . . . please allow me a little time to clarify matters on this front.' In fact no further response on this point was received from the magazine. In the circumstances the Commission could only conclude that the magazine had failed to provide any proper explanation why the Press Office was not consulted. The matter was of importance, not only in concluding that the research was not 'exhaustive' but also in assessing the degree of care which the magazine took to check its facts. In this context the Commission did not accept the contention of the magazine's solicitors that any failure on the part of Business Age to check its facts found no place in the Code. Such a failure may be highly material in deciding whether a complaint under the Code is well grounded.

In his original response to the letter from the Buckingham Palace Press Office detailing over thirty factual complaints and alleged inaccuracies, the editor distinguished between what he described as 'big picture' and 'small picture' areas. The big picture areas included classification of large bundles of assets that had a material impact on the magzine's headline figure of £2.2bn. The smaller picture area included other items and overheads which would have no such impact.

Dealing with large items involving such matters as the Royal jewels, the occupied Palaces and the Royal Collection the Commission noted that while the editor did not accept that any major error had occurred, he did find it necessary to raise a large number of important questions which arose out of the terms of the initial complaint and which might have materially affected any final estimate. The fact that he did so again illustrated that the research carried out by the magazine was far from exhaustive and did not adequately deal with all relevant matters.

In respect of a number of other items the magazine did admit that a number of errors had occurred and said it would correct these in its next valuation. In the view of the Commission this is unsatisfactory as periodicals have a clear obligation under the Code to correct promptly any errors which have occurred. In this case the magazine should have corrected any admitted errors in the next issue of the magazine. It did not do so.

The Commission welcomed the willingness of the magazine to consult fully when it prepares its figures for this year. In the future the Commission will expect Business Age to make clear the factual basis on which any estimate is put forward and the extent to which it is speculative. Where there is substantial and proper arguments to the way in which the figures or information may be interpreted, which might materially affect any final estimate, the Commission would expect the magazine properly to indicate that fact. Business Age provided the Commission with copies of estimates of the Queen's wealth made at various times by The Sunday Times. Some of these estimates drew a distinction between wealth held by the Monarch as Head of State and that of the Queen in her personal capacity. The Commission believed the adoption of such a system by Business Age would do much to eradicate the problems set out above.

The Commission concluded that to the extent set out above, the article presented speculation as established fact, the magazine failed adequately to check its facts and it made a number of errors which were not properly addressed.

On this basis, the complaint was upheld.

CHAPTER TWELVE

A 'failed strategy'? Paparazzi, privacy and the public interest, August 1996–January 1997

'The main aim of the PCC since Lord Wakeham took over has been to fix a deal with Government not to introduce laws against intrusions of privacy by pretending to control them itself. It has succeeded and even Labour is now said to be in line, but the whole thing's a fake.'

Tim Gopsill, NUJ Annual Conference, *UK Press Gazette*, 11 October 1996

'Lord Wakeham is like a eunuch doing his very best in the circumstances.'

Gerald Kaufman MP, National Heritage department select committee, House of Commons, 7 November 1996

When back in May 1996 Wakeham announced that the Commission would be looking into the question of freelance photography and newspaper policy in purchasing pictures from freelances, he could hardly have envisaged the trouble press self-regulation would be in by August over the 'so-called paparazzi'. The immediate origins of his announcement were incidents at Balmoral in April involving disputes about whether certain areas of land were private or public. The Palace was up in arms. The Commission had wrestled with the problem of photography and private property since 1994.[1] The prime source of the current trouble, unsurprisingly, was that most photographed woman in the world, Diana, Princess of Wales. There had already been the scandal of the Princess and the Duchess of York after their divorces holidaying in July in a villa in France, beset by the media in almost siege conditions.

Discoursing on the theme 'In pursuit of Diana the hunted', Alan Hamilton in *The Times* wrote of her 'love-hate relationship with the paparazzi'. At the moment it was hate, and she had succeeded in getting an injunction targeted at one of the more harassing and persistent of the breed. She used to manipulate and tip off the press when it suited her,

Hamilton pointed out. 'But, from her point of view, the affair goes sour when she is no longer in control.' By and large, the national newspapers were not her problem. The great difficulty was not even the attentions of bona fide paparazzi; 'it was the freelance stalkers and obsessives who dogged her to distraction'.[2]

As Ken Lennox, picture editor of the *Sun* put it, 'the guys who do their stuff on Diana are on to us day in, day out'. *Sunday Express* picture editor Les Wilson added:

> It's always difficult for a picture editor because of problems regarding how we go about things. You've got to have a little bit of trust in who you take pictures from. You do tend to rely on regular paparazzi. There is a sort of code there somewhere and you rely on that working relationship.[3]

There being 'a sort of code there somewhere' was not the kind of language which commended itself to the PCC. But nonetheless the PCC had reason to be grateful for even that degree of informal self-regulation. The sale of most of the paparazzi production was to the foreign press, outside the Commission's jurisdiction. 'The paparazzi', as the *Press Gazette* commented, 'are always a weak link in defending the press.' They had no loyalty to individual newspapers and could ignore the Code of Practice and the PCC. The consequence was that the Princess's injunction and the threats of the Palace to set lawyers on to photographers covering Balmoral 'moves the press into dangerous territory'. The Home Office had in view legislation to curb 'stalkers'. A further difficulty for self-regulation was that there was 'not the same level of sympathy towards the Royal Family as there used to be, especially from those readers who buy copies of the tabloid newspapers by the million'.[4]

Media legal experts could see a 'new privacy battle for the press' portended. They drew attention to the Commission's recent laxness in failing to censure long-lens photographs of subjects on private property without their consent, 'particularly when the subject had recently courted publicity'. They warned:

> Whatever the outcome of the actions taken by Diana and the Queen, the result is likely to be a renewed privacy debate bringing closer the day when privacy legislation is introduced into Parliament, perhaps in the guise of an anti-stalking law. It would be wise for the press to prepare for that day and start lobbying sympathetic MPs and other influential people.[5]

2

So far, so bad. Then things quickly started getting worse. The press office at the Palace was fretting again, this time about publication in the *Mirror* of a recorded conversation between the Duke of York and the Greek fortune-teller of his former Duchess. Madame Vasso, counsellor to the Duchess for the past six years, had published a book about her client's irregular relationships with an American businessman and with her former financial adviser John Bryan. The Palace was in touch with the PCC; but it was understood the royal aides decided against making a formal complaint to the Commission in order to minimize the fuss over the tapes and distress for the children. 'A spokesman for the Commission said it would examine privacy issues but would not be giving a formal adjudication.' Letters would be sent to the editor of the *Daily Mirror* and Buckingham Palace within the next few weeks giving them its views.[6] It was an old story: the PCC fighting with one hand tied behind its back.

The stew of royal scandal was further enriched with ingredients provided by the *Sun*. A video had turned up purporting to reveal Diana romping at Highgrove House – Prince Charles's home in Gloucestershire – with her lover James Hewitt. The *Sun*'s editor Stuart Higgins was satisfied as to the genuineness of the stills, evidently taken with some form of spy camera. Hence the paper's public interest defence about 'dirty tricks' surveillance. It soon turned out that the video was a hoax, made with lookalikes in the back garden of a south London house. The *Mirror* permitted itself the *Schadenfreude* of exposing how its rival had been 'conned by cunning fraudsters'. The duped Stuart Higgins issued what *Private Eye* described as 'grovelling apologies' to the Princess and Hewitt.[7]

At least in this instance the rather stark nakedness of self-regulation's condition was granted the modesty of a fig-leaf of apology. Still, Wakeham had to be seen to be doing something. It was reported that he was believed to be under pressure from broadsheet editors and from broadcasters 'fearful that the image of the press was being tarnished by the *Sun*'s Princess Diana hoax video and the *Daily Mirror*'s Madame Vasso revelations about Fergie'.[8] On top of these the *Express* came up with a story about a girlfriend – bogus – of Prince William.

Wakeham wrote a letter to *The Times*. The events of the last few days, he stated, had 'thrown into sharp focus' a matter that had been worrying him for a long time. 'Although these events concern primarily members and former members of the Royal Family, the key issues they raise – invasions of privacy and the use of public-interest defence by newspapers – have wider ramifications.' In the light of these concerns, Wakeham believed, 'we need now to examine all these issues carefully but urgently, to see what lessons can be learned'. In the meantime newspapers should be aware that unjustified reporting of the private lives of public individuals would cast into doubt the system of self-regulation which had, in his view, achieved notable successes over the past few years. 'They should remember, too, that the PCC has powers to raise its own complaints when it needs to – and will not hesitate to use them.' The fact that some victims understandably did not want to undergo the complaints procedure should not lead some news-papers 'to believe that, simply because one of those involved in a story fails to complain, they have carte blanche to invade their privacy without any defence of public interest'. Wakeham concluded gnomically: 'those who seek the limelight of publicity should always be prepared when its glare is returned, sometimes harshly'.[9]

There was no way of avoiding entirely either the futile fist-waving effect or the impotent hand-wringing effect. A shaft of prompt retorts in the *Times*'s letter columns made that very clear. One of the more wounding retorts came from Gerald Isaaman, a local Hampstead editor and a former industry member of the Commission. He dismissed Wakeham's letter as 'another fudge'. So the PCC can now make its own complaints! 'When did the PCC under his energetic leadership last do so? I can recall no such occasion.' The belief unhappily abroad was that the PCC was an 'industry sop'. Where was the stricter and more specific Code promised by Lord Wakeham? 'His reputation is that of a man who can fix things. He ought to get on with it.'[10]

The plot thickened apace. The *Daily Express*, whose editor happened to be on the Code Committee, recklessly published photographs of children at the troubled Ridings School in Halifax. Sir John Gorst MP was highly aggrieved at the Commission's failure to uphold his complaints against the *Hendon Times* and the *Daily Telegraph* for betraying his confidence and 'stitch-ing him up' in the matter of his campaign to save the casualty service at Edgware General Hospital. The Commission's unwillingness to adjudicate on hundreds of complaints about the grossly jingoistic tabloid handling of the England-Germany football match back in July provoked outrage and cartoons of the PCC as Chamberlain appeasing the *Mirror*, *Star* and *Sun*. It was a question, the PCC pleaded, of taste; and while there were grounds for disgust, dismay and shame, there were no grounds for formal censure under the Code. It was enough that Piers Morgan apologized for the

Mirror's excesses.[11] Even the NUJ vote at its annual conference to open negotiations with the Commission (its own attempts to run a code of conduct having collapsed) seemed somehow more threatening than promising.[12] Memories stirred of its kiss of death to the Press Council in 1990.

All this apparent reluctance to tackle the papers was in striking contrast to the confidence exuded in the Commission's *Annual Report, 1995*. The *Press Gazette* judged its implications and consequences matters of high importance needing to be aired. 'Lord Wakeham has lifted the lid of the box. By going public in his letter to *The Times*, the chairman of the Press Complaints Commission has broken the consensus view – which he has done so much to create – that everything was getting better in Fleet Street.' Lord McGregor, as the *Gazette* reminded Wakeham, 'was impaled on the Royals'. Now the 'combination of a Greek soothsayer, a fraudulent video and a lapse at the *Express* by a standard-bearer of the Editors' Code of Practice may have been too much for his successor to bear'.

> Now the lid has been lifted a little in public, there's sense in following the logic of Lord Wakeham's action. He has already said he wants to increase public participation in framing the Code. He and Sir David English . . . now have a chance. Revisions of the Code are due to be announced soon. Let them first be published in green-paper form. Journalists, of all people, shouldn't be shy of public discussion of how they do their job, and should take the initiative in elucidation. It's the only way we'll convince public and politicians that, as well as some disingenuousness, there are real complexities not amenable to simplistic solutions.[13]

3

All depended on whether Wakeham's gamble of lifting the lid of the box in his letter to *The Times* was well-timed: that is to say, towards the end rather than near the beginning of a bad patch. The Commission announced that it was considering altering the Code to authorize it to investigate alleged breaches in the absence of a complaint from the person or persons involved. Under the existing provision the Commission had to get the co-operation of such persons. 'Sources say that new thinking by some commissioners that the Commission should be able to investigate without this co-operation will be a strong argument in favour of self-regulation.' No statutory scheme could entertain it.[14]

Wakeham was about to begin a round of talks with editors and proprietors on the issues raised in the recent squalls, with special reference to the public-interest criteria. Already in the pipeline were ratifications of Code-tightenings on privacy and the protocol on witness payments and payments to criminals. Lord Chancellor Mackay studied the Code changes draft and acknowledged that the government 'recognises and is grateful for the efforts the industry is making to tighten the Code, but remains concerned that payments to witnesses still risk damaging the integrity of the administration of justice'. Self-regulation, he insisted, had failed in the West case.[15] Mackay duly issued his plans to criminalize payments to witnesses. For all that he had been baulked on privacy, Mackay's determination on this front was not to be facilely discounted. He was not a Dorrell or a Bottomley; Wakeham's fingerprints would not be over any of his papers. Roy Greenslade observed, moreover, that 'evidently the commission is not going to introduce a special clause to tackle the paparazzi'. Though there was 'disquiet among PCC members about the way freelance photographers pursue the royal family, it has proved impossible to draft a rule outlawing their activities without threatening press freedom'.[16]

Indications now suggested, even so, that Wakeham had judged his *Times* intervention accurately. The press Richter scale no longer registered alarming shocks. It was true that local education authorities grumbled that disciplinary problems at the Ridings School were aggravated by intense media coverage. There was the tricky problem of dealing with a complaint by the Moors murderer Myra Hindley against the *Daily Mail*'s reporting of her intimate relationship with Rosemary West. The Commission, after five laborious sessions, 'reached a landmark adjudication "reluctantly"' upholding her complaint 'because the report had been published in good faith and was based on confidential sources'. There was a question, however, of reopening the case on the *Mail*'s submission of new evidence, the source of which was not to be disclosed to the PCC.[17] And Roy Greenslade was inclined to question the way editors were exploiting the public-interest justification in the absence of a clear guide to the balance between privacy and public interest, especially in the case of photographers at troubled schools. 'And there are more questions, Lord Wakeham.'[18]

But both the tempo and the temperature of events had now subsided to something like normal levels. Gerald Kaufman, it was true, raised the temperature somewhat at a Heritage committee hearing on witness payments by insulting Wakeham as being 'like a eunuch who is doing his very best in the circumstances'.[19] This gibe reflected a revived sense of possibilities

among the PCC's enemies. After all, as Wakeham's unhappy experiences in
1996 at the British Horseracing Board indicated, he was by no means invariably a Mr Fixit. He had manoeuvred well to protect self-regulation's flank
on the privacy question. But was he not now outflanked on the 'payment
to witnesses' question? The judges wanted it and the Lord Chancellor was
in the field. An Act to ban chequebook journalism might be the thin end
of a wedge that could crack open press self-regulation. Wakeham parried
Mackay: in the past forty years there had been only four high-profile cases
involving newspaper chequebooks – Brady-Hindley, Thorpe, Sutcliffe and
now West – and in no case was there evidence that justice had miscarried.
Against this there was the equally good riposte that there always has to be
a first time. Wakeham fought well; but was there in his plea yet again that
self-regulation be allowed to work an unwonted hint of defensiveness? 'If
it does not, I shall be the first to say, I can't make it work and government
will have to legislate.'[20]

'And there are more questions, Lord Wakeham.' The principal one on the
chairman's mind was the urgency of tackling the conundrum of defining
the uses and abuses of the public-interest defence. Given that the Code
Committee could make no headway as yet on the paparazzi problem,
privacy per se no longer headed the agenda. Inadequacy of public-interest
guidelines and flimsiness of public-interest justifications had taken over. In
his current round of talks with industry people Wakeham was taking
requisite soundings. Jean Morgan for the *Press Gazette* gathered that the
questions being posed by Wakeham were largely prompted by the Countess
Spencer and Selina Scott cases, and were along the lines of: 'If you intend
to use pictures, do you really need them? Are there other ways of demonstrating public interest without using intrusive methods to get the pictures?
Have you considered the impact of your story on vulnerable relatives,
particularly children, and is there any way of minimising this? How old is
the story – is it 30 years old or two? Age of a story has some bearing on
whether intrusion on privacy can be justified.'[21]

Wakeham set forth his findings at a reception at the City Executive Club.
He emphasized that in the first instance it had to be a 'matter of sound
editorial judgment as to what was or was not in the public interest'. In the
vast majority of cases, Wakeham believed, 'editors get it right by agonising
over their decision to publish a story – and applying to it a number of
simple common sense tests'. Wakeham's own distillation of his sense of
these tests emerged as 'the seven tests which will justify a public-interest
defence' to be applied by the Commission to editorial justifications.

1 Is there a genuine public interest involved in invading someone's privacy as defined by Clause 18 of the Code (of Practice) – detecting or exposing crime, protecting public health, preventing the public from being misled – or is this simply a story which interests the public?

2 If there is a genuine public interest, have you considered whether there are ways to disclose it which minimise invasion into the private life of the individual concerned?

3 If you are using photographs as part of the story, which will have to be (or have already been) obtained by clandestine means and therefore compound the invasion of privacy, does the public interest require their automatic publication or are they simply illustrative?

4 If there is a genuine public interest which cannot be exposed in any other way than intrusion, have you considered whether there is any other way to minimise the impact on the innocent and vulnerable relatives of the individual, in particular the children?

5 If you are intending to run a story about someone connected or related to a person in the public eye in order to illustrate a story about that public figure, are you satisfied the connection isn't too remote and there is a genuine public interest in mentioning that connection?

6 Where you are preparing to publish a story seeking to contrast what a public figure has said or done in the past with his or her current statements or behaviour, have you satisfied yourself it is fair to make such a comparison and that the original statement or behaviour was recent enough to justify publication in the public interest?

7 If you are intending to run a story about the private life of an individual where there used to be a public interest, have you applied each of these questions afresh in case such a defence no longer exists?[22]

In this pragmatic, interrogative manner Wakeham hoped to avoid seeming to set principles in concrete and to define 'what so far has proved to be indefinable: the public interest'. At the same time he hoped to make the problem of 'public interest' more transparent to the public.

The seven-tests initiative for the industry coincided with the Commission's publishing its complainants charter for the public. This set standards of service to be expected and performance targets in such respects as the time taken to respond to complaints and the processing of complaints, all to be disclosed in an annual publication of statistics. There were new commitments to aid the disabled, publication of a *How to Complain* leaflet and the Code of Practice in minority languages, and undertakings of unfailing courtesy and helpfulness on the part of complaints staff.

Good public relations on behalf of press self-regulation was never to be underestimated. Here Guy Black was in his element. The Department of National Heritage was still watching, and needed from time to time to be massaged. Good procedure was always good politics. What was most gratifying to Wakeham and the Commission at this particular juncture, however, was probably an exercise in good procedure and good politics offered to the cause of self-regulation by none other than Piers Morgan, editor of the *Daily Mirror*. 'Public interest defence of his story weighed heavily', so Morgan assured the *Press Gazette*, 'in his decision not to publish one of the biggest scoops of all time – the leak of the contents of next day's Budget.' By midday on Monday 25 November Morgan was in possession of ninety-four pages of Budget documents, 'and they were pretty comprehensive and we had just about everything'.

> Obviously then the decision was: a) are these genuine? and b) what is the public interest if we go with these in the morning? At the moment, the public interest defence is being exposed to such scrutiny, and this was a classic example of the press self-regulating. We had, on the face of it, the scoop of all time, but I decided we had a big enough scoop without doing something that would clearly not be in the public interest.[23]

Morgan was not spared 'holier-than-thou' gibes from editorial colleagues and rivals. And variations were revealed as to how other editors would have handled such a potential scoop. But mostly they stressed the public-interest criterion. From the PCC's angle of view, Morgan, a self-confessed 'maverick' and 'not exactly renowned for my circumspection', was by far the best fugleman they could have hoped for as an edifying example to his colleagues. Indeed, the *Press Gazette* fretted that things were getting out of hand. 'The dangerous myth that is being encouraged by this episode is that journalism has an obligation – voluntary or statutory – to take account of the "public interest" before it publishes anything or everything.' Clause 18 of the Code, stressed the *Gazette*, 'is concerned with the public interest, but not as an end in itself'.

> Public interest appears in the Code only as an overriding justification for a derogation from five of the preceding seventeen clauses (and editors' minds will be concentrated on these matters by Lord Wakeham's new, salutary seven tests). Of course editors are free to take account of their concept of the public interest if that's what they want to do, but they should make clear to their readers that their reasoning has no external authority. It is an horrific prospect that editors

should be constructing a concept of public interest for every story they publish. It's not their job to do so and will open doors to intervention in the whole editorial process.[24]

The Commission could take heart from contemplating this horrific prospect. An indelible mark had been left on the industry. But could it be asserted by the end of 1996 that the PCC's confident wordage of late 1995 could be revived and re-employed? That the corner *had* been turned? That 'success' *was* well on the way to being made 'permanent'? That self-regulation *was* manifestly 'delivering the goods'?

It was no doubt salutary for the PCC to contemplate also at this moment a critique of self-regulation's performance from old enemies. James Curran and Jean Seaton published in 1997 the fifth edition of their influential *Power without Responsibility: the Press and Broadcasting in Britain*. Curran especially spoke from an eminent vantage point in press history: he had been an academic adviser to McGregor's Royal Commission in 1975–7. They drew attention to recurring cycles of self-regulatory behaviour. Following Calcutt Phase 2 'the PCC duly appointed a new chairman and promised significant improvements. Once again the cycle of public scrutiny and condemnation, followed by contrition and the promise of reform, was resumed. However, nothing much changed.' How plausible was their finding in 1997 that the industry's 'strategy', in short, had failed?[25]

4

The newspaper industry, at all events, was very ready to proclaim at the opening of 1997 that Lord Wakeham deserved well of it. Pressbof offered him a two-year extension to the three-year contract with which he had commenced his chairmanship in 1995. Harry Roche, chairman of Pressbof, was also staying on, though retiring from his chairmanship of the Guardian Media Group. Roche disclosed that it was a unanimous decision to ask Wakeham to stay on. The industry remained confident of Wakeham's talents at defending self-regulation. Wakeham, it seems, did not need much persuading. 'I've always said I enjoy the job', he told Jean Morgan, 'and I think it's going to take longer than three years to get to the point where you can safely say the threats of legislation have gone completely.'[26]

Such were the sour fruits of Wakeham's hard times in the latter months of 1996. 'I think the press should be aware that one or two adverse cases will bring it right back on the front burner.' The area the press must beware of, Wakeham warned, was still invasion of privacy. 'I do believe there is now a maturity over accuracy. I do not believe that any editor who isn't prepared to put inaccurate statements right is likely to stay very long in his job.' Jean Morgan summed up:

> Wakeham believes the most important thing the PCC has achieved in his first two years is the acceptance of the Code of Practice by the industry: 'Today there is no serious discussion between ourselves and the industry about anything except by reference to the Code. If they disagree, it is about interpretation rather than whether the Code is reasonable and right. The Code is now accepted by the industry, the Government and the Opposition and it's increasingly being accepted by the public as the best way forward.'
>
> He approaches his job neither in a 'spirit of hostility nor a spirit of euphoric support'. He said: 'I try to be a realist and recognise the press serves a very important role in the country. We are here to try and achieve what in a democratic society is an essential balance between the public's right to know what is going on and the public's right to privacy.'[27]

Wakeham also had a lot to say to Morgan about running the self-regulatory apparatus and the development of the PCC. He commended the role of the lay majority of the Commission. 'They don't come with the baggage of the past. All the editors on the Commission try to see issues in a balanced way and to observe the Code. However, it is in the interaction of the lay and press people which gets the right answer. It is the balance time and time again.' The Commission did not do things by votes. 'We find the common position which we all agree is reasonable.' Editors themselves were now dealing with more complaints without resort to the PCC, and, as a result, the complaints which did reach Salisbury Square were more complicated, and unravelling entrenched positions more difficult for its members. Sometimes the Commission consulted lawyers, but not automatically because it liked to run 'a commonsense operation and write adjudications in commonsense language'. One significant indication of the Commission's gaining in authority and reputation, Wakeham held, was that complaints came increasingly from lawyers on behalf of their clients.

The two landmark adjudications Wakeham thought most significant in his first two years as chairman were those on the Julia Carling and Selena Scott complaints. These established a guiding rule that the acceptable degree of intrusion into anyone's privacy was partly determined by themselves. 'If you want your life to be private, keep it private, and you will receive massive support from the PCC in keeping it private.'

Wakeham's old parliamentary role as Mr Fixit continued in his present position. He kept a low profile but invested his influence where it counted. He had known Virginia Bottomley 'for many years and is a great admirer'. He had lately spoken with the president of the Association of Chief Police Officers about press concern at how progress to an open society was being hindered by the way police applied data protection laws. His ambit included also the Palace. Wakeham was in touch often enough to understand Prince William's anti-press feelings. 'Any young person whose parents are so high-profile has a reluctance about the life they lead in the public eye and has a degree of shying away from the limelight.' That was why the Code was adamant that children must be protected. 'The press has to realise that when applying public interest defence to invasion of privacy, in quite a few cases it is the child's privacy which is at stake.'

The last two years' cull of constantly changing editors had added a challenge to his job. But he was careful, when meeting editors and proprietors all over the country, also to spend an hour or two with their reporters, sub-editors and feature writers, to talk about the Commission's work. Grassroots concern was that the PCC would act as a censor. Wakeham assured them it will not.

> 'Editing a newspaper is a professional job and editors will not be told in advance how they should exercise their judgment. That doesn't rule out a hotline but it depends what a hotline is for. . . . A hotline that enables "x" to ring up and say: "A newspaper is about to publish an embarrassing scene about me and some affair I'm having and I'm only really playing chess with them" – I'm not in the business of doing that.'
>
> What he will do is tell an editor the information has been passed to the PCC but it is up to the editor to decide whether he will publish. . . . No one has so far told him to mind his own business. They say thank you and may even add a story or two about the situation.
>
> 'Not everyone who complains gives me an unvarnished account of the truth. There are occasionally people around who deserve exposure in the newspapers. And that's what a free press is about.'

There were rogue editors, as Wakeham admitted, though he would not name them.

> 'But very occasionally and increasingly, we shall make a gentle private inquiry of a newspaper when we see something that looks, on the face of it, difficult to explain. Editors are asked to justify it. No public statements are made because

no one has complained but I think it's interesting and helpful [a quizzical raising of one eyebrow] to editors occasionally to be questioned about things.'

The more significant aspect of Morgan's interview, however, was insights into Wakeham's longer-term hopes. Having now contracted for two further years which would take him to the millennial 2000, Wakeham's ultimate strategy seemed to be to 'put himself and his successors out of a job'. His aim was for 'true self-regulation by individual newspapers and magazines; for the Commission to be an inspectorate rather than an arbitration service, with the press setting its own high standards and taking responsibility for protecting people's privacy – even when the person concerned is unlikely to complain'. Considering that complaints to the PCC were currently running at some 3,000 a year, this, thought Morgan, might seem to be asking a lot. But Wakeham turned to his time at the Energy department for an explanatory analogy.

'We completely reformed and re-did the safety regulations for the North Sea after Piper Alpha. We came up with a system which said: "If you want to operate in this world, you have to have a safety system which you yourself check. We will come round now and then and see how you are getting on checking it."

'Now, if you are a newspaper and you believe in standards, your job is to maintain what you believe in. And I'll talk to you from time to time to see how you are getting on. . . . It's not necessarily the only way of checking on standards to wait till someone complains.'

This seemingly unlikely scenario of the British press monitoring its own behaviour at home base is, surprisingly, already happening, says Wakeham. 'We have editors who have written to us who have spotted serious mistakes in their newspapers, where there has been no complaint, to say: "Frightfully sorry – been a bit of a mess here and we've taken steps to make sure it doesn't happen again." That's showing a maturity I need to encourage.'[28]

CHAPTER THIRTEEN

New Labour, new questions, January–August 1997

'I can only say that I would happily sacrifice the freedom to expose the love-life of a BBC weather forecaster to 11 million prurient eyes if it meant that the courts would give greater protection to serious papers or broadcasters reporting corruption or dishonesty in public life.'

Alan Rusbridger, editor of the *Guardian*, James Cameron memorial lecture,
19 May 1997

'Despite all the posturing of Derry Irvine, Blair is taking a more pragmatic view of the whole thing.'

Piers Morgan, editor of the the the *Mirror*,[1] *UK Press Gazette*, 1 August 1997

Wakeham's vision of the PCC's being transformed into a hands-off inspectorate, rather like his vision of a restored 'Elysian times' when Prime Ministers wrote leaders for the newspapers, was, as Jean Morgan suggested, still some way off. The immediate and pressing concerns at the head of the Commission's agenda for 1997 were paparazzi, 'media scrums', data protection and the Lord Chancellor's recent Green Paper on chequebook journalism.

On the first point, Wakeham was sure that the best way of controlling the paparazzi was to cut off their sources of income; and the best way of doing that was to impress upon editors that it was their responsibility not to use material from unprovenanced sources. 'They must be cautious about the stuff they take from these people.' As for the media-scrum phenomenon, Dunblane, the scene of shocking killings of schoolchildren by a deranged gun fanatic, was an extreme example of a media genre now too common. That 'little town had something like 400 television and newspaper reporters there and, frankly, though every single one of them behaved impeccably, it was just too much for the community'. The PCC was 'going to have to deal with this problem because the scrum is intimidating to ordinary people'. Easy access to worldwide travel and technology for instant relay of stories and pictures had swelled the ranks of the media at disasters and other dramatic events. 'It's got just that much more intense', Wakeham observed. 'Certainly you would not have had 400 or so journalists at Dunblane 10 years ago. The more responsible editors and broadcasters are realising it can't go on as it is.' And as for data protection, serious issues for press freedom would arise if the government signed up to the European Convention on Human Rights, particularly in the area of data-protection legislation. 'The PCC wants to see derogation for the press if this happens and is pressing the Government on the issue.'[2]

The PCC had just sent its response to the Lord Chancellor's Green Paper on press payments to trial witnesses. 'It does not think a case has been made out for new criminal legislation or an extension of the law of contempt to stop this form of chequebook journalism.' The Commission felt particularly sore at Mackay's accusation that self-regulation had 'failed' in the West case. No complaint had been made and the PCC accordingly did not launch its own investigation. 'Furthermore the newspapers concerned have had no opportunity of giving their side of the case, and it is impossible, as a result, to say the PCC would have inevitably reached the conclusion that payments were contrary to the public interest.'

The Commission made five points against the Green Paper. First, the new Code changes should be given a chance to prove themselves. Second, it was not clear there was a widespread problem, and newspapers in any case had played a part in bringing about trials and uncovering witnesses. Third, if government did decide that justice was at risk, the Lord Chancellor's proposals did not meet the case. 'If there is a risk of evidence being slanted because of payment before proceedings, the risk would still exist if the witness knew offers might be forthcoming after the trial ended.' Fourthly, the Commission was concerned that the public's right to know might be undermined. It was arguable that payments assisted newspapers during the West trial in making legitimate comment of public interest about the conduct of the police and social services in Gloucestershire. It would be a matter of considerable concern if newspapers were unable to make these essential comments in future trials because of legislation which barred them from unearthing crucial information. In one of the much-cited earlier cases, the trial of the former Liberal party leader Jeremy Thorpe, the Commission pointed out that its predecessor, the Press Council, found that the cumulative action of the newspapers might actually have led to the launching of criminal proceedings in the first place. Finally, the Commission allowed that if the revised Code failed to work or if there were any objective evidence of a serious problem which could not be corrected by effective self-regulation, then it would support practical proposals for reform.[3]

Having thus dealt faithfully with Lord Chancellor Mackay, the Commission dealt equally faithfully with a 'virulent attack' from Kaufman's National Heritage committee. As the *Press Gazette* saw it, the culture of dignified process and constitutional forms (courts, judges, lawyers, legislators) was pitting itself against the pragmatic and voluntary operations of the press: 'the National Heritage Committee of MPs has combined with the part-lawyer, part-politician Lord Chancellor in a straight run at journalism'. The MPs' report revealed 'a contempt and puzzlement in the face of journalism that is wider and deeper than that generated by activities of some reporters in anticipation of trials'. In particular, 'it lashes the Press Complaints Commission and newspapers' system of self-regulation'. Time and time again, the report alleged, 'the PCC's reaction to criticism is to offer half-measures when radical change is called for'. This was not just about witnesses and trials, concluded the *Gazette*. 'We can't say we haven't been warned.'[4]

Nor had the Data Protection Registrar gone away. Elizabeth France, asked by the *Press Gazette* on her views on 'proper investigative journalism', conceded that 'there must be some limits on journalists'. But 'how can you have a discussion with people who won't even discuss with you where the line should be drawn if they don't think the line should be there in the first place?' The Commission's rebuff of the previous summer still rankled. The European Union Directive, as she saw it, required her to draw lines between breaches of privacy in the public interest and breaches that merely interested the public. It had to be implemented in the UK by 24 October 1998. She thought it 'very disappointing' that the PCC 'don't seem to want to get into constructive dialogue with us'. There were 'things we could discuss which either can be the responsibility of the PCC or it could be something that we introduce'. There was the question about where the right of privacy should override the right of free speech. The PCC had told her it was none of her business to endorse its Code. 'But if there was something in the PCC's own Code that dealt with these things in terms that matched the consideration that I have to exercise under the Data Protection Act, we'd have a common starting point.' Self-regulation would then 'fit in with statutory regulation', and the Data Protection Registrar would be able to say, 'well, that's all right, the first stop's going to be the PCC'.[5]

The PCC did not wish to be a 'first stop' in a self-regulatory role entangled with someone else's role as, presumably, final stop statutory regulator. Nor was Wakeham mollified by France's approval of his recent seven clarificatory questions about public-interest criteria 'which could almost have been her own'. Besides, the Commission had on its hands enough material raising a wide variety of public-interest questions.

2

Back in April 1996, under the auspices of the Commission for Racial Equality, Wakeham had invited complainants to come forward under Clause 15 of the Code dealing with prejudicial or pejorative treatment by the press of matters of race or colour. Perhaps this accounted for the fact that, whereas in 1995 only 1.7 per cent of investigated complaints related to Clause 15, the equivalent figure in 1996 was 6.89 per cent. In any event, the issue now arose in a quite intense but rather oblique manner, disconcerting to the Commission. Dr Vernon Coleman, columnist for the *People* and the Glasgow *Evening Times*, had long been known as a passionate advocate of animal rights. He described in his column a visit to Malta, where he had been horrified at the way the Maltese, as he alleged, mistreated animals. His language about Malta, the Maltese and their cruel habits was unrestrained; and complaints were made by the Maltese High Commissioner and two MPs on grounds of racist abuse.

The problem for the Commission was that Clause 15 allowed for complaints about racist abuse only on an individual as distinct from a collective basis. This issue had come up in 1996 in the case of tabloid jingoism over Euro '96 football coverage.[6] Though it declined to adjudicate on a matter not squarely addressed in the Code and which came under a rubric concerning taste and decency, the Commission did ask the Code Committee to consider changes to Clause 15. The Committee chose to avoid going out looking for trouble. Now, confronted with Dr Coleman's 'hyperbolic' accusations, the Commission found both that it could not uphold the complaints against him on grounds that 'matters of taste and decency quite rightly fall outside the remit of the Commission' and that his language was 'a rare example of the worst type of journalism which all too easily can bring the press into disrepute'. The Commission resolved also to investigate whether the Code needed changing to embrace collective as well as individual application to Clause 15. It was a curious non-adjudication which, predictably, pleased none of the parties concerned. Coleman pleaded that as a columnist he dealt in opinion and not, like a reporter, in fact. His purpose was to shock and arouse. The editors of the *People* and the *Evening Times* had both mitigated the offence, one by judicious censorship, the other by providing ample space for reply. They were, with some reason, irritated at the Commission's having it both ways by disqualifying itself from adjudicating on the one hand but by being free with its opinions on the other.[7]

It remained for Bob Borzello, the veteran anti-racist campaigner and fabled third-party complainer to the Press Council, to come forward with a reminder that it was the weight of third-party complaints which resulted in the Council's eventual willingness to include in its remit collective racist abuse.[8] Perhaps mindful of that very point about the effects of the burden of third-party complaints on the Council, however, both the Code Committee and the PCC persisted in the view that good procedure consists in not as a rule admitting third-party complaints, and that good policy consists in leaving collective racism outside the Code in a category of offences to taste and decency.

A case involving accuracy under Clause 1 also enlivened these months. Described by Roy Greenslade as 'instructive', it concerned a complaint against the *Daily Telegraph* by Victim Support, an organization dedicated to helping victims of criminal acts. The case was instructive because it raised two fundamental points of interest: the supposed distinction between facts and comment, and the 'continued misunderstanding about the limited role of the PCC in dealing with complaints and accuracy'. Barbara Amiel, a *Daily Telegraph* columnist (and wife of Conrad Black, proprietor of the *Telegraph*), attacked Victim Support for abandoning its original vocation as a charity service and becoming a lobby group funded by the Home Office with an increasingly feminist agenda, US-style. The complaint alleged inaccuracy and distortion. The *Telegraph* pleaded that the facts were as stated and so-called distortions were opinions or matters of interpretation. The Commission reportedly gave itself a headache for several months before adjudicating in favour of the paper on the ground that it was not competent, on the evidence submitted, to adjudicate against it.* As Wakeham had remarked, complaints to the Commission were getting more complicated, unravelling entrenched positions more difficult.

It happened that the chairman of Victim Support was Sir Louis Blom-Cooper, never one to let the Commission get away with what he held to be evasive and slovenly procedure. 'What is the PCC's *raison d'être?*' he asked.

---

* See adjudication, pp. 268–9.

It was a conciliation body, not a court of law. And it was not very good, it seemed to him, at conciliation. Greenslade observed that Blom-Cooper was being 'openly hostile to the creation of the PCC, failing to appreciate that when a government minister warned journalists they were drinking in the Last Chance Saloon, the necessary political expedient was to build a new pub and give it a new name and a new chairman. It could be said therefore that Blom-Cooper has an axe to grind, irrespective of the merits of his case.' Nonetheless, on those merits Greenslade came down on Blom-Cooper's side.[9]

Two cases involving harassment were also instructive in their different ways. Diana, feeling harassed by a photographer, ran across the road to demand his film. He was strong-armed by a passer-by and forced to give up the film. Another photographer, whom the Princess's office accused of being present by collusion, recorded the incident. The *Daily Express* sent a reporter to the PCC asking their view on 'Diana and the paparazzo photographer'. Since the Princess had not complained, the Commission's official view, as conveyed to her private secretary, was that there could 'therefore have been absolutely no question of the PCC making any comment on the matter'. Unluckily, however, the *Express* had quoted a 'Commission spokesman' as saying that 'famous and high-profile figures should expect to have their photo taken if they are seen in public – especially if they have courted publicity in the past'. Such, after all, was official PCC doctrine since the *Panorama* affair. All the *Express* needed to do to create a story was to interpret the 'Commission's spokesman's' statement as a 'rebuke' to the Princess. The paper's deputy editor Tessa Hilton insisted that there was no doubt that in this case it was Diana being discussed. The embarrassed PCC wrote to the Princess regretting that remarks by a junior member of staff to an *Express* reporter about principles arising from past adjudications should have been misrepresented. 'It was not a formal statement from anyone in authority at the Commission.'[10] This episode illustrated, a little humiliatingly, the importance for the PCC of not cutting too close to the bone of the 'people's Princess'.

The other case involved a complex relationship between privacy and harassment, and led to the Commission's formulating a concept of 'collective unintentional harassment' as being not subject to the condemnation it visited on harassment by an individual newspaper. It was a matter of a 15-year-old girl being diagnosed (or misdiagnosed, as it turned out) as suffering from CJD, the human equivalent of 'mad cow disease'. Four Scottish newspapers, the *Express*, the *Express on Sunday*, the *Scottish Daily*

Mail and the *Daily Record* homed in in a kind of minor 'scrum'. A complaint was made on two counts: invasion of privacy and harassment. The Commission upheld the privacy complaint but rejected the harassment one.

> In its adjudication, the Commission said it was concerned to learn of harassment experienced by the complainant and her family from repeated and uninvited approaches at home, in person and by telephone, at the workplace and at her children's schools, but said: 'Such pressure inevitably results from the combination of a few enquiries from each of many sources. The Commission believes that this was an example of what was effectively collective (if unintentional) harassment – which could occur when a large number of enquiries from different sources were being made of people who found themselves at the centre of an interesting news story.

The Commission warned, however, that while in this case it did not find evidence to justify criticism of an individual newspaper, 'it would not hesitate to do so in future if it became apparent that an individual paper or reporter played a leading part in unjustified collective harassment or did not desist when personally asked to do so'.[11]

3

In the somewhat fraught circumstances attending on the Lord Chancellor's Green Paper and data protection, the PCC's *Annual Report, 1996* was neither quite so glossy nor quite so confident as its 1995 counterpart. Moreover, its publication in May 1997 coincided with the landslide dismissal of the Conservative government and the election of a 'New Labour' government under Tony Blair. Wakeham no longer had his old political chums at the heart of affairs. On the other hand, there were his old skills as leader of the Commons to call into service. As he had assured Jean Morgan, 'I get on fine with the Opposition spokesman too.'[12]

Still, a new political order made for new uncertainties. On the face of things, press self-regulation did not seem likely to be under threat or hostile interrogation. Blair's landslide majority made him immune from pressure from the Kaufmans and Soleys. David English had helped prepare the way for a revised Labour approach to the press question through his rapport with Mo Mowlam. Murdoch, moreover, had nimbly switched sides as he saw the Conservatives' popularity crumbling. It could be plausibly alleged that he had claims on Blair for services rendered. Hard-core 'Old Labour' had never liked Blair's flirting with Murdoch. The NUJ general secretary John Foster had denounced Blair's 'free for all' policy on media ownership and for abandoning opposition to newspapers taking over television stations, all because Labour 'did not want to displease the Mirror Group and because Tony Blair was "courting" Rupert Murdoch'.[13] But there it was: Blair was 'in bed' not only with the *Mirror* but also with the *Sun*.

Statutory regulation of the press in the by now somewhat traditional manner of Soley and Kaufman, therefore, was arguably at a discount. On the other hand, as Wakeham pointed out in his chairman's introduction to the *Annual Report, 1996*, fresh issues were on the agenda: incorporation of the European Convention on Human Rights, data protection, freedom of information. It was his obvious tactic to draw attention to the PCC's expertise in these areas of concern. 'In some ways, at the heart of each of them is that crucial balancing-act performed by the PCC – and enshrined in the Code of Practice it upholds: reconciling the public's right to know with the legitimate expectation of individuals for privacy.' With the progress made in the last two years in strengthening self-regulation, Wakeham proclaimed 'I believe that the Press Complaints Commission is now in an unrivalled position to show the way in some of these areas.'[14]

It was certainly expedient to get the PCC's word in promptly. The Queen's Speech opening the new Parliament pledged the government to a Data Protection Bill and a preliminary White Paper on Freedom of Information. The point of the data protection measure was 'to balance the privacy of individuals with legitimate investigative reporting'. In the end, it would be for the courts to judge on this balance. Lord Williams of Mostyn at the Home Office, in charge of the measure, emphasized the importance of safeguarding the legitimate interests of the media and undertook to consult fully with media bodies. Frank Rogers of the Newspaper Publishers Association, who had first alerted the industry to the dangers lurking in the data protection directive, returned to his position that exemptions must allow journalists to do their job. The Newspaper Society submitted appropriate proposals about exemptions to the Home Office. The PCC was 'keeping a wary eye on both pieces of legislation, and its chairman Lord Wakeham has made his views on extension of the Data Protection Registrar's powers clear'.[15]

The crucial requirement was to get industry representations in balance to ensure the desired balance in the legislation. Data protection immediately, freedom of information in the short term, and incorporation of the ECHR in the longer term – as Bob Satchwell, chairman of the Guild of

Editors' parliamentary and legal committee, emphasized – were designed to conduce to a 'culture of openness in order to give information, and therefore power, to ordinary people – our readers'. But there was the danger that without careful scrutiny and effectual exemptions press freedoms could be infringed and privacy legislation allowed to slip in 'by the back door'.[16] David Clark, the minister in charge of freedom of information, was reassuring, especially on the point of a 'public interest override', setting aside a long list of statutes barring disclosure or making disclosure discretionary.

It was not long, however, before indicators started popping up through the surface of the new order of things that the seismic shock of the general election would not be without its destabilizing impact on relations between politics and the press. Before May was out Alan Rusbridger, Peter Preston's successor as editor of the *Guardian*, used the James Cameron memorial lecture to 'drive the first wedge into the hitherto unified line of the quality, tabloid and regional press against a law on privacy'. Convinced that Labour would sooner or later bring in a privacy law, Rusbridger wanted to offset any damage to journalism's interests by getting in ahead. He believed privacy to be a fundamental human right. He denounced newspapers that betrayed high standards of journalism in their obsession with trivia and low entertainment. He urged that a law of privacy be hammered out between journalists, politicians and judges. As with the rather similar initiative of Donald Trelford in April 1992, in anticipation of a Labour government,[17] Rusbridger had in mind compensating concessions to the press in the way of libel-law reform and freedom of information. The task was to ensure that decent, serious journalism could flourish in a society without also opening the door to brutalist and intrusive journalism. 'The challenge is to see whether it is possible to restrict the latter while enabling the former.'

Rusbridger had no compunction in breaking ranks. In any case he had sympathetic colleagues: Andrew Marr of the *Independent*, Richard Addis of the *Daily Express*, and the former *Sunday Times* editor Harold Evans. Charles Moore of the *Daily Telegraph* was thought also to be moving in this direction. Under threat from statutory controls, a generation of editors felt the industry had to stand shoulder to shoulder. As a result, lamented Rusbridger, they had been driven to 'defend the indefensible. . . . We have stood by and watched a decade of intrusive stories published and meekly held our silence.' Rusbridger asked whether it was conceivable for journalists 'to admit that this was wrong and that there was a case for a privacy law'. And he asked whether 'the question of self-regulation of the press should not be debated again and a new set of rights constructed – a coherent information policy instead of a ragbag of laws and conventions based on privilege, precedent and prejudice'.[18]

Alarm bells rang throughout the industry. This was privacy law by the front door. 'There is a dangerous new polarisation in the Fleet Street debate on privacy', thought the *Press Gazette*; 'It doesn't just live in the Marr-Addis-Rusbridger call for greater statutory protection of privacy, but in the premature rejection of voluntary regulation.'[19] Wakeham retorted promptly and 'robustly' to Rusbridger. First, it was impossible to draft a privacy law that could blunt 'brutalist, intrusive journalism' without also destroying investigative journalism, and undermining fatally the public's right to know.

> This is a subject about which I know a good deal because, in Government, I chaired the Cabinet Committee looking at a proposed tort of privacy. The answer we always reached then was that privacy laws would never be used by those who found themselves at the receiving end of intrusive media attention – but by those who wanted to use the law to stop any publication investigating and, with merit, exposing them. I have to tell Alan that *The Guardian* would be affected as much as any other paper. And I should remind him that laws would also affect regional newspapers – which do a great deal in their own communities to root out wrongdoing – as well as magazines.

Second, things were no longer as bad as Rusbridger implied. Some of the instances he cited – the Gorden Kaye hospital scandal, for example – were ancient history, predating the Code and the PCC. This was not the time to divert the industry's energies away from attending to immediate problems such as data protection and ECHR, now looming large.[20]

The tabloids were incensed. Piers Morgan intervened on behalf of the traduced 'people's papers'. He thought it a 'very, very sad day for journalism when a national newspaper editor publicly calls for a privacy law'. He believed there was an 'intellectual school of thought, the sole modus operandi of which would be to get rid of the tabloids'. He thought it particularly sad when the editor calling for a privacy law edits a paper 'that has for years been rankly hypocritical in publishing every salacious detail that the tabloids come up with, while at the same time distancing itself by saying: "Isn't it outrageous? Aren't the methods disgusting? But, by the way, here's four pages of it."' The PCC, Morgan insisted, had been 'a fantastic regulator of press behaviour. I think the press as a whole is so much better in its behavioural pattern than it was ten years ago that any need for a privacy law is out of date.'[21]

A debate led by Rusbridger and Morgan – whose mutual loathing was no secret – was set up at the Women in Journalism Forum. Morgan made it clear that 'his very high-placed sources' told him that the UK was *not* going to get a privacy law. This was understood to mean his personal dealings with the Prime Minister. (Rusbridger's reading of it was Morgan's personal threats to the Prime Minister.) In 'a fast-moving and often edgy debate' Morgan yet again mocked the broadsheets for their hypocrisy, and Rusbridger wondered at the paranoia in Britain about laws which other countries took for granted. The PCC's director, Guy Black, threw the weight of its experience into the fray by stressing how few complaints on privacy invasion were made to the Commission. 'Self-regulation is working better than anyone ever thought it would. It has ratcheted up ethical standards. Newspapers and editors are very different today from ten years ago, and that is a tribute to all editors and all journalists.'[22]

For all Morgan's assertions and all Wakeham's and Black's assurances, the privacy issue persisted. Once Rusbridger had opened the lid of the box and let out the genie, it was difficult to stuff it back in again. Things were getting to the point when remarks could be casually made about the 'current vogue for a privacy law'.[23] Suspicions were now forming about Lord Chancellor Irvine's propensities. The industry had been glad to see the back of Mackay; but was it now in danger of exchanging King Log for King Stork? Some of Irvine's earlier encounters with journalists had provoked comment about his 'outrageous behaviour' and about his revealing an attitude to press freedom that 'strikes chill to the heart'.[24] Irvine dismissed all this as 'bizarre'. Had he not for years been a member of self-regulation's Appointments Commission? All the same, his comments on press freedom and responsibility elicited enthusiastic endorsement from, among others, Sir Louis Blom-Cooper, whose advice was that the regulatory system of the press 'deserves the new Government's prompt attention'. Could we now hope, enquired Sir Louis, 'even dare to expect – legislation which will effectively combine press freedom and editorial/journalistic responsibility?' Sir Louis extolled the 'excellent report' in 1993 of the National Heritage select committee, which proposed 'enlargement and extension beyond the sole self-regulatory body, the Press Complaints Commission'.[25]

Then came what the *Gazette* described as 'skipped heart-beats felt by the media' on Irvine's interview in the *Observer*. Irvine told Patrick Wintour and Andrew Adonis: 'The press might think, if they were more intelligent, that they would get a more moderate and politically balanced privacy law out of Parliament.' This was precisely, though less politely, what Alan Rusbridger had been telling it. Irvine expounded on the likelihood of a privacy law being introduced as part of the incorporation into UK law of the European Convention on Human Rights. He suggested that the media and the public should give 'serious thought' to whether privacy law should be developed by the courts or regulated by statute. And he warned that case law developed in the courts might involve the media in 'new and substantial liabilities'.[26]

Alarm bells again sounded loudest in the more populist recesses of the industry. 'We need a privacy law like we need a hole in the head', was the *Sun*'s considered comment. The tabloids immediately turned for succour to the Prime Minister. After interviewing Blair the *Sun* was able to offer reassurance. 'The Prime Minister made it clear he is not in favour of a privacy law. He says: "I believe in self-regulation."' It was important, Blair added, that self-regulation be made to work. In the the *Mirror*'s interview privacy was not even mentioned. Piers Morgan explained loftily to the *Press Gazette*: 'I didn't need to ask him. As I told a recent gathering of Women in Journalism, I already had impeccable sources that assured me there was no intention of bringing in a privacy law.' Morgan declared himself delighted that Blair had unequivocally confirmed that non-intention. 'Despite all the posturing of Derry Irvine, Blair is taking a more pragmatic view of the whole thing.'[27]

Opinion in the industry – again, mainly at the tabloid end – rejoiced that Irvine's 'slap in the teeth' remark on the press's want of intelligence had in effect been repudiated by Blair. 'Maybe the law should be more intelligent before it starts criticising journalists', fumed Piers Morgan. 'I thought it was a snide little remark making out we can't quite get a grasp of what it's all about. Well, WE know what it's all about; we think THEY should get a grasp on it.'[28] As events in Parliament were later to reveal, 'getting a grasp on it' would not be a simple matter for either side in the debate.

4

All the same, 'getting a grasp on it' was obviously what the PCC had to give a lead in attempting. Apropos of Irvine's minatory comments to the *Observer*, a Commission spokesman announced that Lord Wakeham was 'aware of the potential problems raised by the incorporation of the ECHR and is working with the industry and the Government to find a way forward'. The PCC's line was that the ECHR had 'always been intended as a mechanism to protect individuals from the state – not one to create new areas of law'. The Commission held that there were therefore 'a number of practical ways to incorporate it which will prevent the development of judge-made privacy laws encroaching on to self-regulation'. New Zealand had already achieved this and its way forward might provide a guide for the UK. 'These must be fully explored.'[29]

To further that exploration the Commission in June issued a paper, 'The Incorporation of the European Convention on Human Rights, Safeguarding Freedom of Expression'.[30] This drew attention to 'a number of areas of concern to the newspaper and magazine publishing industry'. Its premise avowedly was that the government supported self-regulation and had not proposed a civil tort of privacy. The Commission's concern was therefore to ensure that the industry's Code and its system of self-regulation were not inadvertently 'undermined by the incorporation of the ECHR, and that the freedom of the press is not inhibited in any way by it'. Under the rubric of 'practical considerations' the Commission asked a series of questions which duly turned out to be decidedly awkward.

If incorporating the Convention meant that it could be used in UK courts only against the executive and public bodies, this would, on the face of it, mean that ECHR rights would not enable actions against newspapers and magazines. '*Is this the government's intention?*' If so, strict boundaries would be necessary. The courts have not decided whether the PCC is subject to judicial review (the PCC itself holding that it is not); but if the incorporating Bill could be used against the PCC, that would make the ECHR enforceable in courts against newspapers and magazines by the back door. '*How, therefore, will the legislation define a public body?*' Incorporation will enable UK courts to deal with cases involving public bodies that hitherto went to Strasbourg. But cases not involving public bodies would still go to Strasbourg. '*In policy terms, therefore, how robust and enduring would a restriction be to public bodies?*' Although the government's intentions might be clear, there is nothing in theory to prevent the judges from developing a common law of privacy. '*How will the legislation be drafted to prevent creeping judge-made law which ultimately brings all bodies and persons within the scope of the Convention?*' Finally: Does the government see incorporation as a general statement of principle which would be the first step towards a rights-based approach by the courts – encapsulated eventually in a general Bill of Rights? Or is the government seeking over time to adopt a system of total incorporation? In either case the press will inevitably be subjected to controls incompatible with self-regulation. '*In these circumstances, how does the government see the future of self-regulation – which it has to date supported?*'[31]

Having thus set out its definition of the terms of political and legal engagement, the Commission boldly placed itself in the forefront of the embattled industry. For Wakeham it offered a splendid launching-pad for yet another of his opportunistic exploitations of problems. In July he concocted an occasion to 'present' the Commission's report for 1996, published in May, as plausible cover for an assertion that the PCC was now 'in an unrivalled position to show the Government the way' on issues of freedom of information, data protection and incorporation of the ECHR. 'The bank of experience we've built up over the years on issues like privacy and data protection', he proclaimed, 'shows how difficult some of these things are to deal with. When you start looking at privacy cases, you realise there is no such clear-cut thing as a right to privacy.' The PCC was now really the 'only body in the country which has got such an unrivalled position, having had a look at the whole newspaper industry over the last six years, to see the extent of a problem, if the problem exists, and, in terms of privacy, how difficult it is to adjudicate on these matters'.[32]

This homily on the difficulties of legislating for rights, Wakeham trusted, might be taken by ministers as a cue for their own thinking on the subject. It was gratifying in any case that the *Press Gazette* took the cue about the PCC's unrivalled position and its bank of experience. 'The suggestion by Lord Wakeham that the Press Complaints Commission could extend its role and take the lead on other issues affecting press freedom is signifi-cant.' In the PCC's early days, as the *Gazette* recalled, it shied away from extending its remit, as the whole future of self-regulation was very much in the balance. Since then the Commission and the principle of self-regulation had been accepted by both major political parties. 'It is a sign of the success of the PCC that a change in Government has posed no real threat to self-regulation.' Wakeham's initiative in taking the PCC forward and, in his own words, 'showing the way' on major issues facing the press should be welcomed. 'It is a sign of its maturity that the PCC – which not so long ago represented an industry said to be drinking in the "last chance saloon" – can consider taking on a more pro-active, lobbying role on behalf of the press.' Here the *Gazette* celebrates the realization of what had seemed a rather forlorn hope in 1992.[33] Now, with the advantages of a streamlined secretariat and a skilled lobbyist in Wakeham, with the support of the industry and the growing respect of politicians, the Commission looked poised 'to provide a powerful voice across a wide range of complex issues facing the press', which could 'only be good news for the newspaper and magazine industry'.[34]

5

As the summer of 1997 passed into autumn the Commission had reason to think that it had a grasp on things. Harry Roche's Pressbof report was a serene document, celebrating the way the trade associations in dialogue with the government were able 'to draw on the wisdom and experience of the PCC'. Assuming that the right, pertinent questions had been asked of the government, the big legislative issues of the future could be left over for the new year and the new session of Parliament. Meanwhile, there was always the routine of business and propaganda. Wakeham used the 250th birthday banquet of the Aberdeen *Press & Journal* to bang the drum for the PCC's cheapness, swiftness, straightforwardness, confidentiality and adherence to a 'tough code' which avoided the uncertainties of 'a statutory system of case law and precedent'.[35] A complaint by a Tory MP about a *Mirror* story of his son's suspension from school prompted the Commission to issue editorial guidelines on the handling of stories about children of people in public life.[36] Then came a 'silly season' tabloid outbreak. Bridget Rowe published in the *Sunday Mirror* paparazzi shots of Diana on a luxury yacht in the Mediterranean with her latest *amour* Dodi Fayed, son of the Harrods and Paris Ritz tycoon. 'Maverick' *Mirror* editor Piers Morgan added further enlivenment with electronically manipulated versions of these photographs purporting to show Diana and Dodi in a 'hot lips' relationship. Other tabloids were soon on the same game. The Monaco-based paparazzo Mario Brenna could look forward to £3 million worth of worldwide rights. Morgan showed a bold front to the predictable public outcry. 'With the power of the technology we all now have', Morgan declared, 'it may be the time to have another look at it. If the Press Complaints Commission wants to draw up a new Code to apply to photo manipulation, I think I would agree with it.'[37]

The Commission certainly would want to do that. But the urgent matter at hand was that, with the tabloids in deep water, and throwing photo-ethics overboard, privacy, spiced by paparazzi and what the *Sun*'s editor Stuart Higgins primly denounced as 'cynical deception', was once more a hot issue. This time it was Peter Mandelson, minister without portfolio, who came to the rescue with a statement ruling out privacy legislation and leaving the question in the hands of the self-regulatory body. Magnus Linklater, former editor of *The Scotsman*, observed of 'the Princess and her privacy' that he doubted whether the press-manipulating Diana was the best model to build privacy legislation around. He noted her 'participation in the strange ritual that takes place whenever she is pursued by boatloads of the tabloid press'. One was never quite sure on these occasions 'who is using whom'. It was, Linklater concluded, 'an invasion of privacy, but a privacy of a very public nature'.[38] Alan Hamilton in *The Times* also remarked on the tabloids' 'insatiable' demand for news of the Princess now being 'honed to a particularly keen edge'. He remarked also on the Princess's skills in manipulating the launch-load of the 'British royal ratpack, the so-called *crème de la scum*': 'You are going to get a big surprise at the next thing I do.'[39]

Report No. 37, January–March 1997
The Daily Telegraph

COMPLAINT

Sir Louis Blom-Cooper QC, Chairman of Victim Support, London, SW9 complained that an article in The Daily Telegraph of 26 September 1996, headlined 'Women must be forced to return to Room 101', contained significant inaccuracies, misleading statements and distortions in breach of Clause 1 (Accuracy) of the Code of Practice. In considering the complaint the Commission also had regard to Clause 2 (Opportunity to reply) of the Code of Practice.

A named writer had put forward her views on the work of Victim Support organisations, focusing on its witness service. The complainant alleged that a number of statements in the article misrepresented or distorted the position of the group. There were also significant inaccuracies including the writer's statements that the group had been started up by a grant from an anonymous American donor and that it was funded entirely by the Home Office. In correspondence with the editor the complainant had asked for space for an article in reply by Victim Support. While not ruling this out the editor offered publication of a letter responding to the points made, an offer which the complainant did not regard as satisfactory.

The newspaper did not accept that any significant inaccuracy or misleading or distorted statement had been published. With regard to most of the points raised by the complainant it said these related to opinions or matters of interpretation by the author permitting rebuttal in a letter. It also disputed the factual complaints. For example, it said that although Victim Support as such had not been started by a grant from an anonymous donor, the Victim Support Crown Court witness services had been and the whole article was clearly about witnesses. It understood that in the last financial year 85% or more of Victim Support's funding had come from the Home Office.

ADJUDICATION

The Commission noted that the article was clearly presented as a comment piece. It considered that most of the complaints made concerned matters which was clearly presented as the named writer's personal opinions, which she was entitled to make, as they related to the interpretation and critique of Victim Support's work. The terms of the comparison between the system in the United States and the UK were clear. With regard to the factual complaints the Commission did not find any errors significant within the context of the article taken as a whole.

Any complaint about the article could have been dealt with through the newspaper's offer to publish a letter from the complainant. There was no obligation on the newspaper to give space to a reply article.

The complaint under Clause 1 was rejected.

CHAPTER FOURTEEN

Death of a Princess: the great Diana stampede, September–November 1997

'So within four weeks of her death in Paris, the late Diana, Princess of Wales, has won a posthumous victory that she never would have achieved while she was alive.'

Brian MacArthur, *The Times*, 24 September 1997

'It must be the first time in history that the failings of one drunken driver have changed the way a nation's press can operate.'

Christopher Oakley, president of the Newspaper Society, Young Newspaper Executive Conference, Durham, 5 October 1997

Diana, Princess of Wales, died as a result of a car crash, along with her lover Dodi Fayed, in the Pont d'Alma underpass in Paris on the night of Sunday 31 August. They were being pursued by a gaggle of paparazzi, whom they had tried to elude on departing from the Ritz Hotel. The official French investigation found that the cause of the crash was that the driver was drunk and travelling too fast; but this was not established for some days. In the immediate aftermath of the tragedy, its cause seemed only too apparent. Her brother, Lord Spencer, articulated the general presumption: the press 'has her blood on its hands'.[1]

Another general presumption then was that press self-regulation was thrown back into the crucible. A weary time was foreseeable, going over all the old ground again. Gerald Kaufman wanted the House of Commons to disinter his Heritage committee report of 1993. 'The press will be told that it has not heeded the warnings of successive governments to "put its house in order"', commented Simon Jenkins. 'The familiar arguments will be taken down and dusted off.' Nobody could pretend that yesterday's horror was 'anything but a stain on the journalistic escutcheon', he conceded. 'Yet I cannot think of a remedy.' Privacy legislation was not a remedy. 'Such laws exist in France, Germany, Italy and many American states. The French is one of the toughest. Reformers should note where the past month's gross breaches of personal privacy occurred.'[2]

A crucial point. Had the tragedy, in comparable circumstances, occurred in London, press self-regulation almost certainly would have been swept aside in a mood of public and parliamentary revulsion at tabloid behaviour. The fact that that same public devoured the gossip that the newspapers titillated them with, and ogled the photographs that the newspapers purchased from the paparazzi, would not have been allowed as a plea in mitigation by the industry. There were brave souls who pointed out that those with blood on their hands were the people, themselves included, who bought the tabloids to scrutinize personal details of Diana's life.[3] Their voices were drowned in the din of a nation's exculpatory remorse. As it was, the intensity of the guilty panic in newsrooms all over the country almost amounted to a collective confession: the industry standing over the Princess's corpse with a bloodstained knife in its hand.

Lord Rothermere ordered his papers not to buy paparazzi material without his knowledge and consent. The *Daily Mail* headlined: 'Mail leads way in banning paparazzi pictures.' This infuriated Charles Moore at the *Telegraph*. He denounced Rothermere and English for gross hypocrisy: the *Mail* had been one of the leaders of the pack, he insisted. Then the *Mail* compounded its sin by a sensational front page on 2 September depicting a thoughtful, kilted Prince Charles: 'Charles weeps bitter tears of guilt.' This 'imaginative journalism' provoked enormous outrage, especially of course among pro-Charles circles for whom the *Daily Telegraph* was always the flagship. This spat developed over the coming two weeks into what Brian MacArthur called 'Fleet Street's biggest brawl in living memory'.

As journalists brawled, accusatory presumptions poured forth from the public. Media celebrities led the way. Martyn Lewis, who had fronted the BBC's presentation of the tragedy, demanded legislation. Martin Bell, the much publicized new independent MP for Tatton, saw it as a matter of the press's 'quite literally hounding to death' its noble victim.[4] Alan Rusbridger later told a Guild of Editors' conference that 'in newsrooms there was a lot of soul-searching and a sense of shame'.[5] Assuming that media self-regulation was 'unlikely to satisfy any longer', Frances Gibb assessed 'legal options'.[6] Clive Soley recommended that the first requirement was to redirect anger from the paparazzi to the proprietors and editors who purchased their photographs. A truce was declared in the industry on the privacy issue: the last thing Rusbridger and his allies wanted was a privacy law courtesy of the Diana stampede.

In the shamed and soul-searching *Guardian* Geoffrey Robertson QC, inveterate enemy of self-regulation and despiser of the PCC as a mere million-pound insurance policy taken out by the industry barons, trusted that Diana's untimely death would in due course permit 'a more rational discussion of the need to protect privacy than has come from the present surge of righteous anger against the paparazzi'. Her very absence as an 'example in the debate' Robertson thought would be helpful: 'she never was a paradigm case because of the Faustian bargain she seemed to have made with the media at times'. Surely, it was not beyond 'our wit or our language', insisted Robertson, 'to define laws which protect private places and intimate relationships but not business dealings or exercises of power'.[7]

The industry, naturally, defended itself on the best ground it had. In *The Times* Wayne Bodkin pointed to the 'tragic irony that France, the country with one of Europe's strictest privacy laws, is where Diana, Princess of Wales was killed pursued by paparazzi'.[8] Paul Connew, Mirror Group executive, contributed the thought that 'hard cases make bad law. A cliché, but true nonetheless.'[9] The *Press Gazette* praised the Prime Minister and the Culture secretary for disdaining a knee-jerk reaction to the public backlash. 'It would have been an easy and populist move to announce that it would introduce a privacy law.' As the true events unfolded, ministers' caution proved wiser than the broadcasters' and back-bench MPs' attempts to make the press a scapegoat.[10] And, naturally, the industry looked to its million pound insurance policy.

2

From this moment two dominant facts determine and explain the course of events bearing on Britain's newspaper press industry over the coming three months. The first was the industry's awareness that it was on the run, and that the only defences it could mount would be such as were compatible with retreat in disorder. The second was Lord Wakeham's deftest exploitation yet of opportunities offered by problems.

On 2 September there were reports that the chairman of the PCC was calling for an urgent review of harassment by international paparazzi. Lord Wakeham had begun 'immediate talks with newspaper editors' to discuss the 'seemingly insatiable demand for pictures of public figures'. Wakeham's discussions, it appeared, would assess the difficulties of dealing with a problem which crossed many national boundaries. He insisted that he would make no comment on the circumstances of the Princess's death until the French police had completed their investigations. But he said: 'We can – and must – think very seriously about the problems caused by international paparazzi which the accident has so dreadfully highlighted.' It would be some time before the details of what happened were revealed. Lord Wakeham would keep the Secretary of State for Culture, Media and Sport informed of the progress of their review.[11]

The industry's first respite on the run was an announcement from a Downing Street spokesman reaffirming the Prime Minister's view that self-regulation was the best way ahead. 'Obviously what has happened is going to fuel a huge public debate, and for now he will just let that debate take place without Government having to rush to any significant judgement, and also mindful of the fact that the newspaper industry will be taking a good look at what lessons they may learn.'[12] The immediate lesson was to move quickly in the direction of protecting Diana's children.

The Code Committee was alerted to meet on 17 September, by which time Wakeham and English would have concluded their consultations with national editors. 'Action necessary consequential to the death of Diana, Princess of Wales', was the first substantive agendum.[13] There were calls for a complete ban on newspapers accepting shots from international paparazzi unless within the new strict public-interest definitions; calls for newspapers which published paparazzi pictures to print the name of the photographer and state whether the photos had been taken with or without consent. David English declared himself glad that the government was not rushing to judgment in spite of much incitement from MPs and celebrities. The Code Committee would be discussing 'snatch pictures', he announced, and whether these should be banned completely or whether that would damage publication, 'because some paparazzi pictures are going to have real meaning. If there is a ban, there could be a picture that has gone round the world but might never be seen in Britain.'[14]

A paper, 'Dealing with the Paparazzi', was sent by Wakeham to Chris Smith, the Secretary of State, on 5 September in advance of their planned discussion on the 8th. 'Bluntly', Wakeham told Smith apropos of the relevant Code Clauses 4 and 8, 'very few of these parts of the Code have ever been tested in relation to the foreign paparazzi – partly because Diana, Princess of Wales had, in truth, a patchy record on complaining'. A complaint had been made to the PCC about paparazzi shots published in the *Mirror* of the Princess and the Duchess of York on holiday in France last July. 'That would have been an excellent opportunity to set out ground rules in this area. However, the complaint was soon withdrawn – and speculation followed that the Duchess of York had encouraged the photographs to be taken.' It was not a domestic British problem. And in any case, what precisely distinguished a paparazzo from a freelance? There was also the public-interest aspect. There was unlikely to be a definitive solution. 'The PCC and the media can deal with matters *at publication*, they can – by their actions – reduce the market place; but they cannot change the behaviour of the paparazzi themselves, or be held responsible for it.'

Legal remedies such as stalking legislation or copyright law under the Berne Convention, continued Wakeham, were unlikely to do much. There were possible changes to the Code: tightening requirements for editors about accepting material; a preamble could be brought in with a 'paparazzi clause'; it would be up to editors to demonstrate the checks they had made. The public-interest criterion in Clause 9 might be made more stringent: 'overwhelming'? Photographers could be named. There might be measures to crack down on 'media scrums': harassment by 'creating collectively an intimidating scrum'. Photo agencies might be brought into the ambit of the Code. The definition of private property could be widened to include churches and restaurants.

Some 'private thought' might also be given, suggested Wakeham, to the question of the relationship between press and Palace. The focus of the paparazzi had been on Diana. 'It is likely that in time their attention will turn to HRH Prince William, especially in view of his physical similarity to his mother.' The Code at present covered him only to the age of 16. Wakeham's discussions with, in particular, national tabloid editors were to begin the next week commencing 8 September. 'They will be crucial in agreeing to a tightening of the Code and giving a lead to the rest of the industry.' The PCC would then initiate Code amendments. 'Urgent discussions should take place with St James's Palace to discuss the particular situation of Prince William. Buckingham Palace should also be consulted on the question of Balmoral and Sandringham.' There should be consultations also with press commissions and councils in other countries to assess the scope for international action.[15]

On 5 September, the day of the Princess's funeral, the *Daily Telegraph* had the broadsheet pleasure of announcing the names of the tabloid editors against whom Lord Spencer had a particular animus and who were barred from attending at the Abbey: Stuart Higgins of the *Sun*, Philip Hall of the *News of the World*, Paul Dacre of the *Daily Mail*, Richard Addis of the *Express*, Piers Morgan of the *Mirror* and Bridget Rowe of the *Mirror on Sunday*. Spencer's design was to humiliate the papers 'as publicly as possible by casting them out of the event'. They responded by 'studiously not rocking the boat'. (A report that several tabloids had contacted the Royal National Institute for Deaf People asking for lip-readers 'to examine footage of the funeral and tell them what the grieving members of the Royal Family say to each other', as Joe Saxton, the charity's campaign director put it, 'defies belief'.[16])

Wakeham was due to go public at various industry bodies; English was booked for the *Breakfast with Frost* programme. Earl Spencer had lacerated the press in his Abbey address. Guy Black put 'some lines together' to assist.

> No law in this country or any other could ever have prevented the appalling events that took place in Paris last Sunday. The marketplace for the paparazzi is global – and global legislation on privacy or harassment is not possible. . . .
>
> Where no domestic or global law is a possibility, the obvious answer lies in strengthening self-regulation – and in encouraging editors to think again about their own judgements in the reporting of private lives.
>
> The editors' Code of Practice already does a lot of good – in particular in regard to children. While the foreign press has from time to time carried pictures of Prince William at Eton, no British publication has done since he began there. That is a good start. So the press's treatment of Prince William – which recognizes that he is vulnerable – probably points the way forward. . . .
>
> The Press Complaints Commission is conducting an urgent review of this area to look at possible Code and any other changes. Editors are co-operating fully, and the PCC expects to complete the review very quickly. . . .
>
> Thought therefore needs to be given in the minds of all editors about how far they should go in reporting the lives of public figures, and those who are related to public figures often only by the accident of birth. No law can do that for them. It is up to their own judgement and their own self-regulation.
>
> For all of us, things will never be the same again – but in particular for the public which reads newspapers and for the editors who are responsible for them. Self-regulation has improved a lot of things over the last few years. But self-regulation must also be civil regulation – recognizing the civil responsibilities of editors as well. That is the challenge now.[17]

Wakeham set off on his tour of editorial offices 'in the light of Earl Spencer's attack on the press', to discuss reform and tighter controls on privacy. Sir David English on *Breakfast with Frost* announced that Associated Newspapers 'would never use paparazzi pictures of William while he is growing up'. He believed no other paper would either. 'I believe we in the press have got to listen very much to what Spencer said – you can't ignore him.' Rusbridger confessed to broadsheet guilt for buying from paparazzi. 'The Broadsheets do like to have their cake and eat it.' Piers Morgan undertook to work closely with the PCC to protect the young Princes. 'He concedes that the media must change after the Princess's death, but argues that she had a more complex relationship with broadcasters and publishers than Lord Spencer had indicated in his angry speech.'[18]

The Prime Minister joined calls for newspapers and their proprietors 'to respond to public anger over the activities of the paparazzi'. Mr Blair made plain that he was 'taking a particular interest in the deliberations this week between the Press Complaints Commission and Editors about tightening self-regulation'. Blair, sceptical about the advantages of privacy legislation, was 'looking to the press to order tough new action'. He held that, were proprietors to announce that they would no longer use intrusive photographs from the paparazzi except in cases justified by the public interest, there would be no market in Britain for their work. On *Breakfast with Frost* he said it was a problem requiring 'more than the letter of the law'. Over the past few days ministers had re-examined the arguments for a privacy law, but remained dubious. However, it was possible that legislation could be introduced to prevent harassment by photographers using long-lens cameras if, for example, the press showed no signs of banning such behaviour on its own account.[19]

At the London Press Club on 9 September Wakeham rehearsed the main themes already outlined on behalf of the Commission. A deal relating to the Princes pointed the way forward for editors and the Commission across a wider range of fronts. He believed editors would heed the words of the Prime Minister. A 'watershed in the mood of the country and in the mood of the press' had been reached. The immediate task was to draw up new rules for incorporation in the Code of Practice. 'This is an important time to get a tightening of the Code because I don't want to miss that mood.' Were it missed, 'if action is not rapidly forthcoming, time really could be called in the Last Chance Saloon – and the press would thoroughly deserve it'.[20]

Time was moving on towards the crucial Code Committee meeting on 17 September. An intriguing circumstance relating to this was that the *Daily Telegraph* editor Charles Moore was due to make his debut as a NPA nominee on the Committee. He and David English had been feuding for over a week. Harry Roche felt obliged to assure the *Telegraph* people that English was not really a 'spider figure at the centre of a web of newspaper excess'. Conrad Black, proprietor of the *Telegraph*, likened English to Al Capone and asked: 'Is Sir David English a suitable chairman of the Code of Practice Committee? . . . He should repent or resign.'[21] There were many, including former Tory ministerial grandees, who agreed with him. Paul Dacre, editor of the *Daily Mail*, was scornful of Moore as someone who had been in Fleet Street for five minutes. Explaining the origins of the *Telegraph* 'jihad', he asserted that Diana hated the *Telegraph* as the 'house-organ of that camp of courtiers who, after the separation, had pumped out black propaganda against her, much of its centring on her sanity'.[22] So it was all the odder that when Moore appeared at the Code Committee he had in his pocket a letter from Earl Spencer to be read to the Committee. This letter Spencer had faxed to Moore, not to English. Spencer shared with Moore a loathing of the tabloids: my enemy's enemy is my friend. And Moore was now a convinced advocate of privacy legislation, which was the point of Spencer's letter.[23] All that could be said about the 'biggest brawl in Fleet Street in living memory',[24] at least for the time being, was said by Kathy Marks in the *Independent*: 'Who could guess *The Mail* could not be outdone in righteous indignation? Who ever thought *The Telegraph* could be so passionate?'[25]

3

Grahame Thomson had prepared an agenda for the Code Committee. Paper A read as follows:

Action Necessary Consequential to the Death of Diana, Princess of Wales
I understand that Lord Wakeham will report to the Committee on his round of discussions with editors and publishers.
It may be helpful to note the measures introduced or proposed unilaterally by some of the national newspapers –
Daily Mail, Mail on Sunday, Evening Standard: No paparazzi pictures to be purchased without, Lord Rothermere's knowledge and consent.
The Sun: No intention of carrying photographs which invade the privacy of Princes William and Harry.
The Independent: Will never publish pictures of the young Princes William and Harry in private situations again.
The Express: No pictures of Princes William and Harry if they are unofficial or paparazzi pictures. Will only publish pictures of the Princes with the approval of their guardians. No paparazzi pictures at all will be published. Freelance photographs will be published only if the supplier can show that they comply with the Code. Definition of private property to be strengthened to include places where people clearly believe they are alone.

Reports of Lord Wakeham's speech to the London Press Club on 9 September 1997 suggest a number of areas for consideration:

(1) Extension of the 1995 agreement on Prince William's schooldays to Prince Harry and to continue throughout their education.

(2) Similar provision for all children.

(3) Extending the definition of private property to include areas such as churches and restaurants 'where individuals might reasonably expect a degree of privacy'.

(4) Tightening the requirement for editors to satisfy themselves that photographs from freelances had been obtained in circumstances which did not breach the Code.

(5) Cracking down on publications whose journalists helped form 'the media scrum', playing a part in unjustified 'collective harassment'.

(6) Bringing photographic agencies under the terms of the Code.

(7) Seeking means of bringing paparazzi photographers within the self-regulation culture of the UK press.[26]

'It will be interesting when the Committee meets in London today', wrote Brian MacArthur in *The Times* on 17 September. 'Among the 11 national and regional editors sitting down with Sir David will be Moore. Another will be Bridget Rowe, whose *Sunday Mirror* bought the paparazzi pictures, published three weeks before the princess's death, which first showed the seriousness of her liaison with Dodi Fayed. The same pictures were published the next day in the *Daily Mail* and *The Sun*.'[27] There could also be some nervousness as a consequence of English being quite taken by Alan Rusbridger's idea of adapting the expanded new privacy clause to the wording of Article 8 of the European Convention on Human Rights.[28] Grahame Thomson recalls the occasion as 'cool', chaired very ably by the unfazed English.[29] After helping to ease the tension by disclosing that Canon Oates of St Bride's, Fleet Street, would be offering prayers for their edification, Wakeham, with Black in attendance, made an 'interim report' on his discussions with national newspapers and hoped he would also talk soon to the regionals. Wakeham hoped to catch the mood of the industry as the industry had caught the mood of the public. He defined his own approach: he was an independent chairman of the PCC; the self-regulatory system had made great progress; editing a newspaper required professional judgment; the industry must be responsive to high public expectations; the industry faced very serious threats from implementation of the EC data protection directive and the European Convention on Human Rights.

He said that no one expected Code changes out of this meeting but he would be making his recommendations the following week. His meetings had been encouraging, with evidence of considerable radical thinking. David Newell of the Newspaper Society had been 'helpful'. Wakeham explained his current thinking on (1) Harassment, (2) Privacy, (3) Children, (4) Public Interest, (5) Grief,[30] (6) Sanctions. In his minute reporting a 'prolonged discussion', Thomson's note on 'a new spirit of unity' was undoubtedly the most significant point. This survived Charles Moore's reading a letter from Lord Spencer on privacy and tabling a statement which he felt the Committee should issue. Spencer warned the Committee that if it did not do something adequate about privacy invasion, Parliament would bring in legislation. The new spirit of unity survived the quite intense resistance from the regional editors to Moore's endorsement of Spencer's indiscriminatory indictment of the industry. Moore explained afterwards: 'I wanted to put a bomb under the complacency of the tabloids about their intrusion into the lives of members of the royal family. Earl Spencer and I are both trying in quite separate ways to draw attention to the crisis of confidence in the press caused by the intrusion on privacy.'[31] The Committee eventually agreed to issue the following statement:

> The tragic death of Diana, Princess of Wales, has focused unprecedented public attention on press intrusion, harassment and respect for privacy. As those charged with defining the Code of Practice which sets the benchmarks for the ethical and professional standards of journalism, we recognize this. We are now undertaking an urgent review of the Code. As an industry we emphasize the need for the Code to be followed not just in the letter but in its full spirit. We support Lord Wakeham's calls for wide-ranging and rigorous reforms and recognize that there is a shared determination to rid our publications of practices which we all deplore.[32]

For Wakeham the game was as good as in the bag. Spencer's insolent fax to Moore was probably quite helpful. It certainly heightened consciousness of the 'mood' of the public in editorial minds.[33]

On 26 September Carol Midgley reported for *The Times* Wakeham's plans 'to kill the paparazzi market'. These proposals, drawn up after consultation with editors, were 'expected to be formally approved by the Commission's Code Committee'. Wakeham declared the Code radically overhauled in a statement at a press conference in the Middle Temple. He concluded with 'three important messages':

To the public. We've listened and we've acted. To editors. You've made a great success of self-regulation over the last six years. Let's keep it that way by rising to this new challenge. And to Government. This new Code will be the toughest set of industry regulations anywhere in Europe. It is doing far more than legislation ever could. You are right to put your trust in effective self-regulation.[34]

'So, within four weeks of her death in Paris', commented Brian MacArthur, 'the late Diana, Princess of Wales has won a posthumous victory that she never would have achieved while she was alive.'[35]

Government responded very much in the old style: welcoming the 'press Code improvements', but expecting the Commission and the newspaper industry 'to take the process of self-regulation further so as to give full protection for people of all walks of life, and not only those who are famous or temporarily in the news'. In particular, the government expected newspapers to have the utmost regard to provisions on paparazzi photography and to respect the privacy of the Princes when in private or on private occasions. It hoped also that photo agencies could be brought within the scope of the Code. Culture secretary Chris Smith intended 'discussing these issues further with Lord Wakeham'.[36]

Given that, there was very little likelihood that the next stages of consultation with the industry and approval by the Code Committee would give rise to serious problems or resistance. And given the publicity for Wakeham's proposals and Guy Black's assiduous lobbying, as the *Press Gazette* pointed out, there was an impression that they were already in place. 'In fact, work has only just started in framing the new Code. New clauses have to be written and editors and the industry consulted.' Yet, astonishingly, at the instigation of Stuart Kuttner, managing editor, the *News of the World* had already asked photo agencies to sign an agreement stating that they would abide by the Code. And there were other, equally astonishing, instances of a new kind of voluntary self-censorship. 'It seems', the *Gazette* wonderingly concluded, 'the spirit of the times and changing attitudes since Princess Diana's death are being followed in advance of the revised Code.'[37]

4

This was a line of thinking pushed resolutely by Black and very much encouraged by Wakeham. When presenting the published Code proposals before his press conference, Wakeham had thrown procedural propriety to the winds. He expected editors to 'endorse them with immediate effect'; to deal with this 'pretty dramatic package of improvements' from 'tomorrow, from day one'.[38] Many tabloid editors, he 'suspected' a few days later, 'would be putting his proposals into effect straight away without waiting for the redrafted Code'.[39]

This was to leave English rather dangling in the breeze. One of the most telling effects of Wakeham's deft herdmanship was the splenetic outburst by Chris Oakley, chief executive of Midland Independent Newspapers and current president of the Newspaper Society, who scorned the manipulability of his colleagues. 'It must be the first time in history', he told a Young Newspaper Executives conference in Durham, 'that the failings of one drunken driver have changed the way a nation's press can operate.' The 'self-abasement of editors' had 'allowed Lord Wakeham to boast that he will soon have the strictest Code of Press Conduct in the developed world'.[40] The NUJ had already denounced the whole business as a 'panic reaction, . . . a sham to placate public opinion'.[41] At the Guild of Newspaper Editors' annual conference at Leeds a good deal of evidence accumulated of journalists who felt their profession had been expertly led by the nose. 'There is a revisionist view of the events following the death of the Princess of Wales', declared the *Press Gazette*, 'which claims the Press Complaints Commission acted too quickly. That major changes were being forced on the industry by the actions of a drunken driver and proposed changes to the Code of Practice were announced as an apparent *fait accompli*.' 'Whose Code is it anyway?' was the conference's indignant keynote. 'Some editors may feel', the *Gazette* suspected, 'that the PCC acted too quickly in a "kneejerk" reaction to events and that Lord Wakeham had too high a profile.'[42]

It was English who had to take the flak at Leeds (Wakeham's contribution being by video), with Guy Black spreading oil on the troubled waters of debates on the contentious new privacy proposals. English did nothing to ease the tension by disclosing his plans that the Commission give its privacy commissioner, Robert Pinker, a far higher profile by authorizing him to launch his own investigations into alleged privacy breaches without need of the trigger of a complaint. Black was alarmed to find that Home Office Data Protection officials had been forbidden to discuss privacy questions. He realized the need for swift and radical action. English had put a brave face on it earlier by suggesting that 'the editors would not automatically approve the changes'; but it was the perhaps slightly cynical reporter who guessed 'they will raise little objection'.[43] In fact, a lot of objections were raised in Code Committee meetings working on Wakeham's proposals, mainly by Charles Moore. It was not, as Jean Morgan gathered, 'all sweetness and light'. The regional editors in particular regarded Moore's ideas as 'unrealistic'.[44] A fourth and probably a fifth meeting would be needed. English insisted, however, that it was all going 'quite well'. One or two things 'will be slightly different from the way they were presented earlier by John Wakeham, but he never said they were more than suggestions'. He added: 'There's still quite a lot of tweaking to be done.'[45]

'Tweaking', Wakeham could live with; even, for the time being, lynx-eyed reports about certain provisions being 'watered down'.[46] It was the big impression that mattered. He would have approved the *Press Gazette*'s line that the industry, quite rightly, should examine the minutiae of problems that changes in the clauses of the Code might or might not cause. But the press should also look at it in a wider context. 'It needs not only to get behind the spirit of the Code but also to sell it to the public. If the Code is part of a public-relations exercise, there is nothing wrong with that.'[47] Responses from the industry to the full draft of proposed Code changes locally took that point. Charles Wilson's, on behalf of MGN, was a model of clear-headedness.[48]

By 19 November Guy Black could inform the Commission that the industry's Code Committee had completed its proposed changes to the Code of Practice following the death of Diana. The revised draft Code took account of a number of changes proposed by the Commission's Code sub-committee. It was a peremptory document. It had Guy Black's fingerprints all over it. The word 'must' replacing 'should' now appeared no fewer than thirty-eight times. It was by far the most important change in the mechanism of press self-regulation since the original Code of Practice became effective in 1991. There was a kind of poignant appropriateness in the death on 10 November of Lord McGregor of Durris.

It was now up to the Commission to ratify the new Code. A summary of the major changes to the Code read thus:

> Preamble: Reworded to make clear that the Code should be honoured in the full spirit as well as the letter.
> Clause 1 *Accuracy*: inclusion of inaccurate, misleading or distorted pictures – to take account of picture manipulation. Old Clause 3 (Comment and conjecture) becomes part of Clause 1.
> Clause 3 *Privacy*: substantial changes to stipulations on privacy. Definition of private life included. New rules on taking of pictures 'in private places' – expanding significantly the old definition of private property.

Clause 4 *Harassment*: addition of 'persistent pursuit' to deal with paparazzi photographs and motorbike chases.

Clause 5 *Intrusion into grief*: inclusion of publication – although no restriction on the right to report judicial proceedings.

Clause 6 *Children*: new statement on children's time at school; removal of 16 year age limit – with substitution of 'pupils'; ban on payments to minors except where in interests of the child; new subsection on children of famous or infamous parents.

Clause 7 *Children in sex cases*: rewording and simplification.

Clause 13 *Discrimination*: inclusion of mental illness or disability in subsection (ii).

Public Interest: Introduction of over-riding public interest test for children; editors to give full explanation where they invoke the defence[49].

The Commission ratified on 26 November. A press release by the Code Committee disclosed it to the world on December 19. It was to come into effect on 1 January 1998. Sir David English and Lord Wakeham expressed their gratification that the industry had responded so positively to the recommendations put forward in September.

5

As Lord Wakeham had reminded the fraught Code Committee meeting on 17 September, the industry faced serious threats from implementation of the EC data protection directive and the European Convention on Human Rights. On 14 October David English conveyed to Guy Black at the Commission Associated Newspapers' 'final lobbying' paper on the question of incorporating the ECHR into UK law. The second reading of the Human Rights Bill was due to get under way in the Lords on 3 November. In common with many other media representations, Associated Newspapers lobbied the Home Office for exemptions under Article 8, guaranteeing a right to privacy: 'specific restrictions within the enabling statute to effect its intentions to ensure that Article 8 protects individuals from interference with their rights of privacy by public authorities only'. Such restrictions should ensure, Associated urged, that the courts would not regard themselves as obliged by Article 8 to determine and proscribe on privacy generally, and in any event that infringement of Article 8 should not give rise to compensation or restrictive injunctions.[50]

These were terms of engagement as formally defined within the industry. At the Guild of Editors' conference in Leeds, Les Hinton, executive chairman of News International, demanded that the government 'come clean' and say 'straight up, "we do not see the ECHR as privacy legislation by the back door"'.[51] Tom Crone, legal manager of News Group Newspapers, alleged that judges were 'itching to find a reason to introduce a law of privacy, and ECHR incorporation might well be their opportunity'. 'It won't be the Bill itself which will hit us over the head, but how the judges are likely to pick up this particular ball and run with it.'[52]

This was precisely the point urged by advocates within the press of a privacy law negotiated by the industry: to get in ahead of the wigocrats. Rusbridger saw himself as 'so far a lonely voice pointing out from the wilderness that most editors remain in "blissful ignorance" that we are effectively on the verge of having a privacy law anyway' under Article 8 of the ECHR and the 1997 Harassment Act. 'By the time a few irritable and illiberal judges have begun to play around with piecemeal bits of legislation, it seems quite probable that the very journalists currently inveighing against a privacy law will be begging for one.'[53] An aspect of this argument was put by Adam Raphael: press restraint following Diana's death would not last; commercial pressures once more would lead to breaches of the new Code.[54]

Opinion in the industry by and large doubted any advantage in a negotiated privacy deal. Martin Cruddace, head of the editorial legal department at the *Mirror*, thought Rusbridger naive. 'Once Parliament gets its teeth into a privacy bill you can be assured the result will be a radical and extreme law of privacy, which will be defined to protect MPs and others who are democratically accountable to the electorate.'[55] And what chance would any Bill have, in any case, against the human rights juggernaut now about to get under way in Parliament? The thing to do was not to try to get in ahead of ECHR incorporation, but to fight to ensure that the juggernaut would not crush press and media interests. The industry after all had an insurance policy which had just proved its efficacy – even if perhaps at 'too high a profile' for the comfort of some journalists. In the course of repudiating yet another of Geoffrey Robertson's attacks on the PCC as an 'enormous confidence trick', Cruddace asserted: 'the PCC has slowly and surely developed a status among newspapers I thought not possible four or five years ago'.[56]

On 2 November in the *Mail on Sunday*, the accredited organ of middle England's heartland, Wakeham took up a high-profile stance once more.

The proposed Human Rights Bill, he declared, could threaten freedom of the press and lead to a privacy law 'by the back door'. 'While a privacy law might be established to protect those in the public eye with nothing to hide, it would be used mercilessly by those who had everything to hide. It would be a villains' charter.'[57]

CHAPTER FIFTEEN

Battling the wigocracy: the Commission and the Human Rights Bill, November 1997–June 1998

'In order to remove themselves from the terms of the legislation and protect the position of investigative journalism, the newspaper industry could therefore dissolve the PCC and the Code. Alternatively the PCC could stop dealing with privacy complaints ... that means ordinary citizens – and public figures as well – would lose the protection of the Code.'

Advice to Guy Black, director of the PCC, 8 December 1997

'The only press case against the Human Rights Bill is made by papers with a commercial interest in privacy violations that are indefensible. They will prate most loftily, to defend the money they want to continue making basely. If Blair listens to them, he will show that Murdoch, Montgomery and Rothermere really have got him by the private parts.'

Hugo Young, *Guardian*, 12 February 1998

The problems the Commission had with the Human Rights Bill, 1997–8, stemmed from two unforeseen circumstances.[1] The government originally intended that incorporation into UK law of the European Convention on Human Rights would be a limited, technical measure. In its policy paper before the general election in May 1997, 'Bringing Rights Home', the Labour party stipulated that it would apply only to government and arms of government. It was not intended to introduce a new series of legally enforceable rights whereby private individuals or bodies could act against other private individuals or bodies.

The Bill, however, did not work out that way, because of the government's choice of method to incorporate the Convention. Under the terms of the legislation, those bodies which had to enforce Convention rights included the courts and 'public authorities'. 'Public authorities' were defined as bodies deemed by the courts to exercise some public function, regardless of whether in origin they were private. As a result, the Human Rights Bill revealed itself as bearing more far-reaching consequences than originally intended.[2]

The kind of bodies likely to be caught up under the provisions of the Bill and thus deemed by the courts to be 'public authorities' might be the Church of England (liable particularly under Article 12, right to marry, and Article 14, gender discrimination), City bodies like the Takeover Panel (Article 6, fair and public hearing), the Advertising Standards Authority (Article 10, freedom of expression) and the Press Complaints Commission (Article 8, privacy, and Article 10, freedom of expression). Lord Chancellor Irvine had originally assumed that the PCC was not eligible to be designated as a public authority; but on advice had to change his opinion. But by then the legislative machinery was in motion.

The implications for the PCC were likely to be serious. It would become subject to a new statutory regime, on which it was never consulted, and become part of a system of financial damages for breach of it. 'A judge trying a case must, therefore, give effect to the Convention right of privacy, for example', as an eminent jurist pointed out, 'in a case against a private defendant, such as a newspaper, where there may be no such right at common law.'[3] The notion held at the PCC back in July that the ECHR was to protect individuals from the state and not to create new areas of law no longer obtained. The Convention would allow injunctions to be applied for to block alleged invasions of privacy. The old fear of privacy law 'by the back door' was the new reality. The questions then asked by the Commission as tests of government good faith now transmuted themselves into tests of the slimness of the Commission's chances of survival. The judges, in short, looked to be in a position, by deeming the PCC a public authority under the Act, to succeed where Calcutt, Kaufman and Soley had failed: to confer upon it disciplinary powers and thus make it into their definition of a truly effective regulatory body: powers such as prior restraint of publication, powers to fine, and powers to compensate successful complainants. The Commission would become, in phrases later used by Wakeham, a rung in a legal ladder, a punishment squad rather than a conciliation service.

What to do? It was one thing to raise a hue and cry, as Wakeham had done in the *Mail on Sunday*, against a 'villains' charter'. It was quite another to work out a parliamentary-legal strategy to enable the PCC to emerge unscathed after the human rights juggernaut had passed over it. On 8 December the legal adviser to the Commission sent its director, Guy

Black, a draft paper, 'The Human Rights Bill and the Press Complaints Commission'. This set out the Commission's quandary in sombrely comprehensive terms. As the Bill stood, resolution of privacy complaints under the existing system of press self-regulation would be impossible. Why should an editor of a newspaper co-operate in resolving a dispute if he or she knows that this can simply be a precursor to a court action? Similarly, a critical adjudication from the PCC could lead to complainants going to court to seek remedies. Newspapers would therefore insist on appeals procedures and legal representation.

> In order to remove themselves from the terms of the legislation and protect the position of investigative journalism, the newspaper industry could therefore dissolve the PCC and the Code. Alternatively, the PCC could stop dealing with privacy complaints. . . . Both these courses will mean that the wealthy could have the protection of the courts, but everybody else would have virtually nothing.

How could the Bill be amended?

> The simplest and most logical method would be a provision excluding disputes between private persons – for instance a newspaper and an individual from the obligation on the courts in Clause 6 to act compatibly with the Convention. Similarly public authorities could be defined in terms which excluded bodies like the PCC. . . . In order to cover the problem of injunctions there might be a stipulation that the Bill is not to be used to enlarge the injunctive rights that are already available to individuals.

More discretionary solutions, it was suggested, might include exemptions 'approved by the Secretary of State, or those whose codes were so approved'. But it would be essential that exercise of this discretion be not itself subject to judicial scrutiny through 'another back door'.[4]

2

Amendments along these lines seemed an obvious enough recourse; but they involved daunting political difficulty. There would be strong resistance in both Houses of Parliament to any special 'privileges' being awarded to the newspaper industry to exempt it from compliance with a Human Rights Act. The advice received by the Commission was that 'the best approach is to fasten on government assurances before the Bill was introduced and ask it to make good on these promises that the Bill would really only deal with complaints against public bodies as such'. The problems here were that government assurances then were incompatible now with the 'paradoxical' design of the Bill, and ministers in any case might have little stomach for endowing the press with privileges against human rights.

It was up to Wakeham to do what he could. He would fight the PCC's case on two levels. A first, public level would be mainly in the House of Lords, with speeches and publications elsewhere. A second level would be lobbying ministers, especially Chris Smith at Culture, Media and Sport and Jack Straw at the Home Office, by way of preparing the ground for direct approaches to the Prime Minister. In Sir Brian Cubbon, former permanent under-secretary at the Home Office, the Commission had an invaluable practitioner in the arts of influencing the bureaucratic corridors of power.

In the Lords it was hard going for Wakeham. He struggled against a strong adverse current of opinion. Lord Chancellor Irvine's line was that while he had originally assumed that a body such as the PCC – so clearly voluntary in origin, without statutory functions, without legal sanctions and in receipt of no public money – could hardly be thought of as a public authority, yet so it was; but the PCC should now look upon its newfound public status as a 'happy accident, an opportunity, not a burden, for the PCC'. The opportunity, as outlined by Irvine, was that the courts would look to the PCC as the pre-eminently appropriate public authority to deliver effective self-regulation, fairly balancing Articles 8 and 10. 'The courts, therefore', as Lord Irvine continued, rather like the spider inviting the fly into his parlour, 'would only themselves intervene if self-regulation did not adequately secure compliance with the Convention.' The 'message to the press', Lord Irvine added, 'is plain: strengthen self-regulation, strengthen the PCC'. In that way the press's salvation 'can be in its own hands'.[5]

But what did 'adequately' imply? Lord Lester of Herne Hill QC, an eminent lawyer lord (and, in Lord Russell's words, the 'onlie begetter' of the Human Rights Bill[6]) was, like many of his fellows, impatient with Wakeham's whining. He spelt it out: the existing PCC did not have the power to grant effective remedies for infringement of personal privacy, including the power to order the payment of compensation. 'If the press wishes to avoid unnecessary litigation, this Bill would be a spur to reform because it would be well advised to empower the PCC . . . to grant that crucial remedy.'[7]

The heat was now on. The judges were sure the country needed a privacy law. As Lord Bingham had made clear, they were going to get it one way or

the other. Wakeham proposed amendments. One set sought to stop development of a common law of privacy. The other sought to spare the
Commission from becoming a 'public authority'. 'If Parliament wants a law
of privacy – which would be a fundamental change in our constitutional
balance, to which I am, of course, opposed – it should pass one, not just
acquiesce in the courts' creating one without its approval or scrutiny.'[8]
Wakeham's real appeal was not in his amendments, but to ministers. His
tactic was to get at them by appealing to their parliamentary pride, pressing
the argument that it was the judges and lawyers who had twisted and
deformed the government's original intentions. If ministers were content
that 'we have a *de facto* privacy law on our hands', 'all so well and good'. But
if they took Wakeham's points, they 'ought not to leave them to the discretion of the courts; and they should not leave the Bill unamended'.[9]

This tactic was the essence of Wakeham's strategy: to persuade ministers to accept direct responsibility for the privacy issue, and to put to them
the option that they could have a privacy law or press self-regulation, but
not both. The trick ultimately would be to get ministers to devise amendments that did not expose the press as egregiously privileged.

All that would depend much on time and chance. In the meantime the
PCC defended itself, not disdaining recourse to the tabloids. One indignant
member of the Commission composed a slashing 'outburst' against the
'wigocrats', inveighing at the way eminent law lords glossed over the 'un-
democratic' consequences of the Human Rights Bill. One in particular he
characterized as 'a dyed-in-the-wool economist – with the law as well as the
truth'. It was hoped that this might be palmed off under somebody's name
at 'the *Mail*, or whoever'.[10] Wakeham planted an outburst in the *Sun* on the
horrors of injunctions and prior restraint, 'dangerous and elitist' censorship.[11] But for the most part Wakeham deprecated the industry's making a
fuss and trusted to quiet diplomacy.

'Lord Wakeham will appeal to Chris Smith, the Secretary for Culture,
Media and Sport', reported Andrew Pierce and Frances Gibb in *The Times*,
'to hold urgent talks with ministers and representatives of the newspaper
industry to ensure that the commission is exempted from the Human
Rights Bill.' Smith had already held talks 'with Downing Street officials' to
try to resolve 'the simmering row between the Government and the newspaper industry'. Smith spoke also to Jack Straw, the Home Secretary, and
Irvine. 'Lord Wakeham's appeal to Mr Smith comes amid a feeling of
growing exasperation over the handling of the legislation by Lord Irvine.'
Relations between Smith and Irvine were known to be strained. Irvine had

not informed Smith of his change of opinion on the PCC's eligibility under the Bill. Although the government did not yet appear to accept that an amendment to exempt the PCC would be necessary, Smith was not prepared to swallow Irvine's fait accompli. 'We will see what happens', he was reported as saying. 'There is still time to go before the Bill reaches the House of Commons. There will be detailed discussions.'[12]

The 'simmering row' between the the newspaper industry and the government owed much to the efforts of David Hencke at the *Guardian*, yet again invaluable for his talents in sabotaging governmental plans for press controls, and David Newell at the Newspaper Society. (The NPA, the press barons' club, tended to be prudently recessive when it came to public agitation.) 'The government must not compromise on its commitments to freedom of expression and freedom of information', proclaimed Newell at a press conference on 27 November. 'Its current handling of the Human Rights Bill, data protection and freedom of speech must be challenged.' In helping the judges to develop the very privacy laws it had itself rejected, the government had 'failed to honour its own commitments and policies'. Newell's 'message for the Prime Minister' was spiced with a touch of menace:

1) In spite of the original government statement, the press and self-regulation *will* be severely affected by the Human Rights legislation.
2) We *will* have a privacy law.
3) When they realize what is happening, newspapers *will* be totally united against the government.
4) Self-regulation will collapse under the legal pressures that are placed upon it.
5) The public will then be forced to rely on the courts – which will be too expensive for all but the rich and the crooks. And furthermore, the courts will be unable to deal with all those other areas where the PCC and the Code provide protection – including children, accuracy, misrepresentation, hospitals and so on.
6) I and some colleagues are working with John Wakeham to try and find a way round this to avoid the worst features of the Bill, but we will need your help.
7) The lawyers – including Derry Irvine – are too wedded to the Bill as drafted to change it without your intervention.[13]

Alarm among editors at Irvine's proceedings was attested by Alan Rusbridger of the *Guardian*, no enemy in principle to privacy legislation.

I always suspected that the intention was to use the ECHR as a backdoor privacy law. The whole thing is a terrible mess. The industry as a whole has been misled by the public pronouncements of the Prime Minister saying they didn't want a privacy law and counsel took that on trust and took their eye off this other ball. Either we should get a public interest defence or have a privacy Bill, but at the moment it is a muddle.[14]

Paul Potts, editor-in-chief of the Press Association, put his case directly to Irvine. The Lord Chancellor's response indicated how deeply wedded he was to the Bill as drafted, and that Newell was correct to suppose that only prime-ministerial intervention could deflect Irvine whom Hugo Young described as a man of power, but not yet blooded as a politician. Irvine simply could not understand the reluctance of the industry to empower the PCC, or the reluctance of the PCC to be empowered.[15]

A group of MPs, emboldened by events, sought to cut the Gordian knot by raising yet again the question of a statutory complaints body. Anthony Steen, MP for Totnes, backed by a cross-party group including Clive Soley, Martin Bell and Sir Geoffrey Johnson Smith, begged to move for leave to introduce a Bill to provide for a statutory Press Complaints Commission with legal authority. 'I pay tribute to the present chairman, Lord Wakeham, for his tireless work in trying to make the press barons more accountable to the Code of Practice.' The proposed Bill would not be an attack on the press, insisted Steen, 'but an attempt to gain the support of the House to give real teeth to the Press Complaints Commission, with the aim of outlawing inaccurate, irresponsible or malicious journalism'.[16] Ministers burst this *ballon d'essai* before it reached a second reading; but it counted as a straw in the wind.

One encouraging thing was that Frank Rogers felt content at the way the data protection measure eventually had struck the right balance between protecting personal data and the media's ability to investigate, report and inform in the public interest. Throughout its passage the Commission had worked closely with the Home Office, and 'feels the Government has done a good job in safeguarding press freedom'.[17] Rogers, on behalf of the NPA, now grappled with the Data Protection Bill's manager, Lord Williams of Mostyn QC, under-secretary at the Home Office, to see if at least one sympathetic lawyer lord might also help to get the right balance on the Human Rights Bill ('We had a hand in this!' Guy Black told Wakeham).[18] Wakeham himself was in discussion with Irvine and Smith. The Home Secretary Jack Straw, in answer to a question in the Commons on 22 December, did at least implicitly allow for the possibility of the Bill's being amended.[19] (That a judge should have granted an injunction to prevent publication of the name of Straw's son, involved in a drugs incident, was timely for the PCC. An allegation from a 'source' claimed that the PCC had 'frightened off' identification by lobbying the papers concerned;[20] but in truth the editors frightened themselves off, mainly with the clause in the Code protecting innocent relations. The PCC took it as a gratifying testimony. In any case Wakeham seized the opportunity to draw attention to the 'perils' contained in the Human Rights Bill. 'If the Bill remains unamended, the courts will be given new powers to grant interim injunctions of exactly this sort.'[21])

Ministerial dissatisfaction at the failure of the new Code of Practice quite to measure up to the proposals Wakeham had put forward back in September at least testified to their continuing commitment to press self-regulation. Smith's announcing sternly that he would be 'writing to Lord Wakeham about outstanding problems' reflected an obvious ministerial calculation that if the PCC in its tight corner wanted favours from them, this was the moment to signal further turns of the screw. (It happened that Smith had no screw-turnings on his current agenda.) In any case, as things turned out, it would count for less, at this juncture, than the fact that Smith was at odds with Irvine over the Human Rights Bill. And might not the Commission's having worked successfully with Straw's Home Office people over data protection prove a good augury for similar collaboration when the Human Rights Bill reached the Commons, where Straw would be in charge of it?

3

There was hope also that the Conservative leadership in the Commons might help to play the industry's game. Guy Black was informed that at a meeting with the Conservative shadow Home Secretary, Brian Mawhinney, on 26 January, 'Peter Stothard and other editorial executives of *The Times* discussed the whole question of the Human Rights Bill and what line the Conservative party might take on it when it gets to the Commons'. Although the discussion was 'somewhat inconclusive', there did seem to be a general feeling that 'we should seek to add a clause . . . making it clear that in any "balancing exercise" between Articles 8 and 10, a court must give paramountcy to Article 10'. Black no doubt agreed that it 'would be nice if the press generally could agree that a clause along these lines – not the most controversial suggestion – should be included in the Bill'.[22] As Wakeham mentioned to Norman Fowler, he was keeping 'in fairly regular contact with Brian Mawhinney'.[23]

But the key still remained getting to Blair. The third of 'Four Things to Put to Tony Blair', a PCC propaganda bulletin, was that the Human Rights Bill 'can be amended in a simple way, which will not produce loopholes, to deal with both the public authority point and the issue of injunctions. However, Gareth Williams must have a mandate to negotiate with a view to amendment – nothing less.'[24] Wakeham wrote to 'Dear Tony' on 12 January, setting out his 'serious concerns about the impact of the Human Rights Bill on the Press Complaints Commission'. At the heart of his concerns was a belief that self-regulation would not survive the imposition of the statutory regime that the Bill would establish; and that the Bill would create opportunities for judges to grant new types of interlocutory injunctions that would be deeply damaging to press freedom and investigative journalism. Having heard nothing in reply from Blair, and with the third reading in the Lords imminent, Wakeham tried again on 29 January: 'I have still received no indication as to whether my concerns have been understood or whether the government is prepared to enter a dialogue about the problems and possibly amend the Bill in the very small way that is necessary to meet our concerns'.

Wakeham now put it to Blair that the two primary concerns of his earlier letter were not simply matters of the moment. Both the 'public authority' issue and the injunction issue would 'burn on a long fuse'. They might not cause problems immediately, but would do so from around 2000, when the full effects of the Bill made themselves felt. The scene would then be set for 'a series of highly damaging and high-profile disputes between newspapers and the courts into which the government is bound to be dragged'. Furthermore, if self-regulation itself did not survive, 'the government may be forced in the final years of this Parliament into having to legislate for a statutory press regime which is likely to do nothing for ordinary people and attract condemnation from the press'.

> I have already indicated privately both to the press and to others that I will have to say something at third reading before the Bill leaves the House of Lords – and by far the most constructive thing for me to say is that there are problems but that there is a dialogue taking place to solve them. In order to do that, however, I need *some* indication that this is indeed the position. I genuinely want to find a way forward – because the issues at stake are very dear to me and crucially important in a democratic society – but in order to do so there must be some constructive dialogue between the government, PCC and press, and a willingness to contemplate amending the Bill *in a very minor way*. I do hope you can help us to get things moving – not least because I have no desire to inflame matters at third reading if there is no need to do so.[25]

In the event, all that Wakeham could bring to the third reading debate in the Lords on 5 February was that the questions he raised 'remain under active consideration', that discussions continue, but that 'no decisions have been reached'. He had written that day, Wakeham informed the Lords, to the Lord Chancellor and to Chris Smith; and had also published the letter in view of the public interest involved. But it remained the case that the problems were acute 'and the government have still not indicated to me how they intend to deal with these points'.[26] Matters were inflamed enough in any case as some of the lawyer lords set about roughing up Wakeham for his tiresomeness. Lord Lester of Herne Hill was especially 'robust' – the Lord Chancellor's own slightly apologetic word – on Wakeham's being 'part of an entirely misguided misrepresentation of the effect of this Bill on freedom of speech'. Having acted for newspapers in Strasbourg and in the UK, it stuck in Lester's throat when he read in those papers that they were 'entitled to have the benefit of Article 10 of the Convention on free speech, but they must somehow be immunized against the effects of Article 8 on privacy'. Lord Lester knew 'of no country which has in its legal system what has been advocated by some sections of the press during a campaign against these aspects of the Bill'. He was 'glad that the Lord Chancellor and his colleagues have so far proved themselves to be a rock and not a jellyfish. It would have been easy to cave in to this press campaign.'[27]

Blair, it can be assumed, did not find it in the least easy with Irvine standing stoutly in the way. There was indeed a press campaign, somewhat muted on Wakeham's advice so as to mitigate accusations of browbeating the legislators.[28] A Guild of Newspaper Editors' press release on 5 February drew attention to a statement by Lord Irvine in an interview with the *New Statesman* that he wanted people to be able to go to the PCC to ask for 'prior restraint' to stop stories they claim would breach their privacy. With this touch of indiscreet candour Irvine had indeed blown the gaff. The PCC could proclaim that its fears were now revealed as threatening reality. 'Lord Irvine's pronouncements are deeply worrying', declared Bob Satchwell, president of the Guild and editor of the *Cambridge Evening News*. 'Prior restraint is simply a softer phrase for censorship.' Satchwell suspected that Irvine wanted the recent domestic difficulties of his colleague, the Foreign Secretary, 'kept under wraps'.[29] In the *Guardian* Roy Greenslade pointed to the significance of an adjudication by the Commission against the *Sun* – the first since 1996. The case turned on the verifiability of research on issues of gay sex, HIV and life expectancy. The complainant had rejected the paper's offer of a conciliatory article 'clarifying' the issues; then, in spite of her complaint being upheld, she attacked the Commission for failing to establish the credibility of the research upon which the original article was based. This, as Greenslade commented, was a 'wilful misconception' of the Commission's role: 'It doesn't have the resources to test academic evidence, nor can it call expert witnesses. It must rely on common sense, which was in favour of the complainant.' Guy Black protested at the complainant's Radio 5 attack on the Commission's professionalism. 'In the light of this case', Greenslade concluded, 'Lord Irvine's view that the PCC should levy fines and exercise prior restraint appears very dodgy. Imagine the endless arguments over such monumental matters if this mess is the result of a straightforward breach of the code.'[30] With his *New Statesman* indiscretion Irvine had shot himself, legislatively speaking, in the foot.

On the day following the Lords' debate on the third reading, with Irvine now limping, Wakeham again approached the Prime Minister. He attached a 'formal note' bringing previous correspondence up to date, which he copied to Jack Straw and Chris Smith. 'I spoke very helpfully to Peter Mandelson in your absence on some of these points,' he informed Blair. A compromise could be reached, Wakeham hoped, though the task might not be easy; 'and I am reasonably confident that I can broker one. But I do need somebody with whom to negotiate who has the authority to discuss – if only in principle – amendment to the Bill, subject to your and colleagues' approval.'

The 'sharp end' of Wakeham's concerns was the question of prior restraint. The Lord Chancellor 'has repeatedly confirmed that it will be the result of the Bill as it stands'. Given that, the only conclusion to be drawn, Wakeham contended, was removal of the PCC from the ambit of the legislation. 'Again, I am genuinely grateful for your continued support and for the understanding we now seem to have reached as to what are the problems with the Bill. It is clearly in all our interests to work out a way forward which will not bring courts, government and press to a position of unacceptable constitutional confrontation in two or three years' time after the Act has come into force.'[31]

4

'The Prime Minister's verdict is awaited', announced Hugo Young in a vitriolic *Guardian* comment piece scarifying Wakeham and the newspaper barons for demanding privileged treatment.

There's a plot at the heart of government to eviscerate one of Labour's proud-est bits of legislation. Whether it will succeed is in the balance. In ministerial terms, it ranges the Home Office and the Culture Ministry and possibly the Prime Minister against the Lord Chancellor. In plain language, it's a struggle between high principle and short politics. How it concludes – which means how Tony Blair decides to jump – will tell everything about the heartbeat of New Labour. The question asks ministers to choose between sucking up to press proprietors and standing up for normal law.

Wakeham, Young was sure, overlooked the 'present state of legal reality'. Once the Human Rights Bill was passed, there would be some kind of right to privacy. The climate favoured some privacy, in some form. 'Vapouring against it on behalf of a vested interest group, not all of whom he actually speaks for, Wakeham sounds like a blowhard union boss from the 1970s.'

There was talk, Young disclosed, of sheltering the press behind the Church, which the Lords had exempted from the Bill in certain respects. Normally the government would overturn this in the Commons. By sustaining it now, 'ministers could utter the piety that they were not making the press a special case'.

> In the long run, once the Act is passed, I don't believe a statutory exemption for the PCC will foreclose an emerging privacy law. It might even spur the judges to swifter action on their own. But Wakeham seems to think otherwise and there are people who can get him, as he imagines, off the hook. Jack Straw and Chris Smith make known their pious obeisance before the demands of the press, not to mention their smirking anticipation of victory over the Lord Chancellor.

The only press case against the Human Rights Bill, Young had no doubt, came from papers with a commercial interest in privacy violations that were indefensible. 'If Blair listens to them', Young concluded, 'he will show that Murdoch, Montgomery and Rothermere have got him by the private parts.'[32]

Certainly Blair seems to have listened to Wakeham, whatever the implications that might have borne in relation to his private parts. It is conceivable that Wakeham's arguments – which had a kind of menacing subtext about possible future 'confrontation' – impressed the Prime Minister. At all events, it was decided that a deal would be done. Gareth Williams at the Home Office was important as a facilitator. As Wakeham later recounted to his former colleague Norman Fowler, 'Derry Irvine would have none of it, but Jack Straw saw the point and, after some private negotiations with me, announced on 16 February that he intended to amend the Bill. Since then I have been negotiating with him on the text of an amendment and we have now reached a very satisfactory agreement.'[33] Their initial negotiating session took place in the unlikely location of the VIP waiting room at Heathrow airport. This led some romantically inclined reporters to envisage a dramatic brief encounter between the one flying in and the other flying out. In prosaic fact, it happened that Straw was in the vicinity on Home Office business and Wakeham's sense of urgency made him willing to accept that dismal locale as a convenient rendezvous.

Straw's 'dramatic twist to Parliamentary proceedings', as it was described by one lawyer,[34] came as the Bill was in committee stage in the Commons. His statement indicated that the government wanted to safeguard freedom of expression and to tackle the problem of injunctions by an amendment that would be more comprehensive than providing an exemption for the press. It would apply at large to the arts, literature, the media generally. Wakeham took care to keep the industry barons in the picture. 'As you know', he confided to Lord Hollick, chairman of United News and Media, 'we have made a very great deal of progress with the Home Office – and Jack Straw and his officials have been enormously co-operative and helpful.'[35] Sir Brian Cubbon, it may be surmised, was not entirely without influence in this Home Office helpfulness. Lord Lester was, if not exactly disgruntled, not quite gruntled either. 'I do not understand', he snapped at Wakeham, 'why you think that Jack Straw's announcement is some kind of victory for the press or for the PCC.' Lester thought that proposed attempts to clamp down on injunctions would encourage more prior restraints than at present. 'I therefore think that the Murdoch and the Rothermere press have been entirely misguided in welcoming what is actually a menace to press freedom.'[36]

Doubtless Wakeham and Straw chewed on that arcane prognostication during their negotiations. To facilitate matters, Straw was authorized to convey to Wakeham that ministers would abandon any insistence on the newspaper industry's setting up a compensation fund. That would be left for the industry and the Commission to decide. A 'senior industry figure' was reported as commenting: 'It was important for the issues surrounding the Bill to be sorted out first. If we had been discussing amendments in an atmosphere where the Government was saying, "You have got to have a compensation fund", then we were not going to get terribly far.'[37]

As Wakeham explained to Hollick, what Straw and the Home Office people were proposing was to introduce a separate clause into the Bill on freedom of expression. This would deal with the question of pre-publication injunctions by setting high thresholds which an applicant would have to surmount, and by putting the burden of proof on the applicant as to why publication should be stopped. It would 'enshrine' the importance of freedom of expression by making clear the courts must have 'particular regard' to it. It would give protection to the PCC so long as it acted in accordance with its Code. The courts would have to take account of the Code, including neither compensation nor prior restraint, in making any order. All this, Wakeham trusted, gave the Commission protection 'not just under the Human Rights Bill but also under common law'. 'If you should bump into Jack at any point', Wakeham mentioned to Hollick, 'I would be grateful if you would underline to him what a good job he has done both to protect freedom of expression and the position of effective self-regulation.'[38]

'Further to our recent conversation', Wakeham wrote to Straw, 'I thought it would be helpful to drop you a short line to let you know I have received an enthusiastic response from all publishers I have consulted on the amendment you propose to make to the Human Rights Bill.'

> From the national press, this includes Les Hinton, David Montgomery and David English – all of whom have indicated their warm support. I have also kept in touch with Clive Hollick at United News and Media, and Daniel Colson at the *Telegraph*. As you may know, the *Guardian* has pursued a somewhat different line from the rest of the newspaper industry – with Alan Rusbridger arguing that it would be better to have a fully fledged privacy law than one moulded by the courts. I cannot guarantee what line they will take on this – although it may be supportive. I have also ensured that as many of the regional publishers as possible have been consulted through the Newspaper Society. The Society, too, has indicated its support for the course of action you propose. I should also add that the amendment has been endorsed by Harry Roche, the chairman of the Press Standards Board of Finance – which represents all the national and regional newspapers and magazines.[39]

Jack Straw tabled the amendment in the Commons on 22 June. A Home Office news release that day explained that it followed detailed discussions between the government, the Press Complaints Commission and media representatives. Wakeham thought the announcement of the amendment 'went well'. He was concerned to ensure that the press coverage was 'thoughtful and measured in tone'. 'I was pleased', he told Straw, 'to have the opportunity publicly to welcome the amendment – and my remarks about the amicable and co-operative spirit in which the consultation took place were most sincerely meant. I am really grateful to you, Gareth [Williams] and your officials.' Wakeham wrapped the matter up finally by arranging with Straw an exchange of statements: Wakeham would issue a statement on behalf of the Commission on Thursday, 2 July; and Straw would reciprocate, restating the government's commitment to 'effective and independent self-regulation *as part of* freedom of expression', in his comments explaining the amendment in committee. Ever studious to keep the details neatly wrapped up, Wakeham characteristically forwarded to Straw a draft of 'the statement I should like to make';[40] and, it is reputed, he attached also in his very best chief-whippish manner a draft of the sort of remarks Straw might make in committee.

CHAPTER SIXTEEN

Imbibing the intoxicating liquor of survival, 1998–1999

'Doing this job is a lot more difficult than it was 10 years ago. The goalposts have not only moved, but there's about 15 different sets of posts now, and they're moving all the time.'

David Yelland, editor of the *Sun*, *UK Press Gazette*, 6 November 1998

'After nearly a decade of "drinking in the last-chance saloon", the Press Complaints Commission is imbibing the intoxicating liquor of survival.'

Sir Louis Blom-Cooper, *Guardian*, 5 April 1999

In the Commission's *Annual Review, 1997*, published in May 1998, Wakeham declared his confidence that, because the government – 'to its great credit' – was listening to the industry's and the Commission's concerns, press self-regulation would not suffer damage from either data protection or human rights. This did not mean that 'we can simply rest here and pitch our tents. . . . I have always believed – and feel it in my bones – that self-regulation works far better than any alternative could.' But the public would always remain sceptical. They would never know of the stories which did not see the light of day because of the strictures of the Code. They would never know the inside stories of the politics of self-regulation. Therefore the 'central task' immediately ahead of the PCC in 1998 was, in Wakeham's analysis, to mitigate that public scepticism. The PCC would improve the efficiency of its procedures. It took an average of just forty-four days to resolve a complaint in 1997: 'a speed which the law or any statutory system could never match'. The Code Committee would continue to consider submissions from members of the public and other organizations about the evolution of the Code in 1998 and beyond. It had helped the Commission in negotiations with the Department of Health and the Mental Health Act commission in drawing up new guidelines for media treatment of mental health. And during 1997 the industry agreed that the terms of the Code should extend to those publications on the internet placed there by publishers who already subscribed to the Code of Practice. In thus extending its jurisdiction to the internet, the Commission became, so far as it was possible to tell, the first press self-regulatory body so to do.

This proved to be David English's last report as chairman of the Code Committee. He died suddenly on 10 June. He had served press self-regulation well, both as reformed – up to a point – artful dodger[1] and as industry heavyweight. Replacing him would not be easy. 'The problem is', noted the *Press Gazette* in August, 'that English raised the profile of the post so high, virtually to that of spokesman for the whole British press, which makes him a hard act to follow.' Grahame Thomson, secretary of the Committee, saw no need for haste. 'Had my in-tray been overflowing with problems I'd be urging a quick appointment. But we have time to get it right.'[2] Donald Trelford thought it likely an outsider would be appointed. It was important that the new chairman should be 'above the internal wrangling of the rival newspaper houses'. Tabloid editors were locked in daily cut-throat wars with their rivals. This had been a problem for Patsy Chapman. Not that broadsheet editors were themselves entirely unproblematic. Charles Moore, editor of the *Daily Telegraph* and a member of the Committee, was in public dispute with Peter Stothard over serialization in *The Times* of a book allegedly involving payment to a criminal.[3] A roster of possible contenders included Peter Preston, retired Guardian Group editor-in-chief and former PCC member; Charles Wilson, former editor of *The Times* and former managing director of the Mirror Group; and Brian MacArthur, executive editor of *The Times*. A presumption against *Telegraph* or *Guardian* people was that they had no links to tabloids. Paul Dacre, English's successor as editor of the *Daily Mail*, was held to be ruled out for that dynastic reason.

It was not until October that Leslie Hinton, executive chairman of News International, emerged as the industry's favourite for the job. 'The most obvious man was Les', as Jean Morgan was informed, 'who has enormous editorial experience himself. He is clearly a man of integrity and is liked.' His big task would be to keep harmony between broadsheets and tabloids. 'And it has got to be somebody', another source disclosed, 'with enough stature and clout as far as Government is concerned, because it is the most senior appointment the industry makes.'[4] Hinton of course benefited greatly from the work English had put in to deliver the reformed Code in November 1997. He benefited greatly also from the Commission's efforts to counter public scepticism about the Code by spreading awareness of its existence. Wakeham collaborated with the Newspaper Society's chairman Bob Satchwell in a Guild of Editors' initiative to distribute thousands of copies of a convenient pocket-sized version. Guy Black made a great hit with it on a visit to the *Coronation Street* film set, where all the cast clamoured for copies. 'While it's probably unlikely that we'll see Mike Baldwin and Vera Duckworth discussing the code over a pint in the Rovers', commented the *Press Gazette*, 'there may be a serious point here.'[5]

That editors in general took the point seriously was not in doubt. To some the recent tightening had made the Code 'a minefield to work your way through'. To *Leicester Mercury* editor Nick Carter the Code was 'trying to create a framework that you can hold up to certain stories to and try to get an interpretation. It's much easier to work with than it was, particularly the public interest clarifications which have helped an awful lot.' Brian MacArthur was in no doubt that the PCC had made a 'profound difference. . . . You only have to compare how David Yelland works now with his predecessor of ten years ago to see how profound the change is.' Kelvin MacKenzie's and Stuart Higgins's successor at the *Sun* ruefully confirmed MacArthur's point. 'Doing this job is a lot more difficult than it was 10 years ago. The goalposts have not only moved, but there's about 15 different sets of posts now, and they're moving all the time.'[6]

But the dynamics of editorial interpretation of the changing Code hardly entered into public understanding of the nature of the Code and the Commission's work in relation to it. This applied particularly to critics of self-regulation. Writing of 'a decade of withered hopes', the journalist and author Michael Leapman attributed what he interpreted as the failure of the 'supine' PCC to its lack of 'power to impose a penalty that might serve as a deterrent'.[7] Clive Soley, now chairman of the parliamentary Labour party, deplored not only the lack of punitive 'teeth' but also at what seemed inconsistent application of the provisions. Soley still wanted a much more proactive PCC which could intervene when it suspected a breach of the Code without having to wait for a complaint. To convert the PCC thus into a kind of hit-squad would subvert the very nature of self-regulation, which was in essence the application of editorial judgment to an editors' Code. The Code's whole purpose, as Black explained, was that it should not involve direct interference from the Commission. 'I wouldn't want to be part of a system where the PCC sets about enforcing the editors' code like that.' Codes were meant to evolve over time. 'It's not supposed to be a computer mechanism that you put a problem in at one end and come out with an answer at the other. The PCC and self-regulation is all about editors' judgments.'[8]

2

One of the Commission's tasks was to reconcile those editorial judgments with political expectations on high. 'I have had a number of meetings with Lord Wakeham', Chris Smith informed the House of Commons at the end of June. Smith and Straw would certainly want quid pro quo after their services to the Commission in the matter of human rights. Smith welcomed, in answer to Soley, the strengthening of the Code that was agreed on in December 1997, 'and I have made it clear that further changes should be considered to protect people in all walks of life'.[9] This was New Labourspeak for people other than members of the royal family. A charge often made against the PCC was its alleged readiness to jump through royal hoops. Soley contended that the PCC had been 'proactive in the case of the Royals – particularly with regard to Princes William and Harry – so why not elsewhere?'[10] In dealing with the first complaint lodged by the Prince of Wales's Office in St James's Palace, the Commission insisted that 'Royal complaints are no different from any other'. In this case the *Mail on Sunday* was accused of issuing a special supplement about Prince William at Eton containing 'ill-informed and intrusive material' without any overriding public-interest justification. The Commission succeeded in resolving the matter 'amicably' with an apology from the editor, Jonathan Holborow, stating that he had 'never wished, nor now wishes, to depart from the guidelines laid down from time to time by the Commission'.[11] The significance of this case was that it prepared the way for a later one, involving Prince Harry, in December 1998 which led to agreed revised guidelines on press coverage of the Princes' private lives.[12]

But much happened in the meantime involving 'people in all walks of life'. To start with, at the wigocratic end of the walk, there was something of a stir in February 1998 over plans announced by Lord Chancellor Irvine to proceed with legislation to outlaw press payments to witnesses in criminal trials. The *Press Gazette* suggested that the press was seen as pursuing a 'vendetta' against Irvine; and that on his part the Lord Chancellor, faced with being thwarted in respect to his intentions for press self-regulation in the Human Rights Bill, was intent on getting his own back. Certainly Irvine was markedly tetchy when appearing before the Commons' public administration committee – 'I do not have a particular agenda for enhancing self-regulation' – and Peter Riddell commented that Irvine had 'often appeared touchy in public and thin-skinned about criticism'.[13] Though the question of the planned legislation rather receded because of severe congestion of parliamentary time throughout the 1998 and 1999 sessions, payments to witnesses and criminals became the liveliest issue presently confronting the PCC.

As the *Press Gazette* remarked on publication of the Commission's *Annual Report, 1997* in May, 'at the very point when the Press Complaints Commission is reporting how well it believes it came out of a traumatic year, in 1997, it has been plunged once again into controversy over child murderer Mary Bell'.[14] This 'new backlash against the press' arose over the case of an eleven-year-old girl who, thirty years before, had killed two small boys. *Cries Unheard*, a study of her deprived and damaged life by Gitta Sereny, was serialized in *The Times*. Complaints to the PCC alleged indirect payments to a convicted criminal. Sereny confirmed that she had paid Bell for interviews. For *The Times* Peter Stothard pleaded public-interest justification.

Then came the cases of Lucille MacLauchlan and Deborah Parry, nurses who were convicted of murdering a fellow nurse in Saudi Arabia. The *Mirror* and the *Daily Express* were winners in the 'blood money' bidding war for their stories (the *Daily Mail* and the *Sun* were the losers). MPs raised loud accusations about blatant breaches of the Code. 'It seems that the press will never learn', declaimed the Conservative MP Damian Green. For the Commission, Guy Black announced that the PCC would soon be looking at the 'whole matter of payments to convicted criminals'. It would not proactively stop the payments since they might on examination be within the public-interest guidelines. Simon Jenkins waxed sardonic on the theme of 'media, truth and consequences' and the PCC's efforts to police this war with its own Geneva Convention. 'The PCC rule on media payment to criminals has as its rubric "Coach and horses drive this way".' Jenkins predicted that the PCC would find a way of getting both the Bell case and the nurses case 'off any moral hook'.[15]

In replying to Jenkins, Wakeham rebuked him for failing to make 'one crucial point'. The effectiveness of the Code should not be judged by those few cases – the Guppy and Leeson instances, for example – where the question of such payments had arisen, 'but by the very many cases which had never come to the public eye because the code has stopped editors from making payments'. Moreover, the Code could not function in isolation from the outside world. 'Book publishers, television producers and the World Wide Web are all bound up in this debate and all impact on the functioning of press self-regulation.'[16]

On the way to its adjudication the Commission took into account the case of the *Daily Telegraph*'s serialization of a book by a former IRA terrorist, Sean O'Callaghan. (The notorious case of the *Daily Mail*'s buying the story of Louise Woodward, the British nanny accused of killing a baby in her charge in the United States, was held over for later adjudication.[17]) In the longest and most closely reasoned adjudication yet,[18] the Commission upheld the public-interest pleas of the papers. Roy Greenslade in the *Guardian* saluted this landmark. 'In siding with the editors who have published – and paid handsomely for – the stories of convicted criminals, the Press Complaints Commission shows it is living in the real world.' The PCC's adjudication, released on 22 July, amounted, as Greenslade saw it, to a 'masterly rebuke' to 'hysterical and misguided calls for action' from public, parliamentarians and rival newspapers.[19] 'It's not a whitewash', Guy Black insisted. 'It's a rigorous scrutiny of the public interest defence.'[20]*

3

That magisterial landmark adjudication of July 1998 rejecting complaints against *The Times*, the *Daily Express*, the *Mirror* and the *Daily Telegraph* on grounds of public-interest vindication marked quietly but profoundly an historical 'coming of age' for the PCC. The patterns and rhythms of historical analysis of the Commission's fortunes between 1991 and 1997 featured episodes of high crisis and chances of survival. The materials of analysis were primarily official documents about the nature and purpose and desirability or otherwise of press self-regulation engendered from outside the Commission. From this point onwards, however, the materials of analysis become primarily the documents of self-regulation itself: the cases and adjudications engendered from within the Commission.

Government still took a keen interest in the Code. But legislative ordering of the press, in Brian MacArthur's words in October 1999, was no longer on the political agenda.[21] A Department of Culture, Media and Sport spokesman announced in December 1998: 'An independent press authority set up by the government would be statutory regulation of the press, and the government, in the absence of evidence of a collapse of standards, would be unwilling to consider undermining the authority of the Press Complaints Commission in this way.'[22] Manumission was thus promised. The old questions were still asked, but the new answers got shorter. The government prefer effective self-regulation by the Press Complaints Commission to any form of statutory regulation.'[23]

---

* See boxed adjudication, pp. 317–23.

MacArthur's testimony to the 'success' of the PCC adverted much on the chairmanship of Lord Wakeham, 'the great Mr Fixit of British politics'. Editor members of the Commission 'praise him as a superb and patient diplomat'. Under his leadership, 'ably supported by Guy Black, the director, the PCC has become a streamlined operation, dealing quickly and effectively with more than 3,000 complaints a year, and enforcing its decisions upon editors'. MacArthur had always been a noted advocate for the PCC; but even at that discount his testimony stands as valid evidence of a secure new order of things in press self-regulation.

From that angle of view, a kind of grudging endorsement curiously came from that inveterate detractor of the PCC, Sir Louis Blom-Cooper. Writing for the *British Journalism Review* in April 1999, the former chairman of the Press Council put yet again his case for a 'permanent, independent commission, composed of individuals outside the newspaper industry, but with expertise and experience of the print media and publishing, to keep under constant review the performance of the press', with particular reference to 'mis-information, mis-reporting and distortion of public events'. This was all rather old hat. What was new, surprisingly, was a reluctant concession that, despite newspaper self-regulation's being self-serving and 'palpably' not serving the public interest, under the PCC's supervision it actually worked.

> After nearly a decade of 'drinking in the last-chance saloon', the Press Complaints Commission is imbibing the intoxicating liquor of survival. It has beaten off every threat (some more fearful than others) of legislative intervention in the field of privacy and of statutory regulation. Lord Wakeham, its second chairman, is right when he claims publicly that self-regulation of the press, via the commission, works.

Indisputably, Blom-Cooper admitted, Wakeham had 'skilfully headed off all attempts by the Commission's detractors to persuade government to act'. Although the Labour party in opposition appeared to favour some action against the press, in government it had displayed a hands-off approach. 'Alliance with Rupert Murdoch has dictated a policy of non-intervention.'[24]

Whether the 'alliance' with Murdoch allowed him to be as manipulative as his many enemies liked to think, or whether it was a relationship of mutual convenience which Labour ministers exploited off the record as a reason not to do what in any case they preferred, on balance, not to do, cannot here be determined. What was of moment was one simple word used by Blom-Cooper: 'works'. That was all, in the end, that Wakeham and the PCC needed. The more reluctantly it was offered, the more appreciatively it was accepted.

4

Amid the mass of routine business for the Commission in 1998 and 1999, certain aspects suggest themselves as noteworthy. Adjudication in December 1998 of a complaint against the *Daily Mail* for payment to Louise Woodward, convicted of murdering a child in her care in the United States, was in effect supplementary to the landmark adjudication under Clause 16 of the Code in July. The *Mail*'s public-interest defence was accepted.[25] A contract between the *News of the World* and a witness in the trial of Paul Gadd (Gary Glitter) in 1999 was adjudicated as being substantially within the provisions of Clause 16, but that an ambiguity in its terms constituted a breach of the Code. This case led to police investigation, and renewed undertakings by Lord Chancellor Irvine to outlaw witness payments.

Among many miscellaneous concerns the Commission attended to were complaints that the *Daily Star*'s attack on the way the French football authorities were allocating World Cup tickets was an incitement to racial hatred. Memories of tabloid jingoism against the Germans in 1996 were still vivid. The Commission did adjudicate on this occasion, rejecting the complaints: 'the Code is not intended to stop such robust comment'. The purpose of Clause 13 was to protect *individuals* from prejudice. The Code had not been breached. Wakeham, aware that this would not go down well among the liberal intelligentsia, issued a deprecatory statement.[26] Piers Morgan supportively declared that the *Mirror* had learned the lesson of 1996.

A Dunblane-style consensus among editors was applied to the Omagh bomb atrocity in August 1998. Wakeham expressed his gratification at the self-restraint shown by British papers. He hoped that the rest of the media would follow this 'clear lead'.[27] He was much less gratified when David Montgomery announced that the Mirror Group would complain to the PCC about 'malicious' and 'dishonest' reporting by rival newspapers of MGN affairs. The horror of thus having the PCC dragged into the industry snake-pit was diplomatically deflected.[28] A conflict-of-evidence impasse was the central feature of a complaint involving the actor and comedian

Billy Connolly; another actor, Sean Connery, failed to have his complaint upheld against the Glasgow *Daily Record* for harassment.

A precedent somewhat awkward for the Commission was marked when in January 1999 the Prime Minister and Mrs Blair complained about the *Mail on Sunday*'s story headlined 'Parents' Fury over Blairs in School Place Row'. The treatment, they complained, was misleading in breach of Clause 1 (Accuracy) of the Code, and intruded on their daughter's privacy in breach of Clause 6 (Children). In an elaborate 2,500-word adjudication the Commission upheld the complaints. This was the first occasion on which the Commission considered a complaint about a child of a public figure under the new provisions of Clause 6 of the Code. Its consideration of the case led to the formulation of a guiding concept of 'cumulative intrusion' arising out of 'repetition of unsubstantiated allegations'.[29]*

A matter hanging over from 1997 came to have 'landmark' status. This was the so-called 'death-knock' episode, in which the Commission found against the Newcastle *Evening Chronicle*'s intruding upon grief or shock by sending a reporter to interview a father about his drowned son when the family still hoped he was alive. The *Chronicle* editor, Alison Hastings, challenged the Commission's finding; but in December 1997 the Commission reaffirmed its ruling. In April 1998 the Commission took the opportunity to reaffirm its stance decisively by upholding a complaint against the Dundee *Courier*'s inquiries into the death of a relation of one of its former journalists. The Commission was firm that it was 'not the job of reporters to break the news of a death to the family or friends of those involved'.[30]†

The *Press Gazette*, which had supported the original challenge by the *Chronicle* to the Commission's adjudication, now criticized the 'harsh' verdict against the *Courier*: reactions of people in grief varied widely; it was unfortunate that newspapers normally unlikely to attract complaints could get caught out on such stories unintentionally.[31] (For the PCC the gratifying upshot, as recounted by Brian MacArthur, was that the outraged Newcastle editor 'who spoke her mind and made headlines' was invited to become one of the industry commissioners; 'she has changed her mind about the PCC and is highly impressed by the quality of its work'.[32])

Privacy cases, though always a small proportion of total complaints, as ever tended disproportionately to make headlines. In certain instances it could be a matter of collectivity and guidelines. The 'outing' of sex offenders, especially paedophiles, had been exercising the Association of

---

* See boxed adjudication, pp. 323–7. † Ibid., p. 328.

Chief Officers of Probation. They had the problem of dealing with offenders named by the press going underground and beyond supervision. ACOP put the question both to the Guild of Editors and the PCC in May 1998. Rather than make complaints, ACOP preferred to try to achieve a constructive relationship that served the public by protecting their work, while letting the papers cover the story. 'Our hope is that the PCC can provide the ground rules to make this more commonplace.' Guy Black took the issue to the Commission at its June meeting. 'It might be sensible to produce guidelines in this area, as we have done in the past with mental illness and lottery winners.' It was 'fearsomely complicated and newspapers have a very real public interest role'. A 'fair bit of research and consultation' needed to be done to make sure guidelines were going to work and be practical.[33]

Much more in what might be called the classic tradition was the exposé by the *News of the World* of the irregular private lives of the Conservative MPs Jerry Hayes and Piers Merchant. *Private Eye* had a theory that one of the consequences of Blair's 'cosy relationship' with Murdoch was that Labour sex scandals were spiked while Tories were 'turned over'.[34] That homosexual Labour politicians were not immune from being turned over, however, became clear later in 1998 with the case of Nick Brown, the Agriculture Minister. A public-interest claim was put up by the *News of the World* and taken up by the *Sun* that a 'gay mafia' was running the country. In the background to this was the Ron Davies scandal on Clapham Common, leading to Davies's resigning as Welsh secretary, and Peter Mandelson's 'outing' on BBC's *Newsnight*.

The particular interest of the Brown case was that the minister, in spite of a pressing invitation from Wakeham to make a complaint and put himself in the capable hands of Professor Pinker, resolutely refused. Phil Hall, editor of the *News of the World*, denied any homophobic motive. He thought the electorate had a right to know 'who they are voting for and what they are about'. He pointed out that Ron Davies had outed himself, that Mandelson had been outed by another gay, Matthew Parris, and that Brown wanted to talk to Hall after being told that a former lover was trying to sell the story of their relationship – a story that had been going the rounds for two years but not taken up. Amanda Platell, executive editor of the *Express on Sunday*, argued that all the outrage and public fuss was misplaced. 'The whole gay agenda has changed very significantly. Five years ago it would have been a salacious story, but, reflecting the change in society, the way it was handled was pretty straight up.'[35] David Yelland, editor of the *Sun*, speaking at the Guild of Newspaper Editors' annual conference at Cambridge, put the same case: things had changed, and for the better. The *Sun* no longer did things it used to do.[36]

The PCC did not come out of the affair unscathed. Polly Toynbee launched a ferocious attack in the *Guardian* against self-regulation in general as a tool of the Rothermere and Murdoch bullies, and against the PCC in particular for ignominiously failing to fight on Brown's behalf.[37] Clive Soley on radio likewise denounced the PCC for not acting to defend Brown. That Brown forbade the PCC's doing so was hardly noticed at the time; but it became in its own way a kind of landmark.[38] Provoked by the untoward-ness of this kind of criticism, Guy Black launched a PCC counterattack on its tormenters on the sheer impolicy of pursuing cases against the wishes of the party concerned.

Roy Greenslade took up later in 1999 this issue of victims of intrusion on privacy choosing not to complain. This was apropos of ambitions of Lord Williams of Mostyn to foster a more aggressive and proactive PCC. Citing several recent blatant instances of celebrities who were turned over but did not complain, Greenslade posed the question: was it not scandalous, as critics of self-regulation charged, that in none of these instances did the PCC launch an investigation? Was it not important for the greater good that the PCC become proactive and act on victims' behalf? 'For a minute or two this seems a great idea.' Surely it would result in more adjudications against offending papers? Editors, pressed by public outrage and the publicity of their rivals, would come to heel and refuse to deal in such material. Photographers and reporters would find stalking and ambushing pointless as well as tedious.

Greenslade suggested caution and discretion. Implications of the PCC's 'switching from conflict resolution to adversarial combat, becoming a police officer rather than a social worker' should give pause.

> In the absence of a complaint, what criteria should it adopt on whether or not to launch an inquiry? Should it approach the victim and exhort him or her to complain? If the person still refuses to do so, should it proceed regardless and, in such circumstances, how would it obtain its evidence? If people are persuaded by the PCC to complain, would they not expect the resulting adjudication to go in their favour?

And surely, if it became known that the Commission was looking into stories without the need for a complaint, would not a kind of two-tier system be created? At one level royals and celebrities would expect every story involving them which they disliked to be investigated, while at the other lesser mortals would have to make a formal complaint. And how could the PCC be expected to monitor the whole of the British press – national, regional and magazines? And what of the 'embarrassment factor': people simply not wishing for more publicity about their incidents, even if they were likely to win their case?

It was possible to argue, continued Greenslade, that some newspaper intrusiveness was so flagrant that it demanded the Commission's attention, even without complaint, on the ground that privacy was a human right too important to leave to the individual who had suffered its loss. But it could be a mistake to judge at face value. 'Worse, what if the non-complainer has other reasons to keep quiet?' What if there were things far nastier in the woodshed that a complaint might disclose? An investigative PCC could itself become the intruder. 'A proactive PCC', Greenslade concluded, 'would be a nightmare and could well end up causing more trouble than it solved.' Lord Williams would do well to reconsider his ambitions for it.[39]

5

If the Brown case was important for what the Commission could, or should, not do, the Billington case was important for what it could. It resulted in a landmark adjudication against the *Sunday People* for chicaning its way through the privacy provisions of the Code. Stephen Billington, star of the popular television soap *Coronation Street*, complained that the paper had made speculative and highly intrusive allegations about his private life in the guise of a story purporting to expose peddlers of stories about people in the public eye. In upholding the complaint, the Commission expressly condemned attempts on the part of editors to seek ingenious means of cover to circumvent privacy provisions in the Code.[40]*

Rather different was the case of the 'Lawrence Five', the five white youths suspected of murdering the black teenager Stephen Lawrence. It was a question here of finding a way through an issue involving high emotion in the black community and high vulnerability for families in the white community who had to be considered innocent parties. The five's parents and their Conservative MP complained to the PCC about an article in the black newspaper *New Nation* in September 1998 headed 'Do you know where they live?' The complaints cited harassment as well as breach of privacy. The five had previously declined to take action against the *Daily*

---

* See boxed adjudication, pp. 329–30.

Mail for accusing them of murder, in spite of the Commission's making it clear they would have had a case on grounds of accuracy. The question in this case was the danger of action against their homes and families. It was a delicate issue, touching on very sensitive nerves about race. The editor of *New Nation*, Michael Eboda, 'was shocked to receive the PCC letter. It's another example of them discriminating against the black community.'

The Commission rejected the complaints. It noted that information about the addresses had been 'put firmly into the public domain by the inquest into Stephen Lawrence's death and by the Macpherson inquiry'. It was a matter of clear public interest as well as of high emotion for many people. The Commission expected that in cases such as this editors would take care to consider the vulnerability of innocent families. 'However, in view of the wide reporting of the case and the fact that the information about the complainants' addresses was already in the public domain, the Commission did not find that there was a breach of the Code.'[41]

Different again was the Elton John case. Here was an instance of intrusion on the privacy of a pop celebrity seemingly in the old familiar manner. Roy Greenslade commented on the way many such preferred not to complain. Sir Elton was different. He was different, moreover, in a way that involved an important precedent for the PCC's case law on privacy. Sir Elton complained that long-lens photographs published in the *Daily Star* and the *Sport* in June 1998 of Spice Girl Victoria Adams and football star David Beckham, guests at his home in the south of France, had invaded his privacy. The pictures were taken secretly, without permission.

The Commission was disposed initially to reject the complaint on the ground that Sir Elton himself was not pictured. There were no complaints from Adams or Beckham. Indeed, representatives of one of them allegedly consented to publication. There was no precedent for interpreting the privacy clause in conformity with John's complaint. His solicitors, however, 'forcefully reminded' the Commission that 'the Code had been modified just under a year before and new provisions were introduced including the reference to the privacy of one's home'. What obtained for oneself, they argued, obtained for one's guests. In finding for Sir Elton, the Commission broke new ground in extending privacy protection and in defining the implications of 'home' in ways not foreseen. The press could no longer rely on the express or implied consent of the subject of photographs taken in somebody else's home.[42][†]

---

* See boxed adjudication, pp. 330–1. † Ibid., pp. 331–2.

But the privacy intrusion scandal that defined the tabloid manners and mores of this time, and inflicted a 'torrid week for Lord Wakeham', was the Sophie Rhys-Jones affair. Indignant questions were asked in the House of Lords about obnoxious press treatment of Prince Edward's fiancée. Back in 1988 she had been photographed topless in a beach-party jape. Now that she was about to wed the Queen's youngest son, such a photograph became potentially valuable property. It was purchased and published by the *Sun* at the beginning of June 1999. To David Yelland it was a journalistic jape appropriate to the photo's provenance. It had not been secretly taken. Its existence was not a secret.

To cover himself Yelland promptly published an apology. It took the form of what the *Guardian* described as a 'somewhat tongue-in-cheek full-page editorial', where he protested that there was never any intention of spoiling Sophie's joy over her forthcoming marriage, and calling on readers to send in tin hats so that his staff could protect themselves against the brickbats provoked by the picture. Undisarmed, the Rhys-Jones camp launched a complaint. The Commission, feeling under pressure in a conspicuous matter of what sentimentally interested the public, arranged a prompt resolution through good offices. It issued a statement rebuking the *Sun* for a 'reprehensible' lapse, a 'grave error which should not be repeated'. Editors should not forget that the Commission could ask proprietors to take a view. Wakeham acknowledged Yelland's prompt apology. 'I want to re-iterate that any newspaper intruding into the privacy of an individual must be able to justify itself on the grounds of either genuine public interest or consent.'[43]

Commenting on a new wave of demands for a privacy law, Roy Greenslade drew attention to the fact that the *Sun*, had it wanted to, could have made out an 'excellent case for publication'. Sophie clearly had not protested when the picture was taken. It had 'long been on display on the Capitol Radio notice-board and had, therefore, been in the public domain'. Copyright was held by the woman who took it. 'In law, even with a public interest caveat, the *Sun* would have had a defence.'[44] Yelland, after all, was on record as stating that the *Sun* no longer did things it used to do. He had reason to think that doing his job was a lot more difficult than it had been ten years before.

Having apologized, the *Sun* did not think it would need a defence. It was the PCC that looked vulnerable. The hand-wringing effect was unavoidable. Alan Rusbridger put the boot in. Editorial comment in the *Guardian* dwelt mockingly on the themes of 'a smack on the wrist', and the PCC administering 'er, a ticking-off', and the apparent emptiness of Wakeham's threat that he would not hesitate to bring the breach to the attention of the employer concerned.[45] This was rather to misapprehend the nature of the case. What Ms Rhys-Jones wanted was a prompt and sincere apology from Yelland. This the Commission arranged within a week. Wakeham, amid the uproar, had to be seen doing something signal. It would be absurd to revert to the 1995 precedent of Murdoch's swoop on Piers Morgan. That would be to overmatch the occasion. Yelland had, in a manner, apologized. Wakeham's tactic would be to roast Yelland for his manner.

Private Eye gloatingly took up the story. 'In a further humiliation David Yelland was ordered to make a *second* grovelling apology to Sophie, because his first was deemed to be insincere.' Piers Morgan, in his guise as reformed character, also put the boot in, but in a way supportive of the PCC. The *Mirror*, even more gloatingly, devoted three pages and an editorial to Yelland's travails. 'According to *The Mirror*,' *Private Eye* continued, 'no editor should be allowed to survive such a debacle.'[46] Greenslade offered a word of comfort to the embattled PCC. 'For those who still regard it as toothless, ask *Sun* editor David Yelland to show you his back. It's bleeding. And the wounds might yet prove fatal.'[47]

6

The Sophie Rhys-Jones affair indirectly brought the royal family back into sharper focus. Already in 1998 there had been a storm over Penny Junor's book, *Charles: Victim or Villain?* In this Diana's sons would have read or heard allegations that their mother was a manipulative adulteress and worse. The Commission's negotiations with the Palace to protect the privacy of Princes William and Harry while at school had succeeded in keeping the paparazzi at bay and had opened up, in the *Press Gazette*'s words, a 'useful dialogue' with the royal press offices. But the PCC could do nothing about the Junor book and the press could not be expected to censor itself by not referring to the allegations because it had every right to question where they came from. 'The press and the PCC, as much as the princes, are caught in a cross fire between factions in a family still at war.'[48]

In this stormy context a complaint by the Prince of Wales – 'egged on', as Piers Morgan contended, 'by his team of amateurish press officers'[49] – over intrusive treatment in the *Mirror* and *Star* about a rugby injury sustained by Prince Harry seemed trivial enough. But the way it fed into a row between Piers Morgan at the *Mirror* and Les Hinton in the Code Committee gave it a fortuitous importance. Morgan all but accused Hinton of colluding with the St James's Palace press office and of using his Code Committee chairmanship as cover for giving advantage to News International titles in reporting on the Princes. Morgan drew attention to the *Sun*'s 'getting away without complaint' with a story of the Princes performing a 'full Monty' strip at their father's birthday party. Morgan was irate that stories 'covering the princes' privacy' were repeatedly being fed to the press by St James's Palace 'when it suits them'. Morgan would defend the *Mirror* vigorously against the complaint. 'Les has got a difficult position as chairman, but he's got to look at what his own papers are doing.'[50]

Here was a problem out of which the Commission might profit. It would not do to leave unresolved a question about the Code chairman and a conflict of interest. But beyond that was the opportunity for Wakeham and Black to convert a minor complaint into a major authoritative policy statement that could have strategic leverage in the future. Prince Charles had no chance of winning his case against the *Mirror*. The thing was to avoid adjudicating and open the way for revised guidelines. At St James's Palace, moreover, was Prince Charles's deputy private secretary, the former PCC director Mark Bolland, in a position discreetly to help retrieve the situation. The Commission announced that, as with all other complaints, the first effort would be to try to resolve it by conciliation. By June 1999 it could announce such a resolution. 'The PCC diplomats have won the day', proclaimed Morgan in the *Gazette*, 'shrewdly negotiating a way through the journalistic minefield . . . without upsetting anybody.'[51] Both parties agreed to 'revised guidelines to press coverage on the private lives of Princes William and Harry'. Given that Prince William would become 18 on 21 June 2000, and cease to be a schoolboy on 29 June, it could only be a holding operation in his case. Still, it would stand as a material witness in the next stage of the process of sparing him from his mother's fate at the hands of the media.

The gist of the new guidelines was summed up in the conclusion to the Commission's Report No. 46. It was right, in the light of the complaint from St James's Palace against the *Mirror* and the *Daily Star*, and of representations made by them, to reassess the best way to ensure that the Princes continued to benefit from the self-restraint of editors. The basis for the way forward was twofold. 'In view of the substantial toughening of the Code, the Palace should reassess the amount and type of information they make publicly available.' For their part, all newspapers 'should be aware of the problems posed by an accumulation of newspaper coverage of either of the royal Princes – and, within the spirit of Clauses 3 (Privacy) and 6 (Children) of the Code, seek a view about the likely impact of a particular story on one of the boys when assessing whether or not to publish a story'. In doing so, editors, the Commission stressed, 'should continue to err on the side of restraint as the Code dictates that intrusions into a child's privacy should only be a matter of exceptional public interest'.[52]

It had been a protracted business. Piers Morgan's tribute to the diplomatic skills of the PCC rang true. After the unavoidable embarrassment of the Sophie Rhys-Jones business, it was gratifying that what amounted to a victory for the tabloids over St James's Palace was expediently presented as a triumph for the PCC.

Report No. 43, July–September 1998
The Times, The Mirror, The Express, The Daily Telegraph

1. THE COMPLAINTS
1.0 The complaints. The Commission considered three sets of complaints under Clause 16(ii) of the Code of Practice, which prohibits payments by newspapers or magazines for stories to convicted or confessed criminals, except where publication of such stories is in the public interest.
1.1 The first set of complaints related to the serialisation by The Times of the book *Cries Unheard* by Gitta Sereny about the child killer Mary Bell. Serialisation took place from 29th April to 1st May 1998.
1.2 The second set of complaints related to articles in The Mirror and The Express setting out the story of Deborah Parry and Lucille MacLauchlan, both convicted of a killing in Saudi Arabia but released from prison there following a Royal Pardon. These articles were published in the week beginning 20th May 1998. For ease, these complaints are referred to throughout the first part of this adjudication as 'the nurses'.
1.3 The third set of complaints related to the serialisation by The Daily Telegraph of a book, *The Informer*, by convicted IRA terrorist Sean O'Callaghan. The serialisation began on 16th May 1998.

2. THE CODE AND THE LAW
2.0 Before dealing with the substance of each case in detail, the Commission wished to set out the general principles which it applies to complaints brought under Clause 16(ii) – particularly against the background of the existing legislative framework and the Government's current review of the issue of proceeds of crime.
2.1 Profits from crime. It is a distasteful fact that some criminals can, and do, profit from their crimes and do so in a number of different ways. Some have been known

straightforwardly to exploit their misdemeanours by conducting guided tours of the location of their crimes. Others write books: only recently it became clear that the serial killer Dennis Nilsen is writing a book, for which interested publishers are said to be offering up to £100,000 (reported in The Sunday Telegraph, 31st May 1998).

2.2 The legal framework. The Code of Practice exists outside, and on top of the legal requirements on editors. However, the Commission is aware that in dealing with the matter of payments to criminals, it is dealing not with an ordinary complaint – where there is a victim of a breach of the Code – but with a matter of general public policy. In considering the matter, the Commission has therefore thought it right to have regard to the existing legal structures in this area.

2 3 It has always been, and remains, a matter for Parliament to set down the framework within which people are not allowed to profit from their crimes. There is a good deal of statute in this area – most importantly, the Proceeds of Crime Act 1995, the Criminal Justice Act 1988 and the Drug Trafficking Act 1994, each of which prevents convicted criminals in certain circumstances from profiting from crime. There are geographical and chronological limits to that legislation. Statute does not stop criminals convicted in foreign jurisdictions from profiting from crime – except in very limited circumstances such as drug trafficking. And it does not apply after six years have elapsed following a crime.

2.4 All the cases considered by the Commission therefore fell outside the terms of the law – a point on which the Commission placed some weight. In the case of the nurses, the events and sentencing took place abroad. In the case of Mary Bell, the publication of *Cries Unheard* took place thirty years after the crime had been committed – well outside the time set in statute; in that of Sean O'Callaghan, the book was published eight years after he was convicted. The Commission was therefore mindful that, in interpreting the Code, it should hesitate before enforcing a censorious regime on newspapers beyond that which Parliament itself has put in place. It was also mindful that newspapers and magazines operate under a tough self regulatory regime to which book publishers and broadcasters are not subject: they are subject to the law alone.

2.5 The purpose of the PCC Code. The provisions of Clause 16 of the Code of Practice are not intended to stop all those who have ever been convicted of a crime from being paid for their story in every set of circumstances – for three reasons. First, as set out above, it is for Parliament to establish a legal regime which defines the extent to which criminals should be prevented from cashing in on their crimes through newspaper stories or otherwise. The PCC Code cannot work in isolation from that. Second, it would be unrealistic to demand that all convicted persons should be barred in perpetuity from writing for newspapers or book publishers about their crimes or indeed about other matters. The law itself recognises that offenders can be rehabilitated and convictions 'spent' – and it would be wrong of the PCC to take a different view. Indeed, this point was established in a Commission adjudication on the serialisation by The Guardian of a book by convicted drugs smuggler Howard Marks (McFarquar v The Guardian, PCC Report, October–December 1996). And third, the Commission recognises the importance of freedom of expression and of the public's right to know – both of which are currently being guaranteed by the Human Rights Bill before Parliament.

2.6 The public interest. While the Code is not designed to stop criminals being paid for their stories in all circumstances, it *is* designed to stop newspapers making payments for stories about crimes which do not contain a public interest element. Indeed, the philosophy of the Code is that a payment aggravates the case where there is no public interest, because the glorification of the crime is more of an affront if it is done for gain. The principle behind this is, of course, that it is wrong to glorify crime, not necessarily to write about it: there will be occasions on which the public has a right to know about events relating to a crime or criminals. The key to the Code is, therefore, public interest.

2 7 This is a point established by previous PCC adjudications. One adjudication concerned the publication by Hello! magazine of an interview with Darius Guppy, while he was still serving a prison sentence for fraud. The Commission could not accept that there was any public interest served by the article, which merely served to glorify the crimes that Guppy had committed. It therefore upheld the complaint on the grounds of inadequate public interest (Huins v Hello!, PCC Report, August–September 1993).

2.8 Another adjudication concerned the case of former Barings trader Nick Leeson, whose memoirs were serialised by The Daily Mail soon after he had started his prison sentence. Payment arose because of the television advertising of the book by the newspaper – thus increasing the royalties obtained from increased sales. The Commission concluded that, in this case, there was a public interest justification for the way in which the newspaper had dealt with the matter and rejected the complaints (Gordon v The Daily Mail, PCC Report, January–March 1996).

2.9 Payments – and exclusivity. In each of these cases, the Commission's judgements were determined on the issue of public interest alone. The Code also makes clear that if payment is to be made for a story that is in the public interest, payment must be 'necessary' for this to happen. The Commission acknowledges that payment is increasingly demanded by people (or their agents) whose stories the newspapers want; and that newspapers – which exist in a fiercely competitive environment – in their turn wish to require exclusivity because of the large sums demanded. Although such payments for exclusivity – and the size of them – may be distasteful and offensive, they do not in themselves involve a breach of the Code, because they must in such circumstances be judged as 'necessary'. Indeed, newspapers are not well known for making payments which are *un*necessary.

2.10 The determining factors. In looking at the complaints before it, the determining factors for the Commission are therefore freedom of expression and public interest. The issue of payment – regulated by Act of Parliament, and currently under review by the Government – is only relevant where no arguable public interest can be displayed by the newspaper: if there is no public interest, then payment is in breach of the Code; if there is a public interest, then there is no breach of the Code provided payment is necessary.

3. WAS THERE A PUBLIC INTEREST JUSTIFICATION?

3.0 Mary Bell and The Times. The Commission found the newspaper's public interest arguments in the case of the serialisation of *Cries Unheard* to be compelling. The newspaper summed up that public interest as something that 'runs like a spine through [Gitta Sereny's book] and was the reason why Sereny felt impelled to return to the case she covered at the time of the trial. Does the criminal justice system do real justice to such damaged children? If not, how can it be improved?'

3.1 Many specific issues of public interest were raised by the newspaper. They included: the circumstances in which a child who grew up in surroundings of depravity came to be a murderer; the connection between Bell's own crime and the abuse to which she herself was subjected; and the first authoritative account of how the penal system deals with child criminals. Indeed, the editor had summed up the public interest justification in a way the Commission found highly cogent: 'Only by trying to understand what could conceivably have driven an 11 year old girl to kill two small boys . . . can we come any closer to stopping these crimes.'

3.2 The Commission also noted that the newspaper was only serialising the work – and an argument of freedom of expression, and the public interest attaching to that, therefore also arose. The material had already been put into the public domain – as a result of the willing co-operation of Mary Bell herself – and what she had to say was original material of relevance to a wide range of issues relating to crime and punishment. As such the public – not just those who would buy her book – had a right to access the material. As the newspaper said, '*Cries Unheard* publishes information which should be put in the public domain for no more specific reason than that it is better for important facts to be available for dissection and discussion than for them to remain hidden.'

3.3 The Commission noted that a recent review of the book, by Mary Margaret McCabe of the Department of Philosophy at King's College London, had summed up the issue extremely well. 'Should this book have been published? The answer is a firm "yes" . . . The doubt it provokes, both about this case and how we should deal with it, is a vital component of our reaching proper understanding of how we live our family lives, and of how our institutions might correct them' (*TLS*, 17th July 1998).

3.4 Parry and The Express, MacLaughlan and The Mirror. In both cases, it was not for the Commission to make any finding or pass any judgement on the allegations that had been made about the Saudi justice system. The Commission's role was only to decide whether there was any public interest in newspapers promoting a debate about it.

3.5 Against that background, the Commission found the newspapers' public interest justifications in both these cases to be substantial.

3.6 In the case of Lucille MacLaughlan, the newspaper published evidence that she had allegedly been tortured and sexually assaulted after her arrest by the Saudi police. She had, apparently, been denied access to British Embassy staff and to proper legal representation in advance of a trial in private without a jury and without being allowed to give evidence on her own behalf. Independent experts had analysed her confession and concluded that it was not genuine – as she had always maintained. An independent organisation, Fair Trials Abroad, had been unequivocal in its criticism of the alleged conduct of the police, and made clear its view that the convictions ought not to be sustained. The newspaper believed that the combination of these factors showed that the entire process was carried out by what it described as a 'primitive court dispensing barbaric justice'. The articles, they said, would go some way to prevent such miscarriages of justice in the future and encourage the Saudi Government to examine and reform its judicial system'. The Commission also noted that the Prime Minister and Foreign Secretary had been instrumental in the sentences being commuted – which itself added a substantial element of public interest to the entire story.

3.7 In the case of Deborah Parry, the newspaper said that it was the nurse's family which had convinced it that that the story should be told. There had, the paper said, been a miscarriage of justice. They, too, noted that her story was a 'warning to other people thinking they might make easy money working in the Middle East'. The money that had been given to her, the paper said, would be used almost entirely to pursue this line of public interest: it would be spent on legal costs to assist her in clearing her name; the newspaper would continue to assist her in this.

3.8 Having regard to all the matters set out above, the Commission took the view that the newspapers had an abundant public interest justification.

3.9 First, the British Government itself had been involved in the case – arguing for the commutation of the nurses' sentences and their release. This was therefore a matter of legitimate public interest and debate: indeed, the Government would not have become involved otherwise. To argue that there was no public interest would – in effect – be to say that the public had no right to understand the circumstances of a high profile case involving British citizens abroad, with which their Government was closely involved.

3.10 Second – again emphasising the point that it was not a matter for the Commission to make any judgement whatever about Saudi justice – the Commission noted that 30,000 British citizens currently work in Saudi Arabia. Many thousands of others are no doubt contemplating doing so. Allegations had been made about the way in which justice was dispensed in the country – and it could not be argued that there was no public interest in airing these, whether or not they were well founded. Newspapers have a legitimate role in scrutinising justice in this country, and every other one where British citizens reside. They were fulfilling that role in this case.

3.11 Third, as with the case of Mary Bell, the Commission noted that there was an important argument of freedom of expression and the public interest attaching to the story. The two nurses had a right to give their account – especially against a background in which other newspapers were putting the other side of the story. This was particularly important as the nurses had been convicted following a closed trial – in which their side of the story was never heard by the British public.

3.12 Sean O'Callaghan and The Daily Telegraph. The newspaper provided the Commission with a strong public interest justification. The book they were serialising provided, they said, 'a unique inside account – such as no other book or court testimony has ever provided of the inner workings, thinking and strategy and tactics of the IRA'. The newspaper had said that it was 'proud' to provide this account because of the 'service to truth' that Sean O'Callaghan had performed. Everyone in the British Isles, they added, needed to understand how the most important terrorist organisation in Western Europe worked – and the threat to democracy which 'the fascism of Sinn Fein' posed.

3.13 The Commission agreed with the newspaper that there was a very strong public interest justification in serialising the book. For the first time, an informer had thrown the spotlight onto the workings of a terrorist organisation that had been responsible for many deaths throughout the United Kingdom. The book was an invaluable work – and deserved the wide audience that serialisation gave it.

4. MARY BELL'S DAUGHTER

4.0 The impact on Mary Bell's daughter. The Commission noted that the publication of the book, and to a lesser extent its serialisation. had caused a number of newspapers to begin a search for Mary Bell herself. This led ultimately to allegations of harassment of Mary Bell and her daughter – and to the apparent fact that Bell was forced to reveal her identity to her daughter for the first time.

4.1 The Commission has a very great deal of sympathy for Mary Bell's daughter in this case – although this was clearly not a matter which it could realistically take into account when considering a complaint under Clause 16. Indeed, the Commission had to assume that the furore about payments to Mary Bell would have occurred whether or not there had been a serialisation in the newspaper: concern was being expressed about the book itself in some newspapers long before it became clear that The Times was to undertake the serialisation.

4.2 The Commission also noted that a number of issues relating to the identification of Mary Bell, and intrusion into the private life of her and her daughter, were covered by an existing injunction. In any event, no complaint of harassment was received – without which it was impossible for the Commission formally to investigate.

4.3 The Commission would have welcomed such a complaint from any of the interested parties in order that it could more fully address these issues. That said, the Commission wished to place on record its serious concern about allegations of the harassment of any child – which is always unacceptable – and would have been quick vigorously to censure a newspaper if a complaint had been received, backed up by evidence from one of those involved, and a breach of Clause 4 or Clause 6 proved. This was a point underlined at the time by the Chairman of the Press Complaints Commission in a series of radio and television interviews.

5. PAYMENTS

5.0 As set out above, the Code of Practice allows newspapers to make payments for material in the public interest – provided it is 'necessary' for it to be done. There were two ways for the Commission to look at this issue.

5.1 On one basis, the mere fact that a payment has been made means that it must, in all probability, have been 'necessary'. Individuals who want to give their story for free are able to do so – while newspapers are simply not in the habit of paying for material if they do not have to.

5.2 On another basis, the Commission could have hypothesised about what might have happened if no payment had been made. In the case of the two book serialisations, it would have meant that the material in the books would not have been made available to a wide public audience. In the case of the payments to Parry and MacLaughlan, the material might have emerged in time – perhaps in another country or in another medium – but it might not have emerged at all: the nurses could simply have declined to tell their story until they had written a book. They would have profited from that – perhaps to an even greater extent – and in the meantime the public would have been deprived of information that was in the public interest.

5.3 Looking at it either way, payment was – in the phraseology of the Code – 'necessary' to secure material by which the public interest was served *so far as it was possible for the Commission to determine.*

6. CONCLUSION

6.0 On the two matters before it – public interest and payment – the Commission did not find that any case has been made out for a breach of the Code. In each of the complaints there was a strong public interest justification. These were all matters on which the public had a right to know and about which wide debate was legitimate. Furthermore, payment was in all probability 'necessary' in the terms of the Code to secure the material – or at least it could not be proved that payment was *un*necessary.

6.1 However, there was one further and general matter the Commission wished to address. Like many members of the public – and like many editors – the Commission believes that while payments may in some cases be necessary, they may at the same time be extremely offensive. However. that is a moral and subjective case goes beyond the scope of the Commission and an objective Code at the heart of which is the public interest and the public's right to know. It is a matter of broader public policy for Government and Parliament.

6.2 The Government is presently considering whether the existing law (set out in 2.2–2.4 above) is adequate in this regard – a review which, in the light of its recommendation on these complaints, the Commission welcomes and believes is a sensible way forward. The review will of course need to have regard for the terms of the European Convention on freedom of expression, which is currently being enshrined into UK law through the Human Rights Bill. The Commission will seek to co-operate with the Government on the issues it has covered as a result of this debate.

6.3 The complaints were not upheld.

Report No. 47, July–September 1999
The Mail on Sunday

COMPLAINT AND BACKGROUND

The Prime Minister and Mrs Blair complained that articles and a leader in The Mail on Sunday on 24 January 1999 were misleading in breach of Clause 1 (Accuracy) of the Code of Practice, and intruded into their daughter's privacy in breach of Clause 6 (Children).

The article, including one on the front page headlined 'Parents' Fury over Blairs in School Place Row', and an accompanying leader comment, concerned the decision by the Sacred Heart High School in Hammersmith to admit Kathryn Blair – the Prime Minister's daughter – while rejecting other local children. The article said that some parents believed the Prime Minister had been given special treatment by the school. Thirteen girls had been turned down by the school this year, compared to only two last year. The article said that the parents concerned – two of whom were named in the article – were given no reasons for this decision, despite the fact that eleven of them had been 'promised' places.

A leader said that while Kathryn Blair was 'clearly a bright child', her acceptance into Sacred Heart 'tells us more about choice . . . For while she takes her place in the autumn term, 11 other children, educated in Sacred Heart's adjoining primary school face exclusion'. This leads to the suspicion, it said, that the school was operating an 'under-the-counter' selection policy. The Prime Minister and Mrs Blair were not poor, the leader commented, and could have paid for private education for their daughter instead.

The complainants said that their daughter Kathryn was being raised as a Roman Catholic – and they had always wanted her to attend a Catholic comprehensive school, preferably one which was single sex. The only school in Westminster was mixed and in Maida Vale, some way from Downing Street. Sacred Heart was their first choice: they applied for a place for their daughter and were accepted entirely in line with standard procedures.

They said that the newspaper had contacted Hammersmith and Fulham Borough Council to put to them the allegations that Kathryn Blair had benefited from an 'under-the-counter' selection policy. The Council had made clear that, since the Greenwich judgement of 1989, it has been illegal for schools to refuse admission to children who do not live in the borough. Places at the school were allocated in accordance with published admissions criteria, with preference given to Catholic children who attend Catholic primary schools.

Both the news coverage and the editorial, they said, were designed to invite readers to believe that Kathryn had been given special treatment: only she stood accused of taking a place at the expense of other children, but without any evidence of special treatment to back up these allegations. This was a breach of Clause 6 of the Code – with no exceptional public interest to justify it.

In making the complaint, they underlined that the Prime Minister accepted that the Government's education policies should be properly scrutinised, but believed there were ample opportunities to do so without infringing the privacy of his children. Furthermore, the thrust and premise of the story were false – in breach of Clause 1 of the Code – making the intrusion worse. In response, the newspaper said that the thrust of the story was not special treatment, but a group of parents' justifiable complaint that their daughters had been denied promised places at a school which did accept Mr Blair's daughter, even though she appeared no better qualified. A reporter from the newspaper had tried to interview the Headmistress to ascertain the facts, but she refused to do so.

After the results of the school's selection process had been made known to the parents, those who were disappointed formed the view that the school was taking advantage of its increasing popularity to introduce a policy of back-door selection. This was made worse by the Headmistress's insistence that if parents listed a second choice of school for their daughters on an application form, they would be excluded from consideration. This had placed disappointed parents in an impossible situation and fuelled their anger. In her anger, one of the parents had told the newspaper that 'Tony Blair's daughter got in . . . she had taken my daughter's place.' This was echoed in the comments of some other parents. The newspaper was reporting that anger and the Prime Minister's alleged hypocrisy at taking advantage of a place at a comprehensive school. His conduct in making choices which the policy of his Government is preventing others from making was one of genuine public interest. Such reporting was a crucial role for the press in a democratic society: a successful complaint would place the Prime Minister beyond criticism for his stance on education if scrutiny involved his children.

On the specific point about the privacy of Kathryn Blair, the newspaper said that it had not discussed in any way her private life nor intruded into her school life by disclosing information about her. A deliberate decision was made not to carry a picture of her. It confirmed that it would never publish material about the private lives of the Prime Minister's children simply because he was Prime Minister.

In further comments, the complainants said that the newspaper could have satisfied itself that there was no 'under-the-counter' selection policy simply by looking at the admissions criteria. The admissions policy was made available in full to the newspaper before publication. Kathryn satisfied them all – and it would have been illegal for the school to discriminate against her on grounds of residence. A newspaper should not be able to justify a story about children by repeating a false allegation – when there was no evidence to support it. For a child to start a new school amid allegations that she got in as a result of special treatment was a grotesque attack on her right to lead an ordinary life.

The Headmistress of the school concerned supported the complaint in a lengthy submission which, amongst other things, analysed the admission criteria by reference to both those refused a place and to the position of Kathryn Blair. She strongly refuted any suggestion that Kathryn Blair had been specially favoured, and challenged a number of the other facts.

The newspaper maintained that the reporting was accurate at the time of publication and pointed out that since the articles one rejected child had won a place at the school on appeal. It disputed a number of statements made by the Headmistress and asked for a large amount of supporting documentation to be disclosed. In the event this did not prove necessary as the Commission took the view that, in the light of the newspaper's arguments, the Headmistress's submission and the reply did not add anything to the issues which it had to decide.

ADJUDICATION
Clause 1 (Accuracy) of the Code provides that newspapers must take care not to publish inaccurate or misleading material. Clause 6 (Children) provides that young people should be free to complete their time at school without unnecessary intrusion, and that where material about the private life of a child is published, there must be justification other than the fame or position of his or her parents.

This is the first occasion on which the Commission has considered a complaint about the child of a public figure under the new provisions of Clause 6 of the Code – and it is aware that this complaint raises new issues which it is right for the Commission to address. In the context of this case, the Commission wished to note the following preliminary points.

It is manifestly the role, and responsibility, of the press to scrutinise Government policies and the conduct of those responsible for them. The press should be entitled to relate such scrutiny to the children of politicians where their conduct in matters relating to their children has an impact on policy or gives rise to reasonable charges of hypocrisy. In appropriate cases this might provide the exceptional public interest justification required by the Code.

Although this is the first case of its kind, two recent adjudications offered guidance in dealing with this complaint. In the first, the Commission ruled that unfounded allegations – even though they were presented as such – could create a misleading impression that gave rise to a breach of Clause 1 (Report 43, p. 23). In the second, the Commission ruled that, while an article itself may have been one of public interest, it was wrong to make the complainant the focus of a story which could have been written without mentioning her (Report 44, p. 5).

Finally, the Commission had to bear in mind that at the centre of the article and complaint was an eleven year old child. The Code is rightly designed to give the maximum possible protection to children who in many circumstances may be vulnerable. In this instance Kathryn Blair will now be starting a new school amid a welter of allegations that she might have received preferential treatment in securing a place.

The first question for the Commission was whether the newspaper articles and leader, taken as a whole, gave a misleading impression that Kathryn Blair had been made the subject of special treatment and obtained a place in preference to others who were, at least, equally qualified. The newspaper said that it had not made or implied the suggestion that Kathryn Blair was not entitled on her own merits to a place at the school. It had properly reported the complaints of parents whose children had not been awarded a place.

The Commission concluded that a fair reading of the articles and leader comment led to the conclusion that a breach of the Code had taken place. The articles were concerned with issues relating to the school's admissions policy. There was no evidence to support the allegation that Kathryn Blair was unfairly admitted or had received special treatment, and the newspaper did not provide any. Yet, by the repetition of unsubstantiated allegations about her, the story was presented in a way which implied she had. Linking commentary added to this impression. One parent was said by the newspaper to have 'raised many new questions about how the Blairs secured a place for their own girl when others were refused'. An opposition spokesman was quoted commenting on the premise that it had been established that the Prime Minister's family had enjoyed 'special favouritism.' Specifically referring to Kathryn Blair, the leader said that the actions of the school had led to the suspicion that the school 'was operating an under-the-counter policy of selection.' Only part of a statement by the Hammersmith Council press office was published by the newspaper.

The Commission concluded that the newspaper had reproduced allegations potentially damaging to a child in a misleading way without evidence of special treatment in her case.

The second question which the Commission had to decide was whether there was any justification for making Kathryn Blair the focus of the article and the leader about the admission policy of the school solely because of her relationship to her parents. The newspaper said that the references had arisen during the course of interviews with the parents of unsuccessful children and it should be free to report them.

The Commission believes that an article about the selection procedure at the school could have been written without reference to Kathryn Blair or making her the centre of the story. By herself, she could have been no more responsible for denying a place to the large number of unsuccessful candidates than any other of the girls actually admitted who equally could have been individually highlighted by the articles. To focus on Kathryn Blair in circumstances where there was a breach of Clause 1 of the Code was clearly not within the terms of Clause 6 of the Code and appeared to arise solely because of the position of her father.

Notwithstanding its conclusion on the above question, the Commission went on to consider whether there was any exceptional public interest which justified the reference to Kathryn Blair in the articles and leader. The Commission believes that it would be permissible under the editors' Code to name the children of public figures in newspaper articles – in a manner proportionate to the issues and facts involved – in circumstances where:

* there is reasonable substance to a charge or allegation that provides the exceptional public interest required by the Code; and
* it is necessary to report the story and to identify the child because that child, and that child alone, had to be the centre of the story.

Applying these criteria, the Commission could find no justification for naming Kathryn Blair alone in connection with complaints about the admission criteria of the school. There was no evidence of special treatment in her favour. An opposition spokesman who alleged 'hypocrisy' on Mr Blair's part did so on an inaccurate factual basis that the allegations were true. The newspaper's leader did no more than suggest that Mr Blair would be embarrassed if the unproved allegations of an 'under-the-counter policy of selection' proved to be correct.

Finally, the newspaper noted in its submission that Mr Blair had publicly made reference to his children. The complainants' response to this emphasised the great lengths that the Prime Minister and Mrs Blair go to in order to avoid publicity for their children. The Commission agrees with the contention made to it that if every story about the Prime Minister's children, which relates to their education, is to be justified on the basis that he has made statements about education, then Clause 6 provides no protection for his children or others in a similar position. The Commission intends the industry's Code – drawn up by editors themselves – to be effective and to provide real protection for all children.

The complaint was upheld.

Report No. 41, January–March 1998
Dundee Courier & Advertiser

COMPLAINT

Mr Michael Mulford of Glasgow, complained that approaches made by the Dundee Courier & Advertiser after his niece's death lacked sympathy and discretion, in breach of Clause 5 (Intrusion into grief or shock) of the Code of Practice.

The complainant's niece had been killed in a road accident with her partner. The complainant said that he was unaware of this when, the following day, the newspaper telephoned his office and in his absence spoke with a member of his staff. The reporter had asked if the young woman who had been killed was a close relative of the complainant. In the complainant's view the reporter was left in no doubt that the complainant did not know of the tragedy. However, the reporter then proceeded to page the complainant, clearly intending to break the news to him.

The editor expressed regret to the complainant for the upset caused, but said that his staff were experienced and had acted with sympathy and discretion. The newspaper was at all times sensitive to the need to avoid intrusion into personal grief, but this could not preclude appropriate approaches to members of the public following tragic accidents and other deaths. Such approaches are terminated by staff if this is the wish of the person contacted, and these conditions were met when trying to approach the complainant, whose office had even provided his pager number. The particular reporter had had a 'gut feeling' that the deceased was not a close relative to the complainant. The editor added that, as a former colleague, they had hoped the complainant would have understood their approach and have given guidance as to which member of the family to contact.

ADJUDICATION

Reporters are often involved in seeking comment from those in early stages of grief following a tragedy, and although this form of news gathering can cause distress to those involved, it is not wrong that it should happen – but only, as the Code makes clear, with sympathy and discretion. However the Commission has always held that it is not the job of reporters to break the news of a death to the family or friends of those involved. The Commission noted that the reporter had been provided with the complainant's pager number to facilitate direct contact. However, it should have been clear to him by then that the complainant was unaware that there had been an accident. When the complainant returned his message, another member of staff told him that there had been a death – which, by virtue of the fact that his name is rare, must have been from within his family. In doing so, the reporters had clearly overstepped the mark.

The complaint was therefore upheld.

Report No. 43, July–September 1998
Sunday People

COMPLAINT

Mr Stephen Billington, c/o Granada Studios, Manchester, complained that an article published in the Sunday People on August 23 1998 invaded his privacy in breach of Clause 3 (Privacy) of the Code of Practice. The article detailed how a man claiming to be an associate of the complainant had been prepared to make allegations about the complainant's private life in return for money. The newspaper did not pay the man but described in considerable detail the sort of material he claimed to be willing to disclose.

The complainant said that he did not wish to comment on his private life. However, although the story had purported to be something different – the exposure of a man seeking money in return for salacious allegations – the result had been the publication of speculative and highly intrusive allegations about his private life.

The newspaper contended that the complainant – whom they had contacted about the allegations – had offered an interview to the newspaper in which he would talk about his private life if the newspaper did not run the article. The newspaper thought that in these circumstances – where the complainant was willing to use private details as a bargaining counter – the Commission should not entertain the complaint. The newspaper said that it had not made any further enquiries about his personal life, and had not taken intrusive photographs. Readers would have understood the allegations to be false and that the thrust of the story related to the exposure of wrongdoing, not the complainant's private life. The complainant accepted that he had negotiated about a possible future interview, but this was only a tactic to seek to prevent publication. He claimed the offer had come from the newspaper, not from him, and he had instantly regretted it. He had no intention of talking about his private life.

ADJUDICATION

The Commission noted that one of the newspaper's defences was its duty in the public interest, protected by the Code, to expose wrongdoing. In this instance, it had been uncovering the attempts of an extortionist to obtain money in return for apparently salacious material about a high profile figure. The Commission recognises that it is a fundamental right of newspapers to expose crime or misdemeanour – and it will always protect that right. However, its task in this complaint was to discern whether the newspaper had been doing that, or whether the result of the article was in fact an unjustified intrusion into the complainant's privacy.

The Commission noted that there had been some possibility of an interview with the complainant. Given that no agreement had been reached on this, however, the key to the Commission's consideration was the substantive point of whether the newspaper could have exposed the way in which the attempted extortion had taken place without reporting a great deal of intrusive material about the complainant himself. The Commission believed that it would have been possible to do so. The fact that someone had approached the newspaper demanding money for intrusive material about a star of

Coronation Street was newsworthy in itself; there was no need to report on the substance of the allegations.

In this case, the newspaper repeated the allegations at length – resulting in an impression, whether or not the allegations were founded, about the alleged lifestyle of the complainant. This resulted in a breach of the Code in one of two ways. If the allegations peddled by the extortionist were unfounded, then the impression created by the article was misleading, breaching Clause 1 (Accuracy) of the Code. If there was substance to the allegations, then the amount of information provided intruded into the complainant's privacy in breach of Clause 3 (Privacy) of the Code, for which there was no justification. While the newspaper may have been acting to protect the public interest in good faith, this had been an error of judgement.

The complaint was upheld.

In the light of this case, the Commission wished to underline that newspapers should not seek to circumvent the privacy provisions of the Code by claiming to expose those who peddle stories about people in the public eye as a cover for publishing the gist of those stories, whether founded or not, in colourful detail which results in unjustified intrusion.

Report No. 45, January–March 1999
New Nation

COMPLAINT

The Rt. Hon. Eric Forth MP on behalf of his constituent Mrs Teresa Norris, Mrs P. A'Court, Mr and Mrs Knight and Mr and Mrs Dobson, complained that an article in New Nation on 14 September 1998 headlined 'Do you know where they live?' was in breach of Clause 3 (Privacy) and 4 (Harassment) of the Code of Practice.

The complaint was rejected.

The piece appeared in an opinion column in which the named columnist asked if readers knew the home addresses of the five men accused of murdering the black teenager Stephen Lawrence. The columnist suggested that there were many who would like to visit them and offer their suggestions as to how their media image, 'or indeed their facial features', may be enhanced.

The complainants are the parents of the five men. They objected that the columnist asked for information which would have identified their home addresses and, they believed, put them at risk. Although their addresses had been read out at the Inquest into Stephen Lawrence's death and at the Macpherson Inquiry, it was a different matter to advertise for them in a newspaper which would be read by more people than attended either the Inquest or the Inquiry. They denied that their sons had consulted a 'spin doctor'. They said the newspaper had gone on to publish their addresses in a subsequent article.

The newspaper said that the addresses were read out at the Inquest and the Inquiry and were therefore in the public domain. The reference to enhancing the men's image was a reaction to news that they had been to see a 'spin doctor' to improve their image.

The reference to enhancing their facial features was a tongue-in-cheek reference to what many people were suggesting at the time. None of their readers replied to the request as they all saw it for what it was a rhetorical piece typical of a controversial columnist.

ADJUDICATION

The Commission had to consider whether the article represented an unjustified intrusion into the complainants' privacy or whether the newspaper had sought, without justification, to obtain information through intimidation, harassment or persistent pursuit. The Commission also had regard to the spirit of Clause 10 (Innocent relatives and friends) – although clearly there was no breach of this clause as innocent members of the men's families were not named or otherwise identified in the piece.

Whilst the Commission accepts that newspapers generally have the right to publish individuals' addresses, it has in the past criticised a newspaper for publishing the details of a person's address in Wales in the context of a comment referring to how homes owned by English people in Wales have been burnt down (Blom-Cooper v Evening Standard, PCC Report 7). In reaching its decision on that occasion, the Commission took into account the newspaper's claim that the address was listed in easily available publications. The Commission nevertheless found the newspaper's behaviour in that case 'reckless'.

The complaint under consideration here is different in a number of ways from the earlier complaint. In this case, the Commission noted that the information about the complainant's addresses had been put firmly in the public domain by the Inquest into Stephen Lawrence's death and by the Macpherson Inquiry. The background to the complaint was a high profile case which had attracted a great amount of media attention, including reporting and comment. Many of the details of the case were widely known, including personal information about the five men accused of the murder. The Commission considered that the newspaper was entitled to publish the robust comment of the named columnist on a matter which was clearly in the public interest. It recognised that the case had provoked high emotions in many people and expects that, in cases such as this, editors will take care to consider the vulnerability of innocent family members. However, in view of the wide reporting of the case and the fact that the information about the complainant's addresses was already in the public domain, the Commission did not find that there was a breach of the Code.

Any complaint that the article may have been an incitement to racial hatred would be a matter for the police.

Report No. 45, January–March 1999
Daily Star

COMPLAINT

Messrs Eversheds, Solicitors of London EC4, complained on behalf of Sir Elton John that the taking and publication of photographs of guests relaxing in the privacy of his home in the South of France in the Daily Star on 4 June 1998 was a breach of privacy contrary to Clause 3 of the Code of Practice.

The complaint was upheld under Clause 3(i) of the Code because the pictures had been taken without consent in a way which intruded into the complainant's home life.

The solicitors for the complainant alleged that the photographs had been taken secretly, possibly from the top of a ladder placed against the wall of Sir Elton's property.

The newspaper said that the photographs had been offered to them by a picture agency who said they had been taken from a public footpath adjacent to Sir Elton's property. Before a decision to publish the photographs was taken a representative of one of the two people pictured was contacted on three occasions and gave her consent to publication.

The newspaper said that although it believed the people involved had given their consent to publication of the pictures involved, it realised that there was a separate complaint from Sir Elton relating to his own privacy. It apologised for any distress caused him.

ADJUDICATION

Clause 3(i) of the Code of Practice protects an individual's right to respect for his home life. In this case, the taking of photographs and their subsequent publication had intruded into the complainant's home life, and the privacy to which he and his guests were entitled. No consent was given and there was no public interest justification. The complaint was therefore upheld.

CHAPTER SEVENTEEN

Self-regulation into the twenty-first century, 2000–2001

'In my view, a central pillar of the freedom of the press is the system of self-regulation we have in this country . . . and I think the PCC is to be congratulated for this. Indeed, I would pause here to give praise to John Wakeham who as chairman of the PCC has demonstrated that self-regulation continues to be the best way of ensuring high editorial standards in this country. . . . In short, whatever the future of the news, this government will continue to see that it is produced by a plural and self-regulated press.'

Chris Smith MP, Secretary of State for Culture, Media and Sport, speech to Society of Editors, Cardiff, 17 October 2000

That the Press Complaints Commission had defended itself well was not in doubt. As it entered its tenth year in January 2000, even those who accused it of regulating badly conceded its talent to survive. Looking back to its origins, Naomi Marks quoted David Mellor's notorious quip about the Last Chance Saloon. 'Many drinks later', she observed in the *Independent,* 'it does seem that the PCC has succeeded in at least one respect: it has proved remarkably successful in staving off attempts to introduce privacy and other onerous legislation against the press.'[1] Possibly the Commission could take it as a back-handed compliment that Simon Jenkins now regarded it as 'dormant'.[2] After all, an ambition cherished by the PCC had always been that it would become so familiar an item of the comfortable furniture of public life that no one much outside the industry would ever have more than very occasional cause to notice it. Even when criticizing it as 'not terribly effective' in shielding public figures from press curiosity, Libby Purves admitted 'we're all voyeurs now' and that 'no one can find a satisfactory way to prevent it'.[3]

Still, the larger question remained: to what extent was the PCC's success in self-defence translatable into success for press self-regulation? What criteria are applicable to an essay in resolving that question? Robert Pinker, in a paper written apropos of requests from Hong Kong, Sri Lanka and Kenya for advice on setting up arrangements for press self-regulation – itself some testimony to the general repute of the PCC – outlined the 'institutional preconditions' which had to be met 'before a self-regulatory system can be established and made to work effectively'.

First of these was that publishers and editors must convince politicians that they mean business, and must be able to demonstrate that they possess the ability and goodwill required to make self-regulation work. They must agree to a voluntary code of practice and give it their unqualified support. Having written their own code they must make a public commitment to accept and abide by the decisions of the regulatory body established to administer it. Secondly, membership of the regulatory body must be determined through procedures of an appointments body independent both of government and of the newspaper industry. Membership of the regulatory body itself must also be manifestly independent both of government and the industry it is to regulate in its administration of the code. Thirdly, the industry must provide the necessary funding on pro rata terms that in no way infringe the independence of its regulatory body. Finally, to be effective, a system of press self-regulation must be as open and accessible to ordinary people as it is to public figures and celebrities. With this end in mind it must set up internal procedures for receiving complaints and dealing with them efficiently, fairly and swiftly. It will have to make itself as widely known as possible to the general public.[4]

The latter two of these criteria do not present serious difficulties. Funding and efficiency are not perceived as weaknesses in self-regulation's mechanism. Pressbof does not stint. Begging bowls are not sent around newspaper offices as in the days of the Press Council. The PCC machinery works smoothly. From May 2000 complaints officer Tim Toulmin was promoted to deputy director with responsibility to optimize efficient staff deployment and to expedite especially problematic high-profile cases. The rule now is to deal with most complaints in an average forty working days. In 1999 the PCC logged 4,500 telephone enquiries.

As to the first criterion, the Commission could, especially from 17 October, claim cogently that the politicians were thoroughly convinced of the industry's commitment to its regulatory body and its Code of Practice. For it was on that date, addressing the Society of Editors[5] at Cardiff, that the Culture secretary, Chris Smith, gave the most deliberate endorsement yet offered by government to the self-regulatory regime. 'In my view', he stated, 'a central pillar of the freedom of the press is the system of self-regulation we have in this country.' Over the years, he recalled, that system had 'endured a rocky ride'; and he was 'still asked on occasion why the government supports a voluntary press Code of Practice over statutory regulation'.

> In response, quite apart from not wanting to take any step down the road to censorship, I think it is important to make the point that many of the safeguards contained in the Code go beyond the remit of both civil and criminal law, and thus give complainants an additional avenue for pursuing remedies which is fairly rapid and free. Research shows that the great majority of those people who have needed to approach the Commission have been satisfied with the outcome and I think the PCC is to be congratulated on this. Indeed, I would pause here to give praise to John Wakeham who as chairman the PCC has demonstrated that self-regulation continues to be the best way of ensuring high editorial standards in this country.

This was not to say, Smith added, that self-regulation always worked per-fectly – 'it doesn't'. A free press must strive also to be a responsible press; and there had been occasions – Smith had in mind the Sophie Rhys-Jones topless photographs – of 'less than glorious editorial judgement'. But a free press, 'warts and all', remained an indispensable component of democracy. 'In short, whatever the future of the news, this government will continue to see that it is produced by a plural and self-regulated press.'[6] In his intro-duction to the Commission's *Annual Review, 2000* Wakeham was gratified to be able to quote the Conservative leader, William Hague, speaking at the same occasion and in very much the same approbationary terms.

The great point here was that these political chiefs are no longer speaking in the old customary ways of equivocation or polite blackmail about what hoops the PCC would have to jump through to make the future of self-regulation something better than merely provisional or probation-ary. The manumission promised in December 1998 is formally confirmed. The old Labour predilection for statutory controls is to all appearances a political fossil. Self-regulation has passed all its ordeals decreed by the politicians. To that extent it is safe.

But is it now safe from a more general doubt about its being truly independent from the press industry? Convincing politicians is one thing. After all, politicians themselves are notoriously known to cultivate the press and to be cultivated by the press. A wider general public might well feel itself excused from any obligation to take the claims of either the PCC or the politicians at face value. What criteria are applicable here? That the Appointments Commission is independent is not in doubt. (Currently it consists of Wakeham, Roche – the only industry figure, Lord Mayhew, former Attorney-General, David Clementi, deputy governor of the Bank of England, and Mary Francis, chief executive of the Association of British Insurers.) Does this in turn guarantee the independence of the Commission itself, with its lay majority in place after the recommendation of Calcutt 2? In this respect there will always be unavoidably a degree of doubt. Since it is most unlikely that any lay person would be appointed to the Commission who is not committed in principle to the essence of its purpose, the administration of the industry's self-regulatory Code, and since the industry, with seven editorial representatives on the Commission, is committed to the proposition that self-regulation is in its own best interest, it follows that there is an identity of interest between the PCC and the industry. It is a notorious fact that both directors of the PCC since 1992, first Mark Bolland and then Guy Black, are thick as thieves with the editorial and managerial notables of the industry. 'There is no doubt', as Naomi Marks observed, 'that Mr Black is popular – it is not uncommon for editors to ring him for pre-publication advice on stories they fear might infringe the code. And it is no doubt helpful to have a friend in the palace.'[7] This leads unavoidably to accusations that when it comes to the pinch, the PCC will not challenge or offend the industry which funds it. And it applies the other way round as well. To what extent are public tributes made by editors to the fearsomeness and effectiveness of the PCC discountable as self-interested ploys?

There is no sure answer to that question. The industry set up the PCC as an evil lesser than legislation. Legislation, it is arguable, would be contrary to the public interest. Does it not then follow that it is publicly beneficial that there be an identity of interest between the industry and its self-regulatory body, always providing that while the industry defines the terms and conditions of that interest in its Code, that Code in turn is both validated and administered by the self-regulatory body? It would not serve the public interest if the industry and its self-regulatory body were constantly at odds in the manner of criminals and police. The starting point of the whole arrangement, after all, is the generally accepted axiom that it is in the public interest that the press be free. A free press must persuade itself to be responsible. That is what the PCC does for it. It cannot be other than an intimately internal debate. The more intimate, it might well be argued, the better. Thus Black's expert cultivating of industry notables is arguably the most important thing a director of the PCC has to do. There is no more valuable service he could offer than to interpret informally for enquiring editors the industry's Code to the industry. And as a friend at the Palace he reciprocates the services provided for the PCC by editors who pay it, for whatever mixture of motives, praise and tribute.

2

Of the 2,233 complaints processed in 2000 – slightly fewer than in the previous year, but broadly in line with the recent average – the Commission adjudicated just 57, upholding 24 and rejecting 33. Setting aside the usual one third of total complaints as involving no prima facie breach of the Code or as being disallowed as third-party or unjustifiably delayed, the vast majority of valid complaints were resolved directly with the newspaper or magazine concerned.

Critics of the PCC's management of self-regulation point out that in no year has the number of adjudications upholding complaints exceeded the number of rejections.[8] A bumper year for rejections, for example, was 1996, with only 27 complaints upheld out of a total of 81 adjudications. The Commission's answer to this has been, in effect, to concentrate on resolution and cut back on adjudication. The high peak of adjudication was in 1993, with 244 instances.[9] By 1999 Wakeham proclaimed triumphantly that 'the Commission has had to adjudicate on only 49 complaints'. This was a sign, he insisted, 'not of the weakness of self-regulation – but its strength'.[10] The *Review, 2000* rejoiced that the slight rise to a mere 57 adjudications yet again demonstrated 'our skill in successfully conciliating so many complaints'.

Maximizing nice conciliation and minimizing nasty adjudication could, of course, be interpreted by persistent critics of self-regulation as evasion rather than resolution of the underlying problem of the PCC's independence. The 'hard', or 'landmark', issues involved in controversial cases tend not to be easily conciliated and tend accordingly to go all the way. Ultimately, given the identity of interest binding the press industry to its regulatory body, lay majority notwithstanding, there can be no resolution of the question in anything like absolute terms. It has to be a matter of empirical and pragmatic judgment founded on assessment of the evidence available. What does the evidence offered by the Commission's records of 2000 offer to such an unprejudiced assessment?

Issues relating to the reporting of children (Clauses 6 and 7 of the Code) showed an increase, from 3.5 per cent of total complaints in 1999 to 4.6 per cent. This was reflected in a substantive change in the Code as from

January, as well as in a series of quite tough protective responses from the PCC. The Code change directed editors to pay particular regard to the potentially vulnerable position of children who are victims of, or witnesses to, crime. Hinton's Committee stipulated this in Clause 10 which is retitled 'Reporting on crime'. A further minor change added to the public interest defence in Clause 7 (Children in sex cases). This corrects an anomaly in the Code which precluded identification of a child even when a judge ruled that identification would be in the public interest.

The Commission's protective responses arraigned three national newspapers. They were rebuked on complaints relating to reporting of children under 16 at private parties. As against this, in adjudications involving treatment of children of some public figures, the Commission laid down principles relating to what it held to be the key issue of whether coverage of a child, including the use of pictures, damages the welfare of that child. This question arose in the case of pictures of the eldest son of the Prime Minister and Mrs Blair at a party, and cases involving children of a pop star and the sister of a well-known fashion designer. 'The mere publication of a child's image', pronounced the Commission in its *Review, 2000*, 'unaccompanied by details of its private life, when he or she is in a public place could not be upheld . . . to breach the Code.' An assessment here might conclude that prominent complainants are often unreasonably sensitive.

In a matter of intrusion into grief or shock (Clause 5 of the Code) the Commission decisively upheld a complaint against the Glasgow *Sunday Mail* for intruding on the funeral of the mother of the television presenter Carol Smillie. The paper published photographs taken by a freelance after its own photographer had been asked to leave the private ceremony. The Commission stressed the point that the prominence given to the coverage compounded the fault of the intrusion. Adjudications by the Commission upholding complaints about discrimination relating to mental health and persons suffering from mental illness (Clause 13) prompted Wakeham, in a keynote speech in London on 15 February, to lay down general principles designed to raise standards of press reporting. The Commission's responsibility would be 'to tackle public fear and misunderstanding' by helping the press 'to get it right'.[11] A case of some moment in the matter of payments to criminals (Clause 16) came up with the *Sunday Times*'s deal to pay the convicted perjurer Jonathan Aitken £65,000 to serialize his memoirs. The point here was that the fee would go entirely to his trustee in bankruptcy. Apart from that, however, the Commission found that there was a public interest in the serialization; and that upholding the complaint and prohibiting publication would conflict with freedom of expression as enshrined both in the Code and in law. Complaints about inaccurate reporting (Clauses 1 and 2) are a declining proportion of the total, though still by far the largest component in the PCC's caseload. Of particular note in this category was a complaint by the Prince of Wales's office about a report in the *Sunday Times* purporting to cite sources with knowledge of the Prince's plans for a Scottish wedding to Camilla Parker Bowles. This was the first complaint made directly on the Prince's behalf. Investigation revealed that there was no foundation for the report. An agreed retraction and apology was published by the paper. And a case resulting in rejection of complaints against the *Sunday People* and the *Independent* for alleged harassment illustrated the point that more than a few complainants are bogus. 'It is not the role of the Commission to intervene in the legitimate pursuit of stories which may involve justifiable subterfuge. The Commission will not tolerate complainants seeking to abuse its powers in this way.'[12]

Issues of privacy (Clause 3), although in decline, remained the second largest (14 per cent) component of the complaints total. The year 2000 offered a varied assortment of cases. Granada Television's complaint against the *News of the World* on behalf of its *Coronation Street* star Jacqueline Pirie took on landmark status because the Commission clarified the question of the protection due to popular media figures such as Ms Pirie who are expected from time to time to put matters concerning their private lives into the public domain. Another substantive change made by Hinton's Code Committee had been to expand the public interest defence by making clear that the Commission will have regard to the extent to which material has become available to the public. Even so, the Commission found against the paper's contention that Ms Pirie 'had openly discussed her private life to such an extent that she was disentitled to the protection of the Code'.[13]* This was an instance when the paper bowed to the ruling and published the adjudication in full, but dissented from what Phil Hall, the *News of the World* editor, at first saw as implications inimical to freedom of expression.

Then the Blairs, already sensitive about unwanted press interest in baby Leo and in turmoil about their nanny's breach of trust in negotiating serialization of a book she had written about the family, retaliated by withdrawing co-operation with the usual press coverage of their Italian holiday. This was not matter for adjudication, but it did highlight the perennial issue of privacy for families of public figures and involved the PCC in lengthy

---

* See boxed adjudication, pp. 351–2.

communications with the Prime Minister's press secretary, who requested guidance. At Alastair Campbell's further request, Wakeham stepped into what was described as a 'corrosive atmosphere', calmed frayed nerves and restored peace between the media and Downing Street. The *Press Gazette* thought Wakeham would do both Downing Street and Fleet Street a good turn 'if he makes clear that PCC does not stand for Premier's Complaints Commission'.[14] It was announced that the PCC would attempt to set out some formal guidelines on future practice in reconciling the Blair family's legitimate right to privacy and legitimate public interest.[15]

It was, however, matters involving the privacy of the most conspicuous member of the royal family that most engaged the Commission's attention at this time. Prince William would be 18 on 21 June and would soon after leave Eton. Buckingham Palace was alert to the need to take steps to spare him the media harassment endured by his mother. The Queen was understood 'to have taken a close personal interest in redefining the rules governing media coverage'.[16] The PCC had also negotiated with St James's Palace on the kind of co-operation necessary on legitimate media interest and reasonable access to make a new dispensation work. Wakeham lunched at Highgrove with Prince William, telephoned him at Eton and discussed with him the draft of his forthcoming revised guidelines. After extensive consultation with editors Wakeham prepared another of his preemptive initiatives in a public statement planned for the 14th. There were disturbing signs of media expectations that the Prince would cease to be under what had proved over the last five years to be very effective self-regulatory protection and become 'fair game'. Wakeham also felt it would be expedient to make clear on the other hand that he did not think a 'no change' policy was either feasible or desirable. His plan was derailed by a squabble that erupted between St James's Palace and the *Daily Telegraph* over copyright of a set of birthday photographs of Prince William. The Prince of Wales was outraged. Guy Black at the PCC 'monitored the situation'. The general understanding had always been that all newspapers would be treated equally. A PCC source stated: 'The moment the marketplace becomes involved in Prince William, it will be impossible to protect his privacy.' A meeting was arranged at the Palace to sort things out.[17]

Wakeham meanwhile delayed his statement until 28 June to let the air clear. Then, at St Bride's Institute in Fleet Street, he laid down a revised doctrine on 'Prince William and Privacy'. His point was that as between the 'fair game' line and the 'no change' line realism dictated a middle way. 'He must *absolutely not* be "fair game" – but at the same time, *things will change*.

He *has* left school, he *is* growing up and has become a young adult, he *is* increasingly becoming a public figure – and the way the press covers him will reflect that.'

Wakeham identified the four areas which would need to be handled with a new kind of sensitivity: photographs, factual accuracy, privacy and physical intrusion. While Prince William would need to get used to being photographed in public places 'like any other young adult', the rules applying to harassment, persistent pursuit and snatched pictures taken in private places or where there was a 'reasonable expectation of privacy' still applied. On the question of accuracy Wakeham cited recent cases involving the PCC of bogus stories being run about family arguments and about the Prince's 'set' in relation to drugs and his alleged relationships with young women. Wakeham trusted further that editors would interpret their public interest claims with restraint. And he most decidedly laid it down that 'it would be quite unacceptable for paparazzi photographers to pursue Prince William around whichever university he attends – and quite unacceptable for newspapers to publish photographs which have been obtained in this manner'.[18]

Before the year was out the Commission adjudicated against *OK!* magazine for publishing in contravention of the new guidelines unauthorized photographs of Prince William during his ten-week expedition in Chile. The salient fact was that no other paper or media outlet used them. 'The PCC's ruling', reported Andrew Pierce for *The Times*, 'is the first of its kind about Prince William and will be regarded as a warning shot across the bows of the British press before the teenage Prince takes up his place at St Andrews University in Fife next year.' A St James's Palace source interpreted it as 'a landmark ruling. It was very important to set down as a marker for the future.'[19]

3

The *OK!* indiscretion, while no doubt irritating to the PCC, remained an isolated exotic incident and was not seen as ominous for a breakdown of the 'Prince William and Privacy' understanding with the industry. Since the press had got used to the kind of armistice Wakeham had brokered when William went to Eton, the modified extension of it in 2000 could fairly be assessed as an auspicious feature of its general record. It was a high-profile matter, but it was not unrepresentative of the Commission's more 'bread and butter' activities. Wakeham always stressed that the Prince was not getting privileged protection denied to others of his age. Just as Wakeham had exploited the 'Accrington schoolboy' case for the benefit of the Prince, so he exploited the Prince's case for the benefit of, so to speak, the Accrington classes. David Yelland of the *Sun* testified that 'the PCC's biggest achievement to date has been stemming the use of intrusive pictures by the paparazzi. "I can turn down pictures in the full knowledge that none of my competitors can use them either. The way the two Princes are pretty much left alone by the British press is an amazing achievement."'[20] This achievement, of course rubbed off on the rest of the Commission's record. Where the Commission proved to be vulnerable in 2000 was not as arbiter of any conventional issues of complaint against editors. It was the unconventional behaviour of editors themselves that exposed the PCC to damaging complaint.

The first of the two instances in point was the affair of Piers Morgan and the *Mirror*'s 'City Slickers' share tips. The second was the crusade launched by the new editor of the *News of the World*, Rebekah Wade, in the wake of the tragedy of a brutally murdered 8-year-old girl, to 'name and shame' the nation's paedophiles.

The Piers Morgan affair got under way early in the year. It was a question of a kind of apparent lucrative insider dealing by Morgan in buying shares promoted by his City tipsters the day before the tip was published on 18 January. Morgan had set up the 'City Slickers' column in 1998 to make City gossip as fascinating to his readers as showbiz and celebrity gossip.[21] A Department of Trade and Industry investigation was set in motion. The PCC, given Clause 14 of the Code of Practice prohibiting journalists from profiting directly or indirectly from their knowledge of financial dealings, was bound to take a keen interest in the affair. A complaint was duly lodged alleging share dealing contrary to the Code. Guy Black, it was announced, would handle the investigation and make recommendations to the Commission. This inquiry into the Morgan controversy would be the first relating to Clause 14 and, as *The Times* pointed out, the first 'to examine a national newspaper editor's personal actions'.

Morgan's employer, now Trinity Mirror, on advice from its own investigators and solicitors, accepted the editor's explanations of innocence. The PCC, meanwhile, expanded its investigation to take in the two journalists working on the 'City Slickers' column. David Yelland made a great splash in the *Sun* on the iniquities of 'Mirrorgate'. Heads rolled. The stockbroker concerned was sacked as well as the two tipsters. The DTI inquiry would take a long time. The Commission therefore, as the *Press Gazette* reported, 'is determined to press ahead with its ruling in an attempt not to look ineffective and weak and hiding behind a formal inquiry'.[22]

The Commission was due to consider the case at its regular meeting on 29 March. Guy Black estimated that it might take more than one meeting to get to the bottom of 'Mirrorgate'. A massive influx of written submissions then forced the Commission to postpone consideration until 10 May. 'One of the problems', observed Stephen Glover in the *Spectator*, 'is that the Commission has never had to consider allegations of this nature concerning an editor and prominent journalists. The danger is that its inclination will be to soft-pedal.' Glover was 'somewhat alarmed' to read that Morgan had recently lunched with one of the seven editors who sat on the Commission.[23]

The plot thickened in a way not beneficial to the PCC. Dominic Lawson's lunching, as David Lister commented for the *Independent*, could be discounted as a matter for alarm. ('"We are more worldly than that," said one PCC member. "We would be amazed if editors didn't chat and lunch from time to time."') But in 'Morgan, a suitable case for delay', Lister (unreasonably, but in line with impatient public indignation) asked: 'Why has the PCC failed to comment?' There was the consideration that were Morgan condemned by fellow editors on the Commission known to have cause to be revenged on him, he would have grounds to challenge the finding. '"It is a problem," says a PCC insider. The Commission will inevitably have to take legal advice. And, while lay members are in a majority on the Commission, it may end up having to remit the *Mirror* case to a smaller panel.' The PCC's investigation would, by virtue of its novelty, have lasting repercussions. 'It is proving a learning experience for all parties.'[24]

For the PCC it was not a pleasant learning experience. It came out with its adjudication on 10 May. The industry stood supportively to attention. The Commission did not soft-pedal. Roger Alton, editor of the *Observer*, sensed 'a sobering moment for the newspaper industry as a whole'. The 'nature of this ruling', he thought, 'is astounding. It will make newspaper editors redouble their efforts not to cross the PCC.'[25] Brian MacArthur in *The Times* judged it the harshest adjudication the PCC had issued on the conduct of any national newspaper editor since 1995. 'That editor was also Mr Morgan.' Morgan spread it dutifully over pages 6 and 7 of his 11 May issue. The Commission found that Morgan had not acted corruptly but was in gross breach of Clause 14 and had in multiple respects 'fallen short of the standards demanded by the Code'. His two City journalists had 'engaged in flagrant, multiple breaches of the code over a sustained period of time'. The Commission felt it must register its concern with the Trinity Mirror management. Wakeham announced: 'It was a clear climate of slack. It was all gay abandon. We consider Morgan breached the Code on several occasions and in a serious way.'[26]

The vulnerability of the PCC lay in the circumstance that the harshness of its adjudication echoed in a vacuum of inconsequence. Morgan's head did not roll. Trinity Mirror evidently valued his expertise and flair as an interest more compelling than the reputation of self-regulation. These were hard times for the 'redtop' tabloids. Circulations were down for them all; but under Morgan the *Mirror*'s decline was only half that of the *Sun*'s. As a consequence of the Commission's criticisms Trinity Mirror did require Morgan to apologize and banned any share dealings by its editors. Even so, invidious comment hastened on the scene. David Yelland's declaring at the *Sun* that he knew he would have been fired, as Rupert Murdoch put it on record, had he transgressed as Morgan transgressed, only drew attention all the more to Morgan's survival. 'The danger of the adjudication', Brian MacArthur commented, 'as one editor said yesterday, was that it would seem too restrained.'[27] The *Express* denounced the Trinity Mirror chairman: 'Damn you, Victor Blank. By failing to sack Morgan you have brought disgrace on a great and honourable calling.'[28] This sort of thing had the effect of invidiously suggesting a failure on the part of the PCC to get Morgan sacked. It was a disgrace, somehow, for self-regulation: 'ineffective and weak'. Few would have recalled Virginia Bottomley's raising in 1995 the question of the desirability of the PCC's having that weapon in its armoury.[29] It was never a possibility; but its absence nonetheless now yawned. Public censure, as the *Press Gazette* observed, was 'the limit of PCC power'. Not since McGregor's time had that limit looked so limited. The *Times*'s pocket cartoonist mocked the Commission with an image of guffawing Trinity Mirror executives: 'We take this matter very seriously, Piers – so it's off to bed and NO story.'[30]

More seriously, awkward questions were asked by a public puzzled at self-regulation's anti-climax. When Carlton TV was caught faking part of a documentary on a drugs raid it was fined £2 million. 'You lot may just as well be on a different planet', said television people. 'Press self-regulation is just a joke.'[31] For the PCC the most unpleasant aspect of its learning experience was the way the shock of this affair set loose questions which had remained unasked in 1995. Proto-Morgan was, after all, then arraigned jointly by both the PCC and his proprietor, whose employment he shortly after left. Now there was for many querulous onlookers the paradox of deutero-Morgan arraigned by the PCC to the great admiration of the industry but yet seemingly cherished by his publishers. Matt Wells in the *Guardian* led the new questioners. He remarked upon Roger Alton's applause for the PCC's censure as a 'defining moment': 'So why is it, then, that there is a gnawing feeling of dissatisfaction, a feeling that somehow what the PCC said was not quite strong enough, that Morgan had got away with a slap on the wrist, that there is something unsatisfactory about the whole business of self-regulation?'

Wells had another question: 'So why are newspapers so determined to be seen taking the PCC seriously?'[32] In this instance an answer was forthcoming. Peter Cole, former editor of the *Sunday Correspondent* and now professor of Journalism at the University of Sheffield, wrote:

> There is to a certain extent a sort of tacit conspiracy between the editors and the PCC. The PCC knows it is only there because things had come to such a pass before. The creation of the PCC was a strategic avoidance by the newspaper industry of privacy legislation at the point it came into being. It is in the interests of both parties to be seen to be taking it seriously.[33]

Thus did the deutero-Morgan scandal rip aside the veils of decorum which had thus far in the Wakeham era preserved the oracular dignity of the PCC from rude exposure.

More damage was soon on the way. As with the Morgan affair the PCC, exposed and vulnerable through no fault of its own, was made to look feeble. It was on 23 July that Rebekah Wade, Phil Hall's successor as editor of the *News of the World*, launched her campaign to identify and locate paedophiles. The inspiration ostensibly was the public outrage following the harrowing case of a murdered girl. There were precedents both in Britain and the USA.[34] Wade vowed to continue her crusade with further 'outings'. Vigilante hysteria ignited. Innocent people were assaulted. A paediatrician was allegedly menaced. The *Press Gazette* asked: bold, brave and brilliant? Or mad, bad and sad? Her motives seemed only too cynical and opportunistic: her job was to arrest her paper's sharp drop in circulation. The *Gazette* pointed out also that to fulfil her undertaking to expose all 110,000 convicted or known paedophiles Wade would need, at her launch rate, 43 years and 4,489 pages, not to mention the need to keep pace with current convictions. A storm of criticism denounced Wade for a 'cheap publicity stunt' in 'six stark pages of brutal mixed-up facts' (the *Guardian*), for being 'a nasty piece of work' with her 'rabble-rousing witch-hunt' (*Daily*

Telegraph), and for putting children more at risk by driving offenders underground away from official surveillance and therapy.

The Commission was put in a somewhat embarrassed position by this. Back in 1998 there had been talks with the Association of Chief Officers of Probation on the 'outing' question. PCC guidelines were proposed and then abandoned when the ACOP decided they might be more hindrance than help.[35] It would certainly have been advantageous in the circumstances of July 2000 had the PCC been able to flaunt such credentials of its far-sighted concern. As it was, the PCC became the target of indignant queries as to why it was supinely allowing a tabloid editor to get away with boosting circulation by the most shameless exploitation of human tragedy and mob hysteria. Simon Jenkins put the case for this public indignation. The *News of the World*, he allowed, was part of a great British tradition of press pluralism. Yet papers could go astray. 'They take huge liberties by intruding on privacy and frequently pervert justice and fair play. It was to regulate these liberties that the PCC was brought into being.' Earlier in 2000 the Commission declared apropos of a case concerning Ian Brady that its Code, together with the Human Rights Act, 'confers rights to privacy on everyone, no matter how horrendous their crimes'.

> This is surely an important statement of principle. The *News of the World*'s campaign appears to fly in the face of the PCC's own declaration and must be judged accordingly. The commission may dislike criticising newspapers which pay its bills, but sometimes it must find the courage to take a public stand. So, is the media right to 'name and shame' offenders who have completed their sentences, on the off-chance that they may reoffend? Yes or No? Has the PCC the guts to give an answer? Yes or No?[36]

Confronted in the dock of public opinion with such hectoring, all the Commission could plead was that, as with football jingoism or racial or sexual discrimination, the Code of Practice did not address itself to blanket categories of human behaviour. These have always been regarded as matters of taste and decency, not to be legislated for. Its rule was to attend to complaints made by complainants about specific breaches in the Code. Brady had been a complainant (more than once); any paedophile with a complaint against the *News of the World* would get the same consideration as the Moors murderer. (The Commission as it happened did resolve several complaints by people concerned.) It was decided to revive the discussions broken off in 1998 with the probation officers with a view to drawing up guidelines for press treatment in future. The PCC's response otherwise to the *News of the World* paedophiles adventure was quiet diplomacy behind the scenes by Guy Black and Les Hinton to help Wade stop digging her hole. Jenkins's questions look pertinent but they are null.

But still they bear an enormous weight of public assent. They carry with them, furthermore, a huge baggage of hostile attitudes to the PCC much more broadly spread than merely those provoked by the paedophile controversy. Again, Jenkins articulated this hostility well, spiced with a taking touch of invective. He wrote on 26 July:

> Today a meeting takes place of that august defender of media ethics, the Press Complaints Commission. It is a somnolent body. Its chairman, Lord Wakeham, is known in the corridors of power not as Wakeham but as Let-'em-sleep. Since his appointment five years ago, his profile has been assiduously low. He emerges sometimes, but only to defend the privacy of Britain's royal families, the Windsors and the Blairs. Payments to criminals by newspapers continue. The *Mirror*'s share-tipping scandal goes unpunished. I can recall no *obiter dicta* from Lord Wakeham on media ethics. For such light-touch regulation, this part-time chairman has just won himself a 60 per cent pay rise, from £98,000 to £155,000. His bosses, believe it or not, are the newspapers themselves, who also sit on his commission. How cosy.[37]

This is rich, coming from one who, as a member of Calcutt's Committee, recommended in 1990 the setting up of the PCC with an industry majority. The industry pays Wakeham what it thinks he is worth, just as it does Jenkins. However, leaving that aside, Jenkins's polemic represents faithfully a wide segment of public opinion that will never be satisfied with a press self-regulatory regime without powers to punish (as with the *Mirror* share tipping scandal) or to suppress (as with the *News of the World* paedophile campaign). The industry will never voluntarily pay for such a self-regulatory regime; and any alternative will have to be some arrangement of statutory imposition, which the politicians have made clear they are unwilling to undertake. The result is a comprehensive impasse. Logic is defied, but the system works. It is within the protective embrace of that impasse, like a hugely plump duvet, that the PCC survives all hazards, confounds all critics, and lives.

4

Looking back over the Commission's ten-year history, such an impasse undoubtedly represents a result the industry would have been early and is lately happy to settle for. Wakeham made that point in his introduction to the 1999 *Review*: 'There is no greater crime in public life than resting on laurels. In issues relating to self-regulation and press freedom, I am a firm believer that there is no such thing as final victory.' It is fair to conclude at the same time that the PCC, with all its scars of battles lost as well as won, has good claim to laurels. If there is no such thing as final victory, there is still victory. When he took on the chairmanship of the PCC in 1995, Wakeham declared that his aim was to ensure that the issue of the press industry's self-regulation would be placed beyond the bounds of political debate, and that the Commission and the Code would become part of the furniture of British democracy. 'Of course there will be ups and downs in the future', he cautioned in his introduction to the 2000 *Review*, 'but I am convinced we have achieved that aim. There are no serious commentators now who believe that statutory controls are either desirable or practical – and the Human Rights Act 1998, with its emphasis on freedom of expression, means that it would in any case be almost impossible to introduce such a system.'

In two important areas the PCC can cite independent testimonies to its achieving repute and stature in accordance with its claims to have settled in as part of the accepted furniture of public life. The first is in the calls on it to expand provision of educational expertise, especially in programmes in colleges and in the industry for training journalists. This is a sphere which Robert Pinker has very much made his own. But Pinker is involved also in a newly developing international sphere. His 'Experiences in Persuading Governments of the Benefits of Self-Regulation' of October 2000, relating to Hong Kong, Sri Lanka and Kenya, has already been cited. The PCC has begun working closely with the Commonwealth Press Union as member states have started looking seriously at the self-regulatory option. Australia and New Zealand are also participating, along with the UK, in helping in this area.

Here too Wakeham is emerging as a major figure. 'Although our detractors may not care to know this', he was gratified to announce in the 1999 *Review*, 'the system of effective self-regulation we have built up in this country is a great British export success: the structures of the PCC and the Code Committee are being taken up and adapted the world over – from Bosnia to Sri Lanka – because people can see that they work even in the most competitive newspaper environment in the entire world'. Imitation is the sincerest form of flattery, Wakeham was able to remark in 2000 on taking on responsibility as the first chairman of the newly established

Bosnian Press Council, founded by Bosnian press publishers with the close involvement of PCC staff and assistance from the UN Independent Media Commission in Bosnia. The publishers wanted a chairman of international repute with a record of self-regulatory success.

Demands on the PCC to support such self-regulatory initiatives throughout the world are now a substantial item in the Commission's workload. Help has come from the establishment of the Alliance of Independent Press Councils of Europe. This was a project in which the PCC was much in the vanguard. This was partly because of shared benefits in exchanging information across Europe but partly also with a strategy in view to set up a body with clout to counterbalance the World Association of Press Councils. This initially innocent organization had been taken over by interests pressing for 'some form of a global code of ethics, and a cross-border complaints authority to police it'.[38] Potential dangers in this kind of idea were identified by the PCC in 1996. It was reminiscent of former Unesco plans for a new authoritarian world information order, the sabotaging of which was one of McGregor's finest hours. In Istanbul early in 1998 it was first introduced at a World Association of Press Councils gathering. At a conference of Commonwealth Press Union members later in 1998 in Kuala Lumpur Wakeham forcefully deprecated any notion of a world code of ethics for journalists and any international organ to deal with transnational complaints.[39] This was by way of preparing to put his message across even more forcefully at the World Association of Press Councils in Brisbane in 1999. In the PCC *Review* for that year Wakeham praised the AIPCE for proving 'extremely effective in helping to see off the dangerous plans' of the WAPC. The Egyptian government in particular displayed disturbing keenness in promoting these plans. In March 2000 the PCC formally withdrew from the WAPC, followed by the Australian Press Council. This left the WAPC as a group of state-run press bodies without a European presence. Plans for a global code are currently shelved.

Representatives of some twenty press councils hosted by the German Press Council met in Bonn in 2000 for the second annual conference of the AIPCE. Here, as Wakeham outlined at the biennial meeting of the CPU in Barbados in November 2000, the Alliance consolidated its position as a bastion of self-regulation and press freedom.[40] Ironically, however, it was Europe that confronted the PCC with the signal instance in 2000 of its role in defence of press freedom. It was put to Wakeham that the European Union Commission in Brussels was 'exasperated' by the Commission's refusal to condemn 'paranoid' British newspapers for 'unfair' reporting of EU matters. Here were reminiscences of the *Assises européens de la presse* and the dirigiste plans for replenishing 'national authorities ruling the press' with 'specifically European norms' stemming from Luxembourg and Brussels which had exercised McGregor in 1991.[41] Wakeham had to explain that the PCC was not a national authority ruling the press and that it neither had, nor wished to have, any powers to force newspapers to be 'fair' or to censor opinion and comment. 'We are here to deal with inaccuracy, and I have invited the European Commission to complain to us where they think the Code has been breached and they cannot get satisfaction from a newspaper direct.'[42]

5

In January 1997, looking towards 2000, Wakeham disclosed his ambition to achieve 'true self-regulation', which he interpreted as internal self-regulation by individual newspapers and magazines. The Commission would become an inspectorate rather than an arbitration service.[43] Little or nothing of that high ambition seems to have survived in the following four years. As press self-regulation in the UK under the PCC moves towards its tenth anniversary and into the twenty-first century, the vision is less splendid. But the confidence remains still secure. What Wakeham did assert in January 2001 was that the PCC, with the absolute commitment of editors themselves, and their publishers, had in ten years 'changed the entire culture of British newspapers and magazines'.

> Ten years ago, I doubt if there were very many editors who stopped to ask themselves 'can we get away with it?' – because they knew they could. Today, the application and observance of the Code are part of the culture of every news room and every editorial office. On the central issue of privacy – an area where the PCC and the Code have made huge advances over the last ten years – I am certain that the first question any editor asks of him or herself is: 'Can I justify this if challenged?' And if they can't they won't publish. That is the central achievement of genuine self-regulation – and one which, in my view, the law could never have delivered. Controls imposed on editors from outside are there to be battered down; controls imposed on editors by themselves are observed in letter and spirit.

The other side of that 'central achievement' in cultural turnaround was the corresponding turnaround of the politicians. That was the concluding, and in its way the conclusive, point made by Wakeham in his introduction to the *Annual Review, 2000*. 'There is much still to do: the battles to raise standards and to maintain press freedom are unremitting. But if further progress reports in the years ahead can chart as many successes as this one – and continue to demonstrate that our house is in order – then I for one shall be very content.'

Report No. 49, January–March 2000
News of the World

COMPLAINT
Granada Television complained on behalf of Ms Jacqueline Pirie that an article head-lined 'Street star's 8-month marathon of lust' published in the News of the World on 23 January 2000 invaded her privacy in breach of Clause 3 (Privacy) of the Code of Practice.

The complaint was upheld.

Ms Pirie is an actress in *Coronation Street* and the article was about her relationship with her former fiancé, who was extensively quoted in the piece.

The complainants said that the article was highly salacious and without any shred of public interest. Material contained in the article was of the most personal nature and although the man's right to tell his story was not called into question, the newspaper had not balanced this with Ms Pirie's own right to respect for her private life to which she was entitled under the Code. The complainants asked the Commission to bear in mind two further factors – firstly that Ms Pirie herself was not given the opportunity to comment on the article before publication and secondly that she had not sought pub-licity for herself during her long television career.

The newspaper did not seek to argue that the article was in the public interest but rather that there was a sufficient volume of material about Ms Pirie in the public domain to justify further articles about her private life. It contended that she had actively sought publicity for herself and it sent the Commission several articles which it said showed her willingness to talk about her private life. One of these, for which she had been paid, had been with the News of the World itself. Another article had also been supplied by a former boyfriend and the private material in that article had not been the subject of a complaint. The newspaper suggested that she could not complain selectively.

The complainants thought that it would be untenable for the Commission to hold that Ms Pirie had forfeited all rights to respect for her private life on the basis that she had not complained about one article and had felt obliged to co-operate with another. None of this justified the serious intrusion into her private life contained in the news-paper's most recent article.

ADJUDICATION

The Commission noted that the newspaper had neither sought to justify the article in the public interest or on the grounds of consent, nor denied that the article was intrusive. Its case appeared to rest on two contentions – that Ms Pirie's former fiance was entitled to discuss their relationship publicly and in intimate detail and that Ms Pirie had openly discussed her private life to such an extent that she was disentitled to the protection of the Code.

The Commission, in considering this case, had two fundamental principles to bear in mind. First, the Commission has previously made clear that even when individuals do put matters concerning their private lives into the public domain – as public figures such as Ms Pirie are expected to do from time to time – the press cannot reasonably justify thereafter publishing articles on any subject concerning them. In reviewing the cuttings of interviews with Ms Pirie submitted by the newspaper the Commission could not find any examples of her discussing voluntarily such deeply personal matters as were contained in the newspaper's article. It did not consider that any of them demonstrated a collaboration with the press to publish very intimate material about her private life that forfeited her right to respect for privacy under the Code.

Second, the Commission must also have regard to freedom of expression and the public's right to be informed of matters of public interest. This may include cases where one side in an otherwise private relationship between two parties gives an account of that relationship. In such cases the Commission must consider whether one party's right to freedom of expression – something the Commission generally supports – outweighs the other's right to respect for privacy under the Code.

In seeking to balance these two factors, the Commission considered the extent to which the material was in the public domain. It noted that Ms Pirie had been happy to inform the public about the fact of her relationship with her former fiancé. It would not therefore have been unreasonable for him to have spoken publicly about his relationship with her. However, the Commission has already noted that the complainant had not volunteered the sort of highly personal information that was revealed in the article. Aside from the publication of general details about her previous relationships there was also little in previous articles about the detail of her private life. The newspaper had pointed to the fact that an article in another newspaper by a former boyfriend had been published without complaint. The Commission regretted that Ms Pirie had not complained about the article at the time and would urge individuals to complain to the Commission if they think that an article has invaded their privacy. However, it did not consider that Ms Pirie's failure for whatever reason to complain about this one article implied general consent for further intrusion.

The Commission was concerned about the absence of any proportionality between the subject matter of the article – which was extremely personal and devoid of any public interest – and the material that was already in the public domain about the relationship. In balancing privacy and freedom of expression the newspaper had – on this occasion – made the wrong decision. Ms Pirie deserved her right to privacy on such personal matters and nothing she had done had disentitled her to this.

APPENDIX

Codes of Practice, 1990 and 1999

CODE OF PRACTICE, DECEMBER 1990

The Press Complaints Commission are charged with enforcing the following Code of Practice which was framed by the newspaper and periodical industry.

All members of the Press have a duty to maintain the highest professional and ethical standards. In doing so, they should have regard to the provisions of this Code of Practice and to safeguarding the public's right to know.

Editors are responsible for the actions of journalists employed by their publications. They should also satisfy themselves as far as possible that material accepted from non-staff members was obtained in accordance with this Code.

While recognising that this involves a substantial element of self-restraint by editors and journalists, it is designed to be acceptable in the context of a system of self-regulation. The Code applies in the spirit as well as in the letter.

1. *Accuracy*
   (i) Newspapers and periodicals should take care not to publish inaccurate, misleading or distorted material.
   (ii) Whenever it is recognised that a significant inaccuracy, misleading statement or distorted report has been published, it should be corrected promptly and with due prominence.
   (iii) An apology should be published whenever appropriate.
   (iv) A newspaper or periodical should always report fairly and accurately the outcome of an action for defamation to which it has been a party.

2. *Opportunity to reply*
   A fair opportunity for reply to inaccuracies should be given to individuals or organisations when reasonably called for.

3. *Comment, conjecture and fact*
   Newspapers, while free to be partisan, should distinguish clearly between comment, conjecture and fact.

4. Privacy

Intrusions and enquiries into an individual's private life without his or her consent are not generally acceptable and publication can only be justified when in the public interest. This would include:

(i) Detecting or exposing crime or serious misdemeanour.

(ii) Detecting or exposing seriously anti-social conduct.

(iii) Protecting public health and safety.

(iv) Preventing the public from being misled by some statement or action of that individual.

5. Hospitals

(i) Journalists or photographers making enquiries at hospitals or similar institutions should identify themselves to a responsible official and obtain permission before entering non-public areas.

(ii) The restrictions on intruding into privacy are particularly relevant to enquiries about individuals in hospital or similar institutions.

6. Misrepresentation

(i) Journalists should not generally obtain or seek to obtain information or pictures through misrepresentation or subterfuge.

(ii) Unless in the public interest, documents or photographs should be removed only with the express consent of the owner.

(iii) Subterfuge can be justified only in the public interest and only when material cannot be obtained by any other means.

In all these clauses the public interest includes:

(a) Detecting or exposing crime or serious misdemeanour.

(b) Detecting or exposing anti-social conduct.

(c) Protecting public health or safety.

(d) Preventing the public being misled by some statement or action of an individual or organisation.

7. Harassment

(i) Journalists should neither obtain information nor pictures through intimidation or harassment.

(ii) Unless their enquiries are in the public interest, journalists should not photograph individuals on private property without their consent; should not persist in telephoning or questioning individuals after having been asked to desist; should not remain on their property after having been asked to leave and should not follow them.

The public interest would include:

(a) Detecting or exposing crime or serious misdemeanour.

(b) Detecting or exposing anti-social conduct.

(c) Protecting public health and safety.

(d) Preventing the public from being misled by some statement or action of that individual or organisation.

8. Payment for articles

(i) Payments or offers of payment for stories, pictures or information should not be made to witnesses or potential witnesses in current criminal proceedings or to people engaged in crime or to their associates except where the material concerned ought to be published in the public interest and the payment is necessary for this to be done.

The public interest will include:

(a) Detecting or exposing crime or serious misdemeanour.

(b) Detecting or exposing anti-social conduct.

(c) Protecting public health and safety.

(d) Preventing the public from being misled by some statement or action of that individual or organisation.

(ii) 'Associates' include family, friends, neighbours and colleagues.

(ii) Payments should not be made either directly or indirectly through agents.

9. *Intrusion into grief or shock*

In cases involving personal grief or shock, enquiries should be carried out and approaches made with sympathy and discretion.

10. *Innocent relatives and friends*

The Press should generally avoid identifying relatives or friends of persons convicted or accused of crime unless the reference to them is necessary for the full fair and accurate reporting of the crime or legal proceedings.

11. *Interviewing or photographing children*

(i) Journalists should not normally interview or photograph children under the age of 16 on subjects involving the personal welfare of the child, in the absence of or without the consent of a parent or other adult who is responsible for the children.

(ii) Children should not be approached or photographed while at school without the permission of the school authorities.

12. *Children in sex cases*

The Press should not, even where the law does not prohibit it, identify children under the age of 16 who are involved in cases concerning sexual offences, whether as victims, or as witnesses or defendants.

13. *Victims of crime*

The Press should not identify victims of sexual assault or publish material likely to contribute to such identification unless, by law, they are free to do so.

14. *Discrimination*

(i) The Press should avoid prejudicial or prejorative reference to a person's race, colour, religion, sex or sexual orientation or to any physical or mental illness or handicap.

(ii) It should avoid publishing details of a person's race, colour, religion, sex or sexual orientation, unless these are directly relevant to the story.

15. *Financial journalism*

(i) Even where the law does not prohibit it, journalists should not use for their own profit financial information they receive in advance of its general publication, nor should they pass such information to others.

(ii) They should not write about shares or securities in whose performance they know that they or their close families have a significant financial interest, without disclosing the interest to the editor or financial editor.

(iii) They should not buy or sell, either directly or through nominees or agents, shares or securities about which they have written recently or about which they intend to write in the near future.

16. Confidential sources

Journalists have a moral obligation to protect conWdential sources of information.

CODE OF PRACTICE, DECEMBER 1999

This is the newspaper and magazine industry's Code of Practice. It is written and revised by the Editors' Code Committee made up of independent editors of national, regional and local newspapers and magazines. It is ratified by the Press Complaints Commission which has a majority of lay members who use the Code to adjudicate complaints.

*The Code was revised in December 1999. Items marked * are covered by the exceptions relating to the public interest.*

All members of the press have a duty to maintain the highest professional and ethical standards. This Code sets the benchmarks for those standards. It both protects the rights of the individual and upholds the public's right to know.

The Code is the cornerstone of the system of self-regulation to which the industry has made a binding commitment. Editors and publishers must ensure that the Code is observed rigorously not only by their staff but also by anyone who contributes to their publications.

It is essential to the workings of an agreed code that it be honoured not only to the letter but in the full spirit. The Code should not be interpreted so narrowly as to compromise its commitment to respect the rights of the individual, nor so broadly that it prevents publication in the public interest.

It is the responsibility of editors to co-operate with the PCC as swiftly as possible in the resolution of complaints.

Any publication which is criticised by the PCC under one of the following clauses must print the adjudication which follows in full and with due prominence.

1. Accuracy

(i) Newspapers and periodicals must take care not to publish inaccurate, misleading or distorted material including pictures.

(ii) Whenever it is recognised that a significant inaccuracy, misleading statement or distorted report has been published, it should be corrected promptly and with due prominence.

(iii) An apology should be published whenever appropriate.

(iv) A newspaper or periodical must report fairly and accurately the outcome of an action for defamation to which it has been a party.

2. Opportunity to reply

A fair opportunity for reply to inaccuracies must be given to individuals or organisations when reasonably called for.

3. Privacy

(i) Everyone is entitled to respect for his or her private and family life, home, health and correspondence. A publication will be expected to justify intrusions into any individual's private life without consent.

(ii) The use of long lens photography to take pictures of people in private places without their consent is unacceptable.

Note: Private places are public or private property where there is a reasonable expectation of privacy.

4. *Harassment*

(i) Journalists and photographers must neither obtain information or pictures through intimidation, harassment or persistent pursuit.

(ii) They must not photograph individuals in private places (as defined in the note to Clause 3) without their consent; must not persist in telephoning, questioning, pursuing, or photographing individuals after having been asked to desist; must not remain on their property after having been asked to leave and must not follow them.

(iii) Editors must ensure that those working for them comply with these requirements and must not publish material from other sources which does not meet these requirements.

5. *Intrusion into grief or shock*

In cases involving grief or shock, enquiries must be carried out and approaches made with sympathy and discretion. Publication must be handled sensitively at such times, but this should not be interpreted as restricting the right to report judicial proceedings.

6. *Children*

(i) Young people should be free to complete their time at school without unnecessary intrusion.

(ii) Journalists must not interview or photograph children under the age of 16 on subjects involving the welfare of the child or of any other child, in the absence of or without the consent of a parent or other adult who is responsible for the children.

(iii) Pupils must not be approached or photographed while at school without the permission of the school authorities.

(iv) There must by no payment to minors for material involving the welfare of children nor payment to parents or guardians for material about their children or wards unless it is demonstrably in the child's interest.

(v) Where material about the private life of a child is published, there must be justification for publication other than the fame, notoriety or position of his or her parents or guardian.

7. *Children in sex cases*

(i) The press must not, even where the law does not prohibit it, identify children under the age of 16 who are involved in cases concerning sexual offences, whether as victims or as witnesses.

(ii) In any press report of a case involving a sexual offence against a child –

(a) The child must not be identified.

(b) The adult may be identified.

(c) The word 'incest' must not be used where a child victim might be identified.

(d) Care must be taken that nothing in the report implies the relationship between the accused and the child.

8. *Listening devices*

Jounalists must not obtain or publish material obtained by using clandestine listening devices or by intercepting private telephone conversations.

9. *Hospitals*

(i) Journalists or photographers making enquiries at hospitals or similar institutions must identify themselves to a respinsible executive and obtain permission before entering non-public areas.

(ii) The restrictions on intruding into privacy are particularly relevant to enquiries about individuals in hospitals or similar institutions.

10. *Reporting on crime*

(i) The press must avoid identifying relatives or friends of persons convicted or accused of crime without their consent.

(ii) Particular regard should be paid to the potentially vulnerable position of children who are witnesses to, or victims of, crime. This should not be interpreted as restricting the right to report judicial proceedings.

11. *Misrepresentation*

(i) Journalists must not generally obtain or seek to obtain information or pictures through misrepresentation or subterfuge.

(ii) Documents or photographs should be removed only with the consent of the owner.

(iii) Subterfuge can be justified only in the public interest and only when material cannot be obtained by any other means.

12. *Victims of sexual assault*

The press must not identify victims of sexual assault or publish material likely to contribute to such identification unless there is adequate justification and, by law, they are free to do so.

13. *Discrimination*

(i) The press must avoid prejudicial or pejorative reference to a person's race, colour, religion, sex or sexual orientation or to any physical or mental illness or disability.

(ii) It must avoid publishing details of a person's race, colour, religion, sexual orientation, physical or mental illness or disability unless there are directly relevant to the story.

14. *Financial journalism*

(i) Even where the law does not prohibit it, journalists must not use for their own profit financial information they receive in advance of its general publication, nor should they pass such information to others.

(ii) They must not write about shares or securities in whose performance they know that they or their close families have a significant financial interest, without disclosing the interest to the editor or financial editor.

(iii) They must not buy or sell, either directly or through nominees or agents, shares or securities about which they have written recently or about which they intend to write in the near future.

15. *Confidential sources*

Journalists have a moral obligation to protect confidential sources of information.

16. *Payment for articles*

   (i) Payment or offers of payment for stories or information must not be made directly or through agents to witnesses or potential witnesses in current criminal proceedings except where the material concerned ought to be published in the public interest and there is an overriding need to make or promise to make a payment for this to be done. Journalists must take every possible step to ensure that no financial dealings have influence on the evidence that those witnesses may give. (An editor authorising such a payment must be prepared to demonstrate that there is a legitimate public interest at stake involving matters that the public has a right to know. The payment or, where accepted, the offer of payment to any witness who is actually cited to give evidence must be disclosed to the prosecution and the defence and the witness should be advised of this.)

   (ii) Payment or offers of payment for stories, pictures or information, must not be made directly or through agents to convicted or confessed criminals or to their associates – who may include family, friends and colleagues – except where the material concerned ought to be published in the public interest and payment is necessary for this to be done.

THE PUBLIC INTEREST

There may be exceptions to the clauses marked * where they can be demonstrated to be in the public interest.

   1. The public interest includes:
   (i) Detecting or exposing crime or a serious misdemeanour.
   (ii) Protecting public health and safety.
   (iii) Preventing the public from being misled by some statement or action of an individual or organisation.

   2. In any case where the public interest is invoked, the Press Complaints Commission will require a full explanation by the editor demonstrating how the public interest was served.

   3. There is a public interest in freedom of expression itself. The Commission will therefore have regard to the extent to which material has, or is about to, become available to the public.

   4. In cases involving children editors must demonstrate an exceptional public interest to override the normally paramount interests of the child.

NOTES

PROLOGUE

1. *The Press and the People: the First Annual Report of the General Council of the Press, 1954* (1954), p. 16.
2. See below, p. 120.
3. See below, p. 286.
4. G. Robertson, *The People against the Press: an Enquiry into the Press Council* (1983), p. 3.
5. PCC Paper No. 39, 29 January 1992, Minutes and Agenda File, 1992. PCC, Chatham/217.
6. R. Snoddy, *The Good, the Bad and the Unacceptable: the Hard News about the British Press* (1992), pp. 168–88.
7. A. Jones, *Powers of the Press: Newspapers, Power and the Public in Nineteenth-century England* (1996), p. 130.
8. A. J. Lee, *The Origins of the Popular Press in England, 1885–1914* (1976), p. 15.
9. D. Griffiths (ed.), *The Encyclopedia of the British Press, 1422–1992* (1992), p. 471. Rothermere, Northcliffe's younger brother, took over control of Associated Newspapers, including the *Daily Mail.* The Canadian adventurer Max Aitken, Lord Beaverbrook, took over control of the *Daily Express* in 1917.
10. G. Murray, *The Press and the Public: the Story of the British Press Council* (1972), pp. 19–20.
11. *Royal Commission on the Press, 1947–1949, Report* (1949), pp. 177, 165, 77.
12. Snoddy, *Good, Bad and Unacceptable*, p. 77.

INTRODUCTION

1. *The Press and the People: the First Annual Report of the General Council of the Press, 1954*, p. 3.
2. I. McDonald, *The History of The Times, V, Struggles in War and Peace, 1939–1966* (1984), p. 198.
3. C. Harmsworth King was chairman of the Mirror Group. Roy Thomson, Canadian media magnate, bought *The Times* in 1967; Lord Thomson of Fleet. Esmond Harmsworth, 2nd Viscount Rothermere.
4. C. Seymour-Ure, *British Press and Broadcasting since 1945* (1991), p. 236. In 1990, its last year, the Council received 1,588 new complaints. Of these 128 went to adjudication, with 85 being upheld. The Press Complaints Commission currently processes around 3,000 complaints annually. The PCC conciliates a greater proportion and adjudicates a lesser proportion than did the PC.
5. e.g. H. Phillip Levy, *The Press Council: History, Procedure and Cases* (1967).
6. Murray, *The Press and the Public*, p. 219–20.

7. *The Press and the People: the 37th Annual Report of the Press Council, 1990* (1991), p. 12.

8. PD, Lords 506, 26 April 1989, c. 303.

9. H. Evans, *Good Times, Bad Times* (1983), p. 159.

10. L. Blom-Cooper, Epitaph: Critique of Calcutt. A Personal View, in *The Press and the People: the 37th Annual Report of the Press Council, 1990*, p. 11.

11. *Royal Commission on the Press, Final Report, July 1977*, pp. 196–215.

12. Robertson, *People against the Press*, p. 4.

13. J. Curran (ed.), *The British Press: a Manifesto* (1978).

14. A. Smith (ed.), *Newspapers and Democracy: International Essays on a Changing Medium* (1980).

15. Robertson, *People against the Press*, p. 151.

16. Ibid., p. 2.

17. H. Porter, *Lies, Damned Lies and Some Exclusives* (1984), quoted by Snoddy, in *Good, Bad and Unacceptable*, p. 193.

18. *The Press and the People: the 34th Annual Report of the Press Council, 1987* (1988), p. 8.

19. Director of the Press Council 1980–90. Director of the Press Complaints Commission 1991–2. General Secretary NUJ 1970–7.

20. *The Press and the People, 1987*, p. 10.

21. Blom-Cooper, Epitaph, p. 13.

22. O. R. McGregor, *Press Councils – Statutory and Voluntary* (International Press Institute, 1987) p. 13.

23. In due course Thomson (not to be confused with Lord Thomson of Fleet) would extol McGregor for having chosen 'a good model' for the PCC in the ASA. PD, Lords 538, 1 July 1992, c. 789.

24. *Times*, 13 October 1990, p. 5.

25. Conversation with the author.

26. Conversation with the author.

27. Information from Sir Louis Blom-Cooper.

28. PD, Lords 506, 26 April 1989, cc. 1274–7.

29. PD, Commons 156, 5 July 1989, c. 195.

30. M. Leapman, *Treacherous Estate: the Press after Fleet Street* (1992), p. 203.

31. McGregor to Rogers, 7 November 1989. McGregor Papers (copy).

32. *Times*, 22 December 1989, p. 5.

CHAPTER 1

1. *Times*, 19 March 1990, p. 25.

2. Ibid., 5 February 1990, p. 2.

3. Conversation with the author.

4. M. Killik, *The Sultan of Sleaze: the Story of David Sullivan's Sex and Media Empire* (1994), p. 87: 'Bollocks to the Press Council.'

5. *Press Gazette*, 14 May 1990, p. 4.

6. *Guardian*, 14 May 1990, p. 4.

7. W. Shawcross, *Rupert Murdoch, Ringmaster of the Information Circus* (1992), p. 494.

8. A. Neil, *Full Disclosure* (1996), pp. 27, 190, 355.

9. Members of the BCC were government appointees.

10. *Report of the Committee on Privacy and Related Matters* (Cm. 1102), 16 May 1990, HMSO, pp. 77, 79.

11. PD, Commons 174, 21 June 1990, cc. 1125–8.
12. *Times*, 27 June 1990, p. 16.
13. *Times*, 22 June 1990, p. 6; 30 June, p. 7; *Guardian*, 22 June, p. 7; *Telegraph*, 22 June, p. 7.
14. *Press Gazette*, 25 June 1990, p. 7.
15. *The Press and the Public: 36th Annual Report of the Press Council, 1989* (1990), p. 307.
16. *Telegraph*, 22 June 1990, p. 7.
17. *Guardian*, 22 June 1990, p. 2.
18. *Times*, 22 June 1990, p. 12.
19. *Press Gazette*, 2 July 1990, p. 5.
20. *Sunday Telegraph*, 24 June 1990, p. 20.
21. *Guardian*, 27 June 1990, p. 2.
22. *Press Gazette*, 9 July 1990, p. 7.
23. *Times*, 27 June 1990, p. 6.
24. *Guardian*, 4 July 1990, p. 5.
25. *Times*, 9 July, 1990, p. 3; 17 July, p. 2.
26. *Press Gazette*, 9 July 1990, p. 7.
27. *Private Eye*, 6 July 1990, p. 6.
28. *Guardian*, 5 July 1990, p. 3.
29. *Times*, 1 August 1990, p. 5.
30. Ibid., 8 August 1990, p. 14.
31. Ibid.
32. *British Journalism Review*, 'The tabs defended', vol. 1 no. 3, 1990.
33. *Press Gazette*, 10 September 1990, p. 5.
34. *Times*, 11 October 1990, p. 3.
35. Interview with the author.
36. *Times*, 11 October 1990, p. 3.
37. *Private Eye*, 13 September, 1990, p. 7; G. Taylor, *Changing Faces: a History of* The Guardian, *1956–1988* (1993), p. 242.
38. *Times*, 27 January 1993, p. 19.
39. *Guardian*, 22 October 1990, p. 15.
40. Ibid, 5 February 2001, Media, p. 5.
41. *Times*, 12 December 1990, p. 28.
42. *Guardian*, 17 October 1990, p. 3.
43. *Press Gazette*, 22 October 1990, p. 2.
44. Blom-Cooper, Epitaph, p. 29.
45. *Press Gazette*, 5 November 1990, p. 4.
46. Ibid., 26 November 1990, p. 2.
47. Ibid., 5 November 1990, p. 11.
48. Ibid., 12 November 1990, p. 3.
49. *Self-regulation in Britain: the Cases of the Advertising Standards Authority and the Press Complaints Commission*, p. [29].

CHAPTER 2

1. Lord McGregor of Durris, *Rights, Royals and Regulation: the British Experience* (World Press Freedom Committee, Preston, Virginia, USA, 1995), pp. 20–1. McGregor Papers.
2. McGregor Papers: text of speech (1993).

3. Snoddy, *Good, Bad and Unacceptable*, p. 195; *Press Gazette*, 4 February 1991. p. 2.

4. See Master Memoranda File, 1991, Memo 023/01: 'Do we have a hotline?'. PCC, Chatham/217.

5. *Press Gazette*, 18 March 1991, p. 15.

6. *Press Complaints Commission: First Annual Report, 1991* (1992), p. 7.

7. *Independent*, 1 February 1991, p.

8. Implementation of this discretion was for long a question in both the industry and the PCC: see Commission Papers, Aug–Sept 1992, PCC Paper No. 163, 'Third Party Complaints'. Paper No. 134, Glasser to Cassin, 13 August 1992. PCC, Chatham/219.

9. PCC, Minutes of the 1st Ordinary Meeting of the Commission, 30 January 1991. Minutes of Commission Meetings, 1991–6. The Master Memoranda File, 1991, includes several memoranda on questions of validity of complaints, procedures for handling them, and issues relating to initiation of inquiries. PCC, Chatham/217.

10. *Press Gazette*, 11 March 1991, p. 5.

11. On this point see the protest of Charles Wilson, then managing director of Mirror Group Newspapers, against an adjudication in favour of the *Sunday Express*. *Press Gazette*, 27 July 1992, p. 5.

12. See boxed adjudication, p. 64.

13. *Guardian*, 29 January 1991, p. 19.

14. Ibid.

15. Ibid., 17 June 1991, p. 24.

16. Ibid.

17. *Press Gazette*, 10 June 1991, p. 17.

18. *Guardian*, 30 December 1991, p. 21.

19. *Press Gazette*, 10 June 1991, p. 21.

20. *Guardian*, 17 June 1991, p. 24.

21. Ibid.

22. *Press Gazette*, 1 July 1991, p. 3.

23. Ibid., 24 June 1991, p. 4.

24. *Guardian*, 5 February 2001, Media, p. 5.

25. *Times*, 16 January 1993, p. 4.

26. Ibid., 13 January 1993, p. 2.

27. Ibid.

28. Ibid., 5 July 1991, p. 19.

29. Ibid., 13 January 1993, p. 2.

30. *Guardian*, 12 January 1993, p. 2.

31. *Times*, 2 July 1991, pp. 2, 15.

32. Ibid., p. 2.

33. N. Herbert and D. Flintham, *Press Freedom in Britain* (1991), p. 34.

34. *Press Gazette*, 22 July 1991, p. 4.

35. See boxed adjudication, p. 67.

36. Leapman, *Treacherous Estate*, p. 219.

37. *Times*, 10 August 1991, p. 11.

38. *Press Gazette*, 19 August 1991, p. 2. Maxwell fell off his yacht on 19 November 1991, to incredible industry sycophancy.

39. See Master Memoranda File, 1991: Mark Bolland, 'Public Affairs', July 1991. PCC, Chatham/217.

40. *Times*, 7 August 1991, p. 9.

41. Ibid.

42. See Master Memorandum File, 1991, Memo G31/01, 20 September 1991. PCC, Chatham/217.

43. *Times*, 7 August 1991, p. 9.

44. Ibid., 17 October 1991, p. 20.

45. *Guardian*, 18 September 1991, p. 2.

46. *Press Gazette*, 22 July 1991, p. 4.

47. Leapman, *Treacherous Estate*, p. 220.

48. *Observer*, 29 December 1991, p. 16.

49. *Guardian*, 30 December 1991, p. 21.

50. *Times*, 21 December 1991, p. 2.

51. *Press Gazette*, 8 July 1991, p. 4.

52. See Master Memorandum File, 1991, Memo E18.04: Mark Bolland, 'Organisation and Staffing', 20 June 1991. PCC, Chatham/217.

53. *Press Gazette*, 4 May 1992, p. 4.

54. *Press Complaints Commission: First Annual Report, 1991*, p. 9.

55. *Times*, 11 January 1993, p. 8. Both Baker and O'Donnell later denied McGregor's account of the extent of the information he had given them: *Telegraph*, 13 January 1993, p. 1.

56. McGregor *Rights, Royals and Regulation*, pp. 24–5.

CHAPTER 3

1. See pp. 202–3.

2. McGregor, *Rights, Royals and Regulation*, p. 14.

3. *Press Gazette*, 11 May 1992, p. 15. A complaint by the Economic League against Foot had been upheld by the PCC.

4. Ibid, 27 January 1992, p. 1.

5. Ibid.

6. Sir D. Calcutt, 1993, *Review of Press Self-regulation*, p. 21.

7. *Press Gazette*, 2 March 1992, p. 2.

8. Ibid., 16 March 1992, p. 27.

9. See p. 27.

10. See p. 52.

11. *Times*, 15 May 1992, p. 13.

12. *Guardian*, 6 February 1992, p. 2.

13. *Times*, 7 February 1992, p. 2.

14. PD, Commons 203, 13 February 1992, c. 613.

15. '"Labour and the liberty of the people" – John Wakeham attacks Labour's plans to extend the power of the state and erode the freedom of the British people.' *Extracts from a Speech by the Rt Hon John Wakeham MP to constituents in South Colchester and Maldon, Friday 28 February 1992*. Energy Press Office, 92-02-28. Wakeham's special political adviser at the Energy department assisting policy co-ordination was Guy Black, seconded from Conservative Central Office. See p. 227.

16. *Press Gazette*, 2 March 1992, p. 2.

17. Ibid.
18. *Guardian*, 6 April 1992, p. 29.
19. Ibid.
20. *Press Gazette*, 13 April 1992, p. 17.
21. Ibid,. 6 April 1992, p. 4.
22. Ibid.
23. See *Guardian*, 30 April 1992, p. 2, for the eloquent indignation of John Bennett, of Faversham, Kent.
24. *Press Gazette*, 6 April 1992, p. 6.
25. See p. 23
26. *Press Gazette*, 20 April 1992, p. 5.
27. Ibid.
28. *Times*, 14 May 1992, p. 5.
29. *Guardian*, 15 May 1992, p. 3.
30. *Press Gazette*, 4 May 1992, p. 19.
31. Ibid., 18 May 1992, p. 1.
32. Ibid., 25 May 1992, p. 2.
33. Ibid., 18 May 1992, p. 1.
34. *Times*, 20 May 1992, p. 8.
35. Ibid., 15 May 1992, p. 13.

CHAPTER 4

1. *Times*, 13 January 1992, p. 2.
2. McGregor, *Rights, Royals and Regulation*, p. 28.
3. *Times*, ibid.
4. *Private Eye*, 19 June 1992, p. 6; *Times*, 13 January 1993, p. 2.
5. Neil, *Full Disclosure* (1996), p. 218.
6. See below, p. 89.
7. McGregor, *Rights, Royals and Regulation*, p. 27.
8. *Guardian*, 10 June 1992, p. 2.
9. PCC Paper No. 115, Minutes of the 16th Ordinary Meeting, 24 June 1992. Minute 5: 'Coverage by the Press of the Marriage of the Prince and Princess of Wales'. Minutes of Commission Meetings, 1991–6.
10. *Guardian*, 12 January 1993, pp. 1–2.
11. PCC Paper No. 115, 24 June, 1992.
12. McGregor, *Rights, Royals and Regulation*, pp. 26–7.
13. *Guardian*, 12 January 1993, p. 1.
14. PCC Paper No. 115, 24 June 1992.
15. Interview with the author.
16. McGregor, *Rights, Royals and Regulation*, pp. 27–8.
17. Ibid., p. 28.
18. PCC Paper No. 115, 24 June 1992.
19. *Guardian*, 13 July 1992, p. 27.
20. Ibid., 10 June 1992, p. 2.
21. Interview with the author.
22. Neil, *Full Disclosure*, p. 208; *Times*, 16 June 1992, p. 14.

23. *Times*, 10 June 1992, p. 1.
24. PD, Commons 209, 15 June 1992, c. 371.
25. *Guardian*, 10 June 1992. p. 2.
26. *Times*, 10 June 1992, p. 2.
27. McGregor, *Rights, Royals and Regulation*, pp. 28–9.
28. *Times*, 13 January 1993, p. 2.
29. Ibid.
30. *Guardian*, 12 January 1993, p. 2.
31. Ibid., 10 June 1992, p. 2.
32. The Press Standards Board of Finance Limited, *First Annual Report, 1990–1992*, 10 June 1992.
33. *Press Gazette*, 15 June 1992, pp. 1–2.
34. Ibid.
35. *Telegraph*, 13 January 1993, p. 1.
36. *Times*, 11 June 1992, p. 11.
37. Ibid., 16 June 1992, p. 14.
38. PD, Commons 209, 19 June 1992, c. 685.
39. PD, Lords 538, 1 July 1992, cc. 789, 800, 807.
40. Ibid., cc. 779–81.
41. Ibid., c. 791.
42. See David Newell's comments, *Times*, 4 August 1992, p. 21.
43. PD, Commons 211, 9 July 1992, c. 277.

CHAPTER 5

 1. *Guardian*, 13 July 1992, p. 27.
 2. Ibid.
 3. *Times*, 23 July 1992, p. 2.
 4. Ibid.
 5. Ibid.
 6. *Press Gazette*, 13 July 1992, p. 3.
 7. Ibid., 20 July 1992, pp. 2, 6. Peter Bottomley MP, Virginia's husband, withdrew his complaint to the PCC; the *Independent* in turn published an apology to Virginia's child mentioned in its diary column.
 8. *Times*, 20 July 1992, p. 1; 21 July, p. 13.
 9. *Press Gazette*, 28 September 1992, p. 3.
10. *Private Eye*, 31 July 1992, p. 6.
11. *Times*, 23 July 1992, pp. 1, 16. See also PCC Paper No. 136, Minutes and Agenda File, 1992, 17th Ordinary Meeting, 29 July 1992. Chatham/217.
12. *Press Gazette*, 27 July 1992, pp. 1–2.
13. *Sunday Times*, 26 July 1992, 2/p. 3.
14. Blom-Cooper, with others, had written to *The Times* in October 1991 criticizing the Asylum Bill for 'playing shamefully on the public's fear of foreigners'. The *Standard* pointed out that arsonist Welsh nationalists had a well-developed fear of foreigners such as Blom-Cooper in his Welsh second home. *Guardian*, 23 April 1992, p. 4.
15. *Guardian*, 13 July 1992, p. 27.
16. *Times*, 4 August 1992, p. 21.

17. *Press Gazette*, 24 August 1992, p. 1.
18. Ibid., 7 September 1992, p.1.
19. PD, Commons 217, 29 January 1993, cc. 1304–5.
20. *Press Gazette*, 24 August 1992, p. 1.
21. *Times*, 22 August 1992, p. 10.
22. *Press Gazette*, 31 August 1992, p. 2.
23. Ibid., 7 September 1992, p. 3.
24. *Times*, 22 August 1992, p. 2.
25. McGregor to Bolland, 23 October 1992, PCC, Calcutt II, CR07.
26. McGregor to Phillips, 19 October 1992, PCC, Calcutt II, CR07.
27. *Guardian*, 9 March 1993, p. 3.
28. PCC Paper No. 183, Minutes and Agenda File, 1992, Minutes of 19th Ordinary Meeting, 30 September 1992. PCC, Chatham/217.
29. Thomson to Pressbof, 24 December 1992, PCC, Calcutt II, Box CR07.
30. *Press Gazette*, 12 October 1992, p. 15.
31. Ibid., 19 October 1992, p. 4; 26 October, p. 14.
32. Ibid., 2 November 1992, p. 13.
33. *Times*, 8 October, 1992, p. 2.
34. *Press Gazette*, 26 October 1992, pp. 18–19.
35. *Times*, 27 July 1994, p. 15.
36. Ibid., 15 January 1993, p. 14.
37. See p. 117.
38. *British Journalism Review*, vol. 3 no. 3, 1992.
39. *Guardian*, 16 October 1992, p. 7.
40. *Times*, 9 October 1992, p. 7; *Press Gazette*, 26 October, p. 14.
41. *Press Gazette*, 26 October 1992, p. 14.
42. Ibid., p. 16.
43. *Times*, 11 December 1992, p. 2. See *Freedom and Responsibility of the Press Bill (Clive Soley, MP). Report of the Special Parliamentary Hearings . . .*, ed. Mike Jempson, December 1992.
44. *Guardian*, 4 December 1992, p. 5.
45. *Times*, 10 November 1992, p. 35.
46. *Press Gazette*, 21/28 December 1992, p. 2.
47. *Times*, 8 December 1992, p. 29.
48. Ibid., 15 December 1992, p. 15.
49. Ibid., 3 December 1992, p. 14.
50. *Press Gazette*, 26 October 1992, pp. 18–19.
51. Ibid., 21/28 December 1992, p. 2.
52. Thomson to Pressbof, 24 December 1992. PCC, Calcutt II, Box CR07.
53. Sir D. Calcutt, *Review of Press Self-regulation* (Cm. 2135, HMSO, 1993), p. xi.

CHAPTER 6

1. Calcutt, *Review of Press Self-regulation* pp. xii, xiv, 47.
2. PCC, Calcutt II, Box CR07, B53, B01.
3. *Times*, 11 January 1993, p. 5.
4. See p. 109.
5. *Guardian*, 11 January 1993, p. 00.

6. *Press Gazette*, 18 January 1993, p. 20.
7. Interview with the author.
8. *Times*, 13 January 1993, p. 2.
9. *Telegraph*, 13 January 1993, p. 1.
10. See p. 209.
11. *Press Gazette*, 11 January 1993, p. 1.
12. *Telegraph*, 12 January 1993, p. 16.
13. PD, Commons 216, 15 January 1993, cc. 823, 828.
14. *Guardian*, 12 January 1993, p. 2.
15. *Telegraph*, 14 January 1993, p. 4.
16. See pp. 97, 99.
17. *Times*, 29 January 1993, p. 4.
18. *Telegraph*, 12 January 1993, p. 9.
19. PD, Commons 216, 14 January 1993, c. 1068.
20. *Press Gazette*, 1 February 1993, p. 3.
21. PCC Paper No. 243, Review of Press Regulation. Note by the Chairman on possible changes in appointments to and procedures of the PCC to meet Calcutt's criticisms. Commission Papers, January–February 1993, Chatham/220.
22. PD, Commons 217, 25 January 1993, c. 694.
23. *Times*, 23 January 1993, p. 6.
24. Ibid., 27 January 1993, p. 19.
25. In the hurry to get these reforms in place there were legal anomalies which left the Appointments Commission unconstitutionally in breach of its own articles of association; and nine PCC members later had to have their appointments regularized.
26. See p. 207.
27. *Press Gazette*, 8 February 1993, p. 1. The PCC 'agreed with Pressbof' on 22 April that the line be set up. It was installed in May and eventually launched on 10 June. PCC Papers Nos. 342 and 359, Commission Papers May–June 1993, Chatham/220.
28. *Times*, 3 February 1993, p. 10.
29. *Press Gazette*, 1 February 1993, p. 15. Lindi St Clare, known also as 'Miss Whiplash', was said to have 250 MPs on her file and in her thrall.
30. Ibid., p. 1.
31. *Times*, 26 January 1993, p. 1.
32. *Guardian*, 28 January 1993, 1993, pp. 1, 2.
33. *Times*, 20 February 1993, p. 3.
34. PD, Commons 217, 29 January 1993, c. 1324.
35. *Independent on Sunday*, 7 March 1993, p. 4.
36. *Times*, 31 March 1993, p. 16. Jack was succeeded by Andrew Neil of the *Sunday Times*.
37. *Guardian*, 9 March 1993, p. 3. See above, p. 107.
38. PCC Calcutt II, Box CR07/B53/B01.
39. *Times*, 16 January 1993, p. 13.
40. She was replaced as editor of the *News of the World* in June 1994 by Piers Morgan.
41. The considered opinion of Charles Wilson in conversation with the author.
42. McGregor to Phillips, 28 May 1993. PCC, Calcutt II, Box CR07/B53/B01.
43. PD, Commons 226, 10 June 1993, c. 514. Lady Olga here betrays a common misconception about the relationship of the PCC and the Code Committee.

44. *Press Gazette*, 10 May 1993, p. 4.

45. PD, Commons 226, 10 June 1993, c. 522.

46. *Guardian*, 10 January 1994, p. 4.

47. See p. 26.

48. See pp. 13, 18.

49. *Press Gazette*, 17 May 1993, p. 3.

50. See below, p. 148.

51. See *Guardian* 27 October 1997, Media p. 7; 24 August 1998, Media, p. 7.

52. PCC Paper No. 428, Commission Papers, July–December 1993, 22 September, 1993. The reference was to Mackay's Consultation Paper, Infringement of Privacy. PCC, Chatham/220.

53. *Press Gazette*, 2 August 1993, p. 2.

54. Ibid., 4 October 1993, p. 1.

55. Ibid. See also p. 152 of this volume

56. *Press Gazette*, 4 October 1993, p. 5.

57. Ibid.

CHAPTER 7

1. *Times*, 16 May 1993, p. 32.

2. See p. 123.

3. *Sunday Mirror*, 14 November 1993, p. 9.

4. In conversation with the author.

5. In conversation with the author.

6. *Press Gazette*, 15 November 1993, p. 1.

7. *Times*, 9 November 1993, p. 2.

8. *Mirror*, 9 November 1993, p. 1.

9. *Guardian*, 9 November 1993, p. 4.

10. *Times*, 8 November, 1993, pp. 1, 2.

11. Ibid., 9 November 1993, p. 1.

12. *Guardian*, 9 November 1993, p. 4.

13. *Mirror*, 8 November 1993, pp. 1–2.

14. See p. 95.

15. *Times*, 8 November 1993, pp. 1–2.

16. *Press Gazette*, 8 November 1993, p. 12.

17. *Times*, 9 November 1993, p. 19.

18. *Private Eye*, 19 November 1993, p. 6.

19. *Times*, 8 November 1993, pp. 1–2.

20. *Mirror*, 9 November 1993, p. 6.

21. *Guardian*, 9 November 1993, p. 4.

22. Ibid.

23. *Times*, 9 November 1993, p. 2.

24. Ibid.

25. Ibid., 10 November 1993, p. 18.

26. In an interview on BBC Radio 4 on 1 January 1994, Montgomery made clear his reservations about press self-regulation. 'Now it's commonplace for the *Sun* to publish two or three times a year pretty horrendous things and self-regulation is very useful because

the next day they simply say, oops, we're terribly sorry . . . So self-regulation is a very useful instrument for the *Sun*. We at the Mirror Group are not so sure that commercially some sort of legislation wouldn't be better because taking our chances in the courts, quite frankly, is better and provides a fair trial in a way that trial by the rest of the media does not.' *Guardian*, 10 January 1994, p. 4.

27. *Press Gazette*, 15 November 1993, p. 3.
28. *Guardian*, 11 November 1993, p. 1; *Press Gazette*, 15 November 1993, p. 3.
29. *Press Gazette*, 15 November 1993, p. 3.
30. *Times*, 10 November 1993, p. 18.
31. *Press Gazette*, 15 November 1993, p. 2.
32. *Times*, 11 November 1993, p. 2.
33. Ibid.
34. PCC Paper No. 495, Minutes of the 31st Ordinary Meeting, 24 November 1993. Minutes of Commission Meetings, 1991–6.
35. McGregor to Roche, 25 November 1993. PCC, Calcutt II, Box CR07/B53/B01.
36. *Guardian*, 11 November 1993, p. 1.
37. *Times*, 12 November 1993, p. 2.
38. *Press Gazette*, 15 November 1993, p. 1.
39. *Guardian*, 13 November 1993, p. 4.
40. *Times*, 12 November 1993, p. 2.
41. *Press Gazette*, 22 November 1993, p. 7.
42. *Times Saturday Magazine*, 20 November 1993, p. 12; 4 December, p. 6.
43. *Times*, 6 December 1993, p. 3.
44. *Press Gazette*, 13 December, p. 4.
45. Ibid., 27 December 1993, p. 12.
46. PD, Commons 234, 13 December 1993, cc. 670–1.
47. *Times*, 14 December 1993, p. 2.
48. *Press Gazette*, 20 December 1993, p. 4.
49. McGregor to Roche, 25 November 1993. PCC, Calcutt II, Box CR07/B53/B01.
50. Roche to McGregor, 13 December 1993. PCC, Calcutt II, Box CR07/B53/B01. See also p. 132 of this volume.
51. PCC Paper No. 516, Minutes of the 32nd Ordinary Meeting, 22 December 1993. Minutes of Commission Meetings, 1991–6.

CHAPTER 8

1. *Press Gazette*, 25 July 1994, p. 2.
2. *Guardian*, 10 January 1994, p. 4.
3. Ibid., 22 November, 1993, G2, p. 19.
4. Ibid.
5. *Press Gazette*, 25 July 1994, p. 4.
6. Ibid., p. 2.
7. *Times*, 12 November 1993, p. 2.
8. Ibid., 10 January 1994, p. 4.
9. Sir Harry Roche in conversation with the author.
10. *Press Gazette*, 17 January 1994, p. 2.
11. See p. 152.

12. *Times*, 10 January 1994, p. 4.
13. See p. 162.
14. *Press Gazette*, 17 January 1994, p. 2.
15. PD, Commons 239, 7 March 1994, c. 6.
16. *Press Gazette*, 17 January 1994, p. 2.
17. Ibid., 24 January 1994, p. 2.
18. Ibid., 28 February 1994, p. 1.
19. *Times*, 12 March 1994, p. 10.
20. *Press Gazette*, 28 March 1994, p. 6.
21. See p. 187.
22. *Times*, 30 March 1994, p. 2.
23. *Press Gazette*, 2 May 1994, p. 6.
24. *Times*, 6 April 1994, p. 21.
25. *Press Complaints Commission Review, 1991–1993* (1994), p. 8. These proportions were very much the same in other regulatory bodies dealing with complaints.
26. In 1992 the PCC engaged Research Surveys of Great Britain to survey public attitudes to the PCC. Its findings, in November 1992, on a sample of 2,000 respondents, concluded that the overall response was 'quite satisfactory' within the narrow limits of the sample. Forty per cent accepted that the PCC acted independently of the industry as against 19 per cent dissenting. But of complainants sampled, half declared that their complaint had not been satisfactorily resolved. Commission Papers, October–November 1992. PCC, Chatham/219.
27. *Press Gazette*, 25 April 1994, p. 17.
28. Ibid., p. 2.
29. See p. 156.
30. The Press Standards Board of Finance Limited, *Annual Report, 1994*, p. 1.
31. *Times*, 8 November 1994, p. 1.
32. Ibid.
33. *Guardian*, 6 May 1994, p. 10.
34. Ibid., 27 May 1994, p. 11.
35. *Press Complaints Commission Review, 1991–1993*, p. 5.
36. *Press Gazette*, 12 July 1994, p. 4.
37. *Times*, 27 July 1994, p. 15.
38. See boxed adjudication, p. 164.
39. *Guardian*, 30 July 1994, p. 3.
40. *Press Gazette*, 25 July 1994, p. 2.
41. Ibid., 15 August 1994, p. 2. Blair had recently succeeded John Smith as Labour leader.
42. *News of the World*, 21 August 1994, p. 1.
43. *Press Gazette*, 29 August 1994, p. 1.
44. Ibid., p. 3.
45. Ibid.
46. *Guardian*, 23 August 1994, p. 3.
47. Ibid.
48. Ibid.
49. *Times*, 24 August 1994, p. 28.
50. Ibid., 13 September 1994, p. 4.

51. Ibid., 22 November 1994, p. 2.
52. Preston to McGregor, 1 November 1994. PCC, Chatham/192.
53. R. J. W. Henderson to McGregor, 1 November 1994. PCC, Chatham/192.
54. PCC Paper No. 747. The *Guardian* Newspaper – Mr Jonathan Aitken MP, November 1994. PCC, Chatham/192.
55. Ibid.
56. See p. 73.
57. *Times*, 8 November 1994, p. 23. See p. 158.
58. *Guardian*, 22 November 1994, p. 12.
59. *Times*, 23 November 1994, p. 37.
60. *Guardian*, 9 November 1994, p. 6; *Press Gazette*, 14 November 1994, p. 3.
61. *Guardian*, 21 November 1994, p. 13.

CHAPTER 9

1. See p. 73.
2. *Press Gazette*, 28 November 1994, p. 2.
3. *The Journals of Woodrow Wyatt*, ed. Sarah Curtis, vol. I (1998), p. 494.
4. *Guardian*, 15 January 2000, p. 6.
5. *Press Gazette*, 28 November 1994, p. 2.
6. *Press Complaints Committee, Annual Report, 1995* (1996), p. 2.
7. *Press Gazette*, 28 November 1994, p. 2.
8. *Annual Report, 1995*, ibid.
9. *Press Gazette*, 10 January 1997, p. 19.
10. *Times*, 31 January 1996, p. 21.
11. Ibid.
12. *Guardian*, 11 January 1997, p. 3.
13. *Press Gazette*, 9 November 1994, p. 6.
14. Ibid., 23 January 1995, p. 4.
15. *Guardian*, 31 January 1995, p.1.
16. *Times*, 1 April 1995, p. 7. See p. 122.
17. *Guardian*, 13 March 1995, G2, p. 16. See also Greenslade on 'A job too many for Wakeham', *British Journalism Review*, vol. 6 no. 2, 1995.
18. Bolland to Henderson, 3 January 1995. PCC, Chatham/192.
19. Bolland to Henderson, 11 May 1995. PCC, Chatham/192.
20. PD, Commons 253, 3 January 1995, c. 667.
21. *Press Gazette*, 20 February 1995, p. 2.
22. Ibid., 20 March 1995, p. 2.
23. PCC Paper No. 787, Minutes of the 42nd Ordinary Meeting, 25 January 1995. Minutes of Commission Meetings, 1991–6.
24. *Press Gazette*, 28 November 1994, p. 2.
25. Lord Wakeham, Speech at the British Press Awards, London, 4 April 1995, in *Moving Ahead: the Development of PCC Policy and Practice in 1995*.
26. *Times*, 11 April 1995, p. 16.
27. Ibid.
28. *Private Eye*, 7 April 1995, p. 6.
29. Ibid., 21 April 1995, p. 6.

30. *Press Gazette*, 17 April 1995, p. 1.
31. Lord Wakeham, Speech at the Scottish Press Fund, Glasgow, 21 April 1995, in *Moving Ahead*. See also *Times*, 22 April 1995, p. 6.
32. A complaint by Lord Spencer against the *Mail on Sunday*, which had made enquiries about Lady Spencer but did not publish, was rejected. Another against the *Daily Mirror* was resolved by prompt apology.
33. See boxed adjudication, p. 196.
34. *Press Gazette*, 15 May 1995, p. 1.
35. *Guardian*, 12 May 1995, p. 3.
36. *Times*, 12 May 1995, p. 2.
37. See p. 202. To illustrate its story of the affair, the *Mirror* saw fit to publish the offending photograph of Lady Spencer. For this 'clanger' the *Mirror* had to apologize to the PCC 'in the most abject terms'. *Private Eye*, 11 August 1995, p. 6.
38. 'A kind word for Lord Wakeham', *British Journalism Review*, vol. 6, no. 4, 1995.
39. *Times*, 18 July 1995. p. 9.
40. Wakeham to Murdoch, 15 May 1995. PCC, Chatham/191.
41. *Press Gazette*, 1 May 1995, p. 6.
42. Ibid., 5 June 1995, p. 2.
43. *Times*, 29 April 1995, p. 17; 2 May, p. 21. (BMA = British Medical Association.)
44. See p. 311.
45. *Press Gazette*, 29 May 1995, p. 6.
46. Ibid, 3 July 1995, p. 4.
47. See boxed adjudication, p. 199.
48. *Press Gazette*, 8 May 1995, p. 1.
49. *Guardian*, 31 May 1995, p. 5.
50. *Press Gazette*, 5 June 1995, p. 14.
51. *Guardian*, 3 June 1995, p. 3.
52. *Times*, 10 January 1997, p. 19.
53. *Press Gazette*, 5 June 1995, p. 14.
54. Ibid., 24 July 1995, p. 4.
55. Ibid.; see also *Times*, 18 July 1995, p. 9.
56. *Times*, 19 July 1995, p. 23.
57. *Press Gazette*, 24 July 1995, p. 4.
58. Ibid.
59. Ibid., p. 2.
60. *Times*, 19 July 1995, p. 23.
61. PCC Paper No. 997, Minutes of the 48th Ordinary Meeting, 26 July 1995. Minutes of Commission Meetings, 1991–6.

CHAPTER 10

1. Wakeham to Murdoch, 25 May 1995. PCC, Chatham/191.
2. *Press Gazette*, 24 July 1995, p. 15.
3. *Times*, 1 August 1995, p. 14.
4. *Private Eye*, 25 August 1995, p. 6.
5. Ibid.
6. See boxed adjudication, p. 212.

7. Wakeham, Speech at St Bride's Institute, London 23 August 1995, in *Moving Ahead*.
8. *Press Gazette*, 28 August 1995, p. 2.
9. *Times*, 24 August 1995, p. 6.
10. *Press Gazette*, ibid.
11. Ibid.
12. Wakeham, Speech at St Bride's Institute, p. 8.
13. *Private Eye*, 22 September 1995, p. 4.
14. *Times*, 21 September 1995, p. 2.
15. *Press Gazette*, 23 October 1995, p. 14.
16. PCC, Minutes of 49th Ordinary Meeting, 27 September 1995. Minutes of Commission Meetings, 1991–6.
17. Memo, Bolland to Wakeham, 4 October 1995. PCC, Chatham/191. (DNH = Department of National Heritage.)
18. Lord Wakeham, Away from Damocles: the Harold Macmillan lecture, Nottingham Trent University, 23 October 1995, in *Moving Ahead*.
19. *Press Gazette*, 6 November 1995, p. 6.
20. Wakeham to Fowler, 7 November 1995. PCC, Chatham/191.
21. Code Committee, Definition of Private Life, September 1997. PCC, Chatham/193.
22. Information from Lord Wakeham. Cf. the account in the *Times*, 20 November 1995, 2/p. 13.
23. *Mail on Sunday*, 19 November 1995. p. 28.
24. David Newell had taken over the NS from Nisbet-Smith, with a place on the Pressbof Board.
25. *Guardian*, 27 November 1995, 2/p. 13.
26. *Times*, 21 November 1995, p. 18.
27. Ibid., p. 19.
28. Ibid., 23 November 1995, pp. 1, 2.
29. *Press Gazette*, 4 December 1995, p. 2.
30. *Guardian*, 30 November 1995, p. 6.
31. See p. 16.
32. PD, Lords 567, 20 December 1995, cc. 1647–8, 1668.

CHAPTER 11

1. Bolland, speech to Newspaper Society, 5 March 1996. PCC, Chatham/191.
2. *Guardian*, 1 February 1996, p. 6.
3. *Press Gazette*, 26 February 1996, p. 2.
4. *Times*, 31 January 1996, p. 21.
5. *Guardian* , 1 February 1996, p. 6.
6. Ibid.
7. *Times*, 8 February 1996, p. 5.
8. See boxed adjudication, p. 228.
9. Sir Bernard Ingham's words.
10. Bolland, speech to Newspaper Society, 5 March 1996. PCC, Chatham/191.
11. See boxed adjudication, p. 223.
12. *Times*, 3 January 1996, p. 3.
13. *Press Gazette*, 11 March 1996, p. 4; ibid., 10 January 1997, p. 19.

14. Bolland, speech to Newspaper Society, 5 March 1996. PCC, Chatham/191.
15. *Guardian*, 15 February 1996, p. 10.
16. Code of Practice Committee, Agenda, 17 January 1996. PCC, Chatham/192.
17. See p. 16.
18. *Press Gazette*, 26 February 1996, p. 2.
19. Ibid., 12 April 1996, p. 6.
20. Ibid., 4 March 1996, p. 7.
21. Bolland to Cubbon, 17 April 1996. PCC, Chatham/192.
22. See boxed adjudication, p. 234.
23. See p. 164.
24. *Guardian*, 25 March 1996, p. 5.
25. *Times*, 3 April 1996, p. 21.
26. See boxed adjudication, p. 235.
27. *Press Gazette*, 3 May 1996, p. 13.
28. Ibid., 26 April 1996, p. 3.
29. PCC Press Release, 2 May 1996. PCC, Chatham/191.
30. Ibid.
31. See p. 26.
32. 'Incorporation of the European Convention on Human Rights, Privacy and the Press', PCC [1996], Chatham/193.
33. *Press Gazette*, 31 May 1996, p. 12.
34. Ibid., 14 June 1996, p. 13.
35. Ibid.
36. *Times*, 3 July 1996, p. 25.
37. *Press Gazette*, 9 August 1996, p. 5.
38. Ibid., 16 August 1996, p. 28.
39. PCC Press Release, 'Freedom of the press is sustained by responsibility', 4 July 1996. PCC, Chatham/191.
40. *Sunday Times*, 12 May 1996, p. 5.
41. *Press Gazette*, 17 May 1996, p. 3.
42. *Guardian*, 11 January 1997, p. 3.
43. *Press Gazette*, 9 August 1996, p. 4.

CHAPTER 12

1. See p. 168.
2. *Times*, 17 August 1996, p. 18.
3. *Press Gazette*, 23 August 1996, p. 2.
4. Ibid., p. 10.
5. Ibid.
6. *Times*, 5 October 1996, p. 5.
7. Ibid., 8 October 1996, p. 1; 9 October 1996, p. 1; *Private Eye*, 18 October 1996, p. 6.
8. *Press Gazette*, 18 October 1996, p. 3.
9. *Times*, 10 October 1996, p. 21.
10. Ibid., 14 October 1996, p. 23.
11. *Press Gazette*, 1 November 1996, p. 7.
12. Ibid., 11 October 1996, p. 11.

13. Ibid., 18 October 1996, p. 16.
14. Ibid., p. 3.
15. Ibid., 1 November 1996, p. 3.
16. *Guardian*, 4 November 1996, 2/p. 13.
17. *Times*, 9 November 1996, p. 11. Ultimately the case was reopened but the complaint was refuted because of evidence given by a source with intimate familial knowledge.
18. *Guardian*, 11 November 1996, 2/p. 11.
19. *Times*, 8 November 1996, p. 10.
20. Ibid.
21. *Press Gazette*, 22 November 1996, p. 1.
22. Ibid., 29 November 1996, p. 9.
23. Ibid., p. 2.
24. Ibid., p. 12.
25. J. Curran and J. Seaton, *Power without Responsibility: the Press and Broadcasting in Britain* (5th edn, 1997), p. 296.
26. *Press Gazette*, 10 January 1997, p. 1.
27. Ibid.
28. Ibid., p. 19.

CHAPTER 13

1. The *Daily Mirror* became the *Mirror* as from 1 January 1997.
2. *Press Gazette*, 10 January 1997, p. 19.
3. Ibid., p. 11.
4. Ibid., 24 January 1997, p. 12.
5. Ibid., p. 13.
6. See p. 234.
7. *Press Gazette*, 31 January 1997, p. 8; 7 February, p. 14; 14 February, p. 12.
8. Ibid., 11 April 1997, p. 12.
9. *Guardian*, 10 March 1997, Media, p. 9.
10. *Press Gazette*, 4 April 1997, p. 3.
11. Ibid., 9 May 1997, p. 8.
12. Ibid., 10 January 1997, p. 19.
13. Ibid., 11 October 1996, p. 11.
14. PCC, *Annual Report, 1996* (1997), p. 3.
15. *Press Gazette*, 23 May 1997, p. 8.
16. Ibid.
17. See p. 75.
18. *Press Gazette*, 30 May 1997, p. 4.
19. Ibid., 13 June 1997, p. 12.
20. Ibid.
21. Ibid.
22. Ibid., 20 June 1997, p. 10.
23. Ibid., 18 July 1997, p. 12.
24. *Times*, 13 June 1997, p. 21.
25. Ibid., 24 June 1997, p. 23.
26. *Press Gazette*, 1 August 1997, p. 8.

27. Ibid.
28. Ibid.
29. Ibid.
30. PCC, Chatham/193.
31. Ibid.
32. *Press Gazette* , 18 July 1997, p. 5.
33. See p. 71.
34. *Press Gazette*, 18 July 1997, p. 12.
35. Ibid., p. 5.
36. Ibid., 8 August 1997, p. 9.
37. Ibid.
38. *Times*, 28 August 1997, p. 16.
39. Ibid., 11 August 1997, p. 15.

CHAPTER 14

1. *Times*, 1 September 1997, p. 15.
2. Ibid., p. 24.
3. *South Wales Evening Post*, 6 September 1997, p. 15.
4. *Times*, 2 September 1997, p. 13.
5. *Press Gazette*, 7 November 1997, p. 8.
6. *Times*, 1 September 1997, p. 15.
7. *Guardian*, 2 September 1997, p. 18.
8. *Times*, 3 September 1997, p. 3. The French Embassy Press and Information Service issued a five-page explanation of French privacy law: 'Protection of Privacy: French Legislation.' 'In France, as in many other countries, invasions of privacy have become widespread, aided by advances in science and technology as well as abetted by the claim that "the public has a right to know" and justified by the principle of freedom of expression.' Also: 'France has no equivalent to . . . even a Press Complaints Commission . . . which ensures compliance with rules of professional conduct.'
9. *Times*, 6 September 1997, p. 21.
10. *Press Gazette*, 5 September 1997, p. 12. Not the least of the ironies of the tragedy was that the newspaper industry profited enormously from it. It was estimated that on 1 September, 3.7 million extra national newspapers were purchased, and an extra 2.8 million after the funeral. The *Daily Mail, Mail on Sunday, Times, Sunday Times*, and *Guardian* achieved new sales records. *Times*, 24 September 1997, p. 25.
11. *Press Gazette*, 2 September 1997, p. 13. Smith's department had replaced that of National Heritage; 'heritage' not being a word much liked by New Labour.
12. Ibid.
13. Code of Practice Committee, 11 September 1997. PCC, Chatham/193.
14. *Press Gazette*, 5 September 1997, p. 1.
15. Wakeham to Smith, 5 September 1997. PCC, Chatham/193.
16. *Telegraph*, 5 September 1997, p. 8.
17. Black to Wakeham, 6 September 1997. PCC, Chatham/193.
18. *Times*, 8 September 1997, p. 9.
19. Ibid.
20. Ibid., 10 September 1997, p. 7; *Press Gazette*, 12 September 1997, p. 2.

21. *Telegraph*, 16 September 1997, p. 19.
22. *Guardian*, 15 September 1997, Media, p. 9.
23. Spencer's case at Strasbourg to require the British government to introduce a privacy law compatible with the ECHR was still pending. It was rejected in January 1998.
24. *Times*, 17 September 1997, p. 22.
25. *Independent*, 15 September 1997, Media, p. 2.
26. Code of Practice Committee, 11 September 1997. PCC, Chatham/193.
27. *Times*, 17 September 1997, p. 22.
28. Rusbridger to English, 15 September 1997. PCC, Chatham/193.
29. Conversation with the author.
30. There was currently a complaint against the *Newcastle Evening Chronicle* for a 'death-knocking' story about a missing person, feared drowned. A later PCC adjudication against the paper became controversial. See p. 309.
31. *Independent*, 18 September 1997, p. 15.
32. Code of Practice Committee, 17 September 1997. PCC, Chatham/193.
33. Satchwell to Moore, 18 September 1997; Moore to Satchwell, 19 September 1997. PCC, Chatham/193.
34. Text of a speech by Lord Wakeham at a press conference in Parliament Chamber, Crown Office Row, Temple, on 25 September. PCC, Chatham/193.
35. *Times*, 24 September 1997, p. 25.
36. PCC, Chatham/193.
37. *Press Gazette*, 3 October 1997, p. 10.
38. *Times*, 25 September 1997, p. 2.
39. *Press Gazette*, 8 October 1997, p. 8.
40. Ibid., 10 October 1997, p. 1.
41. Ibid., 3 October2 1997, p. 8.
42. Ibid., 7 November 1997, p. 10.
43. *Times*, 25 September 1997, p. 2.
44. Satchwell to Moore, 18 September 1997. PCC, Chatham/193.
45. *Press Gazette*, 31 October 1997, p. 4.
46. *Times*, 19 December 1997, p. 2.
47. *Press Gazette*, 2 November 1997, p. 10.
48. Wilson to Thomson, 'Proposed Changes in the Press Complaints Commissions Code of Conduct', 11 November 1997. PCC, Chatham/193.
49. PCC Paper No. 1595. Guy Black, 19 November 1997. PCC, Chatham/193.
50. English to Black, 14 October 1997. PCC, Chatham/193. See Brian Cubbon, 'Don't put democracy at risk', *Times*, 30 October 1997, p. 20.
51. *Press Gazette*, 7 November 1997, p. 8.
52. Ibid., 31 October 1997, p. 1.
53. *Times*, 24 September 1997, p. 25.
54. *Guardian*, 28 October 1997, p. 8.
55. *Press Gazette*, 31 October 1997, p. 6.
56. Ibid.
57. *Times*, 3 November 1997, p. 8.

CHAPTER 15

1. 'Human Rights Bill. Briefing on the general issues involved', 9 February 1998. PCC, Chatham/193.
2. On the Human Rights Act as a 'paradox', with its apparent scheme of 'public authorities only' completely undermined by its express provisions, see Sir William Wade QC, *Times*, 1 September 2000, p. 19.
3. Ibid.
4. Glasser to Black, 8 December 1997. PCC, Chatham/193.
5. PD, Lords 583, 24 November 1997, c. 784.
6. Ibid., 585, 5 February 1998, c. 838.
7. Ibid., 583, c. 777.
8. Ibid., c. 772.
9. Ibid., c. 774.
10. Advice to Black, 12 November 1997. PCC, Chatham/193.
11. *Sun*, 15 December 1997. PCC, Chatham/193.
12. *Times*, 2 December 1997, p. 8.
13. Newspaper Society, 'Privacy Laws which Spell the End of Press Freedom', 27 November 1997. PCC, Chatham/193.
14. *Times*, 2 December 1997, p. 8. Rusbridger had a 'Privacy and Defamation Bill 1998' drafted and circulated. It incorporated PCC definitions and strong public-interest clauses, and US privacy precedents. At the PCC opinion was that it would not pass the test of being judged compatible with the Human Rights measure. 'It is now too late for a Privacy Bill on the lines of AR's draft.' Cubbon to English, 7 February 1998. PCC, Chatham/193.
15. Irvine to Potts, 19 January 1998. PCC, Chatham/193.
16. PD, Commons 302, 9 December 1997, c. 813.
17. *Press Gazette*, 23 January 1998, p. 4.
18. Rogers to Williams, 18 December 1997. PCC, Chatham/193.
19. PD, Commons 303, 22 December 1997, c. 640.
20. *Press Gazette*, 9 January 1998, p. 10.
21. *Times*, 15 January 1998, p. 19.
22. Brett to Black, 28 January 1998. PCC, Chatham/193.
23. Wakeham to Fowler, 9 June 1998. PCC, Chatham/193.
24. PCC, 'Four Things to Put to Tony Blair', January 1998. Ibid. Gareth Williams = Lord Williams of Mostyn.
25. Wakeham to Blair, 29 January 1998. PCC, Chatham/193.
26. PD, Lords 585, 5 February 1998, cc. 830, 832.
27. Ibid., c. 835.
28. The World Press Freedom Committee, who had been hosts to Lord McGregor and Sir Frank Rogers in 1995 when McGregor gave his 'Rights, Royals and Regulation' lecture, produced a newsletter, 'Rights Principles are Misused to Hobble Press', on 15 December 1997. It calculated that 'restrictive ideas contained in the European Convention on Human Rights – or functional equivalents – were used more than 1,000 times in 109 countries to justify prosecutions, jailings and other abuses against journalists and news media'. PCC, Chatham/193.
29. Guild of Newspaper Editors, 'Censorship warning by editors', 5 February 1998. PCC, Chatham/193.

30. *Guardian*, 9 February 1998, p. 6.
31. Wakeham to Blair, 6 February 1998. PCC, Chatham/193.
32. *Guardian*, 12 February 1998, p. 19.
33. Wakeham to Fowler, 9 June 1998. PCC, Chatham/193.
34. Stephen Tierney, 'Extra protection for the press', *British Journalism Review*, vol. 9, no. 2, 1998, p. 66.
35. Wakeham to Hollick, 4 June 1998. PCC, Chatham/193. Lord Hollick took over the Express group from Lord Stevens in 1996.
36. Lester to Wakeham, 19 February 1998. PCC, Chatham/193.
37. *Press Gazette*, 27 February 1998, p. 5.
38. Wakeham to Hollick, 4 June 1998. PCC, Chatham/193.
39. Wakeham to Straw, 9 June 1998. PCC, Chatham/193.
40. Wakeham to Straw, 24 June 1998. PCC, Chatham/193.

CHAPTER 16

1. For the alleged 'sleazy and mendacious' aspect of this repute, see *Private Eye*, 26 June 1998, p. 7; and R. Borzello, *Press Gazette*, 31 July 1998, p. 10.
2. *Press Gazette*, 21 August 1998, p. 12.
3. See p. 305.
4. *Press Gazette*, 2 October 1998, p. 1.
5. Ibid., 6 November 1998, p. 11.
6. Ibid.
7. *British Journalism Review*, vol. 10 no. 4, 1999.
8. *Press Gazette*, 17 April 1998, p. 11; 6 November, p. 11.
9. PD, Commons 315, 29 June 1998, cc. 1–2.
10. *Press Gazette*, 6 November 1998, p. 11.
11. *Times*, 19 June 1998, p. 5; 20 June, p. 3; PCC, Report No. 42, April–June 1998, p. 22.
12. See p. 315.
13. *Times*, 4 March 1998, p. 9.
14. *Press Gazette*, 8 May 1998, p. 9.
15. *Times*, 23 May 1998, p. 22.
16. Ibid., 27 May 1998, p. 19.
17. See p. 308
18. See boxed adjudication, p. 317.
19. *Guardian*, 23 July 1998, p. 19.
20. *Press Gazette*, 31 July 1998, p. 11.
21. *Times*, 29 October 1999, p. 41.
22. PD, Commons 322, 7 December 1998, c. 14w.
23. Ibid., 329, 8 February 1999, c. 95w.
24. *Guardian*, 5 April 1999, Media, p. 4. *British Journalism Review*, vol. 19 no. 1, 1999.
25. PCC, Report No. 44 (October–December 1998), pp. 12–17.
26. 'France '98 – the World Cup.' PCC, Report No. 42, April–June 1998. *Press Gazette*, 6 March 1998, p. 2; 15 May, p. 1; *Times*, 14 May 1998, p. 13.
27. *Press Gazette*, 21 August 1998, p. 2.
28. Ibid., 9 October, p. 8.
29. See boxed adjudication, p. 323.

30. *Press Gazette*, 10 April 1998, p. 2.

31. Ibid., p. 10.

32. *Times*, 29 October 1999, p. 41.

33. *Press Gazette*, 24 May 1998, p. 9. Once matters quietened down, ACOP decided that PCC guidelines might be more hindrance than help. The PCC thereupon dropped the project – a matter of some embarrassment in July and August 2000 when the *News of the World* launched its outing campaign. See p. 346.

34. *Private Eye*, 26 June 1998, p. 7.

35. *Press Gazette*, 13 November 1998, p. 2.

36. *Private Eye*, 27 November 1998, p. 6.

37. *Guardian*, 11 November 1998, p. 18.

38. It might be noticed in this regard that PressWise, the charity victim support group run by Mike Jempson, blotted its copybook badly with the PCC by insisting on proceeding with a privacy complaint against the wishes of the complainant. See *Press Gazette*, 9 October 1998, p. 4; 30 October, p. 6.

39. *Guardian*, 7 June 1999, Media, pp. 6–7. See also PCC Paper No. 2009.

40. See boxed adjudication, p. 328.

41. *Press Gazette*, 5 February 1999, p. 6; 7 May, p. 6. *Guardian*, 1 February 1999, p. 2.

42. *Press Gazette*, 12 March 1999, pp. 9, 10, 14.

43. *Guardian*, 3 June 1999, p. 2.

44. Ibid., 7 June 1999, Media, p. 7.

45. Ibid., 3 June 1999, p. 23.

46. *Private Eye*, 11 June 1999, p. 6.

47. *Guardian*, 7 June 1999, Media, p. 6.

48. *Press Gazette*, 30 October 1999, p. 10.

49. Ibid., 7 May 1999, p. 11.

50. Ibid., 27 November 1998, p. 2.

51. Ibid.

52. PCC, Report No. 46, April–June 1999, p. 8.

CHAPTER 17

1. *Independent*, 17 March 2000, p. 8.

2. *Times*, 2 February 2000, p. 20.

3. Ibid., 7 March 2000, p. 20.

4. R. Pinker, 'Experiences in Persuading Governments of the Benefits of Self-Regulation', Commonwealth Press Union (unpublished, 2000), pp. 2–3.

5. An amalgamation of the Guild of British Newspaper Editors and the Association of British Editors in April 1999.

6. The Rt Hon. Chris Smith, Secretary of State for Culture, Media and Sport. Extracts of Society of Editors Speech, Cardiff, 17 October 2000. PCC. The research referred to by Smith was an internal assessment by the DCMS.

7. *Independent*, 7 March 2000, p. 8.

8. This was not so markedly the case with the Press Council. Between 1961 and 1990 (when the issue of adjudications was applicable) upholdings exceeded rejections in eight years, with two years drawn. (Information from Kenneth Morgan.)

9. *Press Complaints Commission Review, 1991–1993*, p. 9.

10. *Press Complaints Commission, Annual Review, 1999.*
11. *Press Gazette,* 3 March 2000, p. 11.
12. Ibid., 18 February 2000, p. 1.
13. See boxed adjudication, p. 35.
14. *Press Gazette,* 4 August 2000, p. 12.
15. *Times,* 2 August 2000, pp. 1, 17.
16. Ibid., 28 June 2000, p. 1.
17. Ibid., 10 June 2000, p. 2.
18. PCC, Report No. 51. Prince William and Privacy. Text of a speech by Lord Wakeham, Chairman of the Press Complaints Commission at St Bride's Institute, Fleet Street on 28 June 2000, pp. 22–4.
19. *Times,* 20 November 2000, p. 1.
20. *Independent,* 7 March 2000, p. 8.
21. *Guardian,* 3 February 2000, pp. 1, 6.
22. *Press Gazette,* 3 March 2000, p. 1.
23. *Spectator,* 20 March 2000, p. 31.
24. *Independent,* 28 March 2000, p. 8.
25. *Guardian,* 15 May 2000, Media, p. 2.
26. *Times,* 11 May 2000, p. 5.
27. Ibid., 12 May 2000, p. 27.
28. *Press Gazette,* 19 May 2000, p. 12.
29. See p. 194.
30. *Times,* 12 May 2000, p. 20.
31. *Guardian,* 15 May 2000, Media, p. 2.
32. Ibid.
33. Ibid.
34. *Press Gazette,* 4 August 2000, p. 12.
35. See p. 309.
36. *Times,* 26 July 2000, p. 16.
37. Ibid.
38. *Press Complaints Commission, Annual Review, 1999,* p. 6.
39. *Press Gazette,* 30 October 1998, p. 1.
40. *Press Complaints Commission, Annual Review, 2000,* 'International Report', p. 18. 'The PCC also continues to maintain close links with other organisations . . . including the World Press Freedom Committee and the International Press Institute.'
41. See p. 56.
42. *Press Gazette,* 21 April 2000, p. 12. 'Indeed, the European Commission itself knows how effective we can be: on the one occasion it made a complaint about a factual inaccuracy in a Sunday newspaper we resolved it amicably and speedily – in fact, in just over 20 working days.'
43. See p. 252.

Index